Theme Parties
Just for Kids...and Families too!

by Pat Nekola

ISBN: 097965232-4
Library of Congress Control Number: 2007933900

Published by:
Kids and Family Activities Ink
A division of: Catering by Design, Applewood Inc.
P.O. Box 181
Waukesha, WI 53187

About the Cover

All the neighbor children love to pick raspberries. They ate more raspberries than they put into each pail for making a raspberry pie. We thought it would be an eye appealing picture with the children on the front cover in front of Mrs. Cola's raspberry patch. I traveled to Indiana to locate the straw hats, and to Paris, Illinois to purchase the red T-shirts. Each child's mom purchased the bib overalls. I found the buckets at our local hardware store. A farmer in a nearby community furnished the bales of hay. The children liked being barefooted and enjoyed sitting on bales of hay covered with a cloth.

If you ever try to take a picture of three pre-school children, you will find it is not easy. The children needed some coaching to smile, sit up straight and pose for the picture. For the most part they did a good job. The raspberries became a big reward for doing a good job. We served them lunch with their favorite foods and of course, raspberry pie.

As Pat Nekola travels the country visiting nursing homes and assisted living facilities, she hears so many heart-warming stories from residents, families, and staff. Pat has decided to share some of these stories in her latest publication, *Elderly Reflections for People Who Care*. The elderly have many stories and experiences to share and they are worth hearing.

Pat hopes these stories will help you feel good while dealing with the everyday "nitty gritty" of an elderly person in need of your care and love.

There are fifty-four short stories by Pat and passed on by friends. Enjoy the book yourself or bring it with you when visiting a family member or friend at home, in a hospital, or care facility.

64 pages, soft cover.
ISBN: 0-9660610-6-3
©Copyright 2003, Catering by Design

To order, mail or fax to:

Catering by Design

P.O. Box 181

Waukesha, WI 53187

Ph: (262) 547-2004

Fax: (262) 547-8594

Customer Name _____

Address _____

City State Zip _____

Phone _____ Fax _____ E-mail _____

Qty:	Price @	Ext.
	$14.95	$
Shipping	$4.50	$
Total		$

MasterCard and Visa accepted.

WI residents please add 5.5% sales tax.

Signature _____

Date _____

Invoice Number _____

Picnics

Catering on the Move:
A Cookbook and Guide
by Pat Nekola

Learn to cater your own picnic for family and friends, for church or service club gatherings, or open a catering business. This cookbook has a variety of recipes designed especially for picnics. View buffet layouts, decorations, and various styles of picnics from simple to elegant. Recipes serve groups of 12-100, some up to 1,500!

Snacks and beverages, salads, grilled meats, hot vegetables, and desserts recipes are all designed for the picnicker's appetite.

From the owner of Pat's Party Foods, Caterers.

Pat Nekola has a long history of fine catering with her own business, Pat's Party Foods, in Wisconsin. She cooked many delicious recipes in *Picnics, Catering on the Move.* Picnics were her favorite parties because she enjoyed watching families and friends relax and have fun.

242 pages, hard back with spiral binding.
ISBN: 0-9660610-0-4
February 2000, Catering by Design

Pat Nekola began writing *Picnics, Catering on the Move* when her mother was diagnosed with Alzheimer's disease. Alzheimer's is a progressive, degenerative disease of the brain causing confusion, personality, and behavioral changes. Eventually many people with Alzheimer's are not able to care for themselves. A family member loses them twice: first to Alzheimer's, then to death. Taking care of a person with Alzheimer's takes a lot of patience and love.

- *Kitchen-tested recipes.*
- *Picnic ideas.*
- *Quantities shown for small to large groups.*
- *Decorations for theme parties.*
- *Diagrams to guide the reader.*
- *Buffet layout diagrams act as a learning tool.*
- *Heartwarming stories accompany recipes.*
- *Easy-to-follow instructions.*
- *Garnishes to make food attractive.*
- *Catering for crowds for fun and profit.*

Picnics

Catering on the Move:
A Cookbook and Guide
by Pat Nekola

Mail or fax to:	**Catering by Design** P.O. Box 181 Waukesha, WI 53187 Ph: (262) 547-2004 Fax: (262) 547-8594

Thank you for your order!

Customer Name _____

Library _____

Address _____

City State Zip _____

Phone _____ Fax _____

Qty:	Price @	Ext.
	$27.95	$
Shipping	$4.50	$
Total		$

MasterCard and Visa accepted.

WI residents please add 5.5% sales tax.

Signature _____

Date _____

Invoice Number _____

An Alzheimer's Guide

Activities and Issues for People Who Care

242 pages, soft cover.
ISBN: 0-9660610-8-X
February 2002, Catering by Design

When Pat Nekola's mother and aunt were stricken with Alzheimer's disease, she found help and information from a number of public and private sources. She also found that there were many others—families, caregivers, residential facilities' staff—just like herself, that could make use of the same types of information. With this in mind, Pat set out to accumulate the education and information to write this handbook to help others going through the same trying personal experiences.

This handbook is easy to read and to understand. Pat's writing approach is like a one-on-one conversation with a friend that has "been there and done that". Everyone needs to read this book, we are all dealing with the disease whether on a personal level, or as members of our local communities. It is an informative and warm approach to helping the Alzheimer's patient live to their fullest and enjoy each day—no matter what their present situation.

Information included in Part One of this Handbook:

- *Easy to understand information on each stage of the disease.*
- *How to deal with the different stages for families and caregivers.*
- *Coping strategies when caring for the patient at home.*
- *What to look for when selecting a care facility.*
- *Resources including telephone numbers, websites, and questions to ask.*

Information and Activities Useful for the Care Facilities' Activity Directors included in Part Two of this Handbook:

- *Directions for different craft activities.*
- *Color graphics for use with the activities.*
- *Recommended music for patient participation.*
- *Recipes.*
- *Patient assessment forms.*

An Alzheimer's Guide
Activities and Issues for People Who Care

Customer Name _____

Library _____

Address _____

City State Zip _____

Phone _____ Fax _____

Mail or fax to:	**Catering by Design** P.O. Box 181 Waukesha, WI 53187 Ph: (262) 547-2004 Fax: (262) 547-8594

Thank you for your order!

Qty:	Price @	Ext.
	$39.95	$
Shipping	$4.50	$
Total		$

MasterCard and Visa accepted.

WI residents please add 5.5% sales tax.

Signature _____

Date _____

Invoice Number _____

Acknowledgments

Thanks to Sue Schmitzer for her sincere interest in my progress and for also editing my book. She always has time to listen and encourage me. She has stayed in touch for several years. I appreciate her help and kindness.

Thanks to Leo Hickok for perfecting the final draft.

I also want to thank the staff at Barking Dog Publishing for their diligent work to make this book a reality. They have listened willingly as I have gone through the process of compiling my book.

I want to thank all my neighbors and church family for their kind support and for always being there for me.

Thank you Glen Victorey, owner of "Let's Celebrate" for lending cake pans and finding just the right products and giving party advice to do every party to perfection.

A special thanks to my husband, Steve, for his encouragement and financial support while compiling my books. I wanted to be an author and he made it possible to fulfill my dream. Thanks Steve for caring and loving me.

Disclosure

I do not proclaim to be an expert in Child Development. However, my career started as a Home Economics teacher with strong emphasis on family activities, food and diet, and Child Development. I ran a pre-school program in high school to teach the seniors about activities and how to care for pre-school children.

I also have had many parties for the neighborhood children. In addition I share my experience and creative ability to meet the children's emotional and psychological needs.

I ran my own catering business for 18 years and did many parties for families and also children parties.

I have authored *Picnics, Catering on the Move* with many creative party ideas for many family events.

I plan to continue to help families to enrich the lives of their children, and I hope your family will add this book to your library and apply some of my ideas in your activity planning.

—Pat Nekola

When you were born you cried and the world rejoiced. Live your life, so that when you die the world cries and you Rejoice!!!

—Old Cherokee Saying—

As a child my father taught me, if you can dream it, you can do it. He reminded me almost daily, that you can accomplish anything you so desire, if you are willing to put the time and effort into your dream. His encouragement helped me realize my dreams into reality throughout my life.

—Howard Evans—

Catch the winning spirit of a child.
Love, protect, and nurture a child.
Rejoice, as that child returns his
love to you for your love, time,
and kindness to him.

—Author unknown—

Love is the greatest gift of all!!!

Preface

Family is the social unit of the world. Whether it is a biological, church, or extended family, it is healthy to be a part of a supportive family. People need people to cope with their daily trials and tribulations. I like to call problems challenges. A family can make or break a person's spirit. Family can build a child's self-esteem and self-worth or the child can also be destroyed in a dysfunctional family unit. A good attitude is important when dealing with daily challenges with family.

Juggling activities in the family can be challenging with today's busy life, but also rewarding. The knowledge gained for having parties for your children and family is a huge gift. It is an opportunity to bond family members together, to relax, and to enjoy each other's company.

I personally enjoy getting the children together to help do the food preparation and setting up the buffet table. It is amazing how many ideas I gain from the children. Just when I think they are not paying attention, they surprise me with some new party ideas. Of course, I brag them up at the party for their help and ideas. The children respond with pride and they are willing to help me again at our next family gathering.

When my mother turned 80, my husband and I gave her a memorable birthday party. I still see her smiling as all the guests arrive to congratulate her on her 80th birthday.

Children and family parties create beautiful memories and good will. I can reflect on my childhood. My mother made my favorite maraschino cherry cake year after year. The recipe can be found in my *Picnics, Catering on the Move Cookbook and Guide* on page 127. Each year family and friends sang to me and made me feel so special. It is a pleasantry I have always cherished through my life.

As I approached adulthood and left home, mom stopped making my favorite cake. She said, "you are talented enough to make your own cake." I had to agree. Instead, each year she sent me a pretty card with a lovely saying and always signed the card with Love and Prayers, Mom. The card really meant more to me than the cake.

From age 8 on up, I liked to help mom cook and I enjoyed family parties. I really liked to see the children get involved while teaching pre-school. I invited the neighbor children and church children to many of my parties. I saw how wonderful it was to see the children interact with each other and also with the adults attending the party.

I began to put various parties together that would not only be fun but also educational. There are crafts, recipes, menus, word searches, and music with every theme party. Each party is well designed to walk each reader through the steps to have a beautiful and successful party.

The ready-reference book is easy to follow. You can build in your own ideas and make your activity as simple or elaborate as you desire. The information I have shared works. Observe the smiling faces of the children while using the ideas in this book. Good Luck!

—*Pat Nekola*

Introduction

Information on How to Create a Perfect Party

About the Recipes

Every recipe has been tested with many notes to the reader in order to create a successful product. There are lists to help the reader know what to purchase for the recipes and many tips. There are a variety of menus and theme cakes for each party. The ingredients are common enough to be purchased at most local grocery stores.

About Decorating for the Party

The colored pictures and step by step explanations of how to set up each party lends ease for making a beautiful party, even if you have not accomplished many parties.

About Arts and Crafts

Each art and craft explains the age level of the child to make for a successful project. A list of items needed are in order with the directions. I have experienced that children have enjoyed doing the projects with the supervision of an adult.

About Special Diets

Some children are allergic to peanuts and are also lactose intolerant. Always check with the child's parents what a child can eat or needs to avoid problems. Be sure you follow their special diet for their health.

About Music

Many children enjoy music. I personally play the accordion and I entertain the children with music. However, not everyone plays an instrument. I used my local library to locate just the right CD for several of the parties.

About References

The back of each chapter has references for each party. This ready reference list can help you decide what you might like to read to the children at the party. There are many stories for each unit that may give you many ideas for the party.

General Comments About the Book

The book is divided into two sections. Section one has a variety of children's parties and section two has family parties. The Theme party book is filled with many exciting themes such as rocket, train, fire truck, princess and many more. It is the parent or guardian that will be responsible for the making of the child's party.

What to Remember as You Work with Children

Teach them how to be polite and gracious at a party. Have the parents help their child write a thank you note after the party. Work with their ability and help them enjoy the party. Do not scold a child that does not eat every item on his plate. Encourage every child to participate in the various activities. Make sure that every child says, "please" and "thank you" at the appropriate times at the party. Every child must be safe and comfortable while attending the party. Be sure to have plenty of adults on hand to help the children with projects and serving the food. Remember to laugh a lot and have fun with the children while attending the party.

Dedication

I would like to dedicate this book to all the librarians in the United States. They have been very supportive and have encouraged their patrons to use my books. I especially want to thank all the staff members at the Waukesha Public Library for their help and support. Their concerns and diligent work have helped me in compiling the material in this book.

Theme Parties *Just for Kids...and Families too!*
Color Section of Projects and Parties:

Contents

Theme Parties
Just for Kids...and Families too!

Introduction

Theme Parties Section Part I
Rocket Ship Party

Half Birthday Party

Indy 500 Theme Party

Train Party

Airplane Party

Fire Truck Party

Mrs. Cola's Raspberry Party

Pony Party

Bowling Party

Ladybug Tea Party

Dinosaur Party

Clown Party

Pizza Party

50's Party

Princess Party

Family Section Part II

Kindergarten Graduation Party

Bridal Shower Party

Reunion Party

Music Camp Party

Bell Party

Baptism Party

Rocket Party

The Rocket Cake
Shopping List

Cake Decorating Supplies for Rocket Cake

- 1-16x16x3 inch high round Styrofoam®
- 1 piece 28x32 inch blue plastic table covering
- 1 roll duct tape
- 1-¼ inch wooden dowel rod, 29 inches long
- 1-12x12 inch square cardboard
- 6-10 inch cardboard circles
- 6-12 inch dowels ¼ inch thick
- 1-#506 star cake tube
- 1-12 inch cake decorating bag
- 2-8 inch star cake pans

Rocket cake plates
Rocket cake size napkins and cups (optional)
Plastic dessert forks (one per person)
- 1 small package miniature flags toothpicks
- 1 small package multi-color plastic stars picks
- 1 small package plastic flag picks
  with saying forever (optional)

Home Supply Company

½ inch copper pipe, 8 inches long
(Pipe is from the plumbing Department)

Department Store

1 twin size bed ruffle with rocket print
   (cut ruffle to fit diameter of circle)
   (about 1 yard 23 inches)

Equipment at Home

1 kitchen mixer and beaters
1 mixing bowl
1 stainless steel bowl for storing extra frosting
scissors
tall glass
can opener
measuring spoons
measuring cups
2 rubber spatulas
1 cake spatula with six inch blade
1-8$\frac{1}{2}$ inch stainless steel shish kabob rod or
   (1-10 inch wooden chopstick)

Grocery List

Note: You can purchase any food desired as long as the can sizes are the same as listed below. I made chili with the tomato products. Of course, I added the meat, onion, chili beans, and seasonings to complete the chili.

Can Sizes

1-6 pound 10 ounce can (Institutional size)
1-46 fluid ounce can tomato juice
1-1 pound 13 ounce can black beans
1-15 ounce can diced tomatoes
1-8 ounce can tomato sauce
1-6 ounce can tomato paste

Other Items Needed for the Cake

1-16 ounce box angel food cake mix
3-18.25 ounce cake mixes of choice
2-3 pound cans white shortening
1 pound butter
1-pound 10 ounce box iodized salt
5 pounds sugar
5 pounds flour
2-net 1 fluid ounce almond extract
5-2 pound powdered sugar, total 10 pounds
2 dozen grade A large eggs
1-14 ounce double acting baking powder
1-15 fluid ounce 100% lemon juice
1-3 ounce container red sugar crystals
1-8 ounce container red, white, and blue
   assorted jimmies
1-1.69 ounce package milk chocolate M&M's®
   (assorted colors)
1-16 ounce package licorice cherry bites
3-8 ounce chocolate candy bars, total 24 ounce
1-16 ounce package miniature marshmallows
1 box round wooden toothpicks
1-16 ounce non-dairy whipped topping
2-3 quarts fresh strawberries, total 6 quarts

Note: I have a five-quart Kitchen Aide mixer that holds two batches of batter. A regular or smaller kitchen mixer holds only one batch. You will have to make the one-half batter twice if you have a regular or smaller kitchen mixer. If you have a five-quart mixer double this recipe. Thus, the two half batters will make enough batter for the first layer of:

Grandma's Old-Fashion Pound Cake

Yield: One-half of batter for 6 pound 10 ounce can cake or 12 servings

1 cup solid vegetable shortening
1-$\frac{1}{2}$ cups sugar
1 teaspoon vanilla
2 teaspoons lemon juice
6 eggs
2 cups flour
1 teaspoon baking powder

Preheat oven to 325 F. Grease and flour the 6-pound 10-ounce can and the copper pipe. In a mixing bowl, cream shortening, sugar, vanilla, and lemon juice together until fluffy. Add eggs. Beat well. Add flour and baking powder. Mix well. Place copper pipe in the middle of the can. Pour batter into prepared can around the copper pipe. Repeat single batch recipe. Add the second batch to the can. Bake at 325 F for 1-$\frac{1}{2}$ hours or until wooden chop stick or shish kabob skewer comes out clean. Cool in the can for 15 minutes. Loosen edges with spatula or knife. Turn can over. Remove bottom lid with can opener. Gently push cake through the can and remove the copper pipe. Discard can. Cool for 2 to 3 hours. Wrap and store in cool dry place for 24 hours. **Do not refrigerate.**

Note: The copper pipe holds the cake in place and conducts the heat to ensure even baking through the entire cake. Without the pipe the cake center will not bake completely. For extra cake batter, double the recipe to make 24 servings.

Angel Food Cake Recipe

Yield: One 46 fluid ounce can 8 slices, one 1 pound 13 ounce can 6 slices, one 15 ounce can 4 slices, one 8 ounce can 3 slices, one 6 ounce can 2 slices **Total Servings 23**

Follow directions on the cake mix very carefully. *DO NOT GREASE CANS OR CAKES WILL FALL.*

Fill each can a little less than two-thirds full. Place all 5 cakes on the bottom rack in oven. Set timer for each cake starting from the smallest to largest size cake. Bake at 375 F for times listed below, or until toothpick inserted in the center comes out clean.

Note: Use the wooden chopstick to check doneness for the 46 fluid ounce cake. If cakes are baking too quickly turn oven down to 350 F.

Approximate Time for Each Can Size

Angel Food Cake batter Size	Time
One 46 fluid ounce can	50-60 minutes
1 pound 13 ounce can	40-50 minutes
15 ounce can	30-35 minutes
8 ounce can	15-20 minutes
6 ounce can	10-15 minutes

Cool cakes in cans for 10-15 minutes. Turn can over. Remove bottom lid with can opener. Gently push cake through the can. Discard cans. Cool on baking racks. Wrap cakes once cakes are thoroughly cooled. **Do not refrigerate.**

Note: Trace star pan onto six 10 inch cardboard circles. Add on $^1/_4$ to $^1/_2$ inch. Cut out each cardboard. See the example in the photos below.

Star Cakes

Yield: Six 8 inch star cakes or 36-48 pieces

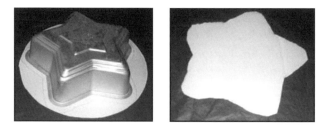

3 boxes 18.25 ounce (each) cake mix
Eggs
Water
Vegetable oil

Grease and flour each cake pan. Following cake mix box directions, make one cake mix. Divide batter between 2 prepared pans. Place on bottom oven rack. Bake at 350 F for 25-30 minutes or until wooden pick inserted in center comes out clean. Cool in pans for 10 minutes. Place a star-shaped cardboard on top of each cake. Turn each cake over onto the cardboard. Wrap and refrigerate for a day. Repeat with the remaining two cake mixes for a total of six cakes.

Note: It takes almost five batches of the following frosting to make the rocket cake and the six star cakes. Keep the extra pound of frosting for touch ups. Luckily, I did not have to use the extra frosting on the rocket cake project.

Creamy Cake Decorating Frosting

Yield: One batch

$1^3/_4$ cup shortening
2 tablespoons butter
$^1/_2$ teaspoon salt
1 teaspoon almond extract
2 pounds powdered sugar
$^1/_3$ cup water

Cream shortening and butter together. Add salt and almond extract. Blend. Alternate powdered sugar with water. Beat mixture until smooth and creamy. Repeat 4 more times. Place frosting in bowl (two batches per bowl) or make one batch at a time.

How to Assemble the Rocket Cake

1. Place hole in center of the board and square feet on the bottom of the board.
2. Foil 24x24 inch board with three pieces of foil (dull side up).
3. Cover 16x16 round x 3 inch deep Styrofoam® with blue plastic.
4. Tape plastic table cover to back of the Styrofoam® round with duct tape.
5. Run the 29 inch dowel through the Styrofoam® and board.
6. Frost bottom of the pound cake.
7. Slide the 6 pound 10 ounce cake at the center hole through the 29 inch wooden dowel rod. The bottom should touch the Styrofoam®. This size pound cake becomes the first layer to the rocket cake.
8. Place four dowels, evenly spaced (one on each 4 sides) into the first layer of cake. The four dowels are about an inch to 1$\frac{1}{2}$ inch from the middle dowel.
9. Mark and remove dowels.
10. Saw four dowels on marking with cake decorating saw and miter box and return dowels to the four holes in the cake.
11. Frost the top of the pound cake.
12. Trace all six cans sizes on a 10x10 inch square cake cardboard.
13. Cut out each circle.
14. Mark a circle $\frac{1}{4}$ inch diameter in the center of each cardboard.
15. Poke hole through the marked circle of each cardboard with the points of a scissors.
16. Slide the largest cardboard circle over the 29 inch dowel rod onto the frosted cake layer, letting the cardboard circle rest securely atop pound cake layer and covering the short support dowels.

17. Center 46 fluid ounce can size cake. Slide cake over the 29 inch wooden dowel rod. This size angel food cake is the second largest cake.
18. Place two dowels, one on each side of the center dowel.
19. Mark and remove the dowels.
20. Saw the two dowels and re-place dowels back into the holes of this cake.
21. Frost top of the cake.
22. Slide the cardboard circle through the 29 inch wooden dowel rod onto surface of cake and covering support dowel rods.
23. Frost bottom of the 1 pound 36 ounce cake.
24. Slide the center of the 1 pound 13 ounce cake through the 29 inch wooden dowel rod onto cardboard circle.
25. Frost the top of the 1 pound 36 ounce cake.
26. Place two dowels, one on each side of the 29 inch wooden dowel.
27. Mark and remove the dowels.
28. Saw the two dowels and replace dowels back into the holes of this cake.
29. Slide the cardboard circle through the 29 inch wooden dowel rod onto cake surface top of the third cake.
30. Frost bottom of the 15 ounce size can cake.
31. Slide the center of the cake through the 29 inch wooden dowel rod.
32. Frost top of the cake.
33. Slide the cardboard circle through the 29 inch wooden dowel rod onto cake surface.
34. Frost bottom of the 8 ounce can size cake.
35. Repeat steps 31-34 for the 8 ounce cake.
36. Frost the bottom of the 6 ounce can cake.
37. Slide the center of the 6 ounce can cake through the 29 inch wooden dowel rod onto surface of cake.

Assemble the cake decorating tube (#506) into your cake-decorating bag. Fill cake decorating bag a little more than half full. Roll top of bag over (about 1 inch) to stop frosting from escaping the bag. Do not frost the cakes. Using frosting in the cake-decorating bag, start decorating the cake, top to bottom, with frosting lines all around the cake. Using the same cake tube, pipe frosting stars around the second layer and cover. Repeat the third cake just like the first cake. Repeat the star design for the remaining top cakes. Arrange six mini marshmallows into a cone shape. Gently frost the top layer of the 6-ounce can cake. Place the marshmallow cone on top of the cake. Pipe frosting onto marshmallow cone to form the nose of the rocket.

Decorations for the Rocket Cake

Cut two 8-ounce chocolate bars on the diagonal. Use a ruler to make a straight angle line. Mark the angle with a knife. Prevent the chocolate bar from cracking by using a sharp paring knife. While sawing the chocolate, dip knife into a tall glass of hot water several times. Gently saw the chocolate on the line. The chocolate becomes two pieces. Repeat this method to make two more chocolate pieces. Place a little frosting on each angled edge. Place chocolate pieces on the cake on center front and back and one on each side. Gently push each chocolate piece into the sides of the bottom layer of the cake to form the wings on the rocket. See picture on page 1 in the color section.

Decorate the bottom of the cake by alternating cherry mini bites licorice with yellow M&M's®.

Place plastic stars at random around the top of the bottom layer of cake. The I love USA is in the center of the bottom layer of the cake (above the front center chocolate wing).

Place a ring of blue M&M's® around the top of the second layer of the cake.

Place a ring of cherry flavored mini bites licorice at the top of the third cake.

Cut 4 chocolate squares from the third candy bar. Place the squares around the 5th layer. The squares act as windows or just a design (your choice). Place a red M&M® centered above and below the four pieces of chocolate. The body of the rocket cake is completed.

Note: The cake will collapse if you delete the short and long support wooden dowel rods in the cakes or use butter cream frosting and a very moist cake mix. For best results use the pound cake recipe and the angel food cake mix. The assembled rocket cake sat on my dining room table for 48 hours without any problems. I served the cake with rave reviews for both style and taste. My friend's son has his order in for his next birthday

Star Cakes

Place a little frosting in the middle of each star shaped cardboard. Center one star shaped cake on each cardboard. Continue using the #506 star tip. Cover sides and top of each cake with frosting stars. Sprinkle three of the six cake tops with red sugar crystal and the remaining three with the red, white, and blue jimmies. Show off the space theme bed ruffle by evenly spacing star cakes around the bottom of the blue covered Styrofoam®. See picture on page 1 in the color section.

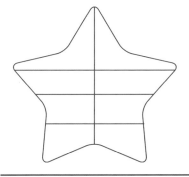

How to Cut Eight Pieces from a Five Point Star Cake

1. Cut a vertical line through the center of the cake.
2. Cut three horizontal lines through the cake as evenly as possible.

How to Cut Six Pieces from a Five Point Star Cake.

1. Cut a vertical line through the center of the cake.
2. Cut two horizontal lines through the cake as evenly as possible.

How to Cut the Rocket Cake

Remove one layer of angel food cake at a time. Lay angel food cakes down on its side and slice into circles. Serve with fresh sugared strawberries and non-dairy whip topping.

Remove the four chocolate wings from the bottom layer of the space-ship. Select four guest names from a hat or guess a number to win the chocolate space-ship wings. Cut the cake into four pieces slicing top to bottom using the chocolate wing markings for a guide. Each section yields 6 pieces or a total of 24 servings per pound cake.

Note: The body of the rocket space-ship serves 47. The star cakes serve six to eight pieces per cake or a total of 36-48 servings. I suggest that you use a couple of the star cakes for door prizes. The young guests are very happy to take home a decorated cake.

Transporting the Cake

Use an air-conditioned van to transport the cake. A person should sit with the cake. Shield side windows on a very hot day. Carry the star cakes separately. Carry extra frosting for touch ups. It is not a good idea for this cake to travel very far. Set up the cake upon arrival.

Items Needed for Transporting the Cake

Cake decorating bag	#506 star cake tube	1 blue plastic tablecloth to cover the cake table
Cake spatula	Rubber spatula	Space-ship fabric to go around cake base.
Extra M&M's®	Extra licorice cherry bites	(This is made from the bed ruffle).
Tall glass for water	Extra bowl of frosting	

Note: Find out in advance the size of the table. Purchase the tablecloth to fit the specified table.

Steps Taken After Arriving with the Cake

Cover table with the blue tablecloth. Place rocket cake on the center of the table. The table should be very sturdy to hold the weight of cakes. Place rocket theme skirting around the bottom of the blue covered Styrofoam® circle. Place the six star cakes around the bottom of the Styrofoam® circle.

How to Construct a Rocket Space-ship Centerpiece

Each child can make a rocket space-ship to enjoy during the party. They can take the rocket space-ship home. One of the boys attending the party placed his rocket ship on his dresser. His mother told me that no one is allowed to touch his rocket ship. She dusts with caution around Robby's rocket ship masterpiece. Ages 8-10 can put together the larger space-ship. Ages 5-7 can put together the mini version of a space-ship.

A Rocket Art Project for Ages Eight to Ten

Suggested Supplies for Each Rocket Space-ship

Wallpaper	Heavy Duty non-stick foil
Tape	Various colors of ribbon
2¹/₂ yards (each rocket) wide ribbon	2-3inch (each) Styrofoam® circles, 2 inches thick
2¹/₂ yards (each) ⁵/₈ inch red and gold	1-4 inch Styrofoam® circle
Jumbo Metallic Rick Rack	1-15 ounce can
Newspapers	1-6 ounce can
1-8 ounce can	1 small package decorative gold stars stickpins
Glue stick	Pencils
Fabric Glue	Q-tips
Washable Glue	Scissors

Note: Use your imagination. Perhaps there are supplies in your home for this fun project.

How to Assemble the Rocket Space-ship *(ages 8-10)*

1. Place newspapers on top of the table.
2. Place one set of the 3 cans and the 3 Styrofoam® circles at each participant's place setting.
3. Place other materials in center of the table.
4. Cut two pieces of foil. Cut the second piece of foil in half. Wrap the 15 ounce can.
5. Wrap the remaining two cans with foil.
6. Place the 6 ounce can on the 4 inch Styrofoam® circle. Place one 15 ounce and one 8 ounce can on each of the 3 inch Styrofoam® circles. Be sure to center the 6 ounce can on the Styrofoam® circle.
7. Push each can through each Styrofoam® circle. Reserve the Styrofoam® with the hole for the rocket base.
8. Wrap donut shaped base with the 2¹/₂ yards of ribbon going through the hole several times.
9. Tuck edge of ribbon inside the ribbon in the hole; fasten with three stickpins.
10. Cut strips of ribbon and Rick Rack to fit each size can.
11. Glue each ribbon piece on each can. Use fabric glue for best results.
12. Trace the bottom of the 15 ounce can on red construction paper to form the circle.
13. Make a line from the edge to the center of the circle. Cut out the circle and also cut a slit from the edge to the center of the circle.
14. Glue on gold stars on the circle.
15. Fold over the slit side to make the raised cone. Glue the slit sides together.
16. Glue the cone onto the top of the 6 ounce can. Be sure the Styrofoam® is at the top of the can.
17. Place toothpick flag through the center of the cone and the Styrofoam® base.

18. Starting with the largest can, glue can to the base. Continue gluing each can one on top of each other until cans are fastened in place. Glue the rocket to the Styrofoam® base. Enjoy your rocket project!

Note: Adults should help each child understand the project's instructions. The children should have plenty of time to enjoy and complete the rocket project. See picture on page 1 in the color section

A Rocket Art Project for Ages Five to Seven

Suggested Supplies for Each Rocket Space-ship

Heavy Duty non-stick foil	1 piece red construction paper
1 small package American flag	Toothpicks
1 small package gold stars	2 ¼ yards wide blue ribbon (base)
1-9 inch wide ribbon strip	1 package ⅝ inch gold Jumbo Metallic rick rack
Glue stick	Fabric glue
Q-tips	1-6 ounce can
1-15 ounce can	1-4 inch Styrofoam® circle
Small scissors designed for children	Pencils

Note: The Styrofoam® circles can be found in a craft store in the floral department. It will save time to prepare a rocket kit in a bag for each child.

1. Place newspapers on top of the table.
2. Set each place setting with 1 star flag, one small piece of red construction paper, 7-10 gold stars, 2-9 inch strips rick rack, 1-9 inch wide ribbon, 2-½ yards blue ribbon, 1-4 inch Styrofoam® circle, ½ sheet foil, one Q-tip, 1-15 ounce can, 1-6 ounce can, 1 pencil, and 1 pair of scissors.
3. Center 6 ounce can on top of the Styrofoam® circle. Push can through the Styrofoam® to make the circle. The Styrofoam® base looks like a donut. The center of the Styrofoam® will be inside the 6 ounce can.
4. Foil the can.
5. Glue the wide ribbon in the center of the can.
6. Glue the rick rack on top and bottom of can.
7. Make sure the Styrofoam® shows and is even at the top of the 6 ounce can.
8. Trace bottom of the 15 ounce can on red construction paper to form the circle.
9. Draw a line from the center to the edge of the circle. Cut out the circle; cut a slit from the edge to the center of the circle.
10. Circle slits should meet each side to make the raised cone. Glue the slit sides together.
11. Glue the cone onto the top of the 6 ounce can.
12. Place toothpick flag through the center of the cone and through the Styrofoam® base.
13. Use the 2½ yards of wide blue ribbon and wrap the Styrofoam® donut ring base around the hole several times.
14. Tuck edge of the ribbon inside the hole in ribbon edge and fasten with three stickpins.

Inside of the Invitation Should Say.

You are invited to a surprise birthday party
in honor of Glen's memorable 5th birthday.

For: Glen Green

Date: Sunday April 7th

Time: 2-5 p.m.

Place: Mrs. Cola's Home

R.S.V.P
Call Glen's mother by April 1.

Grandma's Birthday Wish for Glen

May this rocket cake remind you to soar
As you learn life skills and so much more.

May you grow up big and strong
Always knowing right from wrong.

May you celebrate your daily life
Being kind and living without strife.

May the many hours we spend and share
Provide pleasant memories of fun and care.

May we cook together and cook in style
Creating pleasing parties all the while.

May you know you are always in my heart
I have loved you, Glen, from the start.

Happy Birthday!!!

Love,
Grandma

A Birthday Cake Story

Grandma made Glen a rocket ship cake at age five. Five friends came to celebrate Glen's special birthday. He studied the cake and his eyes became as large as saucers. He loved chocolate and could not believe the size of the chocolate wings on the cake.

Glen never forgot the exciting rocket ship party. He said, "Grandma rocks."

Glen and Grandma dedicated many hours together making cakes and party foods for family and friends. She was very creative with foods and crafts. She could make any design to please the palate.

Glen is grown. Grandma has passed on. Glen continues to savor the times spent with Grandma. Just before she died, he told her he could not live without her. She said, "My dear Glen, I will always be with you in spirit. Be good and do well."

Today, Glen runs a party store. He has carried on Grandma's party ideas with great enthusiasm. He has taken Grandma's advice. He practices Grandma's wishes.

When I made the rocket cake, I invited the neighborhood families to come over and enjoy the cake. We took many pictures of the cake and each family. We surprised Glen. We invited him to stop by the house. He looked at the rocket cake and, just as many years before, his eyes became as large as saucers, and he spoke about Grandma in a very tender manner. She will always be in his heart.

Note: Children may enjoy making their own rocket sandwiches. This project is best for a small group.

Rocket Sandwiches

Yield: Eight sandwiches and thirty salami cones

1 loaf white or wheat bread
$\frac{1}{4}$ pound butter (softened) or margarine spread
8 thin slices deli ham or turkey
8 thin slices American cheese
2-8 ounce (each) container whipped Garlic 'N Herb cream cheese spread
15 thin slices salami
1 package frilled toothpicks
2-10 or 12 inch round doilies
1-12 inch serving tray
1 pound bag baby carrots
1 ounce package mint leaves
1-quart dill pickles
1-16 ounce jar olives

Stack 12 slices of bread. Cut off crusts. Place 12 slices bread across counter top. Use rolling pin to slightly flatten the bread. Butter the bread. Place one slice of ham or turkey and cheese on the bread. Roll the bread, meat, and cheese into a long pinwheel. Seal edges of pinwheel by placing cream cheese along the edges of pinwheel from top to bottom. Cut salami in half. Form salami into a cone. Hold cone together with a frilled toothpick. Complete the remaining salami cones. Fill the salami cones with cream cheese. Place one salami cone on the top of the sandwich. Place one or two doilies on a 12 inch serving tray. Arrange rocket sandwiches and remaining salami cones on tray. Garnish platter with salami cones, baby carrots and mint leaves. Serve with side dishes of dill pickle spears, and olives. See picture on page 1 in the color section.

Connect the dots using the numbered dots below; start with 1 and keep connecting the dots until you are finished making the rocket. Color the rocket.

For More Information Write

National Aeronautics and Space Administration
Langley Research Center
Hampton, VA 23665

National Space Society
922 Pennsylvania Avenue, SE
Washington, D.C. 20003

Space USA
Kennedy Space Center
Cape Canaveral, FL 32899

Places to Visit

Hall of Science
47-1 111th Street
Flushing Meadows
Corona Park
Queens, NY 11368

Museum of Science and space
Transit Planetarium
3280 S. Miami Avenue
Miami, FL 33129

Rocket Theme Related Resources and Book References

Loomis, Christine
"Astro Bunnies"
Publisher: G.P. Putman's Sons
Published Date: c2001
The story is about bunnies going to space and what happens in space. The process is explained in very simple terms with many pictures. (ages 2-4)

Morris, Ting
"Space"
Publisher: F. Watts
Published Date: c1994
The "Space" book is from a Sticky Fingers Series. This book teaches the children how to make things, various activities, and facts about space. Check out page 14 for the rocket art project called, "Blast Off!" (ages 8-10)

Rey, Margret
"Curious George and the Rocket"
Publisher: Houghton Mifflin Company
Published Date: c2001
Every human being is too large to fit into the rocket so Curious George volunteers to go to the moon to help out his professor friend. George becomes the first space monkey.

Scarry, Richard
"The Space Shuttle, Basic First Aid, Manholes, Mailing a Letter"
Publisher: Simon Spotlight
Published Date: c1997
The book is divided into four titles: "The Space Shuttle", "Basic First Aid", "Manholes", and "Mailing a Letter". The book has many colored pictures to go with each title (ages 3-5)

Todd, Traci N.
"A is for Astronaut: Space Exploration from A to Z"
Publisher: Chronicle books
Published Date: c2006
The book explores an out-of-this-world mix of vintage illustrations and contemporary photos to make this book as entertaining to look at, as it is to read. (ages 4-8)

DVD Resources

"NASA, The Story of America's Courageous Space Explorers!"
(Video recording:)
"50 Years of Space Exploration"
Publisher: Madacy Entertainment Group LP
Published Date: c2003
The information on space has 5 videos with 11 hours and 6 minutes. (young adults and family)

Wind Party

Introduction to the Wind Party

The Webster's Dictionary describes the wind as "a large body of air in rapid natural motion, its speed often being expressed in terms of the force it exerts on an obstacle to its motion. Its direction is that from which it comes, a west wind, air set locally in motion. He felt the wind it made as it rushed past him."

Children are fascinated by the wind. It is a great party for ages 3-7. The 3 year olds can color the pinwheel but they need help cutting out the pinwheel and more guidance on this project. We did the Wind party at the Public Library in Shell Lake, Wisconsin. The children had a wonderful time.

The smaller children talked to each other at their table. One three year old said to the boy across from her, "I like your pinwheel". How do you like my pinwheel?" The boy answered, "It's ok." "Oh!" she exclaimed. Her face and big blue eyes revealed her disappointment for a lack of a great compliment.

Facts About the Wind

We can feel and hear the wind and also watch it blow. The wind helps the birds, butterflies, and airplanes fly and even scatters plant seeds. A sailboat sails as the wind blows against their sails. Air is across the entire world. A windmill's blades move when the wind blows. It has been a power machine and used for many centuries. A windmill can help make electricity or grind grain. The wind makes waves; makes trees bend; helps the leaves to fall and also uproots trees. The wind can move clouds. The wind can make a storm and cause a tornado or a hurricane. The wind can whistle and also chill our bones or warm our face.

A blizzard is produced when wind blows snow very hard. A tornado travels in a funnel form. When a tornado touches the ground, it does a lot of damage to the area. A hurricane has an eye that is still. When the eye passes, the winds blow in the opposite direction. A thunderstorm can bring strong winds and is accompanied by an atmospheric electrical discharge. Webster Dictionary states that, "lightning is due to the explosive expansion of suddenly heated air." Cold air is very heavy while hot air is light. There is always a movement of wind either cool or warm. Hot air rises. The sun heats the air.

Did you know that way back in 1752 Ben Franklin flew a kite in a thunderstorm? He wanted to prove that there was electricity in storm clouds. The lightning caused a spark. He did not understand that he could have been hurt badly, due to the electrical current. Did you know that Mount Washington recorded winds of 231 miles per hour?

Pinwheel Project
Supplies Needed and Directions

| pattern for windmill | markers | crayons |
| scissors | pencil with eraser | pushpin |

1 Color the pinwheel different colors.
2. Cut out the square along the solid lines.
3. Cut into the square along the_____solid lines—but not inside the circle.
4. Bend (Don't fold down) each of the corners marked with a "X" along the —— broken lines. Tape in place.
5. Put a straight pin through the four corners and the center of the circle.
6. Put the pin into the eraser of a pencil.
7. Take your pinwheel outside. It will spin when you run with it or blow on it.
Note: See pinwheel pattern on page 26.

Suggested Snack Menu
Windmill Cookies and Juice or
Kite Shaped Cake and Juice
Windmill S'mores
Kite Pizza Snacks

Note: Windmill cookies come 12-15 to a 9 ounce package. Some of the cookies were broken in each of the 2–9 ounce packages for my wind party.

Story About the Wind
My husband and I celebrated our 25th wedding anniversary a number of years ago. We decided to have 25 balloons filled with one card inside each balloon. At the end of the ceremony we released the balloons on a very windy day.

The Saying Inside of the Balloon Said:

In Celebration of 25 years of marriage, we released 25 balloons
As full as our hearts, to soar as high as our dreams
To journey, as we have, into an unknown destiny.

Love has allowed us to sail safely through life's storms,
And has taught us to savor the sunshine and blue skies.
We would love to know how far our anniversary
balloons traveled. Please indicate where you found
this note and return it to us.

Composed by Julie Wohlt (a dear friend)

We also placed our return address on the card. We received a letter back approximately three months later. Phyllis said that her husband found the anniversary note in their woods. She also told us that they lived in Mason County just east of Lake Michigan in Manistee, many miles away.

We have pictures of the wind soaring the balloons into the air. So, Mrs. Cola thought it would be a great idea to have a wind party and make windmills and kites. She also wanted to share her pictures of the wind flying the anniversary balloons. She would make a kite cake and talk about how kites originated. In addition she would help the children make a simple diamond kite and fly the kites on a moderately windy day. Springtime in the Midwestern states U.S.A. is a great time to fly kites.

History of Kites.

There are several ideas about the origin of kites. One story states that two Chinese brothers had to bang pots and pan lids together to scare away the birds. The birds were eating the rice in the family's rice field. The boys put their heads together and began to think of other ways to scare away the birds. They came up with an idea for a kite made from paper and chopsticks. Their idea worked. Soon the boys' family opened a factory to make many kites. The kites were made of various colors and shapes such as dragons, fish and flying tigers. Some kites made in China were also made to have musical sounds like that of a flute or a harp.

It is believed that an ancient Chinese philosopher flew a kite more than twenty four hundred years ago. Kites were first recorded in 500 BC. Inexpensive kites were made with paper in the second century AD. The more beautiful kites were made with silk and bamboo. Kites were used in the military in 200 BC. Lawrence Hargrave invented a box kite in 1893. Did you know that the National Weather Service used box kites for about 35 years from the late 1800's to the near mid 1930's? They were equipped with thermometers and other weather-measuring devices.

Chinese people still celebrate festivals with kites both in the fall and spring. They believe that the kites scare away the demons and also bring good luck.

Kites are not new to many nations. People began to realize that kites could be fun and a great pastime. Today many families work together to make a kite for recreation. The diamond and bowed shaped kites are the most common. William Eddy invented these two styles of kites. However, there are many styles and shapes made into kites.

Here Are a Few Names of Styles of Kites:

Box	Diamond	Fighter
Butterfly	Fish delta	Soft
Stunt	Bowed	Yakko

For more information on how to make these kites please check out the book called *The Ultimate Kite Book*, by Paul and Helene Morgan.

Other Styles of Kites:

Adelino's Phillipine	Kelly Improved	Arrow
Four-W	Chinese	Octopus
Scott Sled	Half Sheet	Cylindrical
Triangle Box	Bird	A.G. Bell
Four Sheet	The Sky's the Limit	

For information on how to make the above kites and diagrams please check out the book called *Kites on the Wind,* by Emery J. Kelly.

Make a Diamond Shaped Kite

Supplies Needed

Light construction paper	Knife or saw
Two sticks or dowel rod type	Scissors
Transparent tape	Waterproof white glue
Ball of strong string	Needles and pins
Material such as silk or rip-stop nylon	

Note: Newspaper, brown wrapping paper or crepe paper can be used to cover the kite. However,these materials will not hold up as well as the rip-stop nylon or silk. There is a cross stick on the diamond kite, the top horizontal cross stick should be two-thirds the length of the other vertical stick. If the covering is too heavy, the kite will not fly.

While I was working in Topeka, Kansas I found a hobby shop. I purchased several kite kits such as Spongebob, Mickey, Butterfly, Froggy, and the nova kite. The shop had many selections. The various shaped kites are made by Nickelodeon. Their Website is www.nick.com. Go fly a Kite is a division of Jakks Pacific, Clinton, Ct USA. The ready-made diamond shaped kites come sized 33 inches across by 39 inches down. The smaller ready-made kite for a younger child comes sized 20 inches across and 25 inches down.

How to Assemble a Diamond Shaped Kite

1. Make a cross with the two sticks, one stick shorter than the other. Lay the long stick vertically and center the shorter stick across the longer stick $1/3$ the way down.
2. Tie the cross together at the intersection of the two sticks.
3. Dab a little glue on the end of a piece of string. Dry the string.
4. Notch ends of sticks. Have an adult do this step.
5. Place the string into the notches. Pull it tight, going from notched stick end to the next all the way around to make the diamond kite frame. Be sure to go all the way around the notched sticks. Knot the two ends of string together.
4. Make a newspaper pattern to fit the frame of the kite with a 1 $1/4$ inch extra margin all around the kite frame.
5. Place the pattern on the material. Lay the frame onto the material. Outline the diamond shaped kite. There should be a 1 $1/4$ inch margin all around the kite frame.
6. Cut out the body of the kite.

7. Trim the four corners of the cover.
8. Bend the edges of the cover over the string of the frame.
9. Glue edges in place.
10. The bridle string is about three times as long as your kite. Tie one end of the string around the top of the spine. Make a loop one-third the way down the string. Knot it.
11. Tie the other end of the string to the bottom of the spine. Cut off the extra string.
12. Fold construction paper into 2 inch x 3 inch strips (accordion style)
13. Tie the strips onto the string 7 inches to 8 inches apart.
14. Tie the tail to the bottom end of the kite.
15. Tie the kite line to the loop. The kite is now completed. Get ready! Get Set! Up, up and away as the wind sends the kite to the sky. Remember practice makes a perfect kite- flying day! Well almost! Wait!!! Review the rules before first beginning your adventure.

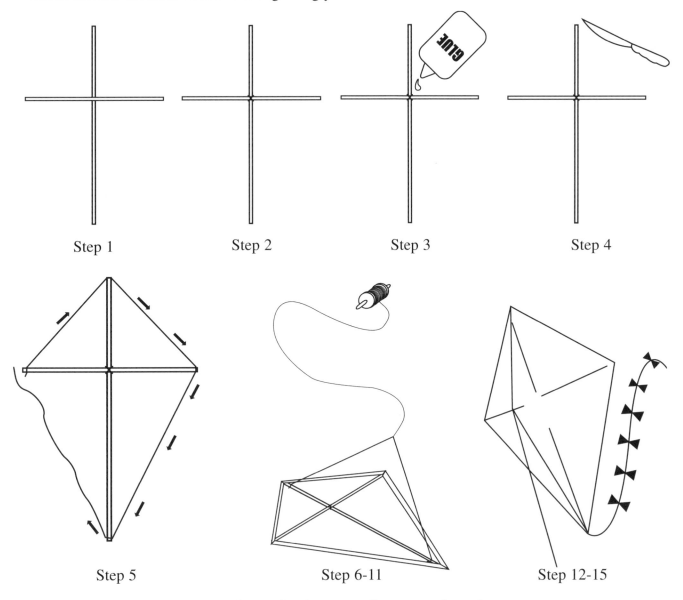

Step 1　　　　Step 2　　　　Step 3　　　　Step 4

Step 5　　　　Step 6-11　　　　Step 12-15

Note: You can make a simple reel out of soda can or flat piece of wood.

What to Wear While Flying a Kite

1. Wear comfortable shoes such as tennis or walking shoes.
2. Wear comfortable slacks and shirt to avoid wind burn.
3. Wear a ball cap to protect your head on a very sunny day.
4. Wear gloves to protect your hands.

Remember Rules for Flying a Kite

1. Fly a kite on top of a hill or in an open field.
2. Know when and how to launch a kite.
3. The wind must be to your back to get your kite to soar upward.
4. Hold the kite in the air.
5. When the wind starts blowing, let go of the kite but hang onto the reel of string.
   As the wind tugs at the kite, give the kite more string. With your help the wind will do the job.
6. Fly a kite with a friend or an adult.
7. To bring a kite down walk toward the kite, in the direction the wind is blowing. Reel in the kite line as you walk.

When Not to Fly a Kite

1. Avoid flying a kite near the edge of a steep slope.
2. Avoid using metal on a kite. Metal attracts electricity.
3. Avoid flying a kite in a rain or a thunderstorm. Electricity will travel along a wet kite line.
4. Avoid flying a kite near electrical wires, poles or trees.
5. Avoid flying a kite in strong winds.
   Now you should be ready to fly your kite. Have a great day!

Note: You can buy ready-made kites from a hobby shop. They are very easy to assemble. They come in all sizes, shapes, and styles. There is a diagram of the diagonal kite on page 21. Dihedral angle means the angle between two intersecting planes. The dihedral angle is found on the kite in the middle of the horizontal dowel.

A smaller kite is ideal for a preschool child. An adult can help a child fly and manage the kite.

Pin the Tail on the Kite Game

Supplies Needed

One diamond or nova shaped kite   Corsage pins
One hand made kite tail for each child   One scarf for a blindfold

Hang a nova kite or square ready-made kite from the ceiling or hang a diamond shaped kite on a nail on the wall. Make up a tail for each child with construction paper. Give each child one chance to pin the tail on the kite. The tail closest to the end of the kite wins the kite. The younger children seem to enjoy this game at a birthday party. See picture on page 2 in the color section.

Note: I find that most young children do not like peppers, onions, or pepperoni. When I have adults and children I make the pizza snacks half with pepperoni and half with just cheese. There are always some broken Triscuits in each box. Guests can leave the carrot on the tray and just eat the Triscuit.

Kite Pizza Snacks
Yield: Forty pieces

$^1/_3$ cup soft margarine or butter
1-9.5 ounce Tricuits® (original)
1-6 ounce tomato paste
$^1/_4$ teaspoon onion powder
$^1/_4$ teaspoon garlic salt
1 $^1/_2$ teaspoon Italian seasoning
20 slices pepperoni (sliced thin)
$2^1/_4$ cups mozzarella cheese
1-10 ounce bag shredded carrots
2 doilies

Preheat oven to 400 F. Spread margarine or butter over each Triscuit®. In a medium bowl, mix together the tomato paste, onion powder, garlic salt, and Italian seasonings. Spread each cracker with $^1/_4$-$^1/_2$ teaspoon tomato paste mixture. Place one slice of pepperoni over 20 individual pizza snacks. Top all 40 pizza snacks with the mozzarella cheese. Bake for 3-5 minutes or until cheese melts or microwave for one minute doing 10 snacks at a time or until cheese melts. Place on a serving tray with doilies. Place the pizza snack down on the tray in the shape of a diamond. Place three pieces of shredded carrot per Triscuit® to form the tail at the point of the bottom of the diamond. Pass Triscuits. See picture on page 1 in the color section.

Note: You can decorate the cake any color or colors and also use any shapes of candy such as fish with a number style candle. See picture on page 2 in the color section. The children helped Mrs. Cola decorate the kite cakes.

Note: Each square cake yields 9 servings.

Kite Cake

Yield: Eighteen servings (two cakes)

1-box 18-2.25 ounce cake mix
Eggs
Water
Vegetable oil

Follow box mix directions. Grease and flour two 8x8 pans. Divide the batter between the two pans. Place cakes on the bottom oven rack. Bake at 350 F for 25-30 minutes or until wooden pick inserted in center of cake comes out clean. Cool in pans. Place each layer on an 8 inch square cardboard. Beforehand, be sure to cover the cardboard with foil and tape the foil to the back of the cardboard. Place cakes on two separate 16x18 rectangular trays making each cake into a diamond.

Make 1 batch of the creamy cake decorating frosting on page 4. Frost both cakes. With icing-filled cake tube bag and writing tip, pipe on kite frame and border. Place star candles into the cake. Pipe in kite tails. On each tail lay one candle down. See picture on page 2 in the color section.

Windmill S'mores

Yield: Eighteen s'mores

4-9 ounce boxes (each) windmill cookies
1-13 ounce jar marshmallow cream
2-8 ounce milk chocolate bars

Place the windmill cookie face side down on the cookie sheet. Spread the marshmallow cream on the surface of each cookie. Center one square of chocolate over the marshmallow cream. Bake at 350 F for five minutes or until chocolate melts. Remove cookies from oven. Place the second windmill cookie on top of the S'more to form the sandwich. The imprint of the windmill should be on the top. Cool. Arrange on a tray. on page 1 in the color section.

Mrs. Cola's Hat Story

Mrs. Cola's mom liked to crochet. Her mother made her a surprise Christmas gift. It was a warm tassel hat and a long scarf. It was just perfect for the winter season. When Mrs. Cola opened her Christmas box she could not believe her own eyes. The hat and scarf were made of white wool. It was the perfect gift. Mrs. Cola's old hat was tattered and worn looking. She wore her new hat and scarf back to school after Christmas vacation. The other teachers and Mrs. Cola's students were very complimentary. One day there was a gust of wind in her sub-division. Her hat blow off. She chased the hat, but the wind carried it away. She could not find it and longed to have the hat back. She could not tell her mother that the hat was lost. Finally, spring arrived. She went out to her mailbox one day to get the newspapers. She looked across the field beyond her home still wishing to find her hat. There, on a far away tree, was her hat, hanging from a twig. She dashed to the tree and retrieved her hat. It was wet and cold but still in good condition. She brought the hat home, cleaned it and dried it.

To this day Mrs. Cola still wears this beautiful hat. It is a sentimental treasure. Mrs. Cola's mother became afflicted with Alzheimer's and could no longer remember how to crochet. So, Mrs. Cola wears this hat and scarf in honor of her mother's Alzheimer's. Every person has a special treasure. Can you share a treasure or tell a story that makes you think of someone special in your life?

The Wind Poem

Wind, Wind, Wind please go away,
I want to go outside and play.

I think of the wind as I ride my bike,
And hope in Spring I can fly my kite.

I like to see the flowers gently swaying on a windy day in May.
I like to feel the breeze brush my face on a sunny August day.

The wind itself I cannot see,
But I hear it blowing through the leaves on our tree.

I get the chills and I feel oh so cold,
As the wind whips mercilessly when storms unfold.

Sometimes, high winds will destroy land,
And sometimes, they move mountains of sand.

Sometimes the wind has me guessing,
However, most of the time, the wind is a blessing.

Pinwheel Pattern

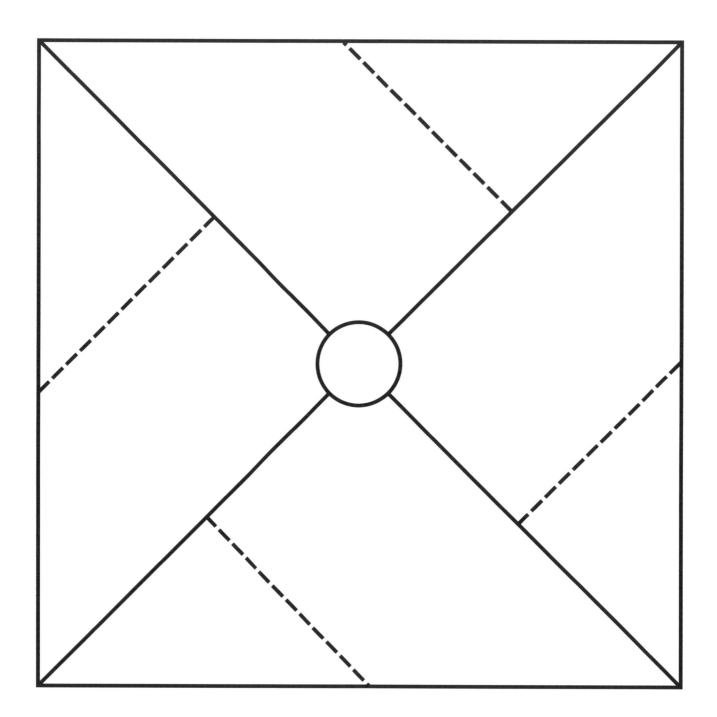

Connect the dots using the numbered dots below; start with 1 and keep connecting the dots until you are finished making the kite. Color the kite.

Diagram of a Diamond Shaped Kite

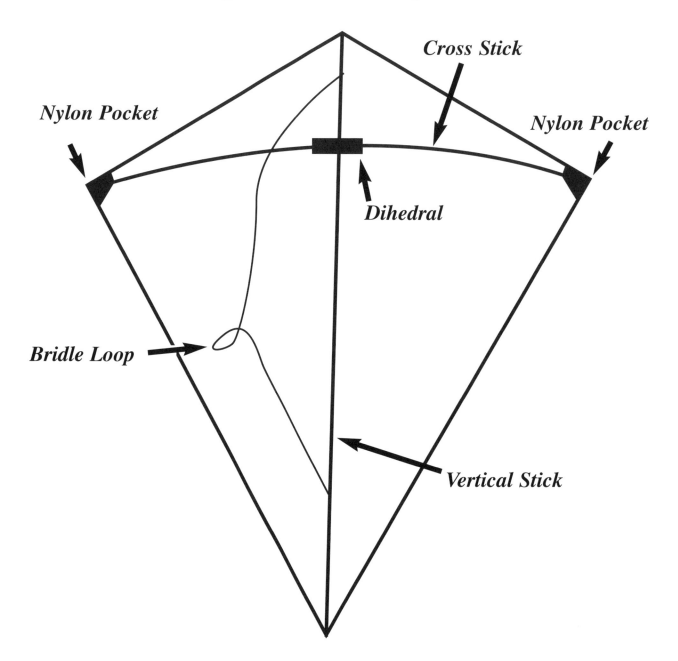

Nylon Pocket

Cross Stick

Nylon Pocket

Dihedral

Bridle Loop

Vertical Stick

Wind and Kite Theme Related Books

Bauer, Marion Dane
"Wind"
Publisher: Aladdin
Published Date: c2003
This is a simple text that makes it fun to learn about the weather. (ages 5-7)

Cobb, Vicki
"I Face The Wind"
Publisher: HarperCollins
Published Date: c2003
The author is a scientist and tells about the scientific principles in easy format. There is a simple hanger and balloon project to demonstrate the air. (ages 3-5)

Dorros, Authur
"Feel The Wind"
Publisher: Crowell
Published Date: c1989
You can feel the wind on your face and hear the wind whistle through your window. Wind travels faster than a car. Learn how to make your own weather vane. (ages 4-6)

Flanagan, Alice K.
"Wind: (A Level One Reader)"
Publisher: Child's World
Published Date: c2003
The book is a simple text that describes the wind and the effects on the world. (ages 3-5)

Fowler, Allan
"Can You See The Wind?"
Publisher: Children's Press
Published Date: c1999
Young readers discover the intriguing facts about the fascinating world around them and information on the wind. (ages 4-6)

Hoban, Julia
"Amy Loves The Wind"
Publisher: Harper & Row
Published Date: c1998
"While walking in the park on a windy day, Amy and her mother feel what the wind can do." (ages 4-6)

Madokoro, Hisako
"Buster's Blustry Day
Publisher: Gareth Stevens Children's Books
Published Date: c1991
Buster stays in his doghouse because he is afraid of the strong winds. When he goes out to play he discovers that the wind can be great fun. (ages 3-5)

Moore, Lilian
"While You Were Chasing a Hat"
Publisher: Harper Festival
Published Date: c2001
The wind takes off the little girl's hat. She chases her hat and she can see how the wind affects everyone and everything. There are full color illustrations (ages 3-5)

Pitcher, Caroline
"Run with the Wind"
Publisher: Little Tiger Press
Published Date: c1998
A foal does not want his mother to go off without him. When the mother finally leaves, the foal has fun with the wind. It is a cute story. (ages 3-5)

Shannon, George
"Dancing The Breeze"
Publisher: Bradbury Press
Published Date: c1991
Papa and his young daughter go out into the evening breeze. They dance among the flowers in the front yard while the moon rises. (ages 4-5)

Taylor, Barbara
"Wind and Weather"
Publisher: Franklin Watts
Published Date: c1991
You can see what makes the air move and how the wind effects our environment. How does pollution affect the weather? (ages 7-8)

Dixon, Norma
"Kites: Twelve Easy-to-Make High Fliers"
Publisher: Morrow Junior Books
Published Date: c1996
The book provides instructions for making and flying all kinds of kites (ages 8-12)

Kelly, Emery J.
"Kites on the Wind"
Publisher: Lerner Publications Company
Published Date: c1991
The book has instructions on how to make thirteen different style kites that fly without sticks.
There are diagrams and flying tips. (ages 10-12)

Michael David
"Making Kites"
Publisher: Kingfisher Books
Published Date: c1993
It gives step-by-step instructions on how to make different style kites and how to decorate the kites
such as stick and box kites. It also shows how to make a windsock. (ages 8-10)

Morgan, Paul
"The Ultimate Kite Book"
Publisher: Simon and Schuster
Published Date: c1992
There are diagrams and instructions on how to make different styles of kites. (ages 10-14)

Schmidt, Norman
"The Great Kite Book"
Publisher: Sterling Publishing Company
Published Date: c1997
The book teaches a person how to make different animal shapes kites such as dragonfly, falcon,
multicolor peacocks, and even a zebra. (ages 10-12)

Valentine Party

Note: You can purchase any of the items from a caterer or buy some items at the Grocery store and make some items. Time is the biggest factor. Mrs. Cola likes to cook and has the time to create a beautiful tea party.

A Special Valentine Tea

Menu

Cheese Heart Finger Sandwiches
Radish Rose Centerpiece
Cucumber Finger Sandwiches
Mini Quiches
Chocolate Covered Strawberries
Banana and Strawberry Fruit Kabobs
Mini Apple Muffins
Heart Shaped Mini Cherry Cheesecakes
Mini Pecan Tarts
Heart Shaped Sugar Cookies
White Chocolate Truffles
Raspberry Sherbet Punch
Green Tea
Raspberry Flavored Decaf Coffee

Cheese Heart Finger Sandwiches

Yield: Twenty-four

1-20 ounce loaf all whole grain or 100% whole wheat bread
1-2 ounce loaf white bread
Butter, softened
24 cheese slices
1 red pepper
1-2 inch wide heart cookie cutter

Lay out 12 slices whole wheat bread and 12 slices white bread. With cookie cutter, cut out heart shape finger sandwiches. Butter each heart. Cut out 24 heart shaped cheese. Place one slice of heart shaped cheese on the bread. Place two doilies down on a 14 inch platter. Place the heart shaped sandwiches on the platter. Cut red pepper in half. Discard the core. Cut the red pepper into short strips. Cross 2 strips on each sandwich top to form an x. See picture on page 2 in the color section.

Radish Rose Centerpiece

Yield: Twenty

20 radishes
Cold water
4 ice cubes
20 round toothpicks
1 grapefruit or large orange
Parsley

Make radish roses. Place into cold water with ice cubes. Radish rose leaves will fan out. Drain water. Place a toothpick into the center of each radish rose. Insert bottom of toothpick into the grapefruit to attach radish roses. Place the grapefruit centerpiece on a glass plate. Garnish with parsley.

Note: One slice of bread makes four 1½ inch bread rounds. One half of the cream cheese mixture makes 24 finger sandwiches. Cover leftover cream cheese mixture and refrigerate. The mixture will keep for a week. Do not freeze.

Cucumber Finger Sandwiches

Yield: Twenty-four

1-8 ounce package cream cheese, softened
1 teaspoon Worcestershire Sauce
¼ teaspoon garlic powder
6 slices of white or wheat bread
½ cup butter or margarine, softened
1 cucumber, peeled and sliced in 24 slices
Dill weed
2 doilies

Beat cream cheese. Add Worcestershire sauce and garlic powder. Beat ingredients until blended well. Cut out bread rounds with a small cookie cutter. Butter bread rounds. Spread cream cheese mixture over each bread round. Thoroughly dry sliced cucumbers with paper towel. Place one cucumber on each bread round. Lightly sprinkle dill weed over each cucumber sandwich. Place doilies on a 12 inch silver tray. Place finger sandwiches on the tray. Serve cold.

Note: Mini quiches can be reheated in the microwave, 12 at a time, for 1 minute or until the chill is removed.

Mini Ham Quiche

Yield: Twenty-two to twenty-four

Crust

3 ounces cream cheese, softened
$^1/_2$ cup butter
1 cup flour
No-stick vegetable spray
Mini-muffin tins

Quiche Filling

3 ounces cream cheese, softened
4 large eggs
$^1/_4$ teaspoon garlic powder
2 teaspoons onion flakes
$^1/_2$ teaspoon Worcestershire sauce
$^1/_2$ cup smoked ham, chopped fine

Crust Directions:

Preheat oven to 350 F. Beat cream cheese and butter together until smooth. Gradually add the flour. Beat until smooth. Lightly flour the board and rolling pin. Roll out the dough $^1/_4$ inch thick. Cut out dough with a $1^1/_2$ round cookie cutter. Spray no-stick vegetable spray into mini muffin tin. Place each round into the mini muffin tin to form the crust.

Filling Directions:

Beat cream cheese and eggs. Add garlic powder, onion flakes, Worcestershire sauce and ham. Beat all ingredients until smooth. Pour egg mixture into a glass-measuring cup with a spout. Fill each mini quiche crust with egg mixture. Bake at 350 F for 20-22 minutes or until golden brown. Cool in pan for 5 minutes. Run a knife around the outside of the crust. Remove the quiche. Place quiches on a 12 inch tray, lined with a doily. Serve warm.

Mini Crab Quiche
Yield: Twenty to twenty-two mini crab quiche

Crust
Repeat the crust as used for the mini ham quiches.

Quiche Filling
4 ounce cream cheese, softened
4 eggs
$^1/_2$ teaspoon Old Bay seasoning®
$^1/_4$ teaspoon garlic powder
1 teaspoon Worcestershire sauce
2 teaspoons dehydrated onion flakes

Preheat oven to 350 F. Spray mini muffin pan with vegetable spray. Roll out crust, $^1/_4$ inch thick, on floured cutting board. Cut out dough with $2^1/_2$ inch round cookie cutter. Place each round into the mini muffin tin to form the crust. Beat cream cheese and eggs. Add Old Bay seasoning®, garlic powder, Worcestershire sauce, and onion flakes. Beat until smooth. Pour mixture into a glass-measuring cup with a spout. Fill each mini quiche crust with the egg mixture. Bake 20-22 minutes or until golden brown. Cool in pan for 5 minutes. Run a sharp knife around the outside of the crust. Remove the quiche. Place quiches on a 12 inch tray lined with a doily.

Chocolate Covered Strawberries
Yield: Sixteen to eighteen strawberries

1 pound strawberries with hulls
1-7 ounce container dipping chocolate

Follow the directions on the box for best results for making chocolate covered strawberries.

Banana and Strawberry Fruit Kabobs
Yield: Twenty-four

3-8 inch bananas, peeled
1-12 ounce can frozen concentrate orange juice
24 frilled toothpicks
24 strawberries with hull
Parsley

Cut each banana in eight 1 inch pieces. Thaw and pour $^1/_3$ cup orange juice concentrate into a small bowl. Dip each banana piece into the concentrate. Drain on a paper towel. Place the toothpick through middle of banana and strawberry to make kabob. Place kabobs on 12 inch silver tray. Garnish with parsley. See picture on page 2 in the color section.

Note: I use 3 to 4 large Granny Smith apples for the apple muffins. Cortland and McIntosh apples are also very good for baking apple muffins. My mini muffin pan makes 24 muffins at a time.

Mini Apple Muffins

Yield: Forty

2 cups all-purpose flour
2 teaspoons baking powder
$^1/_2$ cup white sugar
1 teaspoon ground cinnamon
$^1/_4$ teaspoon salt
1 cup milk
1 egg, beaten
$^1/_4$ cup butter
1 cup apple-peeled, cored and chopped fine
mini apple muffin pan
Heart pattern mini muffin liners

Streusel Topping

Yield: Streusel topping for 40 mini muffins

$^1/_2$ cup butter (softened)
$^1/_2$ cup brown sugar (packed)
1 cup flour

Beat butter and brown sugar together. Slowly add flour. Mix together all three ingredients until well blended.

Preheat oven to 375 F. Place the heart mini muffin liners in the mini muffin pans. Stir together flour, baking powder, sugar, cinnamon, and salt. In a separate bowl, stir together milk, egg, and butter. Make a well in the dry ingredients. Stir egg mixture into flour mixture just until combined. Fold in chopped apples. Spoon an unmeasured teaspoon of batter into each muffin liner. Top each muffin with Streusel Topping. Bake for 10-12 minutes or until toothpick inserted in center of muffin comes out clean.

Note: I purchase cherry pie filling in a 2-pound pouch at a cake-decorating center. I used half of the pouch. Purchase cherry pie filling in a one-pound 5 ounce can at your local grocery store.

Heart Shaped Mini Cherry Cheesecakes
Yield: Sixty

Pastry Crust
1-$\frac{1}{2}$ cups flour
$\frac{1}{3}$ cup sugar
$\frac{1}{4}$ cup unsweetened dark cocoa
$\frac{1}{2}$ cup butter, softened
$\frac{1}{2}$ teaspoon cinnamon
3 tablespoons water
No-stick vegetable spray
Petite Heart pan

Cream Cheese Mixture
2-8 ounce cream cheese, softened
$\frac{1}{2}$ cup sugar
2 eggs
2 teaspoons almond flavoring
1-2 pound pouch of cherry pie filling or 1 pound 5 ounce can cherry pie filling
1-12 inch doily
1-12 inch tray

Preheat oven to 350 F. Spray petite hearts pan with vegetable spray. In a small bowl, combine flour, sugar, and cocoa. Cut in butter until pieces are the size of small peas. Sprinkle with water, tossing until moist. Form into 1 inch diameter log. Divide pastry into 48 balls. Press into petite heart pan making an even shell. Beat cream cheese until light and creamy. Gradually add sugar; mix well. Add eggs, mixing well. Stir in almond flavoring. Fill prepared pan with cream cheese mixture. Top each heart with one pie filling cherry. Bake for 10-18 minutes or until cheese filling is firm. Remove from pans. Cool completely. Arrange on a tray.

Mini Pecan Tarts
Yield: Forty-eight

Crust
1-8 ounce package cream cheese, softened
1$\frac{1}{2}$ cups butter
1 cup sugar
3 cups flour
No-stick vegetable spray
Mini muffin pans

Pecan Filling
$\frac{1}{4}$ cup butter, softened
$\frac{1}{2}$ cup sugar
1 cup dark corn syrup
3 eggs
$\frac{1}{4}$ teaspoon salt
1 cup pecans, chopped fine

Preheat oven to 350 F. Grease the muffin pan with vegetable spray. Beat cream cheese and butter together. Add sugar and beat. Add flour, one cup at a time. Roll out dough $\frac{1}{4}$ inch thick onto floured board. Cut out dough with a round cookie cutter. Place each round into mini muffin pan. Cream butter and sugar together until fluffy. Add the corn syrup and salt. Beat well. Add eggs one at a time beating thoroughly after each egg. Stir in pecans. Spoon pecan mixture into each tart. Bake for 12-15 minutes until golden brown.

Note: Flour board with just a little flour at a time so cookies will not stick to the board or rolling pin. Place 12 cookies on a cookie sheet 3 across and 4 down. Roll out cookies $\frac{1}{4}$ inch thick. Many people have the tendency to roll out sugar cookies too thin.

Heart Shaped Sugar Cookies
Yield: Twenty-four cookies

1 cup butter
1 cup sugar
1 egg
1 teaspoon vanilla
pinch of nutmeg (optional)
3 cups flour
1 teaspoon baking soda

Preheat oven to 350 F. Set aside $\frac{1}{2}$ cup flour for rolling out cookies. Cream the butter and sugar. Add egg and vanilla and beat. Mix together 2$\frac{1}{2}$ cups flour, baking soda, and nutmeg. Add dry mixture to the butter, sugar, and egg mixture. Beat until smooth. Roll out cookies on a floured board. Use a heart shape cookie cutter to cut out the cookies. Place twelve heart cookies on a baking sheet, 3 across and 4 down. Bake cookies 10-12 minutes. Cookies will be golden brown on the bottom of the cookie and white on the top of cookies.

Note: The glaze used on the sugar cookies is thick. One batch of glaze frosts 12 cookies. You may need to make 3 batches to frost 36 cookies. If the glaze is too thick, add a little more water. If the glaze is too thin, add more powdered sugar. I like to make small batches of glaze for best results.

Glaze for Sugar Cookies
Yield: Thirty-six

1 cup powdered sugar
2 tablespoons water
1 teaspoon almond flavoring
a pinch of salt
1-2.25 ounce container of pink crystal decors

In a mixing bowl add powdered sugar, water, almond flavoring, and salt. Beat all together until smooth. Frost the tops of each cookie with glaze. Sprinkle pink crystal decors over the frosted cookies. Arrange on a large tray lined with doilies.

White Chocolate Truffles
Yield: One pound box

Arrange the 1-pound box white chocolate truffles on a tray lined with a doily.

Note: Hawaiian punch usually comes in gallon size and bottled 7 Up comes in 2-quart size. My punch bowl holds 4 quarts with sherbet.

Raspberry Sherbet Punch
Yield: Three quarts

2 quarts Hawaiian Punch
1 quart 7up
1 quart raspberry sherbet

Mix Hawaiian Punch with the 7up in the punch bowl. Scoop raspberry sherbet into the punch. Serve in glass punch cups.

Green Tea
Yield: Ten cups

10 cups cold water
4 tea bags
1 lemon

Heat water in a teakettle. Turn off the stove. Add 4 tea bags to the hot water and steep for 5-8 minutes. Serve tea in teacups. Cut lemons into wedges. Serve with a small tray lemon wedges.

Raspberry Flavored Decaf Coffee

Yield: Eight cups

8 cups cold water
$^1/_3$ cup raspberry flavored decaf coffee
1 coffee filter

Place coffee filter into top of coffee pot. Place 4 tablespoons raspberry flavored decaf grounds into the coffee filter. Pour eight cups water into coffee tank. Perk coffee. Serve with glass coffee cups with sugar and cream.

The Purpose of the Tea

Mrs. Cola invited some of the youth church group and neighborhood friends to her home for a special tea. She saw a need to help teach some polite social behavior and forms of etiquette to children, ages 5-13.

The teatime was set for two to four p.m. She set up two guest tables with valentine tablecloths. She placed red cloth napkins through teapot napkin holders. Roses were placed in the center of each table and the buffet table. There were valentine cards and puzzles around the flower vase. Mrs. Cola made several tea items for her buffet. She also had tea, punch, and coffee for beverages. China and silverware were used for service.

Guests arrived promptly at 2 p.m. I gave them time for introductions. Five adults chaperoned the party; they also helped clean up. The children warmed up to each other very quickly. They also called the adults by Miss or Mrs. Ten children attended the party (3 boys and 7 girls). The boys were very comfortable with the girls. Mrs. Cola created a welcoming atmosphere for her tea.

Mrs. Cola's Goals for Learning About a Tea

1. Who was St. Valentine?
2. What is the real value of Valentine's day?
3. What is the importance of friendship, family, and respect for each other?
4. What types of manners are necessary while attending a tea?
5. What types of foods should be served at a tea party?
6. How to decorate for a theme tea party.
7. How to set up a buffet.
8. How to go through a buffet to select food.
9. How to use china, place napkin on lap, and drink punch or tea from a china or punch cup.
10. What topics should be discussed at the table with other guests?
11. How to include all guests in a good conversation.

Mrs. Cola also asked each family to bring a dozen cookies to donate to the Women's Center. The children made Valentine cards for the families' children in the Women's Center. Mrs. Cola delivered the cookies and cards on Valentine's Day to the Center. The children warmed Mrs. Cola's heart because they were so eager to help others and learn about a formal tea.

Mrs. Cola began the tea by reading two stories to the group. She used two reference books titled *"St. Valentine"*, Robert Sabuda and *"Valentine's Day"*, Michael Deas.

Both the St. Valentine and Valentine's Day books were on Valentine's Day. St. Valentine was a Christian and a kind man. He treated patients with his herbs and medicine. He wanted to help people feel better. He did not charge for his services. He was executed on February 14, 270 for standing firm about being a Christian. St Valentine left a message for the jailer's daughter and a violet. While roses are mostly given on Valentine's Day, the violet is also a Valentine's Day flower.

The Valentine book explains how we send cards and flowers to people we love. We should really be nice to people all year round. Cards are sent out and often say, "Be my Valentine." The Roman gods celebrated Valentine's Day. Cupid is affiliated with Valentine's Day. It is a day to celebrate love for all generations but especially for the young.

One of the guests said she was born on Valentine's Day. She celebrates two separate parties (one with family and the other with friends). She is a beautiful Valentine and a treasured friend to Mrs. Cola.

Mrs. Cola explained the rules of a formal tea. The children were very attentive. They enjoyed participating and exchanging their feelings and ideas in conversation.

After the tea the children went into Mrs. Cola's living room and played board games. The older children and younger children got along with each other very well.

At the end of the day, Mrs. Cola received many thanks and hugs. She also received thank you notes. There are two examples of the thank you notes from the children.

A Valentine Poem

Be my Valentine
'cause you're so fine

Roses are red
Violets are blue

I love you Valentine
'Cause you're so true.

Theme Related Resources and Book References

Bauer, Dane
"A Recipe for Valentine's Day"
(A Rebus Lift-the-Flap-Story)
Publisher: Little Simon
Published Date: c2005
The book uses 25 flaps that the reader can lift words such as hearts, ribbons, and cupid to make "A Recipe for Valentine's Day." (ages 3-5)

Cooper, Jason
"Valentine's Day, Holiday Celebrations"
Publisher: Rourke Publishing
Published Date: c2003
The book explains about Valentine's Day. It tells how it began, information on sending out Valentine cards, where the first Valentine cards were made, with symbols such as hearts, cupid, and roses. Legend has it that St. Valentine was put to death on February 14th in 270 AD. (ages 5-8)

Erlbach, Arlene
"Valentine's Day Crafts"
Publisher: Enslow Publishers
Published Date: c2004
"Hearts candy, hugs, and kisses...it is Valentine's Day. It is a great time to show others you care! In "Valentine's Day Crafts" author Arlene and Herbert Erlbach present step-by step instructions on how to make ten simple crafts with material that can be found around the home or in the classroom. (ages 5-7)

Lexau, Joan M.
"Don't Be My Valentine: A Classroom Mystery"
Publisher: Harper Collins Publishers
Published date: c1999
"Don't bug me, Amy Lou." She is always trying to help Sam, and it bothers him. So, when it is time for Valentine's Day Sam makes a mean card for Amy Lou. The Valentine card is delivered to the teacher instead of Amy Lou. The question is how did that happen on Valentine's Day? The sweet card from Sam goes to Amy Lou. It is a mystery. (ages 5-7)

Sabuda, Robert
"St. Valentine"
Publisher: Atheneum
Published Date:c1992
The book gives information about St. Valentine's life. (ages 4-7)

Sandak, Cass R.
"Valentine's Day"
Publisher: F. Watts
Published Date: c1980
The book tells about Valentine's Day and how it began. (ages 5-8)

Scarry, Richard
"Be My Valentine"
Publisher: Simon Spotlight
Published Date: c1999
"Be My Valentine" shows Huckle and Lowly chase a Valentine gift through the park when Hilda Hippo's good intentions go away. (ages 3-5)

Warricha, Jean
"Who Will Be My Valentine?"
Publisher: Harper Entertainment
Published Date: c2004
"Advice columnist Michelle gets a letter from a boy with a secret crush on a girl in his class—a girl who sounds a lot like Michelle. Does she have a secret admirer? Michelle is smart, friendly, and has strawberry-blonde hair. He thinks she is friendly and very nice. (ages 5-7)

DVD

"Be My Valentine, Love, Barney"
{Video recording}
Publisher: Lyons Partnership
Published Date: {2005} c2000

"Love is in the air as Barney and his friends celebrate Valentine's Day. They are invited to the Valentine Castle by the Queen of Hearts. (ages 1-8)

Half Birthday Party

Story

Marcy and Mark wanted to have a family. They were only children. For several years, she dreamed of having a baby. She even bought baby clothes and continued wishing she could get pregnant. At age 40, she gave up and decided to go back to school to work on her doctorate degree. One year later she learned she was pregnant. In disbelief she and her husband Mark celebrated. They had been married 12 years and at last their wish had come true. They decided not to tell anyone until the end of the first trimester. Then, after the three months were up, they gathered their parents and friends to tell them the big news. Marcy's mom asked when the baby was due. Marcy said, "Christmas day." Nine months went by with great anticipation. John Mark was born on Christmas Day. He weighed eight pounds seven ounces. Marcy counted his fingers and toes. The doctor announced that Marcy and Mark had a healthy baby boy. The grandparents came to see John Mark and to welcome their new grandson. He was their first grandchild. They felt that John Mark was a precious gift. Marcy and Mark were very close to their parents. In fact, Grandma announced that she was born on December 27th. Her mom always felt bad that her family would give her a gift and say "Merry Christmas" and "Happy Birthday." Marcy remembered her mom's remarks. Marcy and Mark decided to celebrate John Mark's half birthday every June 25th. He would be remembered at Christmas and also in June so he would not feel slighted like his grandmother.

John Mark is now grown and in college. Every year he and his family celebrate his half birthday. Marcy said, that now, John Mark was in his last year of college and they probably would skip the half birthday. He was getting older and most likely he didn't care about the special celebration any longer.

On June 25th John Mark called his mom after 7 p.m. "Hi mom, I thought I should call you to see how you are doing." There was a long pause from John Mark. Finally, he asked if they had forgotten to put something in the mail. His mom said, "No", I don't think so." He replied, "Oh" well, ok mom, I guess I will be going for now". He said goodbye. Later his parents learned from his best friend that John Mark was hurt because they did not remember his half birthday. At Christmas he wrote a note to his parents thanking them for all the years they celebrated his half birthday. He was very blessed to be remembered in such a special way. He knew that he was so lucky to have great parents. The next year he helped his parents prepare food and celebrated his half birthday.

John Mark's Favorite Menu

Lasagna
Romaine Lettuce Salad
Italian Dressing
Red and Green Grapes with Strawberry Garnish
Garlic Bread
Half Birthday Cake

His mom made this menu every year to please him. Actually this menu was his mom's favorite menu when she was a youngster. She began to celebrate his half birthday at age 6 months. From age 5 on, John Mark always requested his mom's favorite menu.

Note: Marcy cooked her lasagna noodles 6-8 at a time. She had a smaller pan. She filled her pan half full of cold water with two tablespoons olive oil per batch. She claimed the smaller batches cooked up better. I have tried her recipe and I tend to agree. No-cook lasagna noodles are also available at many supermarkets. Follow directions for the no-cook lasagna noodles for best results.

Lasagna

Yield: Ten-twelve servings

1 pound lasagna noodles
Olive oil
Cold water
Salt

Sauce

1 cup water
1 pound pork sausage
1 pound ground chuck
1 small onion, diced fine
2 tablespoons garlic, minced
$^1/_2$ cup fresh parsley, chopped fine
$^1/_3$ cup fresh basil, chopped fine
2 teaspoons pizza seasoning
1 teaspoon oregano
1 teaspoon salt
1 teaspoon pepper
1-29 ounce can tomato sauce
1-29 ounce can tomato puree
2-6 ounce cans tomato paste
$^1/_3$ cup red wine (optional)
2 cups zucchini peeled, shredded fine

Ricotta Filling

1 pound ricotta cheese
1 egg, beaten
$1/2$ teaspoon garlic salt
$1/4$ teaspoon onion salt
$1/4$ teaspoon white pepper

Extra Cheese

1-6 ounce package Parmesan cheese, natural finely shredded
1-16 ounce package mozzarella cheese, shredded

How to Cook the Lasagna Noodles

Add water to a 5-quart pan. Bring water to a boil. Add olive oil and salt. Add the lasagna noodles and cook until al dente. Drain and rinse lasagna noodles with cold water. Place noodles flat onto paper towel. Pat noodles with paper towel to remove excess water.

How to Prepare the Sauce

Sauté sausage and ground chuck. Drain and rinse. Add onion, garlic, parsley, basil, pizza seasoning, oregano, salt, pepper, tomato sauce, tomato puree, tomato paste, wine and zucchini. Cover and simmer for one hour over low heat. Stir every few minutes.

How to Prepare the Ricotta Cheese Mixture

In a medium size bowl, mix together ricotta cheese, egg, garlic, onion salt, and white pepper.

How to Assemble the Lasagna

Preheat oven to 350 F. Spray 9x13 inch deep lasagna pan with no-stick cooking spray. Place 3 lasagna noodles lengthwise in the pan. Spread a thin coat of the ricotta cheese mixture over noodles. Sprinkle $1/2$ cup shredded Parmesan cheese over the ricotta cheese mixture. Spread about 3 cups sauce over the Parmesan cheese. Sprinkle 1 cup mozzarella cheese over meat mixture. Repeat two more times. Top with noodles going crosswise. Place a thin layer of sauce over noodles. Top with one cup mozzarella cheese. Bake for 50 to 55 minutes. Cover lasagna with a piece of foil if mozzarella cheese becomes too brown. See picture on page 3 in the color section.

Romaine Lettuce Salad

Yield: Eight servings

1^1/$_2$ heads romaine lettuce
1 cup broccoli flowerets, chopped
1-8 ounce package fresh mushrooms, sliced
1 cup shredded carrots
1 cucumber, sliced
1 pound of grape tomatoes or cherry tomatoes
1-16 ounce bottle Italian Dressing

Wash and dry all the vegetables. Tear romaine into bite size pieces. In a large salad bowl mix broccoli, mushrooms, and carrots into the lettuce. Garnish the lettuce with cucumbers and grape tomatoes. Serve the dressing on the side. See picture on 3 in the color section.

Red and Green Grapes with Strawberry Garnish

Yield: Eight servings

6 romaine leaves
1^1/$_4$ pounds green grapes
^{3}/$_4$ pound red grapes
1-16 ounce container fresh strawberries

Wash romaine leaves and dry each one. Arrange in the shallow salad bowl. Wash grapes and dry. Reserve one large clump of green grapes and set aside. Cut remaining grapes into small clumps. Arrange the red and green grapes alternately in the bowl with the large green clump of grapes in the middle. Wash the strawberries and dry. Arrange a circle of strawberries around the large clump of grapes. Reserve remaining strawberries and replenish as needed.

Garlic Bread

Yield: Eight

1-12 ounce loaf of bread, French Baguettes style
1 teaspoon garlic salt
^{1}/$_2$ teaspoon granulated onion
^{1}/$_2$ teaspoon white pepper
^{1}/$_2$ cup butter, melted

Slice the bread into 1 inch thick slices. Mix the garlic, granulated onion, and pepper into the butter. Brush garlic butter mixture over each slice of bread, top and bottom. Bake at 400 F for 5 minutes on each side or until golden brown. Serve warm.

Note: The Christmas wreath cake can be found on page 294 in the book called an Alzheimer's Guide, Activities and Issues for People Who Care, by Pat Nekola. This cake could be used instead of the chocolate cake.

One Half Chocolate Cake

Yield: One bundt cake or two half cakes

1³/₄ cups all-purpose flour
¹/₄ cup dark cocoa
1¹/₂ teaspoons baking powder
¹/₂ teaspoon cinnamon
2 cups sugar
1¹/₂ teaspoons baking soda
¹/₂ teaspoon salt
2 eggs
¹/₂ cup vegetable oil
1 cup milk or half and half
2 teaspoons vanilla
¹/₂ cup boiling water

Combine dry ingredients in large mixing bowl. Add eggs, vegetable oil, milk, and vanilla and mix all together. Stir in boiling water last. Pour into greased bundt pan. Bake at 350 F for 45-55 minutes or until toothpick inserted in the center comes out clean. Cool 10 minutes on rack. Remove from pan; cool completely. Cut the cake in half to represent the half birthday. Frost cake with butter cream or white chocolate frosting. See picture on 3 in the color section.

White Chocolate Frosting

Yield: One bundt cake cut into two half pieces

2 cups butter, softened
2 pounds powdered sugar
$^1/_3$ cup evaporated milk
1 teaspoon water
1 cup white chocolate chips
2 cups non-dairy whipped topping
2 teaspoons coconut extract
4-4.3 ounce cups snack pack pudding
1 package cake decoration with blue flowers and saying happy birthday
4 blocks saying baby
1 happy birthday candle
Half card sign
$^1/_3$ cup chocolate jimmies

Cream butter. Gradually add powdered sugar alternating with milk. Set aside. Add water to white chocolate chips. Microwave 1$^1/_2$ minutes. Stir chocolate until smooth. Add chocolate to the frosting. Beat. Add the non-dairy whipped topping and beat. Add coconut extract and beat until smooth and creamy.

Cut cake in half vertically. Slice each half crosswise to make two layers. Fill bottom layer of each half cake with 2 puddings. Place the top layers over bottom layers. Bring a pan of water to a boil. Frost both cake halves. Dip cake spatula into hot water to help smooth the frosting. Decorate cake with flowers and place happy birthday on the cake plate. Place the four blocks on top of the cake spelling out baby. Place birthday candle in between the a and the second b. Make a half card and a sign. The card should say, "Happy One-Half Birthday, 6 months old." Place the card to the left side of the cake.

Note: When John Mark started school, his mom made peach and blueberry muffins for his teachers to celebrate John Mark's birthday. Substitute ¹/₄ cup brown sugar and ¹/₂ cup white sugar for the ³/₄ cup white sugar for a different flavor even for the blueberry muffins. I like to use the light brown sugar in the muffins for it has less molasses.

Note: Canned blueberries muffins yield 16 while fresh blueberry muffins yield 15.

Blueberry Muffins

Yield: Sixteen

¹/₄ cup butter, melted
³/₄ cup sugar
¹/₂ cup sour cream
1 egg
¹/₄ cup buttermilk
1¹/₂ cups flour
2 teaspoons baking powder
¹/₂ teaspoon cinnamon
2 teaspoons vanilla
¹/₂ cup pecans, chopped (optional)
1-15 ounce can blueberries, rinsed and drained or 1 cup of fresh blueberries

Topping

¹/₃ cup sugar
¹/₂ teaspoon cinnamon
¹/₄ cup butter, melted

Preheat the oven to 375 F. In a 5 quart mixing bowl combine butter, sugar, sour cream and egg. Mix by hand. Add buttermilk, flour, baking powder, cinnamon and vanilla. Gently stir in ingredients. Fold in nuts and blueberries. Place cupcake liners into cupcake pans. Fill each muffin ²/₃ full. Combine sugar and cinnamon. Melt butter. Brush butter over the top of each muffin. Sprinkle cinnamon/sugar mixture over top of each muffin. Bake for 20 minutes or until toothpick in center comes out clean. Serve warm. Cut muffins in half for the half birthday breakfast.

Breakfast Peach Muffins

Yield: Sixteen

¹/₄ cup butter, melted
¹/₄ cup brown sugar, packed
¹/₂ cup sugar
¹/₂ cup sour cream
1 egg
2 tablespoons peach juice
2 tablespoons buttermilk
1¹/₂ cups flour
2 teaspoons baking powder
¹/₂ teaspoon cinnamon
¹/₄ teaspoon cloves
1-15 ounce can diced peaches, drained

Topping

¹/₃ cup sugar
¹/₂ teaspoon cinnamon
¹/₄ cup butter, melted

Preheat the oven to 375 F. In a 5-quart mixing bowl combine butter, sugars, sour cream and egg. Mix by hand. Add peach juice, buttermilk, flour, baking powder, cinnamon, and cloves. Stir until mixed well. Fold in the peaches. Place cupcake liners into cupcake pans. Fill the muffins ²/₃ full. Combine sugar and cinnamon. Melt butter. Brush butter over top of each muffin. Sprinkle sugar and cinnamon mixture over the top of each muffin. Bake for 20 minutes or until toothpick in center comes out clean.

Welcome John Mark Poem

The doctor announced,
"You have a healthy baby boy."

I counted your fingers and toes.
I snuggled you against my breast
And gently touched your tiny nose.

For years, I purchased baby clothes,
Frilly things with buttons and bows.

God gave me you, John Mark.
You are perfect right from the start.

Today, I am celebrating with joy
Because you are our little baby boy.

I promise to take good care of you
And teach you many good things to do.

I will celebrate your half birthday each year
And make you feel wanted for I am sincere.

I will protect you in your crib as you sleep.
I will be excited to watch you take your first step.

I will be there always to watch you grow.
My heart is pounding and my eyes are a glow.

I am so proud to be your mother,
John Mark, I will keep you, my son, above all others.

Welcome John Mark to our family from grandparents,
Friends, godparents, mom and dad
With a loving heart, we say, "You make us happy and glad."

I love you,

Mother

Connect the dots using the numbered dots below; start with 1 and keep connecting the dots until you are finished making the present. Color the present.

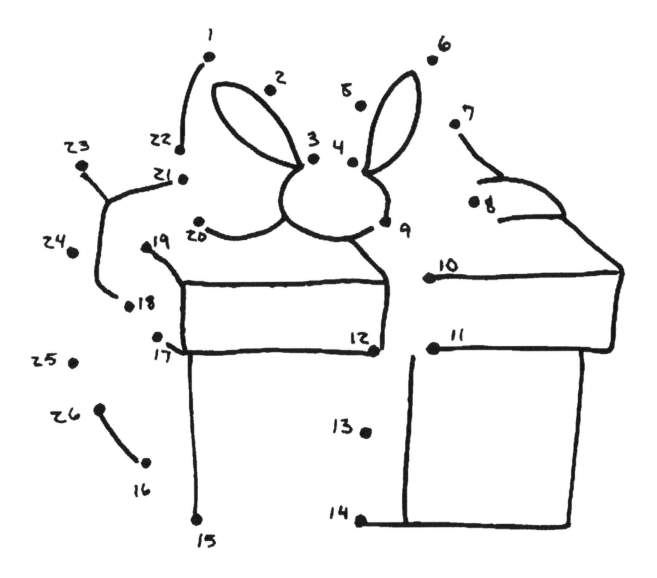

Indy 500 & NASCAR® Party

Indy 500 Trivia Questions

1. The title of a person in charge of all race functions *(crew chef)*.
2. The color of the flag the official waves when the winner crosses the finish line. *(black and white check)*.
3. What does NASCAR® stand for? *(National Association for Stock Car Automobile Racing)*.
4. The term used for a job as a racecar driver *(ride)*.
5. This is a small, open wheel racer used by a young driver *(go-kart)*
6. What does ARCA stand for? *(Automobile Racing Club of America)*.
7. What is the famous race held each year on Memorial Day weekend in Indianapolis (Indy 500).
8. A stock car that does not exceed three years is called a *(late model)*.
9. This is a special area of a racetrack where winners go there to receive their prize *(victory lane)*.
10. A race team is made up of the following three categories of people: *(mechanics, owners, and drivers)*.
11. The Busch series is the top "minor league" circuit of *(NASCAR® races)*.
12. The Nextel cup series is sponsored by NASCAR® for drivers to earn points toward a *(national championship)*.
13. The first race held in Indianapolis 500 was *(1911)*.
14. The average speed in the Indy 500 race in 1911 was *(74.60 M.P.H)*.
15. A driver must *(qualify)* in order to become a part of the race.
16. When a driver goes around the track once, it is called a *(lap)*.
17. Race cars in the old days did not have *(seat belts)*.
18. Pit row at Indy 500 is where *(drivers)* pull in for *(repairs)* and refueling during the race.
19. Spectators that go to see their favorite racecar at the Indy 500 are called *(fans)*.
20. A driver who is new at racing is called a *("rookie")*.
21. In 1911 only 27,000 fans attended the first race in Indianapolis. The following year the crowd almost tripled. How many fans attended the race in 1912? *(80,000)*.
22. *(Ralph De Palma)* was America's first auto racing super star.
23. The ultimate goal of a racecar driver is to *(win)* the race.
24. The *(pit)* crew is in charge of making sure the racecar is safe and running properly.
25. A great driver must have racing in his *(blood)*.
26. What type of glasses does a driver wear? *(sun glasses)*.
27. In the early days of racing only *(men)* were allowed to race.
28. To win races several times is considered to be true *(victories)*.
29. Today's Indy 500 racecars have high speeds of (200) miles per hour.

30. During World War II, the Indy *(500)* was cancelled from 1942-45.
31. In order for a racecar driver to win a race, he must have within himself a *(competitive)* spirit.
32. If a racecar driver becomes too warm while racing, he/she can be overcome by *(heat exhaustion)*.
33. A racer that crashes during a race can be *(killed)*.
34. By the time Jeff Gordon was age 20 he had won more than *(500)* races.
35. One of the most popular spectator sports in America is *(automobile racing)*.
36. A race car driver is always at risk of a *(crash)*.

A Racecar Driver's Dream Poem
By Pat Nekola

Catch the spirit to win,
Feel the anxiety of family's loved one.

Hear the heart beat,
of the driver in his seat.

Racing is in the driver's blood,
And he will drive again and again,
With the desire to win.

He travels the racetrack,
Knowing he could lose.

There is a thrill of speed,
He desires to take the lead.

He races each lap with determination
Brings him closer to a win.

The checkered flag hails the racer to the finish line,
He is a winner that shows joy to mankind.

He is ecstatic as he greets victory.
Celebrate your winning day and life.

The Racecar Driver
by Sue Schmitzer

Hear his heart quicken and skip a beat
As he walks to his car and climbs into the driver's seat

"Gentlemen, start your engines." A green flag cuts through the air.
The race is on with man and machine, the perfect pair.

Again and again he travels around the oval track
Coming from behind, working his way up through the pack.

The crowd is cheering; there is such a din
As each lap brings him closer to the win.

The checkered flag comes down as he crosses the finish line.
Victory is his. He grins and gives the fans the "high sign".

Laps in life's course are marked with celebrations of each birthday.
You and the racecar driver are winners, each in your own special way.

You will meet green flags, yellow flags and sometimes red,
But keep your eyes focused on the checkered flag-it can be just ahead.

Mrs. Cola's Racecar Story

Mrs. Cola grew up in Mishawaka, Indiana. Her father loved to go to the Indy 500 race. He lost his son at birth and had three daughters. He took his daughters to Indy 500 every year to tailgate and watch the trial runs. He knew all the names of the racecar drivers and every detail of the race. His best male friend passed away at age 40. So, he adopted his friend's son and introduced Jon to racecars. Jon also came along year after year starting at the age of 10. Jon now lives in Indianapolis and watches the race on TV every Memorial Day. He talks tenderly of my father for introducing him to racing. Last year a bunch of his friends went together and purchased a ticket for him for the Indy 500. It was his 60th birthday. This was a wonderful birthday present for Jon. His oldest grandson was born in May and soon would be five. Jon's wife Susie put together an Indy 500 party for Jay. She made up a racetrack with cars, a flag centerpiece, and a checkerboard cake. She gave her grandson and husband an Indy 500 blanket. She also gave Jay the NASCAR® "Jumbo Color & Fun" book with a huge box of assorted crayons. She said Jay could color while waiting for the race to begin. She made the families favorite picnic meal. Susie was from Atlanta, Georgia. Her family kidded her because it seem like everything she made had to be with peaches (not quite, but almost).

She kept the meal for lunch very simple with a racetrack theme. Little Jay always told Grandma Susie that she was the "bestest" cook.

Grandma liked to read. She said she was a racecar widow. She was a good sport around racing season. She always had something educational for the entire family such as a word search, trivia or a crossword puzzle. She read up on racing and took the time to teach Jay and the entire family the history of the Indy 500. Jay had the best of both worlds with grandma's time and a wonderful birthday party. He watched the race with grandpa. He ate lunch with the entire family. His wonderful family was full of life and a winning spirit.

The Indy 500 Menu
Grandma Susie's Special Hamburgers

Potato Chips

Taco Chips

Peach Salsa

Assorted Chilled Relishes

Checkerboard Cake and Ice Cream

Note: Grandma Susie always made her hamburgers in advance. She wrapped each hamburger patty in a plastic sandwich bag. She place the hamburgers in a larger freezer bag, labeled and dated the package. A day before the party she thawed the hamburgers in the refrigerator. The meat was already for the gas grill. Cook over low heat turning them 3-4 times until cooked through or fry. Add water to the frying pan as it will evaporate and prevent the ham burgers from burning.

Grandma Susie's Special Hamburgers

Yield: Fifteen - $\frac{1}{3}$ pound each

2 pounds ground chuck
3 eggs
2 tablespoon dehydrated onion
1 tablespoon minced garlic
$\frac{1}{4}$ cup catsup
2 tablespoons yellow mustard
1 teaspoon Worcestershire sauce
$\frac{1}{2}$ cup milk
$1\frac{1}{2}$ cup seasoned breadcrumbs
$\frac{1}{4}$ teaspoon salt
1 teaspoon pepper
Hamburger press
Wax paper

Place meat, eggs, onion, garlic, catsup, yellow mustard, Worcestershire sauce, milk, seasoned bread-crumbs, salt, and pepper in a large bowl. Mix thoroughly by hand until all ingredients are blended together. Cut 15 pieces waxed paper into 4 x 5 inch pieces. Shape each hamburger into a ball. Each ball should weigh $\frac{1}{3}$ pound. Place each ball on waxed paper. Place hamburger ball onto the press with waxed paper side up. Press down hamburger ball on the counter top to shape a perfectly round hamburger. Gently take the hamburger off the press, leaving the hamburger on the waxed paper. On the day of the party place the hamburgers on the gas grill over medium low to low heat. Turn hamburgers over as needed. Cook until the meat is no longer pink inside or fry in a pan with 1 tablespoon olive oil and $\frac{1}{2}$ cup water over medium low heat until no longer pink inside. Serve with catsup, mustard, mayonnaise, dill pickle slices, onion, and tomato slices, and cheese slices.

Peach Salsa Recipe

Yield: Twelve half pints

7 large ripe peaches
1-6 ounce can (number 10) diced tomatoes with juice
1 teaspoon fajita seasoning
1 teaspoon ancho chili pepper
3-1 ounce packages simple mild salsa mix
$\frac{1}{3}$ cup minced garlic
2 green peppers, diced fine
2 medium onions, diced
$\frac{1}{3}$ cup plus $\frac{1}{4}$ cup light brown sugar

Boil peaches in skins for 8 to 10 minutes. Peel off skins. Remove the pits. Dice peaches. Stir peaches into diced tomatoes. Add fajita and ancho chili pepper seasoning. Add the simple mild salsa mix. Stir thoroughly. Cook mixture for 30 minutes over medium heat. Remove from heat. Using a blender, place two cups at a time into the blender. Puree the salsa. It takes only a split second for each batch in the blender.

Boil canning jars, lids and rings to sterilize the canning equipment. Place salsa into pint or half pint jars. Leave a $\frac{1}{2}$ -1 inch space on top so the lids can seal. Place lid and ring on top. Tighten lids. Place into hot water bath and boil for 30 minutes. Take out of bath and set on counter top. When you hear a ping and see a slight indentation, the lid is sealed. Label and date the product.

Note: My friends went to Chile for a visit. Her husband lived in Chile when he was a teenager. He always wanted to go back to visit old friends. While traveling in Chile, they fell in love with a salsa called Pebre. (You roll the "r" as you pronounce the dish.) Every restaurant serves this type of salsa. I thought it would be fun to include the Pebre recipe. It is very delicious. My friend served this recipe at her dinner party. I just could not get enough of this great dish. I like it with taco chips.

Pebre

Yield: Ten to twelve

1 bunch fresh cilantro, (cleaned and chopped fine)
1 small onion, chopped very fine
Juice of 1 lemon
1 tablespoon balsamic vinegar
3 cloves fresh garlic, minced
3 tablespoons olive oil
3 jalapeno peppers, seeded and chopped very fine
1 tomato chopped fine

Mix cilantro, onion, lemon, balsamic vinegar, garlic, olive oil, jalapeno pepper, and tomato together. Refrigerate overnight to blend flavors. Serve with taco chips, bread or crackers as an appetizer.

Note: Make a simple salsa with the following recipe.

Quick and Easy Salsa
Yields:Eight

1-14.5 ounce can tomatoes, diced
1-8 ounce package salsa mix

Mix the tomatoes and the salsa mix together. Cook for 8-10 minutes on low heat. Cool and refrigerate. Serve with taco chips.

Southwestern Style Cheese Dip
Yield: Eight servings

1-14.5 ounce can tomatoes, diced
1-8 ounce package salsa mix
$^1/_2$ pound pasteurized cheese, sliced
4 vine sweet mini red peppers or
$^1/_2$ red pepper, diced
1-6 ounce can black olives, sliced
1 bunch of green onions, tops only, chopped

Mix the tomatoes and the salsa mix together. Microwave for 3 minutes. Stir. Lay cheese slices over the entire pan of salsa. Microwave for 3 minutes or until cheese melts. Core mini red peppers and cut into circles or remove core from red pepper. Garnish with ripe olives and red pepper circles or diced red peppers and chopped green onions. See picture on 4 in the color section.

Note: The checkerboard cake pan set comes with three 9x1½ non-stick pans and one plastic divider. Do not put plastic divider in oven or it will melt into the cake and make a real disaster. The batter weighs 4½ pounds. The checkerboard cake can be made all white. Use any color food coloring to make different colors of the checker theme. Chocolate frosting can be used in place of the butter cream frosting.

Checkerboard Cake

Yield: Ten to twelve

1 cup butter, softened
2⅔ cups sugar
3 eggs
2 teaspoon almond extract
2 cups half & half
4 cups flour
1 tablespoon baking powder
½ teaspoon salt
⅓ cup dark cocoa
½ cup milk
3-10 inch cardboard cake circles.

Preheat oven to 350 F. Spray pans with vegetable pan spray. In a five quart mixing bowl, cream butter and sugar with mixer until light and fluffy. Add eggs, one at a time, and almond flavor. Mix well. Combine flour, baking powder, and salt. Add butter to the mixture alternately with half&half. Divide batter in half. Add the cocoa and ¼ cup milk to one of the half mixtures. Beat until smooth. Add remaining milk to the other half mixture. Beat until smooth. Place batter dividing ring in the first prepared 9 inch pan. Pour chocolate batter in outer and center sections and white batter into the middle section. Remove ring from pan by gently lifting straight up on handles. Wash off any extra cake batter and dry. This will be the bottom layer of the cake. Repeat steps one and two for the top layer of the cake. Place ring in third cake pan. Place white cake batter in outer and center section and chocolate batter in middle section. Fill each cake pan not quite half way. This cake will become a checkerboard cake. Bake for 25 to 30 minutes or until toothpick inserted in the center of cake comes out clean. Cool in pan 8 minutes. Gently, remove from pans onto cardboard cake circles. Cool thoroughly. See picture on 4 in the color section.

Butter Cream Frosting

Yield: One 9 inch three layer cake

1 cup shortening
1 cup butter, softened
1 teaspoon vanilla or almond flavor
2 pounds powdered sugar
⅓ cup water

Cream shortening and butter together. Add almond flavor and beat. Add powdered sugar alternately with water. Beat until smooth. Frost cake. Place first layer of cake with the chocolate cake on the outside. Spread with butter cream frosting. Place second layer with yellow cake on outside on top of the first layer. Spread top with frosting. Place final layer. Frost the entire cake with the frosting.

Easy Chocolate Butter Cream Frosting

Yield: One whole 9 inch cake

2 cups butter, softened
1 teaspoons almond flavor
1 teaspoon vanilla flavor
$\frac{1}{2}$ cup dark cocoa
2 pounds powdered sugar
$\frac{1}{3}$ cup evaporated milk

Cream butter. Add almond and vanilla flavor. Beat. Add cocoa and beat until smooth. Add powdered sugar alternately with milk. Beat until smooth and creamy. Frost the cake.

Decorations and Supplies for the Checkerboard Cake

1 plastic 54x108 inch checker table cover, cut into strips
1-13$\frac{1}{2}$ ounce box graham cracker crumbs
3 racecars
1 number 5 white candle (with red outline)
5 black candles (with star at the top of each candle)
1 pkg toothpicks with check flags (Use a total of 17 toothpick checkered flags on top of the cake)

Mark a circle 1-$\frac{1}{2}$ from the edge of the cake to form the racetrack. Gently sprinkle $\frac{1}{4}$ to $\frac{1}{3}$ cup graham cracker crumbs on racetrack. Cut two 1$\frac{1}{2}$ yard strips from checkered table cover (4 inches wide). Make an accordion like strip and tuck it in around the bottom of the cake. With a number 30 star tip, pipe on the border, both top and bottom. Pipe the edge of the racetrack with stars. Place three racecars on the racetrack area. Place the number 5 in the middle of the cake. Place 5 black star candles at random on the cake. Place flat toothpicks at the top border about 1-$\frac{1}{4}$ inch apart. Place 3 flag toothpicks by the number 5 candle.

Note: The vase is 9 inches tall, 24 inches in diameter in the middle, 5 inches down from the top and 12 inches in diameter around the neck of the vase.

Indy 500 Centerpiece

Yield: One centerpiece

1 glass vase
4-12 ounce bags each 16mm-18mm flat marbles
1-1.5 ounce package black metallic strands
2 large black and white check flags (18 inches across x 11 inches long)
3 small black and white check flags (6 inches across x 4 inches long)
1 piece of cardboard (7 inches long and 3 inches across)

1 racecar (8 inches in length and 4 inches across)
Glue
7 black and white check flags on a toothpick
1 miniature trophy (4 ¹/₂ inches tall)
1-13x6x2 piece flower arranger (floral Styrofoam®)
1-2 inch strip duct tape
1 package black foil spray (onion grass)
1 package black and white serpentine

Place the 4 bags of marbles in the bottom of the vase. Place metallic strands over the marbles. Place the large black check into the vase one on each side and the small check flags one each side in front of the large flags and one off to the side. Glue racecar onto cardboard. Place racecar on top of the vase opening. Place 5 toothpick check flags at random in the front and side of the car. Using the top of the trophy for a pattern, draw a circular piece of floral Styrofoam® around the top outer edge of the cup. Cut out a one inch thick piece of Styrofoam® and place into the trophy. Fan out the onion grass and cut off the bottom end for the proper height of the trophy. Using a number 28 star tip, pipe on the meringue frosting on the florist Styrofoam®. Tape the trophy onto the car so tape is hidden in the back of the car. Place 2 toothpick check flags in the front into the trophy. Tie black and white serpentine around the neck of the vase and let the serpentine roll out around the racetrack underneath the cake on the buffet table. See picture on 4 in the color section.

Note: Meringue frosting hardens. Always cover the bowl of frosting with a damp cloth to prevent frosting from becoming hard. Also cover the cake tube with a damp cloth when not in use.

Meringue Frosting
Yield: One small batch

2 tablespoons meringue powder
²/₃ cups powdered sugar
3 ounces water (a little more than a ¹/₄ cup)

Add the meringue powder to the powdered sugar. Gradually add the water and beat the frosting until slightly less than a stiff batter. Use for the racecar favors and/or around the racetrack beneath the checkerboard cake on the buffet table.

Note: Purchase the Easter Hunt marshmallow candy at Easter. They will keep until May unless you have a husband with a big sweet tooth. If the racecars are used for table favors, pipe each person's name on each marshmallow racecar. Easter Hunt Eggs Marshmallow candy eggs are individually wrapped.

Racecar Party Favors
Yield: Fifteen per bag

1-14 ounce bag milk chocolate M&M's® (assorted colors)
2-7 ounce bags (each) Easter Hunt Eggs Marshmallow candy
1 batch of meringue frosting (see recipe above)

Using a number 3 writing tip, pipe meringue frosting on each M&M®. Place two M&M's® on front of car and two in back of the marshmallow candy eggs to form the wheels. Pipe on a circle for the driver's head and stick arms making one arm on each side of the head. Place on a racecar napkin at each place setting and/or place around the edge of the mirror for the racetrack area. See picture on 4 in the color section.

List of Equipment for Buffet

1 package black and white checked paper luncheon plates
1 package black and white checked luncheon napkins
Black forks, knives and spoons
2 packages Serviettes NASCAR® print napkins
2 packages 6 ¾ inch NASCAR® cake plates
Cake forks
1 basket for buns
2 small bowls for taco dip
1 black tray for taco chips
3 custard cups for mustard, mayonnaise, and catsup
5 bowls for tomatoes, dill pickles, bread and butter pickles, onion slices and green olives
1 basket for buns
1 black napkin to line basket
2 large checkered flags
1 oval shape glass mirror
1 cup of chocolate Oreo® cookie crumbs
1 cake stand
Salt and pepper

How to Set up the Buffet

Cover the table with a black tablecloth. Place the centerpiece to the left on the buffet table. Place the oval mirror in the center of the table. Sprinkle Oreo® crumbs around the outer edge of the mirror to form the track. Place the candy racecars on the Oreo® track going all the same way. Arrange taco chips and two taco dips on the black tray. Arrange the Southwestern style cheese dip next to the black tray. Place the cake stand in the center of the mirror. Place cake on top of the cake stand. Place the bowls of condiments and hamburger fixings to the right of the cake. Slice buns. Place the black napkin in the basket and then the buns. Place two large checkered flags (one on each side) in the basket. Get the hamburgers from the grill or at the stove area in the kitchen. See more pictures on 4 in the color section.

```
Y M A R K D O N A H U E T T Y Y I O K L M N B G R R E T G T
M M Y T R E W K J H B Y T R K K E N N Y B R A C K O Y I P P
F R E W Q A S C R G T Y Y U J M J I L H B I L L E L L I O T
A J F O Y T G E R R T I N M E D H D A L E E A R N H A R D T
S A P O I U Y E J K M A R I O A N D R E T T I S T W K M J T
O J C H G R F E D B B V C D E N B E R I C K M E A R S D H A
B O B B Y U N S E R Q W E R T N E I J O E D A W S O N H P N
S H I P R U N H O P S C O N T Y S R L H H Y Z D G E M T Y Y
D N D A Q W E R T R P J Y R E S S Y U L O H A S B F E W E G
O N P L A N D S H O I S T O P U I T E T Y E L E I X H S T A
O Y R E A D F M N D S Y I O P L T O S U I V L V J U Y T Q R
D R F G H C K I M N I I K Y T L O O E X W E U T P N B O E I
C U A K G E T G O N E F O E P I T O O R T U Y K R K T U I E
O T O N Y G H U N B I H O P E V T Y U T H U J I O O L W F L
D H E I J D I T J I E J I T C A J U H T F R D E J V V M W U
Y E J K L M N B V C E D C X S N N E T H G F R B F I I I H Y
Y R I C H A R D P E T T Y I C M I S E G E Q W E U T G C C E
O F O E E M T R E W M U M I M I P A T O C O N N O R E N H N
W O R T Y P O I K J U Y H T G R F E B V C D E R O Y T R Y D
M R N U J H G T R F E D F G T H J U H Y U I K J T Y H G Y Y
H D I U T F R A L U N S E R S E N I O R N Z X C U A R F T K
```

Winning Racecar Drivers for Indy 500

Billy Vukovich	Danny Sullivan	Mario Andretti
Rick Mears	Richard Petty	Kenny Brack
Pat O'Connor	Joe Dawson	Bobby Unser
Bill Elliot	Al Unser Senior	AJ Foyt
Mark Donahue	Dale Earnhardt	Arie Luyendyk
Johnny Rutherford		

```
Y M A R K D O N A H U E T T Y Y I O K L M N B G R R E T G T
M M Y T R E W K J H B Y T R K K E N N Y B R A C K O Y I P P
F R E W Q A S C R G T Y Y U J M J I L H B I L L E L L I O T
A J F O Y T G E R R T I N M E D H D A L E E A R N H A R D T
S A P O I U Y E J K M A R I O A N D R E T T I S T W K M J T
O J C H G R F E D B B V C D E N B E R I C K M E A R S D H A
B O B B Y U N S E R Q W E R T N E I J O E D A W S O N H P N
S H I P R U N H O P S C O N T Y S R L H H Y Z D G E M T Y Y
D N D A Q W E R T R P J Y R E S S Y U L O H A S B F E W E G
O N P L A N D S H O I S T O P U I T E T Y E L E I X H S T A
O Y R E A D F M N D S Y I O P L T O S U I V L V J U Y T Q R
D R F G H C K I M N I I K Y T L O O E X W E U T P N B O E I
C U A K G E T G O N E F O E P I T O O R T U Y K R K T U I E
O T O N Y G H U N B I H O P E V T Y U T H U J I O O L W F L
D H E I J D I T J I E J I T C A J U H T F R D E J V M W U U
Y E J K L M N B V C E D C X S N N E T H G F R B F I I H Y
Y R I C H A R D P E T T Y I C M I S E G E Q W E U T G C C E
O F O E E M T R E W M U M I M I P A T O C O N N O R E N H N
W O R T Y P O I K J U Y H T G R F E B V C D E R O Y T R Y D
M R N U J H G T R F E D F G T H J U H Y U I K J T Y H G Y Y
H D I U T F R A L U N S E R S E N I O R N Z X C U A R F T K
```

Winning Racecar Drivers for Indy 500

Billy Vukovich	Danny Sullivan	Mario Andretti
Rick Mears	Richard Petty	Kenny Brack
Pat O'Connor	Joe Dawson	Bobby Unser
Bill Elliot	Al Unser Senior	AJ Foyt
Mark Donahue	Dale Earnhardt	Arie Luyendyk
Johnny Rutherford		

Indy 500 Crossword Puzzle

Answers across

1. Title of a person in charge of all race functions. (2 words)

6. The initials for National Association for Stock Car Automobile Racing.

8. In the early days of racing only_____ were allowed to drive a racecar.

11. A driver has to qualify in order to enter the_____.

12. A type of car used for racing is the_____.

14. The driver will accomplishes this when he goes around the track once.

15. A stockcar that does not exceed three years is called a late_____.

16. A great race driver must have racing in his_____.

17. What the name of the race held every year on Memorial Day in Indiana is called.

18. Spectators that go to see their favorite racecar at the race are called_____.

Answers down

2. A type of car driven at the Indy 500_____.

3. When the winner sees his family, they will all give him a big_____.

4. This is what the official waves when the winner crosses the line_____.

5. A special area of a racetrack for winners to go to receive their prize_____. (2 words)

7. This term is used for a job as a racecar driver_____.

9. The place where the racecar stops to make sure the racecar is safe_____.

10. A small open wheeled racer used by young drivers _____.

11. A driver who is new at racing is called a_____.

12. Racecar drivers go at a very high_____.

13. A race car driver wears a special type of glasses to protect him from the_____.

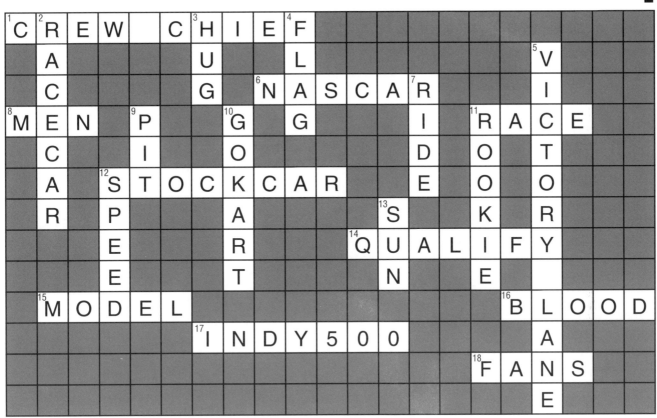

Indy 500 Crossword Puzzle

Answers across

1. Title of a person in charge of all race functions. (2 words)

6. The initials for National Association for Stock Car Automobile Racing.

8. In the early days of racing only_____ were allowed to drive a racecar.

11. A driver has to qualify in order to enter the_____.

12. A type of car used for racing is the_____.

14. The driver will accomplishes this when he goes around the track once.

15. A stockcar that does not exceed three years is called a late_____.

16. A great race driver must have racing in his_____.

17. What the name of the race held every year on Memorial Day in Indiana is called.

18. Spectators that go to see their favorite racecar at the race are called_____.

Answers down

2. A type of car driven at the Indy 500_____.

3. When the winner sees his family, they will all give him a big_____.

4. This is what the official waves when the winner crosses the line_____.

5. A special area of a racetrack for winners to go to receive their prize_____. (2 words)

7. This term is used for a job as a racecar driver_____.

9. The place where the racecar stops to make sure the racecar is safe_____.

10. A small open wheeled racer used by young drivers _____.

11. A driver who is new at racing is called a_____.

12. Racecar drivers go at a very high_____.

13. A race car driver wears a special type of glasses to protect him from the_____.

Indy 500 Theme Related Resources

Barber, Phil
"Bill Elliot: The Fasted Man Alive"
Publisher: Tradition Books
Published Date: c2004
The book gives an account of Bill Elliot's racing career. (ages 10 and older)

Brinster, Richard
"Jeff Gordon"
Publisher: Chelsea House Publisher
Published Date: c1999
The book is a biography of the racecar driver who, at the age of twenty-four was the youngest ever to win the Winston Cup title. (ages 10 and older)

Prentzas, G.S.
"Mario Andretti"
Publisher: Chelsea House Publishers
Published Date: c1996
Mario could win any kind of race. He was a racecar legend. The book also talks about racecar legends. (ages 10 and older)

Steward, Mark
"The Indy 500"
Publisher, F. Watts
Published Date: c2003
This book gives the background of Indy 500 and all the winners since 1911. (ages 10 and older)

Automobile Racing Books for Young Children

Audette, Roger
"My First NASCAR Book"
Publisher: Bendon Publisher International
Published Date: c2005
It is a cute child's book on racing and it is juvenile fiction. (ages 3-5)
For more information on the NASCAR books and other titles such as "My Big Race", My First Race!" and "My NASCAR Colors and Shapes Book" research the search engine Google, the eBay store, or call Bendon Publisher International in Ashland, Ohio (409-207-3600) I found the "NASCAR Jumbo Color & Fun Book" at my local Dollar Store. The children enjoyed coloring. I also purchased racecar pads from our neighborhood party store. I used the pads at each place setting and the children could doodle or draw a picture at the party. Many children took their pads home as a present.

A Video on Racing

"NASCAR For Kids: A Day at the Races"
{Video recording}
Publisher: Vision Media
Published Date: c1995
The video explores the garages where mechanics work on the cars, meet the race crew drivers and learn all about their jobs. The children will also learn about the high speed of a racer. It can be as high as 200 miles per hour. (ages 3-8)

Train Party

Note: The train party is for ages 4-8 with various activities according to the age groups. The adults enjoy trains and love to be around the kids to celebrate this very special party.

The Half Train Sheet Cake
Yield: Thirty-five servings

Supplies

2 11x17x1½ inch deep
  (each) foil cake pans
2 boxes (each) 18.25 ounces
  dark chocolate cake mixes
6 eggs
Oil
Water
1 number 5 birthday candle
1 glue gun
1 glue stick
5 flags picks, 1-¼ long
  and 2½ inches wide
1 package 14 decorative glitter
  Happy Birthday candles
1 decorative wooden train
1-2.75 ounce package cherry sours

1½ cups butter
3 pounds powdered sugar
1½ cups shortening
Vanilla flavoring
1 piece cardboard 14 inches long
  and 2½ inches wide
1-7 ounce bag star chocolate candy
1-10 ounce package black licorice
Green food coloring
1-15 ounce box Oreo® cookie crumbs
1 cake decorating metal spatula
2 cake decorating bags
1 number 30 star tip
1 number 234 hair tip
1-15 ounce box Oreo® cookie crumbs

Note: The 11x17 inch cake takes two cake mixes. Two cake mixes fit in a five-quart mixer. Stack two 11x17x1½ inch deep disposable foil baking pans together for strength. I used chocolate cake mixes but you can use the cake mix of your choice. I prefer cooling the cake overnight but it is not necessary. I used two dozen (each) star candies and cherry sours for decorating the border. I purchased the wooden train design at the Hobby Lobby store in Florence, South Carolina. There are many Hobby Lobby stores and other hobby stores throughout the country. There are many grandfathers who would be only too happy to make a wooden train for the cake.

Note: The Train Quarter Sheet Cake serves 12 and uses one 18.25 ounce cake mix. Use the butter cream frosting recipe on this page to frost the cake. Mix 2 cups frosting yellow with a number 30 tip pipe on the border. Sprinkle the top of the cake with multi-color sugar. Decorate with the plastic engine and train car set. Place candle into car candle holders. See picture on page 5 in the color section.

Sheet Cake
Yield: Thirty-five servings

2 Boxes 18.25 ounce cake mixes
6 Eggs
Water
Oil

Follow the directions on the back of the box mix, remembering to double the recipe. Spray the pan with no-stick spray. Place cake batter in pan. Spread batter out evenly in the pan. Bake at 350 F for 30-35 minutes or until toothpick inserted in center of the cake comes out clean. Cool cake thoroughly.

Butter Cream Frosting Number One
Yield: Frost $^1/_2$ sheet cake

1 cup butter
1 cup shortening
2 pounds powdered sugar
$^1/_3$ cup water
2 teaspoons vanilla flavor

Cream butter and shortening together. Add powder sugar, a little at a time, alternating with the water. Add vanilla and beat frosting until smooth and creamy.

Butter Cream Frosting Number Two
Yield: Frosting for grass

$^1/_2$ cup butter
$^1/_2$ cup shortening
1 pound powdered sugar
3 tablespoons water
1 teaspoon vanilla
Couple drops green food coloring

Cream butter and shortening together. Add powdered sugar a little at a time alternating with water. Add the vanilla. Beat frosting until smooth and creamy. Thoroughly mix in green food coloring until the color is evenly distributed.

How To Frost the Sheet Cake

Boil a pan of water. Place frosting on top of the cake using the cake spatula. Spread frosting over the entire cake. Place the spatula in hot water. Smooth the frosting on the entire top of the cake. With a number 30 tip, pipe on the border. Alternate the chocolate star candy with the cherry sours around the four sides of the border.

Hot glue two flags to the smoke stack of the engine and three flags onto the star of the second car. Hot glue "HAPPY BIRTHDAY" picks onto the back of the train with the letters facing the front of the train. Cut off the wicks on the happy birthday candles. Prevent a fire by not burning the candles on the wooden train.

Cut out a three inch wide cardboard, the length of the cake, into a serpentine shape. Frost the top of the cardboard. Place frosted cardboard centered on the top of the cake. Place the train onto the frosted cardboard to fasten the train in place. Make the track by placing strips of licorice along the outline of the cardboard and strips of licorice in between the wheels of the train to complete the track. Sprinkle Oreo® cookie crumbs onto the white frosted area of the cardboard to form the dirt on the track.

Using the number 234 hair tip, pipe on the green frosting to make the grass on the front of the cake and lines to form grass on the back of the cake alternating with Oreo® cookie crumbs. Place the number five candle onto the cake near the engine. See more pictures on page 5 in the color section.

Note: One 5x9 inch loaf pan serves 8 children.
Note: The spelling of Stixx® is correct. It really does have 2 x's.
Note: Stixx® is a candy shaped into logs. It is a dark chocolate covered wafer and Chocolate
crème. There are six per package. Other suggestions for the logs are:
1.65 ounce (each) S'mores bars. They are made with milk chocolate, marshmallow, and
graham cracker bites, or 2-3 ounce (each) chocolate cake rolled with creamy filling. Each
chocolate cake is one ounce. There are three per package.

The Smile Candy Train

Supplies
4-5x9 inch loaf pans
4-6x10 inch cardboard pieces
1 birthday candle with number of age
1 package of four jungle animal cake decoration and party favors
1-3½ x ½ x 2½ inch cardboard
2½ x 3½ cardboard pieces
1 plastic balloon bouquet party favor (12 balloons)

Lumber Supply Store
1-10x44 inch long finished wood or shelving board

Groceries for the Smile Candy Train Cake

4-18.25 ounce boxes (each) cake mixes

1 dozen eggs

4-1 pound containers (each) creamy chocolate frosting

2-1 pound containers (each) white creamy frosting

1 yellow food coloring

Oil

Canola oil no-stick spray

1-8 ounce package mini Oreo® cookies

1-14 ounce package chocolate Oreo® sandwich cookies

½ pound milk chocolate candy with rainbow sprinkles

2-2.75 ounce (each) cherry sours

5-4 inch individually wrapped (each) tootsie roll

1-6.25 ounce package lifesavers (with five flavors)

1 pound miniature bubble gum balls

1 pound bag animal crackers

2-2.5 boxes (each) gumdrops

1-3.14 ounce package milk chocolate M&M's®

2-3.64 ounce boxes (each) crunch dark Stixx® candy

1-5 ounce box waffle cones

1-3.5 ounce box of ice cream cones

How to Make the Cakes for the Smile Candy Train Cake

Prepare the four loaf pans with no-stick spray. Mix one cake mix at a time following the directions. Pour batter into prepared pans. Bake at 350 F for 45-55 minutes or until toothpick inserted into the center of the loaf cake comes out clean. Cool thoroughly before frosting.

How to Assemble the Train Cake

Frost four 6x10 inch cardboards with the chocolate frosting. Place one loaf cake per cardboard to make train cars. Cut the first car down by slicing off a 1 inch thick layer of the cake straight across the top. Cut a well into the second and third car leaving a one-inch edge around all four sides of each cake. Frost all four cakes with the chocolate frosting. Frost the center of the wooden board. Place all four cakes in a line in the center of the board to form the train. See more pictures on page 5 in the color section.

How to Decorate the Engine

FRONT CAKE

Trace pattern below on cardboard. Cut out sides and front of the engine from the cardboard. Frost the edges of the cardboard pieces. Place cardboard together to form the sides and front of the engine. Using chocolate frosting and a number 501 star tip, pipe on squiggly lines at random over the three cardboard pieces. Place engine front onto the front of the cake. Pipe on a circle of yellow frosting in the middle of the front of the cardboard to form the light. Place one yellow M&M® in the middle of the circle to form the headlight on the front of the train. With a number 501 star tip, pipe on a border of chocolate frosting on the top and sides of the cardboard to finish off the front of the train. Alternate orange and yellow M&M's® around the border. Place one ice cream cone with point down into the cake, centered in the front of the cake. With a number 3 writing tip, pipe a face onto the front of the cone. Fill the cone with yellow frosting. Place various colored M&M's® on top of the frosting. Place a bouquet of plastic balloons into the center of the frosting filled cone. Cut down a cone with the flat bottom to two inches tall. Place the cone on top of the back of the engine with flat side up. With a number 32 tip, pipe on yellow frosting up and around all the cone to cover. Place one red gum drop centered on top of the ice cream cone. Place eleven red gum drops around the bottom of the ice cream cone. Alternate red, yellow and green M&M's® with red cherry sours on the sides and front of the engine to form the candy border.

Engine Pattern

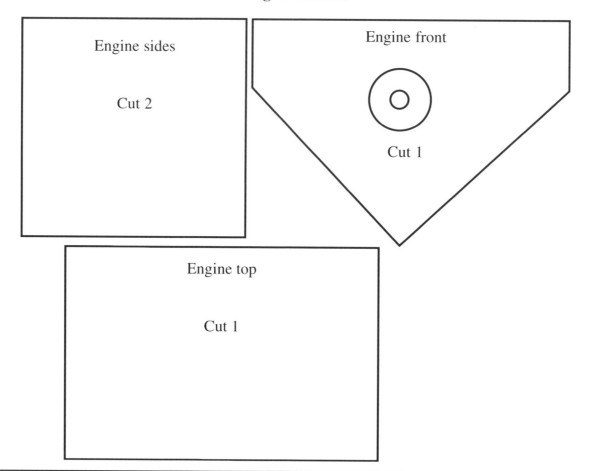

The Log Car Number One

Frost the top of the cake yellow. Place 5 Tootsie Rolls® off centered. Place 3 Stixx® candies to one side of the tootsie rolls and 9 Stixxs® to the opposite side of the tootsie rolls in a stacking fashion. With a number 32 tip, pipe on the border on all four sides of the log car. Place the candy on the border alternating the various colors of lifesavers with blue M&M's®.

The Animal Car Number Two

Place animal crackers at random into the well of the car, stacking up the various animals. Place the 4 jungle animals into the center of the cake into the animal cracker area with animal faces facing the front of the cake. With a number 32 tip, pipe on the border with yellow frosting. Place chocolate candy with rainbow sprinkles around the border of the cake.

The Bubble Gum Car Number Three

Fill the well with the assorted colored bubble gum balls. With a number 32 tip, pipe on the border with yellow frosting. Alternate green with red gum drops around the four sides of the border of the cake. Place the number "6" birthday candle into the cake or the number for the age of the child.

Placement of Wheels for the Train

Note: Take seven large Oreo® cookies apart.

Engine Wheels

Place one large Oreo® cookie in the front and back on each side of the engine.
Place two mini Oreo® cookies next to each large Oreo® cookie on the front and back of each side of the engine.

Cars 1,2,3 Wheels

Place one large Oreo® cookie in the front and back and each side of the cake for car 1, 2, and 3. Place one mini Oreo® cookie next to each large Oreo® cookie on all three cars.

With a number 32 tip and yellow frosting, pipe on a line connecting the large and small Oreo® cookies together on the three cars and the engine. Pipe in yellow frosting into the middle of each lifesaver. Place each lifesaver into the center of each large Oreo® cookie.

How to Make Railroad Tracks

Outline the entire bottom of cardboard with licorice all the way around the train. Cut licorice pieces to fit onto the cardboard (touching the cake and the licorice outline). This will form the links of the track. Place one link of licorice in between each car. Take lots of pictures and enjoy!

Note: One miniature train serves two children. There are a total of 8 miniature cakes.

The Miniature Train

Yield: Sixteen servings

Supplies

1 train set with tracks, engine, 2 cars, caboose
8-2/₂ x 5¹/₂ cardboard pieces
1 package miniature flags on picks
1 package plastic red stars on a pick
1 package jungle animals cake decorations and party favors
8-2¹/₂ x 4-¹/₂ inch loaf pans

Grocery Supplies

1 pound package miniature gumballs	3 eggs
1-6.25 package lifesavers (five flavors)	1-7-ounce package Whoppers® (malted milk balls)
1-3.14 ounce package M&M's®	1-8 ounce box dark cocoa
1-12 ounce package mini tootsie rolls	1 pound butter
1-18.25 ounce white box cake mix	1 pint fat free half and half
Oil	Vanilla
Water	No-stick cooking spray

Spray loaf pans with no-stick cooking spray. Follow directions on the box cake mix. Fill the loaf pans a little more than half full. Bake at 350 F for 18-20 minutes or until toothpick inserted in the center of the cake comes out clean. Cool thoroughly.

Microwave Fudge Frosting

Yield: Frosting for 8-2¹/₂ x 4¹/₂ loaf cakes

1 pound powdered sugar
¹/₂ cup dark cocoa
¹/₂ cup butter
¹/₂ cup fat free half and half (divided)
¹/₂ teaspoon vanilla

Place powdered sugar, dark cocoa, butter, and ¹/₂ cup half and half in a microwave bowl. Microwave ingredients for 2¹/₂ minutes. Remove bowl from the microwave. Place ingredients into a mixing bowl. Add the vanilla. Beat frosting, while slowly adding the remaining half and half. Beat until smooth and creamy. Refrigerate the frosting for 30 minutes.

How to Frost and Decorate Cakes

Frost 8 cardboards. Place one cake per cardboard.

Cut down one cake by slicing off a $1/2$ inch thick layer of cake across the top of the cake. Frost the cake and place four rows of miniature tootsie rolls on the top of the cake. Place 3 flags in the front of the cake. Place 1 birthday candle in the center of the cake. Place 1 lifesaver per wheel on each side of the cake, both front and back. (4 total)

Using four cakes, cut out a well in each cake leaving $1/2$ inch thick sides and bottom. Frost the cakes by smoothing frosting on each cake with hot water. Fill the four train car cake with animal cookies and one party favor jungle animal per cake. Outline each of the four cars with M&M's®. Place 4 mini Oreo® cookies for the wheels (one on each side of the car, both front and back). Place three flags in front of each car. Place 1 star pick in back of the animal car for two of the cars. Center 1 birthday candle in each of the other two cars.

Frost the remaining 3 cakes by smoothing frosting on each cake with hot water. Two cakes have gum-balls on top of the cake with mini Oreo® cookies for the wheels, 1 birthday candle centered in the middle of each cake and 3 flags in the front of each cake. Place mini Oreo® cookies one on each side on the car both front and back to form the wheels.

Fill another of the eight cars with gumballs, malted milk balls, 1 animal cracker and lifesavers on top of the cake. Place 3 flags in the front of the car. Place miniature Oreo® cookies on the bottom of the car with one on each side (both front and back). Put together the train tracks to form a circle. Place track on the buffet table. Place the engine on the track in front of the decorated cake cars. (four cakes on each side). Place the caboose on the other side of the track with the remaining four cakes in front of the caboose. Place the wooden patriotic train with bears and "Happy Birthday" sign centered to the back of the track. See picture on page 5 in the color section.

Place the Following Foods in the Center of the Track

1 tray of quesadillas (cheese and chicken)
1 bowl of scoop tortilla chips
1 bowl sliced ripe olives
1 dish of re-fried beans
1 dish of Mexican rice
1 bowl of guacamole dip
1 dish of pica de gallo sauce
1 dish sour cream

Note: See recipes below for the Mexican buffet placement in the center of the train tracks.

Note: The Spanish word "queso' means "cheese". The tortilla has shredded cheese. Mexicans often use a soft farmer's cheese such as Chihuahua cheese. They also use light colored melting cheese. Some quesadillas include beans or meat filling. The various methods for cooking quesadillas are fried, deep-fried, toasted, griddle or open fire. Some quesadillas include spicy salsa. Most Mexicans use corn tortillas and the "Oaxaco" cheese. This is a type of Mexican cheese, which originated from the Mexican state of Oaxaco.

Note: The quesadillas are cut into wedges in most Mexican restaurants. Some quesadillas are used as appetizers. The most common quesadillas are made of two tortillas, like a sandwich with cheese and meat. Some Mexican restaurants fold over the quesadillas.

Note: There are 8-12 inch tortillas to a 14-ounce package. Cut each 12 inch cooked quesadilla into 6 sections. Most children will eat a cheese quesadillas. The chicken quesadillas are a favorite of many adults.

Cheese Quesadillas

Yield: Six

1 quesadilla maker
2-12 inch flour tortillas
1 cup four cheeses, shredded

Heat the quesadilla maker. When the machine is hot, the light shows the machine is ready. Place 1 flour tortilla on a cutting board. Sprinkle 1 cup cheese over the tortilla leaving a $1/2$ inch space around the outer edge of the tortilla. Place the second tortilla over the cheese. Place tortilla onto the quesadilla maker. Place lid down onto the quesadilla and bake for 4 to 5 minutes or until golden brown. Cut into 6 quesadillas. Arrange on a platter.

Chicken Quesadilla Filling

Yield: Six

1-14 ounce can vegetarian vegetable broth (100% fat free)
2 tablespoons olive oil
2-6 ounce chicken breasts (Boneless and skinless), diced
1 large bell pepper, cored and chopped
1 small onion, diced fine
$1^1/2$ cups pico de gallo sauce
1-14 ounce package 12 inch flour tortillas

In a large frying pan add 3 tablespoons vegetable broth and 1 tablespoon olive oil. Add chicken and stir-fry. Remove the chicken from the pan and set aside. Wipe the pan clean. Add 1 tablespoon olive oil and 3 tablespoons vegetable broth. Stir-fry the bell pepper and onion. Add the chicken to the bell pepper mixture. Set this mixture aside.

Pico de Gallo Sauce

Yield: Three cups

1 pound ripe Roma tomatoes, (chopped fine)
1²/₃ ounce package fresh cilantro,(chopped)
1-11.5 ounce mild sliced green Jalapeno peppers, (seeded and chopped fine)
2 green onions with tops and bottoms,(chopped)
1 tablespoon fresh lime juice
1 teaspoon sugar
2 teaspoons olive oil
1 teaspoon red wine vinegar
1 teaspoon pepper
¹/₂ teaspoon salt
1 teaspoon fajita seasoning

In a medium size bowl stir together tomatoes, cilantro, Jalapeno peppers, green onions, lime juice, sugar, olive oil, red wine vinegar, pepper, salt, and fajita seasoning. Add 1¹/₂ cups pico de dallo sauce to the chicken quesadilla recipe. Cook over medium heat stirring constantly. Simmer to cook down excess juice from the tomatoes. Use the remanding pico de gallo as a condiment with the cooked quesadillas or with the scoop tortilla chips.

Note: The quesadilla maker makes 6 pie shaped sandwiches.

Note: Leave ¹/₂ space around the edge of each tortilla to prevent ingredients oozing out.

Chicken Quesadillas

Yield: Twelve

4 flour tortillas
2 cups chicken quesadilla mixture
2 cups four cheeses, shredded
No-stick olive oil spray
1 quesadilla maker

Lay out 2 flour tortillas on counter top. Place 1 cup of chicken quesadilla mixture on top of each tortilla. Top each tortilla with one cup four cheeses. Place second flour tortilla over each of the bottom tortillas. Spray the no-stick olive oil spray over the top and bottom of the quesadilla maker. Place quesadilla into the quesadilla maker. Close lid. Bake for 6-9 minutes or until quesadilla is heated through and golden brown. Repeat steps for the second quesadilla.

Note: Stir the rice every few minutes to keep rice from burning.

Mexican Rice

Yield: Six servings

3 tablespoon olive oil
1 cup white rice
1-14 ounce can chicken broth
1 cup mild picante sauce
2 tablespoons chopped onion
1 tablespoon minced garlic

Heat skillet. Add the cold oil to the bottom of the pan. Stir in the white rice and sauté until golden in color. Add the chicken broth, picante sauce, onion, and garlic. Stir. Cover and cook 10-15 minutes or until liquid has been absorbed and rice is tender. Serve with the quesadillas

Refried Beans

Yield: Six

1-15 ounce can refried beans
1 teaspoon southwest seasoning
$\frac{1}{3}$ cup picante sauce
1 teaspoon minced garlic
No-stick olive oil cooking spray
1 cup four cheeses

Place refried beans in a medium size bowl. Add southwest seasoning, picante sauce, minced garlic and stir. Spray medium baking dish with no-stick olive oil cooking spray. Place refried beans into the dish. Top with the 1 cup of four cheeses. Bake at 350 F uncovered for 15 to 20 minutes or until heated through and the cheese is golden brown. Serve with the quesadillas.

Sour Cream

Yield: Six

1 pound sour cream
Paprika

Place sour cream into a small bowl. Lightly sprinkle paprika on top of the sour cream for color. Serve cold with the quesadillas.

Guacamole Dip

Yield: Six

2 ripe avocados, peeled, cored
1 Roma tomato, seeded and finely diced
2 tablespoons guacamole mix
$^1/_2$ fresh squeezed lime

Note: The dry guacamole mix comes in a 1.5 ounce package in the produce department.

Mash avocados with a fork. Add the Roma tomato, guacamole mix, and lime juice. Mix thoroughly. Serve with the quesadillas.

Ripe Olives

Yield: Six

1-6 ounce can ripe olives, drained

Slice olives and place olives into a small bowl. Serve with the quesadillas.

Note: I always serve the olives separate because some children and adults are not lovers of ripe olives.

Con Queso Appetizer Dip
Yield: Fifteen servings

2 pounds ground beef, browned drained and rinsed
1 medium onion, diced fine
1 tablespoon minced garlic
1-15 ounce can crispy corn
1-15 ounce can chili beans
1-15 ounce can back beans, drained and rinsed
2-16 ounce jars (each) mild picante sauce
1-10$^{3}/_{4}$ ounce can Pepper Jack soup
$^{1}/_{4}$ teaspoon salt
$^{1}/_{2}$ teaspoon pepper
1 teaspoon chili powder
1-16 ounce package fancy 4 cheese Mexican shredded cheese
1-13 ounce package nacho cheese chips, crushed
1-11 ounce package tortilla chips, scoops style
No-stick baking spray

Preheat oven to 350 F. In a large pot, brown the ground beef with onion. Add garlic, corn, chili beans, black beans, picante sauce, Pepper Jack soup, salt, pepper, chili powder, 2 cups cheese, and $^{1}/_{2}$ of the crushed nacho chips to the beef and onion mixture. Cook over low heat for 5 minutes, or until all the ingredients are heated through. Spray no-stick baking spray into a 9x13 casserole dish. Place the dip into the dish. Top with the remaining 2 cups of cheese add second half of the bag of the crushed nacho cheese chips. Bake the dip uncovered for 15-20 minutes or until the cheese is melted and nacho chips are crisp. Serve with tortilla chip scoops.

Scoop Tortilla Chips
Yield: Six

1-11 ounce bag scoop tortilla chips

Fill one bowl with scoop tortilla chips

Note: Purchase a mini train pan at your local cake decorating shop. There are 6 mini trains per pan. The Sundae Neapolitan Coconut candy is sold at local grocery stores in bulk. You may want to substitute another type of candy if your store does not sell this style of candy. I cut off the pink on the Neapolitan candy for the front of some of the engines. If a child is allergic to coconut be sure to select another style of candy for the entire group to avoid problems. Have extra candy in case the children eat a piece of the candy. I have two extra tootsie rolls and one extra Oreo® cookie for them to eat while they decorate their crisp rice cereal train. See picture on page 5 in the color section.

Individual Crisped Rice Cereal Trains

Yield: Eight

3 tablespoons butter
4 cups miniature marshmallows
6 cups crisped rice cereal
Pound container prepared chocolate fudge frosting
1 package Thomas the Train plates (12 per package)
Portion control cups (one per child)
Plastic knives (one per child)
8 decorated boxes to hold candy pieces
1-14 ounce package Oreo® cookies
2-2.25 ounce boxes (each) gumdrops
1-5.30 ounce package M&M's®
2-6.25 packages lifesavers
1 pound package cherry bites
1–12 ounce package mini tootsie rolls
8 milk chocolate with rainbow sprinkles
6-ounces bulk Sundae Neapolitan Coconut Candy
A sample of the decorated train
1 package Thomas the Train cake napkins (16 per package)
1 roll of paper towel

Melt butter in a large pan. Add marshmallows and stir constantly until marshmallows are melted. Add crisped rice cereal. Stir until marshmallow and butter mixture sticks together with the cereal. Butter the mini train pan generously. Place mixture into the train pan in each of the six sections. Form the individual trains. Remove formed trains. Repeat in two more times. Cool train thoroughly. Place one crisped rice cereal train on a Thomas the Train cake plate with a portion control cup filled with frosting, and one plastic knife. Place the plate at each child's place setting. Place a cream cheese box covered with Thomas the Train material at each place setting. See pattern on page 91. Each box is filled with 2 Oreo® cookies, 1 red gum drop, 10 assorted M&M's®, 2 lifesavers, 2 pieces of cherry bites, 2 miniature tootsie rolls, 1 milk chocolate with rainbow sprinkles, and 1 Neapolitan block of candy. Help each child frost the train border and areas where candy adheres to the train. Give each child the opportunity to decorate his/her own train and decorate the train by piping on the frosting as a border. The children can eat train while at the party or take it home. See picture on page 5 in the color section

Decorated Cream Cheese Box

Yield: One box

1-8 ounce cream cheese box
1-11 inch long piece of Thomas the train material
2-1¹/₂x1³/₈ inch pieces of Thomas the Train material
Scissors
Hot glue gun
Hot glue

Lay open the cream cheese box. Tuck in side flaps to the inside to make the box flat. Lay box onto the material and trace the pattern adding on one-inch to the lid area. The extra material is tucked inside of the box. Cut out the pattern. Trace the sides of box. Place pattern on the material and cut out two sides. The pattern is on page 90. Wrap the material around the box ending at the inside of the lid and bottom of the box. Hot glue the material to the sides and the body of the box. See pattern on page 90 and picture of the finished box on page 5 in the color section.

Pretend Cone Train Horns

1-4 inch cone
1-6 inch cone
1-8 inch cone
¹/₂ yard Thomas the Train material
3 Thomas the Train pictures on a circle with pick
3 sets plastic balloon bouquets

Details on Patterns for the Thomas the Train

Note: Each pattern is shaped like a circular skirt

1. **The 4 Inch Cone Pattern**
   5 inches long on the left side
   5³/₄ inches long on the right side
   2³/₄ inches (half circle shape) at the top
   10 inches (half circle shape) at the bottom

2. **The 6 Inch Cone Pattern**
   6¹/₂ inches long on the left side
   5¹/₂ inches long on the right side
   3¹/₂ inches long across top and
   4¹/₂ inches (half circle shape) across the top
   11¹/₂ inches (circular skirt style) across the bottom

3. **The 8 Inch Cone Pattern**

$8^1/_2$ inches long on the left side

$9^1/_2$ inches long on the sight side

$7^3/_4$ inches (half circle shape) across the top

15 inches wide (circular skirt style) across the bottom

Follow patterns for each size. Lay pattern on material. Cut out 1 pattern per size of cone. Wrap each piece around the prospective size cone and hot glue seam in place. Put the Thomas the Train picture on a pick into the center of the top of the cone and balloons behind Thomas the Train picture. See pattern on page 91. See picture on page 5 in the color section.

The Thomas the Train Table for the Children

Cover the table with a plastic blue tablecloth. Place a Thomas the Train runner down the center of the table. Place the pretend horns in the middle of the table on the Thomas the Train runner. Place decorated crisped cereal train engines and miniature car trains down the center of the runner (some on each side of the pretend horns).

Note: Each child can wear his/her visor once he/she sits down at his/her assigned seating.

Each Child's Place Setting

1 train engine visor with name of the child

1 train whistle

1 Thomas the Train plate with the crisped rice cereal train

1 cream cheese box decorated with Thomas the Train material,
  filled with candy

1 Thomas the Train napkin

2 pieces paper towel above the place setting

Place the visor, whistle, Thomas the Train plate with crisped rice cereal train, 1 cream cheese box decorated with Thomas the Train material and filled with candy for decorating the crisped rice cereal train. See picture on page 5 in the color section. Also place the napkin and paper towel at each place setting.

Note: I play the accordion and played train songs for the children. Some of the train songs are "Casey Jones", "Do the Locomotive", "Night Train," and "I've Been Working on the Railroad". The live music is a plus for the children.

Suggested Activities for the Train Party

*Musical trains: Line up chairs per number of children. Play a CD or audio tape of train songs. Use a train whistle as you stop the music. The last child to be seated wins the game. The children enjoyed this game.*Hand out a jigsaw puzzle featuring Thomas the Tank Engine. Have the older children work with the younger children to put the puzzle together.

*Get the children to guess how much candy is in each car if you make the larger train cake.

*Have a sing- along with Thomas the Train

*Decorate the crisped rice cereal trains.

*Have a map of the United States. Ask the children to place a dot in their state and a dot in each of the states where other relatives live. Have the children connect the dots. This exercise is for 8 and older children or can be accomplished with adults.

*Watch a 40 minute video on Thomas & Friends. The title is Songs from the Station. Get the children to sing and interact with the video. This video is great because it teaches the children about kindness, teamwork and patience. See if the children can remember the names of Thomas's friends after the video. They are Thomas, James, Percy, Gordon, Emily, Henry, Edward, and Toby. The songs are very upbeat. For more information visit Thomas & Friends at www.thomasandfriends.com.

*Take the children to a train museum to watch the trains and learn about the history of trains. This could be a family outing with a small group of friends.

Train Story

There are three neighbors that have large areas with miniature train sets. My one neighbor added on to his home so that he could expand his train hobby. He raised 4 daughters. He always wished to have boys. Finally, he realized he would not have boys. He went out and bought a male dog. All of the neighbors have kidded him for years about his male dog.

He got a couple of his daughters to take an interest in his train hobby. His daughters are now married and have sons. Grandpa Bill is very excited to have his four grandsons come to the house to see how his toy trains run and they enjoy his fancy train yard.

Train Thoughts Poem
by Pat Nekola

Ride the train,
Hear the whistle blow,
See the wheels blaze the track.

Listen to the brakes squeak,
Count the boxcars,
Wave at the engineet.

Enjoy the ride,
Make a new friend,
Sing a Choo Choo song.

After the ride,
Stop, look, and listen,
For the red flashing lights.

Be aware of the train,
Wait for the gate to be upward,
Cross the tracks cautiously.

Avoid walking on the tracks,
Respect the signals,
Be safe and watch for the train.

Pattern for the Cream Cheese Box

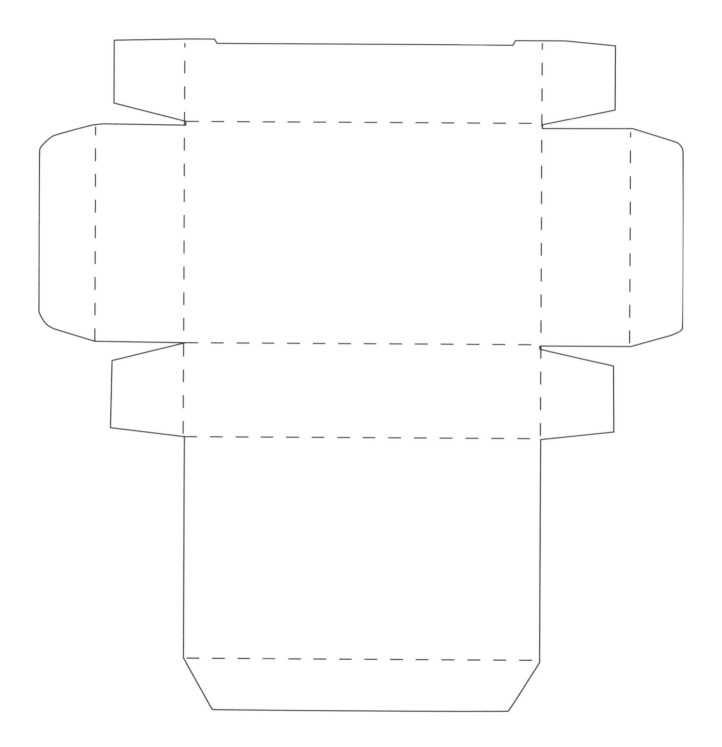

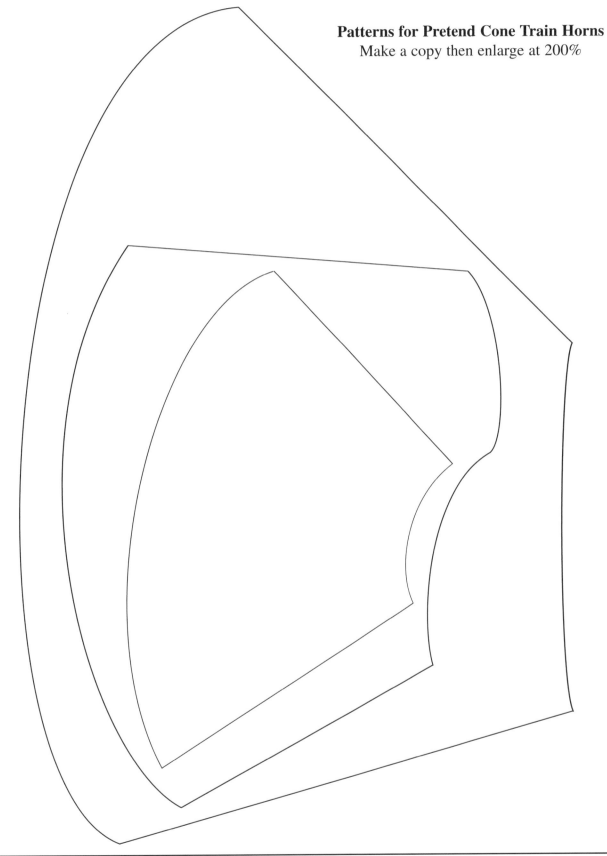

Patterns for Pretend Cone Train Horns
Make a copy then enlarge at 200%

Train Theme Related Resources and Book References

Balkwill, Richard
"The Best Book of Trains"
Publisher: Kingfisher
Published Dates: c1999
This book explains trains of the various ages (ages 8-10)

Booth, Philip
"Crossing"
Publisher: Candlewick Press
Published Date: c2001
It has many illustrations of the parts of the train such as the boxcars and a caboose. It teaches safety. The book tells the story of trains from laying the tracks to traveling as a passenger. (ages 5-9)

Culicutt, Paul
"This Train"
Publisher: Farrar Straus Giroux
Published Date: c1999
There are many pictures and few words to describe the kinds of trains such as long, short, and the color. The book is designed for a young reader.(ages 2-6)

Hillenbrand, Will
"Down by the Station"
Publisher: Harcourt Brace
Published Date: c1999
Ride the train and learn about the animals at the zoo (ages 3-4)

Hubbell, Patricia
"Trains" Steaming! Puffing! Huffing!
Publisher: Marshall Cavendish
Published Date: c2005
This preschool book talks about all kinds of trains. (ages 3-4)

Lenski, Lois
"The Little Train"
Publisher: Random House
Published Date: 2000 (c1940)
Mr. Small does it all! In this adventure, Engineer drives his little train from Terry town to city-and-back. Along the way, the train passes tunnels and stops at stations to pick up cargo and passengers. The book is in full color. (ages 3-5)

Piper, Watty
"Little Engine That Could"
Publisher: Philomel Books
Published Date: c2005
It is an excellent book for preschoolers. "Although he is not very big, the Little blue Engine agrees to pull the standard train full of toys over the mountain." It is a good book to help build self-esteem. (ages 3-5)

Note: Both my husband and I had this book when we were youngsters. To this day, I have a framed picture in my kitchen saying "I think I can, I think I can." The saying and the picture give me encouragement when I am uncertain of accomplishing a task.

Ray, Mary Lyn
"All Aboard"
Publisher: Little, Brown
Published Date: c2002
Climb aboard this train with Mr. Barnes and travel the train, both day and night to enjoy the sights and sounds of the train ride. (ages 1-3)

Rey, Margret
"Curious George Takes a Train"
Publisher: Houghton Mifflin
Published Date: c2002
While waiting for the man with a yellow hat to buy train tickets, Curious George causes trouble by mixing up numbers on the schedule, but he makes up for it when a little boy's toy rolls toward the track.

Stutson, Caroline
"Night Train"
Publisher: Roaring Brook Press
Published Date: c2002
"This rhyming text presents a nighttime train ride through the countryside. There is lightening on the tracks, rattling cars, and welcoming lights at the station at the end of the journey. The book has many beautiful illustrations with few words to caption the illustrations. It shows the train traveling and stopping at the station. (ages 1-4)

Train Material on Cassette

Buckwheat Zydeco (Musical group)
"Choo Choo Boogaloo"
{Sound recording}
Publisher: Music for Little People
Published Date: c1994
It is a lively cassette. The children can sing, clap, dance, and play bells with this cassette.(ages 3-5)

Video Materials on Trains

"Thomas the Tank Engine and Friends: A Big Day for Thomas"
{Video recording}
Publisher: Anchor Bay Entertainment
Published Date: c2007
Travel with Thomas when he gets to pull his own train for the first time. (3-5)

"Thomas & Friends: Come Ride the Rails"
{Video recording} (DVD)
Publisher 20th Century Fox Home Entertainment
Published Date: c2006
Ride the Rails to fun and adventure with Thomas and friends as they make tracks to great destinations on Sodar and beyond. Gordon learns a lesson about respect and Emily would like to be Queen for the day. (ages 3-5)

"Traveling with Ooga Booga on Trains"
{Video recording}
Publisher: ALA Video/Library Video Network
Published Date: c1992
It is a 15-minute video presentation on trains. It is part of a transportation series. It explains the names of people affiliated with trains and the different parts of the train such as the Pullman car and the caboose. (ages 4-6)

"Cars, Boats, Trains, and Planes"(Kidsongs)
{Video sounding}
Publisher: Warner Reprise Video
Published Date: c1986
This video is excellent on transportation. It is lively, fun, and informative. (ages 3-5)

For More Information on "Thomas the Train" Books and Videos
Look up Thomas the Train Websites.
www.stepintoreading.com
www.thmasthetankengine.com

Airplane Party

Styles of Airplanes for The Airplane Birthday Party

Note: 1-16 ounce bag of whole carrots makes 10 carrots airplanes. It takes one round, but less full carrot to make one airplane.

The Carrot Airplane Relish

Yield: One airplane

One carrot
3 toothpicks

Peel carrots. Cut carrot in half crosswise in center of the carrot. Cut top part of the carrot lengthwise to make two wings for the airplane. Round out edges of the carrot wings. Lay flat side of carrot down to form the bottom wing. Place the cylinder shaped carrot on top perpendicular and in the center of the bottom wing. Place other half top carrot flat side down, perpendicular onto cylinder shaped carrot to form the top wing. Cut two circles from the smaller end of the carrot to form the wheels. Toothpick wings through center of the carrot. Place toothpicks through wheels at the back of the cylinder shaped carrot to make the back of the plane. Leave $\frac{1}{2}$ of the toothpick sticking out in the center of the bottom wing so the plane stands up. See picture on page 6 in the color section.

Note: This airplane is very easy for the children to make at the party. Each airplane has two sticks of gum, 2 rubber bands, 2 lifesavers and one package of Smarties®.

A Gum and Candy Airplane

Yield: Ten airplanes

2 Packages (each) Fruit Stripes® (10 per package)
1 2.25 ounce package Smarties®
1-1½ packages assorted rubber bands (assorted sizes) (1-1½ inch)
2-.84-ounce (each) mint lifesavers

Place one stick of gum on top and bottom of the Smarties® candy. The Smarties® is centered and sandwiched between and near the top of the gum. Place one rubber band through each lifesaver and loop through the lifesaver to form each wheel. Wrap the rubber band around the two pieces of gum on each side to hold the gum in place and to construct the airplane.

Note: There are 80 multi-color jumbo craft sticks per package. Each plane requires 4 craft sticks to construct the plane (2 for the wings and 1¼ for the tail). There are 24-3⅜ (84 mm) spring clothespins per package. Each airplane takes one clothespin.

Simple Craft Stick Airplane

Yield: Twenty airplanes

1 empty gallon milk jug
1 package multi-color jumbo craft sticks
1-3⅜ package spring clothespins
2-6.25 ounce packages (each) 5 flavor lifesavers
1 50 cent or quarter piece
1 thin tip magic marker
1 4 ounce bottle clear gel Tacky glue
1 jig saw

Cut milk carton into squares to help make the pieces lay flat. Trace the quarter or 50 cent piece on the milk carton to form the circle for the front of the airplane. Remove the spring from each clothespin. Glue the two flat sides of the clothespins together, matching the shape, both top and bottom, using 3 craft sticks, saw pieces for the tail. Each piece must be cut off of the end of a craft stick to make the rounded edge of the tail, 1 inch in length. Glue the two short pieces with straight edges butting together and then glue the top piece in the center of the two glued pieces. The third piece should stand up with the rounded area at the top to complete the back wing. Center the completed tailpiece onto the topside of the clothespin and glue it to the bottom (back) edge of the clothespin. Glue one craft stick to the bottom and one to the top of the clothespin about 1 inch from the top of the clothespin to form the wings. Glue the plastic circle to the front nose of the clothespin. Glue the two lifesavers on the bottom craft stick with a 1 inch space between the lifesavers. The front of the clothespin will be centered between the lifesavers and the lifesavers will be glued to the bottom wing of the plane. Let the plane dry.

Note: There are 1½x1¹⁄₃₂ inch stack checkers that come 6 to a package. This could be used for the front of the engine. However, they would need to be painted and painting is time consuming and messy. One grandfather insisted on making a plane as a gift for each child at his grandson's birthday party. He sawed and painted every piece to perfection and even put wooden wheels on each airplane. They were beautiful and well received. It made grandfather feel proud. His grandson bragged on his grandfather. See grandfather's plane on the cupcake tree. I believe it is more fun for the children to make their own airplane. Keep it simple, so each child feels good about assembling his/her own airplane.

Note: The metal rings can be purchased at a craft store.

The Airplane Luncheon Napkin

Yield: One per airplane

1 yard of material with airplanes (or of your choice) (9x9inch square per napkin)
1 spool of thread (to match material)
1-1$\frac{1}{2}$ metal ring
1 ball of yarn

Cut the napkin out of the material. Hem the edges with a sewing machine or by hand. Measure and cut off a 24 inch piece of yarn. Fold the yarn in half to meet the ends. Place the center of the fold of the yarn around the body of the airplane about 1/2 inch above the tail. Tie yarn into a knot. Tie each end of yarn onto the ring. Place the napkin through the ring to form the tail to the airplane. It looks like a bow.

Note: There are three styles of lunch boxes.

The Lunch Box - Style One

Yield: One lunch box

1 decorative bag
1 wooden craft pre-finished airplane
1-4 fluid ounce clean tacky glue

Glue airplane onto front of the bag. Let the airplane dry onto the bag.

Note: To speed up time, have pictures of several different bears or people dressed up to represent a country. A person can cut out different states to have the children color the state and glue the state onto the top of the box.

The Lunch Box - Style Two

Yield: One lunch box

1 corsage box
1 pre-finished airplane
1-4 fluid ounce clear tacky glue
Wallpaper from children's book

Cut out the wallpaper of the children's choice. Cut the wallpaper to fit the body of the box. Glue on the wallpaper onto the outside of the box. Find wallpaper pictures of bears or animals dressed up representing their country such as Mexico or a state such as Hawaii. Cut out the bears and glue their pictures on top of the box. Glue the airplane onto the front of the box.

The Lunch Box - Style Three

Yield: One lunch box

1 children's shoebox (size 7)
$1/2$ yard colorful material
1 piece 10x10 inch square material (airplane print) (optional)
1-4 fluid ounce clear tacky glue

Cut one piece of fabric to fit around the entire sides of the box. Glue material to the box by putting dots at random on the box and firmly pressing material onto the box. Cover and glue top of the box with the airplane print. See picture on page 6 in the color section.

Note: My friend's mother always made the banana cake for the family birthdays. She didn't like to cook much, unlike her daughter, but she always remembered her children at birthday time. This particular banana cake recipe was a family favorite. She also was a very kind person. She remembered people, doing good deeds for many folks, until her death. I felt like a privileged character to know Marion, a beautiful woman, with a kind heart.

Banana Cake

Yield: One 13x9 inch cake

2 cups plus 2 tablespoons flour
$1/2$ teaspoon salt
1 teaspoon baking powder
1 teaspoon baking soda
$1/2$ cup shortening
$1^1/2$ cups sugar
2 large eggs
1 cup mashed ripe bananas (about 3 medium bananas)
$1/2$ cup buttermilk
1 teaspoon vanilla

Preheat the oven to 375 F. In a mixing bowl mix together the flour, salt, baking powder, and baking soda. Whisk together and set this mixture aside. In a mixing bowl, cream together the shortening and sugar. Add the eggs and bananas and mix together. Alternate adding the buttermilk and vanilla with the flour mixture. Stir the batter until blended together. Pour the batter into prepared 13x9 inch cake pan. Bake for 30 to 35 minutes or until toothpick inserted into the center of the cake comes out clean. Cool thoroughly.

Note: Wash out mixing bowl with hot soapy water, rinse and dry thoroughly. Chill the mixing bowl for best result.

Mary's Frosting
Yield: Frosting for one 13x9 inch cake

1 cup sugar
$\frac{1}{2}$ cup fat-free half and half
2 egg whites, beaten until stiff
$\frac{1}{2}$ cup butter
$\frac{1}{2}$ cup shortening
1 teaspoon vanilla

Add sugar to the half and half. Wire whip together. Microwave for 2 minutes. Stir again. Place the mixture into the freezer until cooled. Do not freeze the mixture. Beat the egg whites until stiff. Add to the butter and shortening mixture and beat until creamy. Add the vanilla and beat again. Slowly add the milk-sugar mixture and continue to beat until the frosting is creamy and fluffy.

How to Make the Airplane Cake
Yield: One airplane cake

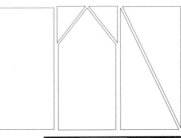

1 13x9 inch cake
1 18x18 inch cake cardboard
1 batch of Mary's Frosting
1 ounce blue sugar
1-16 ounce bag cherry mini bites (red licorice)
1-2.75 ounce cherry sours
1 USA sign on a pick, optional
2 red stars on a pick, optional
1 candle with age of the child, optional

Cut the 13x9 inch cake into three equal horizontal sections. See the diagram and picture above on how to cut and assemble the cake to form an airplane. The plane will be at a slight angle to fit the cardboard. Fill a cake tube, using a number 30 tip, and pipe on straight lines across the top and bottom of the airplane, covering the entire cake with frosting. Sprinkle blue sugar over the top of the cake. Outline the border, both top and bottom, with the cherry mini bites. Place the cherry sours vertically at the nose and two front sides-of the airplane (three in each row) to make the lights on the airplane. Place an I love USA sign on a pick and a red star on each side of the sign centered on each side of the wings. Place the birthday candle at the back of the airplane. See picture of the decorated cake on page 6 in the color section.

Note: Wilton sells Cupcake 'N More dessert stands in size 13 and 23 per stand. *I personally own the large stand. My friend owns the small stand. Both are nice for a party.*

Note: The Décor sprinkles have 4 varieties, one ounce each, red, white, and blue stars; red sugar, blue sugar; and red, white, and blue jimmies.

Airplane Cupcake Tree

Yield: Twenty-four cupcakes

1 banana cake recipe
24 cupcake liners
2 cupcake pans (12 per each)
22 cupcakes (to go onto the cupcake holder)
1 batch of Mary's Frosting
1-4 ounce container of décor sprinkles
1 package decorative pick candles (1 large star, two small stars)
1 Cupcake'N More Dessert Stand
2 airplanes
7 packages birthday candle bougies (4 per package)

Set oven to 350 F. Make the banana cake recipe on page 98. Place cupcake liners into the cupcake tin. Divide the batter to make 24 cupcakes. Bake for 20 minutes or until toothpick inserted in the center comes out clean. Cool thoroughly. Make up the frosting recipe on page 99. Frost the cupcakes. Place one variety of the colored sugar, jimmies or stars onto each cupcake, using all 4 varieties. Place one birthday candle bougie in the center of each cupcake. Place one cupcake on each cupcake holder to make the tree, leaving the top cupcake holder free for the decoration. Arrange 2 airplanes, 4 candle bougies, 2 small stars and one large star into the top of the tree stand cupcake holder. See picture on page 6 in the color section.

The Apple Basket

Yield: Ten apples and bananas

1 napkin
1 basket
10 apples
10 bananas

Place napkin into the basket. Fill the basket with apples and bananas. See picture on page 6 in the color section.

Note: There are 10 biscuits per 5 ounce can. The tiny pricked holes let the steam escape and prevent the biscuit sandwich from coming apart. You can find the prepared biscuits at your local grocery store in the dairy case. This is a very easy project for the children. Each child can make his/her own sandwich.

Aircraft Landing Sandwiches

Yield: Ten sandwiches

2-5 ounce cans (each) prepared biscuits
1-16 ounce package Mexican mild pasteurized prepared cheese
$^1/_2$ cup butter, melted
Sandwich Baggies

Flatten out two biscuits per sandwich with the heel of your hand. Place one thin slice of cheese on top of the bottom biscuit, leaving the cheese about $^1/_2$ inch from the edge. Place the second biscuit on top of the cheese. Seal edges with a fork and prick tiny holes on the top of the biscuit. Microwave butter in a custard cup for 20 seconds. Brush the top of each biscuit with melted butter. Bake at 375 F for 8 minutes until golden brown and cheese melts. Cool and place one sandwich per baggie. See picture on page 6 in the color section. If you decide to have a buffet, place the sandwiches and the carrot airplanes onto a tray. Place the basket of apples and bananas, sandwich tray, cupcake tree, and airplane cake onto the buffet table. Lay out napkins and silverware. Set up a small table area for the beverage with cups and beverages napkins. See the arrangement of the different food items for the buffet.

If you decide to take the children on a field trip, let each child pack his/her own lunch from the buffet. Each lunch box contains finger foods. The following items can be found in the lunch box:

Food in Each Lunch Box

Apple or banana
1 sandwich
1 carrot airplane
1 cupcake decorated with the gum airplane and a birthday candle
1 airplane with a napkin at the tail of the airplane
See picture on page 6 in the color section.

Suggested Activities for the Party

Color Book Activity for Ages 5-7

Give each child a box of crayons and a coloring book called Airport Adventure published by the Playmore Inc., and Waldman Publishing Corp., New York, New York. Go through the book with the children and do the activities in the book. Some examples are as follows:

Color the biggest plane blue and color the smallest plane red.
There are two pictures on the page that look exactly alike.
Find 3 places where they are different.
Shadow Match the airplane.
Count and Color.
Find 5 mistakes in the picture.

The coloring book also tells the story of the airport and traveling. It is a very cool book for the younger children. I received a big positive response at the party with this activity book.

Note: I get wallpaper books free of charge from various paint and wallpaper companies. There are many themes for traveling in each kid's wallpaper book.

Lunch Box Activity for Ages 7-8

Tear out sheets from several kids wallpaper books. Let each child select a friend to take an imaginary trip and also pick out the animals that are ready for the trip. Cover the body of the box with wallpaper and the top of the box with the animals dressed to represent a country or a state such as Hawaii or Mexico. Have props in a couple of boxes for the children to match up with the country. The box could have a Mexican hat for Mexico, a hula skirt for Hawaii, or an Irish hat with shamrocks for Ireland. In another box have different picture books on different countries. The children can wear the hats, match the country with the lunch box and find a couple ideas to share with the group.

Note: If you decide to make the planes in advance, you could play the game "Hide the Planes."

Hide the Airplanes

Each child will search to find a airplane and bring the plane back to the table. They can show off their planes to the group while eating cake and ice cream. They can also have the privilege of trading their planes with another guest.

Note: There is a gentleman in our church who makes model airplanes. He flies the planes in the open field next to the park. The children pack a lunch box. Mrs. K enjoyed helping the children pack their lunches for Tommy's special birthday. The children walked to the nearby neighborhood park to see the model airplanes. It was a favorite outing for Tommy and his friends as they got to fly some of the airplanes.

Lunch Box for Airplane Exhibition Field Trip Ages 6-9

See the lunch box section for packing the lunch on page 101. Each child gets three airplanes and also pack his/her lunch off the buffet table. The children jabbered with excitement and wore happy facial expressions while packing the lunch box. They ate their lunches at the park and Mrs. K also served a huge container of lemonade.

Plane identification Activity Ages 5-8
Read the plane poem to the children. Have pictures of the different styles of planes. Have the children identify the planes and color the picture. Have various airplane pictures and let the children connect the dots or letters to shape the plane. They can color each plane.

Notice the Airplane
Poem
by Pat Nekola

Fly your wings.
See the cargo plane
And what it may bring.

Watch the hot air balloon.
Go high to the sky
As you wave a good bye.

Observe the blimp.
Flying high in the sky
Advertising a camping show.

You will find Wilber and Orville Wright
Recorded in many books,
For making the very first flight.

Read about World War I planes in flight.
As they took photographs and sent messages,
To save the US with their prowess and might.

Helicopters are the eyes of the air police,
Along with rescuing people, helping wherever needed
And saving lives as far as Greece.

Military Jets fly with great speed.
Their long sleek slender shape and nose
Decrease air friction that would impede.

A special plane sprays
Over the fields to kill bugs
For healthy crops to stay.

People ride glider planes for fun
Lifted up on the wings of the wind
Soaring through the sky under the sun.

Travel the country by air with care.
Airplanes fly around the world.
Travel with a friend and have adventures to share.

Arita's Airplane Story

Arita's father was living in Milwaukee, Wisconsin. She was teaching in Michigan at the time. Her father had three days of vacation and invited her to come and visit. Arita had not seen her father for three months because he had just moved to Milwaukee and opened his new restaurant. She was excited and curious about his adventure. Arita got a flight to Milwaukee late on a Friday evening. She decided to make a pizza and carry the pizza on the airplane. She would surprise her father. She wrapped the pizza in an airtight container. When she arrived in Milwaukee, she got a big surprise. She opened the container at her father's apartment and found that the pizza had risen and looked like it was ready to explode. She had no idea that the altitude would govern the size of the pizza. She decided to bake the pizza. When it came out of the oven, the pizza was very flat and not very appetizing. Her father was a good sport. They had a great laugh about the experiment. They ate the pizza and enjoyed the evening. To this day Arita and her dad still laugh about the strange looking pizza. He said it looked like a one-eyed-purple-people-eater.

Connect the dots using the numbered dots below; start with 1 and keep connecting the dots until you are finished making the plane. Color the plane.

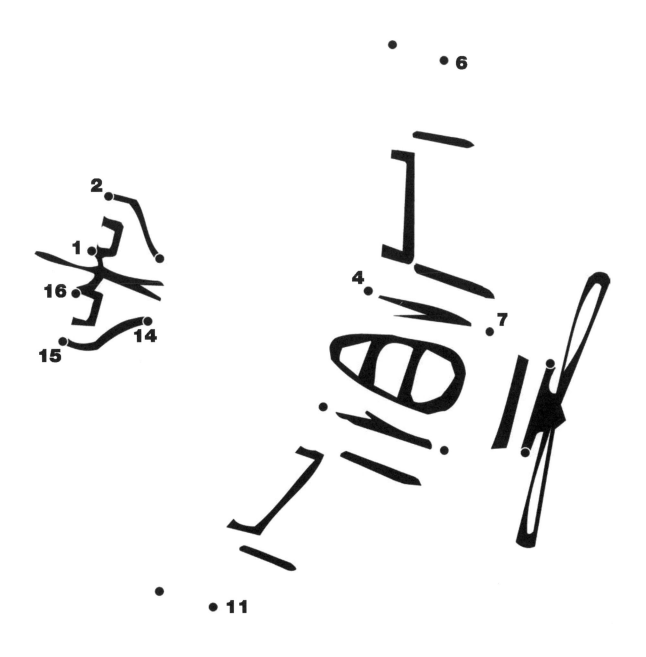

Connect the dots using the letters below; start with **a** and keep
going down the alphabet until you are finished making the plane. Color the plane.

Connect the dots using the numbered dots below; start with 1 and keep connecting the dots until you are finished making the plane. Color the plane.

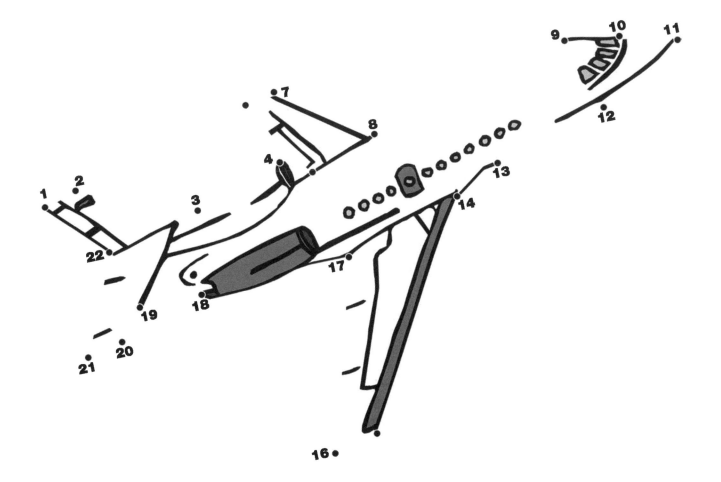

Connect the dots using the letters below; start with **a** and keep
going down the alphabet until you are finished making the plane. Color the plane.

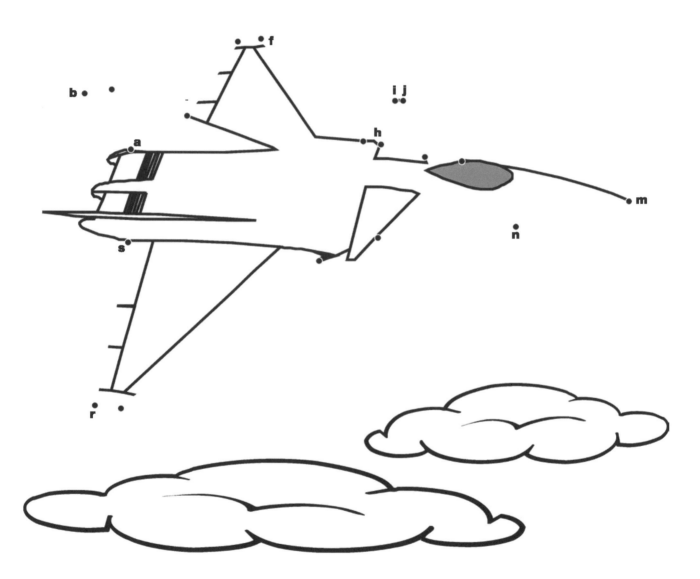

Body to the Airplane Pattern

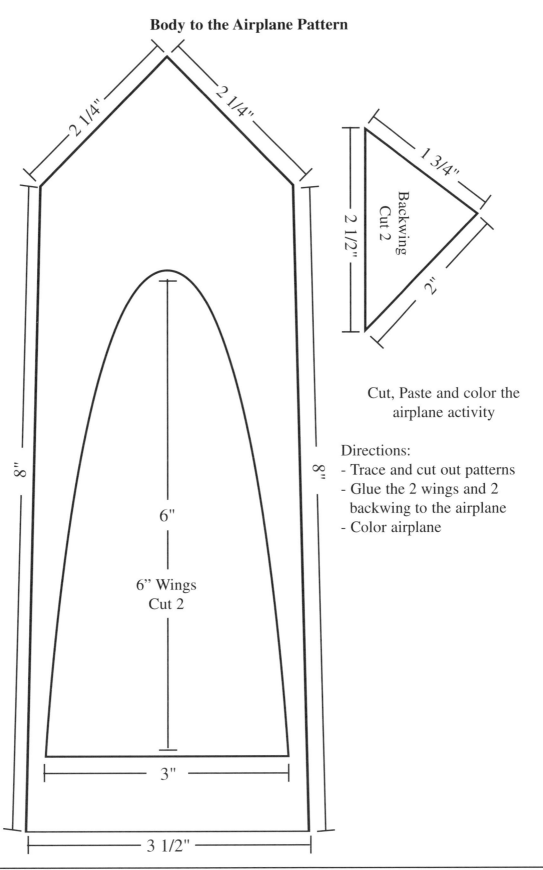

2 1/4"

2 1/4"

Backwing
Cut 2

1 3/4"

2 1/2"

2"

8"

8"

6"

6" Wings
Cut 2

3"

3 1/2"

Cut, Paste and color the
airplane activity

Directions:
- Trace and cut out patterns
- Glue the 2 wings and 2
  backwing to the airplane
- Color airplane

Airplane Theme Related Book Resources

Ashley, Susan
"Going by Plane"
Publisher: Weekly Reader Early Learning
Published Date: c2004
The book tells the history of the early planes to the present day. This book has excellent information and it is very simple for a younger child to understand. "The author talks about crop dusters, seaplanes, cargo planes, military aircrafts, and helicopters." The (ages 3-5)

Barrett, Norman
"The Picture World Air Rescue"
Publisher: F. Watts
Published Date: c1990
The book has information on helicopters, military rescue and air ambulances. (ages 8-10)

Berenstain, Stan
"The Berenstain Bears Fly-It: Up, Up, And Away"
Publisher: Random House
Published Date: c1996
"after visiting the hall of fight at the Bearsonian Institution, the bear cubs decide to invent their own airplanes. The book includes information about the history flight and instructions for making various balloon-powered aircrafts."

Busby, Peter
"First to Fly: How Wilbur & Orville Wright Invented the Airplane"
Publisher: Crown
Published Date: c2002
This book tells how Wilbur and Orville invented the airplane. (ages 7-10)

Collicutt, Paul
"This Plane"
Publisher: Farrar Stroux Gioux
Published Date: c2000
This picture book explains all the different types of planes in the U.S.A., France, Germany, and the United Kingdom. (ages 2-4)

Dudko, Mary Ann
"Barney's Book of Airplanes"
Publisher: Lyrick Publishing
Published Date: c1998
 Preschool readers will love following the dino-friends on a trip to the airplane Museum where they learn all about airplanes. (ages 2-5)

Grist, Julie
"Flying Just Plane Fun"
Publisher: Spoonbender books
Published Date: c2003
Grandpa builds a home-style plane. He takes his grandson on his first flight. The book explains how airplanes stay up in the air. (ages 7-9)

Ingoglia, Gina
"Airplanes and Things That Fly"
Publisher: Western Publishing Company
Published Date: c1989
The book has wonderful illustrations with few words to describe the different styles of planes. (ages 2-4)

Lord, Suzanne
"Radio Controlled Model Airplanes"
Publisher: Crestwood House
Published Date: c1988
The book teaches a person how to fly a model airplane. (ages 9-10)

Mitton, Tony
"Amazing Planes"
Publisher: Kingfisher
Published Date: c2002
The story explains how you fly. It takes a child from start to finish with rhyming text that introduces air travel from the airport to the flight deck, safety rules and air traffic control. It also explains the parts of the airplane. (ages 2-5)

Munsch, Robert
"Angela's Airplane"
Publisher: Annich Press
Published Date: c1998
A little five year old explores the plane and tries to fly. It crashes but she is safe. She grows up to become an airplane pilot. (ages 3-5)

Potter, Tony
"See How It Works, Planes"
Publisher: Aladdin Books
Published Date: c1989
The book explains the inside of a plane in picture form and diagrams. There are also pictures of different styles of planes and the use of each plane. It tells the duties of the captain and the co-pilot. It shows the airport and various trucks that help the airplane before the take off. (ages 3-5)

Schmidt, Norman
"Incredible Paper Flying Machines"
Publisher: Sterling Publishing
Published Book: c2001
The book teaches kids how to make a model airplane from paper. (ages 6-10)

Schomp, Virginia
"If You Were A Pilot"
Publisher: Benchmark Books
Published Date: c2000
The books teaches a person about a pilot and business jets, and cargo planes and describes the training and skills of an air pilot (ages 5-6)

 Sturges, Philemon
"I Love Planes"
Publisher: Harper Collins
Published Date: c2003
This is an excellent book that explains the various kinds of aircrafts. There are pictures of each type of aircraft. (ages 3-5)

Videos on the Jay Jay Series

There are many of the Jay Jay Series on "The Jet Plane". Each video lasts 40 minutes.

"Friends Take Flight"
{Video recording}
Publisher: Columbia Tristar Home Entertainment
Published Date: c2002
There are three cartoon clips in this video. The titles are Snuffy's Favorite Color, Super Loop-De-Loop and Brenda's Mother's Day. Each clip has a lesson. What is Snuffy's favorite color? Is it red, blue, or green. Find out by watching "Friends Take Flight. (ages 2-5)

"First Flights and New Friends"
{Video recording}
Publisher: Columbia Tristar Home Entertainment
Published Date: c2002

There are three cartoon clips in this video. The titles are "Snuffy's First Day of School", "Jay Jay's Speedy Delivery", and "The Buddy System". Snuffy is afraid to go to school but an Old Oscar admits he too was afraid to go to school. In the "Jay Jay's Speedy Delivery" clip the lesson is it's better to be safe than sorry! In "The Buddy System" clip the lesson is use the "buddy system" for two heads are better than one. (ages 2-5)

Website for the Jay Jay Series

http://pbskids.org/jayjay/

Fire Truck Party

Grandpa M's Story

When Grandpa M was growing up, he was very fascinated with fire. Every time he heard the fire truck going to a fire, he followed the firemen. One day a policeman knocked on grandpa's door. His mother answered the door. They were looking for Grandpa M. They believed he had started the fire. He was finally proven innocent. It was the last time Grandpa M arrived at the scene.

Grandpa M grew up and became a firefighter and the fire chief in his hometown. He worked for 30 years helping people. He said that helping people was one of the best things a man could do for his community. He firmly believed that in giving, a person received. He never understood why people would be so thoughtless and call in false alarms or become heartless to their fellow man.

Grandpa M trained many firefighters and watched their families grow up. He attended many family functions, including their family weddings.

Every spring Grandpa M helped with the pancake breakfast. The firemen cleared out the firehouse and set up tables and chairs for the people to come in and enjoy Grandma M's pancakes. She had a reputation for making the best pancakes in town. The kids and their families had the opportunity to tour the firehouse and check out the fire trucks.

Grandpa and his committee, with the approval of the town's people, gave the proceeds to a family dealing with cancer like little Timmy's. Every year grandpa made sure the money raised from the pancake breakfast went to a charity or family in need. Grandpa also sold firemen hats and T-shirts for the cause. Several businesses also helped with donations.

Grandpa M talked a lot to his triplet grandsons (Jon, James, and Jacob) about the firehouse. They all said they wanted to be fire fighters just like Grandpa M. They enjoyed listening to Grandpa M's story about Del the fire station Dalmation mascot. Once when Del rode to the fire, he went into the large apartment building. Del helped save a beautiful baby girl with the biggest and prettiest crystal blue eyes. Del made the community newspaper. Grandpa M and his crew put the blaze out and he complimented the firemen and Del for a job well done.

Grandma M said that Grandpa M was the big influence on his grandsons' desire to be firefighters. Of course, she admitted that they were only 5 and they could very well change their minds. For now, it pleased Grandpa M that one day his grandsons might become firefighters.

Grandma M promised her triplet grandsons that she would make each of them a birthday cake for their fifth birthday. She also would have a grand party. Jon wanted a white cake with banana frosting. Grandma M found birthday candles shaped into fireman symbols. He also liked pecans. So, she made a French vanilla cake using her 2-8inch square pans and a yummy banana frosting for Jon. She decorated the sides of the cake with pecans. Jon wanted a flag with his name in the center. Grandma M also found stickers and used the fireman hat and truck stickers on the flag. The flag pattern is on page 125 and Jon's cake is on page 6 in the color section.

The Triplet Poem

Surprise, surprise, surprise,
Three new grandsons,
Grandpa said, three new firemen.

Grandma shouted, "Party time!"
She beamed and her eyes shined,
Saying, always celebrate life.

The newborn babies looked alike,
Jacob, James, and Jon,
Named after their great uncles.

The baby boys are a joy.
Mom is full of smiles.
Dad is ecstatic about his boys.

Neighbors rallied around
The newborn triplets,
They were the talk of the town.

Note: Take out the 2 pieces of bay leaves at the end of the cooking time. Grandma M uses the bay leaf seasoning. Do not over cook the fine noodles or they will turn to mush. If you cannot find Bavarian seasoning, make your own recipe.

Bavarian Seasoning

Yield: One ounce

4 bay leaves, crushed
1 teaspoon thyme
2 teaspoons sage
1 teaspoon minced dehydrated garlic
2 teaspoons basil
2 teaspoons rosemary
$1/2$ teaspoon white granulated onion powder

Mix all ingredients together. Store in an airtight container.

Note: Penzey Spice Company sells the bay leaf and Bavarian spice. You can have these spices shipped to your door. They also have a Penzeys Spices catalog of seasonings and order blank. Just write to Penzeys Spices, 19300 West Janacek Court, P.O. Box 924, Brookfield, WI 53008-0924 or place the order by phone, 1 (800) 741-7787 (262) 785-7676 or fax your order at (262) 785-7676. Fax your order at (262) 785-7678 or order at the website address: www.penzeys.com.

Grandma M's Simple Chicken Noodle Soup

Yield : Ten to twelve servings

2 quarts chicken stock
2-14 ounce cans vegetarian vegetable broth
2 pounds boneless, skinless, chicken breast tenders
1 bunch green onions, diced fine with tops
1 leek, diced fine without the top
2 teaspoons minced garlic
$1/2$ teaspoon white pepper
1 teaspoon Bavarian seasoning or Italian seasoning
1 teaspoon bay leaf seasoning or two bay leaves
1 tablespoon olive oil
1 teaspoon salt
1 pound enriched egg noodles (fine)

In a large stockpot, pour in 2 quarts chicken broth and 2 cans vegetarian vegetable broth. Add the chicken and boil until chicken is cooked through. Add onions, leek, garlic, white pepper, Bavarian and bay leaf seasonings. Simmer on low heat for about an hour. In a 4 quart pan bring water to a boil with the olive oil and salt. Add the noodles and cook for 35 minutes or until tender. Drain and rinse the noodles with cold water. Add to the soup. Stir thoroughly. Serve with soup crackers.

Note: Grandma M had a pot of soup going most of the time. She made the chicken noodle soup for her grandchildren. Her two favorite soups are turkey vegetable and Mexican potato soup. Grandma is Polish. We all thought it was very strange that she liked Mexican potato soup. She enjoyed making her favorite soups for everyone.

Grandma M's Turkey Vegetable Soup

Yield: Twenty servings

3 quarts chicken stock
1 turkey carcass
1 bunch scallions with tops, chopped
1 leek without the top, chopped
2 tablespoons minced garlic
1 red pepper, diced
1 yellow pepper, diced
1 orange pepper, diced
1 teaspoon white pepper
2 teaspoons Bavarian seasoning
2 teaspoons bay leaf seasoning or 4 bay leaves
Water
2 tablespoons olive oil
1 teaspoon salt
1 pound package enriched egg noodles (fine)
2-1 pound (each) frozen mixed vegetables

In a large stockpot, pour in 3 quarts chicken broth. Place the turkey carcass into the chicken broth. Add the scallions, leek, minced garlic, red pepper, yellow pepper, orange pepper, white pepper, Bavarian and bay leaf seasonings. Simmer on low heat for 5 hours.

In a 4 quart pan bring water to a boil with olive oil and salt. Add noodles and cook for 3-5 minutes or until tender. Drain and rinse noodles with cold water. Set aside. Thaw frozen vegetables. Remove the turkey carcass, making sure there are no bones in the broth mixture. Pick the meat off the carcass. Stir in the turkey meat, noodles, and frozen vegetables. Simmer for 5-7 more minutes over low heat.

Grandma M's Mexican Potato Soup

Yield: Eight to ten servings

1 pound bacon, diced, fried and drained
2 thinly sliced leek without the tops
2 bunches scallions, with tops
5 pounds red potatoes, peeled, cubed
1 teaspoon minced garlic
2 teaspoons white pepper
1 teaspoon chili powder
2 cans (48 ounces each) chicken stock
2 cups non-fat cream
2 cups 4 cheese shredded Mexican Blend
Ingredients for thickening soup:
2 cups milk at almost room temperature
6 tablespoons cornstarch

Fry bacon until almost crisp. Add the leeks, and scallions and sauté. Drain grease off and dab up excess grease with a paper towel. Boil the potatoes in jackets until tender, then drain, peel, and dice. Mix together potatoes, leek, scallions, minced garlic, bacon, white pepper, and chili powder in a soup kettle. Add chicken stock and cream. Heat through over moderate heat, while occasionally stirring. In a separate bowl mix the cornstarch and milk and wire whip until smooth. Add this mixture slowly to the hot soup while stirring constantly to prevent lumps. Remove from the heat. Slowly add 1 cup of Mexican cheese. Whisk in the cheese until the soup is smooth and creamy. Return to stove and heat. Serve hot with soup crackers.

Grandma M's Finger Hoagie Sandwiches

Yield: Thirty finger sandwiches

6 club rolls
$1/2$ pound butter or margarine
6 slices ham
6 slices beef
6 slices turkey
6 slices salami
6 slices American cheese
30 frilled toothpicks (with red frilled top)

Slice rolls. Butter club rolls, both top and bottom. Place 1 piece each of ham, beef, turkey, salami, and cheese on each sandwich. Place the top of the roll onto the meat and cheese to make a whole sandwich. Place toothpicks, 5 across, and about $1/2$-$3/4$ inch apart. Cut each roll into 5 finger sandwiches. 20 finger sandwiches fits on a 14 inch tray without stacking sandwiches.

Grandma M's Yummy Granola

Yield: Approximately eight cups

3 cups oatmeal
1-12 ounce jar wheat germ (3 cups)
2-25 ounce packages (each) pine nuts (1 cup)
2-25 ounce packages (each) pecans (1 cup)
1 teaspoon cinnamon
$^1/_4$ teaspoon salt
$^1/_2$ cup dark brown sugar
$^1/_2$ cup butter
$^3/_4$ cup honey
1 teaspoon hazelnut flavoring or vanilla
$^1/_2$ cup raisins
$^1/_2$ cup golden raisins
$^1/_2$ cup craisins
No-stick spray
1 package stickers with firemen symbols
1 package nut cups in primary colors (16 per package)

Preheat oven to 300 F. In a large bowl mix oatmeal, wheat germ, pine nuts, pecans, cinnamon, salt and brown sugar. Melt butter in a saucepan over low heat. Add the honey and stir until smooth. Whisk in the hazelnut flavoring. Remove from the heat. Stir the honey/butter mixture into the oatmeal/wheat germ mixture. Coat mixture well. In a small bowl mix together the raisins and craisins. Set aside. Spray no-stick spray onto a 15x10 inch baking pan. Spread the granola onto the baking pan. Bake for 40 minutes, stirring every 10 to 15 minutes. Place granola pan on a cooling rack. Stir the raisins and craisins into the cooled mixture. Place a fireman's sticker at the top of each nut cup. Fill cups for the party. Extra granola will freeze in an airtight bag and keep for 3 months or store in an airtight container for a week.

Jon's Fire Truck Cake

Yield: Two 8 inch square layers

No-stick spray
1-18.25 ounce box French Vanilla Cake mix
3 eggs
Water
Oil

Preheat oven to 350 F. Spray no-stick spray into the two square pans. Follow the directions on the box mix. Divide the cake batter between the two pans. Spread cake out evenly. Bake for 25-30 minutes or until toothpick inserted into the center of the cake comes out clean.

Note: The banana frosting is a softer frosting and it is very sweet. Frost cake and place cake into the refrigerator for a half hour or into the freezer for 15 minutes to harden the frosting. Three cups powdered sugar equals 1 pound.

Grandma M's Banana Ice Box Frosting

Yield: Two whole 8 inch cakes

1 small ripe banana ($^1/_3$ cup)
$^1/_4$ cup sour cream
1 teaspoon vanilla or banana flavor
2 cups non-dairy whipped topping
$^1/_4$ cup butter
5 cups powdered sugar

Mash the banana in a mixing bowl. Add sour cream, vanilla, and 1 cup non-dairy whipped topping. Beat until smooth. Beat butter in a separate 5 quart bowl. Alternate the powdered sugar with the banana mixture, ending with the powdered sugar. Fold in the second cup of non-dairy whipped topping into the frosting. Beat slightly until smooth.

Note: Grandma M placed the candles toward the back of the cake so the candles would not interfere with cutting the front of the cake. You can center the candles and pipe "Happy Birthday" onto the cake instead of making the flag. Jon helped Grandma M make the flag. He is the computer whiz of the triplets. Grandma M said that Jon puts her to shame when it comes to computers. She knew little about the computer world.

How to Decorate Jon's Fire Truck Cake

Yield: One whole 8x8 inch cake

1-2.5 ounce bag whole pecans, (optional)
1-1 ounce container assorted red, white and blue jimmies
1 package firefighting candles (1 Dalmatian dog, 1 pair of black boots,1 fire hydrant,
   and 1 fire fighter's hat)
1 extra birthday candle (any style)
1 number 30 cake tube
1 cake decorating bag
1 12x12 cardboard
Foil
2-10 inch (each) doilies
1 round toothpick
1 roll clear tape
1-8x11 sheet construction paper
1-8x11 sheet copy paper
1 glue stick
1 package stickers with firemen symbols

Cover the cardboard with foil. Tape the foil onto the back of the cardboard. Center the first cake layer on the cardboard. Frost the top of the first layer. Place the second layer of cake onto the first layer of the cake. Complete frosting the entire cake. Place the pecans in a group of three, with three groupings on each side for a total of 36 whole pecans. Sprinkle the jimmies on top of the cake. Place the candles on top of the cake forming a semi circle toward the back of the cake. Cut each doily in half. Place the flat edge of each half doily around the bottom edge of the cake. With a number 30 tip, pipe a border around the top and bottom of the cake. Trace the flag onto red construction paper. Type in happy birthday on the computer (using the child's name) with the size 18 font and all capital letters. Print the copy. Trace the second pattern on the white print out sheet. Cut out both patterns. Glue the Happy Birthday sign onto the red flag. Place a fire truck and fireman hat sticker at the left edge of the red flag (one above each other). Tape top of the toothpick to the bottom left edge of the red flag. Place toothpick flag into the cake behind the birthday candles. See the pattern for the flag on page 125 and the picture of Jon's cake on page 6 in the color section.

Note: James wanted a cinnamon swirl cake decorated with a real fire truck and firefighters. James liked cinnamon toast and any breakfast roll or sweets with cinnamon. Grandma M found a cinnamon swirl box cake at her local grocery store. She said it was made very much like a marble cake.

James' Fire Truck Cake
Yield: 13x9 cake

No-stick spray
1-21.5 ounce cinnamon swirl cake mix
3 eggs
Water
Oil
1-12x16 inch cardboard
Foil
Tape

Preheat oven to 350 F. Spray non-stick spray into 2-9 inch cake pans. Follow the directions on the box mix. Pour batter into the cake pans. Spread cake evenly. Bake for 35-40 minutes or until toothpick inserted into the center of the cake comes out clean. Cool on cooling rack for 5 minutes. Cover the top of the cardboard with foil. Tape the foil to the back of the cardboard. Place the front side of the foiled cardboard over the cake pan. Turn cake onto the cardboard.

Note: Grandma M used a wire whip to beat in the brown sugar and powdered sugar. It was smooth and tasty.

Cinnamon Caramel Frosting

Yield: One 13x9 cake

$^1/_2$ cup butter
1cup dark-brown sugar, firmly, packed
$^1/_3$ cup fat free half and half
2-$^1/_2$ cups powdered sugar
1 teaspoon cinnamon
$^1/_2$ teaspoon maple flavoring or vanilla

Melt butter for about 40-60 seconds in the microwave. Place melted butter in a medium sauce pan. Add the brown sugar, stirring until smooth. Bring mixture to a boil over low heat. Add the cream. Boil over low heat for another minute, stirring constantly. Remove from the heat. Using a candy thermometer, cool to 110 F or the bottom of the pan feels lukewarm. Beat in the powdered sugar and cinnamon until frosting is thick and smooth. Add the maple flavoring and beat. Place pan into a bowl of cold water until frosting holds its shape and it is ready to spread on the cake. Frost the top and sides of the cake and smooth the frosting with warm water and a cake spatula.

Decorations for James' Fire Truck Cake

1 cake decorating package with fire truck and firemen
1-7 ounce package chocolate stars
1-2 ounce jar cinnamon red hots

Place chocolate stars around the border on top of the cake. Place the fire truck in middle of the cake with the three firemen to the left of the fire truck. Place the number 5-birthday candle to the right of the truck. Place red hots around the bottom of the border leaving about a 1 inch space between each red-hot. Place red hots around the fire truck and firemen to form a path leading to the fire. Place a dab of frosting at the end of the ladder to help hold the ladder up. Follow instructions for making the sign on Jon's cake. Place the Happy Birthday sign at the back end of the ladder as the sign rests on the length of the ladder. See picture on page 6 in the color section.

Note: Jacob wanted fire truck cake. Grandma found a pan shaped like a fire truck at her local cake decorating shop. He also wanted his cake to be red. Grandma M picked up a red velvet cake mix at the local grocery store to also please Jacob. She asked Jacob if it would be all right to use the butter cream frosting. She thought it would be best for decorating his cake. Jacob agreed and knew Grandma M would have a neat birthday cake just for him.

Jacob's Fire Truck Cake
Yield: One fire truck cake

1-18x18 inch cardboard
Foil
Tape
Non-stick spray
1-18.25 ounce red velvet cake mix
2 eggs
Water
Oil
1-l pound bag of black licorice
1-11.5 ounce package white stripes cookies 'n crème cookies

Before making the cake, lay the fire truck cake pan face down onto the cardboard. Trace two extra inches around the entire pan. Cut out the cardboard. Wrap foil around the cardboard. Tape foil onto the back of the cardboard. Preheat oven to 350 F. Spray non-stick spray into the fire truck pan. Follow the directions on the box mix. Place the batter into the fire truck. Spread cake out evenly. Bake for 35-40 minutes or until toothpick inserted into the center of the cake comes out clean.

Note: Follow the butter cream frosting recipe on page 73. There is a picture of the decorated fire truck inside the cake pan. Grandma M used her imagination and made a couple of changes. She used licorice for the ladder and the cookies for the center of the wheels. Grandma M uses powdered food coloring. However, liquid food coloring is acceptable.

In one small bowl set aside white frosting. Mix another bowl of frosting with gray or black food coloring and another with yellow. Color the remanding frosting red. Fill four cake decorating bags with each of the frostings. With the number 30 tip, pipe on the windows and outline the bottom of the cake and around the wheels with the white frosting. With a number 13 tip, pipe the yellow frosting around the front and back bumper, the front headlight, and the outline of the front door, and windows. Using a number 30 tip, pipe the entire body of the truck with red frosting. Place 2 pieces of licorice parallel to each other. Cut another piece of licorice into 7-1 inch pieces. At the top of the fire truck, place licorice pieces about 1 inch apart horizontally in between the two pieces of licorice to form the ladder. Place a dab of frosting in the middle of the imprint of each wheel. Place one cookie on each side of the bottom of the fire truck to form the wheel. With a number 13 tip, outline the cookie in red. With a number 30 tip, outline the wheel in black or gray. With a number 13 tip, outline the wheel in yellow. With a number 30 tip, pipe the front bottom side of the cake with white frosting and use the remaining frosting to complete the other three sides. Make a flag saying "Happy Birthday Jacob" using the same directions for Jon's birthday cake. See picture on page 6 in the color section.

Making a List for the
Firemen's Theme Guest Table for Six children

Firemen's tablecloth

Firemen loot bags

Firemen hats

Firemen pencils

Pads

Granola nut cups

Note: An eight foot table takes 9 feet of material. You need extra material for a 1 inch hem on each side and 8 inches extra length to drop for the ends of the table.

How to Set up the Firemen Theme Guest Table

Grandma M purchased 2-1/2 yards of firemen print material and made a tablecloth for the guest table. She covered the table with the tablecloth. She placed the fire truck shaped cake onto the center of the table. Each chair had a loot bag over the back. Each place setting had a fireman's hat, a fireman's pencil and pad, a portion cup filled with granola, a red napkin folded in half diagonally with a Dalmation dog sticker in the middle of the folded napkin, and a fire truck luncheon plate. Place plate in the center of each place setting. Place the napkin to the left of the plate. Place the fireman's hat to the left above the napkin. Place the granola cup to the center, above the plate. Place the pencil and pad next to the napkin. See picture on page 6 in the color section.

Grandma M served up a cup of soup and a finger sandwich to her guests first and then her grandsons. She placed the food onto the fire truck plates. She also passed fresh strawberries in her favorite strawberry design bowl.

Note: Grandma M and her three grandsons put the cards together for the game. They enjoyed the time together. The boys were excited about playing the game with their friends.

Note: Each package contains 4 sheets of acid free stickers. There are four designs (Dalmation dog, fireman's hat, fire truck and fire hydrant).

Note: The purpose of the game is to teach the children to concentrate and use their memory and also have fun.

Fireman's Memory Drill Card Game
4-6 players

2-9x12 inch sheets red construction paper
2-9x12 inch sheets yellow construction paper
2-9x12 inch sheets orange construction paper
3 packages (each) fireman designed stickers
2 glue sticks
Scissors

How to Make the Cards

Follow the pattern on page 125 for making the cards. Trace pattern onto the red construction paper, 18 size 4$\frac{1}{2}$ inches long and 3 inches wide to make the body of the card. Cut out the card. Trace 16-3 inch long rectangles by 1$\frac{1}{2}$ inches wide in both the yellow and orange construction paper. Cut out all 32 pieces. Draw a diagonal line across the orange pieces. Cut along the diagonal line. Glue one yellow piece in the center of each red card. Glue one orange piece at an angle, gluing from left edge to right top edge of the card. Glue the second orange piece from bottom to top of the right side. The two orange pieces go over the yellow and partially on the red. Place a Dalmatian dog sticker at the top left side and a fire hydrant sticker at the top right side of the card. Place a fire truck sticker at the bottom left side and a fire hat sticker at the right side of the card. Trace two circles from the pattern for the wildcard. Type up the words "fireman's wild card", twice on the computer (or just print it). Run off the copy. Cut out the fireman's wild card wording. Glue the yellow circle onto the center back of two separate cards. Glue the "fireman's wild card" onto the center of the yellow circle. Place one sticker in the center on the backside of each of the 16 cards. Each group of four cards has one symbol on each card (dog, fire hydrant, fire truck, and fireman's hat). See picture on page 6 in the color section.

How to Play the Card Game

Place cards onto the table face down. Mix the cards around. Line up 3 rows with 6 cards each in the center of the table. Mix the different fireman sticker symbols in each roll. Each child gets a turn to pick two cards to try to match the symbol, such as the fire hat with the fire hat. If he does not get a pair he returns the two cards back to the space in the center of the table. If he selects a pair, he will keep the cards at his placesetting (face down). A prize is given to the two children who draw a wild card. The game ends when all the cards are picked up and matched. The child with the most matched cards wins the prize. A second prize can be given to the same child if he seleced the second wild card. It is your judgment call.

Suggested Activities

Take the children on a tour to the firehouse. They can see the trucks and the firehouse.They will learn how the firemen live and do their jobs as a firefighter. Grandma M set up a couple tables for the adult friends and family members. She told the guests to wear their firemen hats or Grandma M would not serve any guest not wearing a firemen's hat. People giggled, but wore the hats. She got Grandpa M to take pictures of the guests with the firemen hats. The guests later admitted it was great fun to wear the hats and the hats made for a great conversation.

Patterns for the Fireman's Memory Drill Card Game
Card sizes and card designs

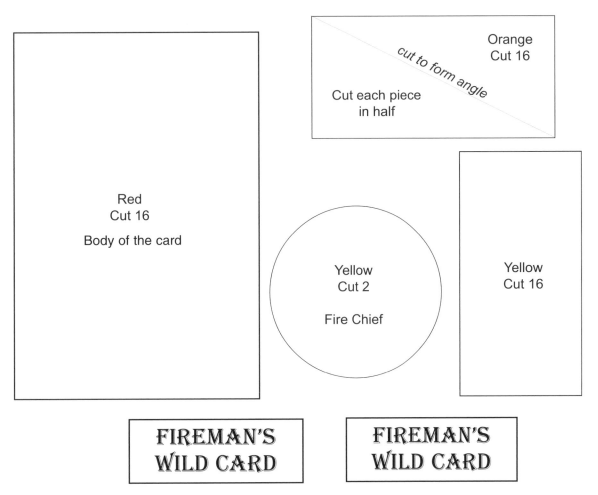

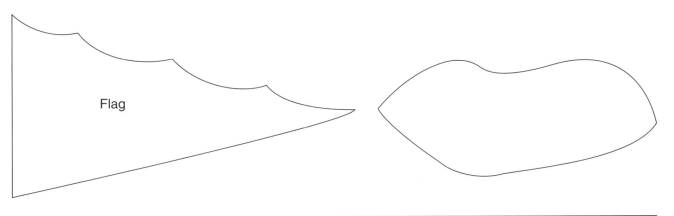

Patterns for Jon's Birthday Cake

Fire Truck Theme Related Book Resources

Bernthal, Mark S.
"Barney & BJ Go To The Fire Station"
Publisher: Barney Publications:
Published Date: c1996
Barney and BJ visits the fire station. The book shows the life of the firefighter, where they live, and discusses fire safety. (ages 1-4)

Bowman-Kruhm, Mary
"A Day in the Life of a Firefighter":
Publisher: PowerKids Press
Published Date: c1997
The book explains the fireman's job. (ages 4-6)

Cohen-Jango, Judith
"Fire Trucks"
Publisher: Lerner Publications
Published Date: c2003
The book explains the tools in a fire truck, the fire tanks, hoses, ladder and the bucket at the fire station.

Lenski, Lois
"The Little Fire Engine"
Publisher: Random House
Published Date: c2000
The book explains the fireman's job with many illustrations. "Mr. Small does it all! This fireman rushes to battle a fire in town. He roars down the street with his red fire engine to put the fire out. (ages 3-5)

London, Sara
"Firehorse Max"
Publisher: HarperCollins
Publisher Date: c1997
A peddler has a horse name Bubba who becomes too old to pull the peddler's wagon. The peddler purchases a horse called Max. The peddler realizes afterwards that Max is a firehorse. When Max hears the fire bell, he runs toward the fire to help the firemen put out the fire. (ages 3-6)

McGuire, Leslie
"Big Frank's Fire Truck"
Publication: Random House
Published Date: c1996
This book has illustrations in full color. Ride along with big Frank and the rest of the crew to find out the fireman's day and night on the job. (ages 3-6)

Raatma, Lucia
"Fire Safety"
Publisher: Child's World
Published Date: c2004
The book "explains various ways to stay safe near fires, and what to do in emergencies. Photographs and sidebars further describe more complex issues and concepts." The author asks a question on "how can you prevent a fire or what should you do in case of a fire?" The book also gives tips on how to escape your home if there is a fire and also safety fire tips at home. There is information on smoke alarms, kinds of fire, and what to do in case of a fire. (ages 7-9)

Scarry, Richard
"A Day at the Fire Station"
Publisher: Golden Books
Published Date: c2003
Drippy and Sticky are painters for the Busytown Fire Station. Fire fighters are busy fighting fires. There are several painting mishaps. The book is filled with information about firefighters. (ages 3-5)

Sis, Peter
"Fire Truck"
Publisher: Greenwillow Books
Published Date: c1998
"Matt loves fire trucks all sizes and all shapes. When he wakes up in the morning his first words are "fire truck." Children will love and enjoy the author's depictions of the trucks and they will have no trouble relating to Matt's fascination to fire trucks. (ages 2-5)

Smith, Dennis
"Brassy The Fire Engine Saves the City"
Publisher: Little, Brown
Published Date: c2005
The story is about a fire engine, named Brassy. The fire engine Brassy saves the day. Brassy is the only fire truck small enough to reach the city fire. Brassy and his friend Captain Bill put out the fire. It is a cute story. (ages 2-4)

Raspberry Party

Mrs. Cola's Raspberry Story

Mrs. Cola had a community bucket for picking raspberries. She said the kids could pick raspberries and put them into the bucket. The kids were very funny and yet so serious about their raspberry picking assignment. They ate more than what went into the bucket. Enjoying every bite, they did not share too many raspberries. They did pick enough raspberries for Mrs. Cola's quick and easy Raspberry Picnic Pie. The adults ate the pie but the children wanted Oreo® cookies. They got tired of Mrs. Cola's homemade cookies and they thought it was cool to eat store-bought cookies. Mrs. Cola found the children's idea about the cookies to be very amusing. Yet, when the kids grew up and went away to college, they again welcomed Mrs. Cola's homemade cookies.

Mrs. Cola has so many wonderful memories of her children's parties. The children became a highlight in her life and she enjoyed each child's personality.

Mrs. Cola's Raspberry Patch Poem
by Mrs. Cola

Children she could not bear,
But God answered her prayer.

Surrounding her with many children to share
In her love, respect, understanding and care.

Mrs. Cola created lots of activities for learning and fun,
And in return was rewarded with children's hearts she had won.

She taught them about being kind and polite.
She taught them to fly a model airplane and even a kite.

The real fun began with raspberry picking time,
And a chance to find the hidden lime.

Her raspberry party was a hit, providing good times,
For each child, picking and eating his/her way through the vines.

They gathered around the picnic table,
And listened to stories told by Aunt Mable.

In Mrs. Cola's big back and side yards,
They played hide and seek and memory cards.

Mrs. Cola sat in the raspberry patch,
With a camera focused for a picture to catch.

The children's smiling faces at the raspberry party,
And the laughter of each child was ever so hardy.

Mrs. Cola set up a hobo buffet on her wide Corian counter top (with no tablecloth). She used her colorful votive candles with garden leaves and purple flowers that intertwined the hobo pie tins filled with the following foods. Each pie tin had coleslaw, potato salad, tomatoes, lettuce salad, cucumbers and carrots, crackers, raspberries, black cherries, pretzels, peanut butter sandwiches, tuna and chicken salad sandwiches, cantaloupe and strawberries, grapes, and blueberries. Use any types of foods that you wish. Purchase many items at the deli if you do not want to prepare the food yourself or refer to *"Picnics, Catering on the Move"* cookbook by Pat Nekola for many of the recipes used for this raspberry party. See pictures of Mrs. Cola's raspberry party on page 7 in the color section.

Mrs. Cola's Picnic Raspberry Pie

Yield: Eight servings

1 prepared deep-dish 9 inch piecrust
1 pound prepared vanilla pudding
1 cup fresh/frozen raspberries, thawed
1-8 ounce container non-dairy whipped topping
1 2.5 ounce package sliced almonds
1 tablespoon mini chocolate chips
Maraschino cherry with stem, drained and dried

Preheat oven to 375 F. Poke tiny holes into the pie shell with a fork to prevent blistering. Bake the crust for 10 minutes or until the crust is brown. Cool. Fill the pie shell with the pudding. Drain and dry raspberries with paper towel. Mix raspberries into half of the non-dairy whip topping. Spread raspberry mixture over the pudding. Place the remaining non-dairy whip topping into a cake-decorating bag. With a number 849 cake tube, pipe on a border and a mound of whipped toping onto the center of the pie. Sprinkle the sliced almonds around the border. Sprinkle chocolate chips onto the center mound of whipped topping. Top the mound with one red maraschino cherry. Cover and refrigerate. See Picture on page 7 in the color section.

Note: Each year Mrs. Cola picked and froze raspberries into 1 cup bags. She could make a picnic pie. At Christmas she trimmed the border with green sugar and used a green maraschino cherry garnish. For Memorial Day, July 4th, and Labor Day she trimmed the border with blueberries andpecans. Aunt Maybel usually requested this pie for her birthday, because she didn't like cake. We put candles on her pie.

Pony Party

Horse Stories

When Charity was a little girl, she wanted to ride a horse. Charity was born without arms. Her mom read her daughter every horse story from their library. Every year Charity requested a horse theme birthday table. Charity turned eight at her last birthday. Her folks purchased a horse for her. Charity gleamed with joy. It was a big surprise. At last she had a pony. It was Charity's dream came true. She named her pony Jewels. Her parents discovered a wonderful horse club for disabled children. They took her to a meeting and met wonderful instructors. The warmth of the instructors at the training ranch made Charity feel very comfortable. She also was very excited about learning how to ride her pony. Her parents assured Charity that she was very normal and a big blessing to their family. They were there for Charity every step of the way. Charity was a happy and well-adjusted child. Charity learned to ride her pony with assistance.

My friend Mary had polio when she was a child. The horse learned to lie down so she could get up onto the horse.

Robert was a rambunctious child. His folks got him a rocking horse for Christmas. He bounced up and down on the horse. His family nicknamed Robert, "Bronco." To this day everyone calls him Bronco.

My friend Barb raised five children and a corral of horses. When we worked parties Barb talked constantly about her children and her horses. Her daughter Joan kidded her mother. She said, "Mom, I am not sure if you like the horses better than us kids." Where is the order? Is it horses and then kids or kids and then horses?." Barb just giggled. We never did get an answer from Barb on that subject.

Story About Muffin and Aunt Beatrice

Muffin was a beautiful pony. Muffin was always getting sick. All of the other horses looked after Muffin. Silverton was very protective of Muffin. He was the fatherly type. One night, Silverton heard Muffin crying for help. Silverton trotted to Aunt Beatrice's house and pounded on the door with his hoof. She got help for Muffin. Silverton saved Muffin's life. Aunt Beatrice said, "We are going to have a Pony Macaroni party to celebrate Muffin's recovery". Plans began for the big macaroni feast. By the way, Aunt Beatrice does not like to be called Aunt "B". One time her neighbor lady called her "B" and she received a five-minute lecture on why Beatrice was her name, not "B". So, when you see her, be sure to call her Aunt Beatrice. She makes good macaroni dishes and beautiful cakes for everyone who calls her Aunt Beatrice. She is very proud of her name. Everyone has a name and each person should be addressed properly.

Johnny's Birthday Dream Horse Poem
by Pat Nekola

I want a real horse
Of course, of course.

Mom gave me a horse for rocking,
And a puzzle in my Christmas stocking.

I want a real horse,
Of course, of course.

Dad gave me a horse on a broom stick,
That was fun for a while and very slick.

I want a real horse,
Of course, of course.

Auntie Joan gave me a horse storybook,
And she said, "Johnny, let's have a look".

I want a real horse,
Of course, of course.

Uncle Sidney has a lot of charm,
One day, he took me to a horse farm.

I want a real horse,
Of course, of course.

Uncle Sidney gave me a pony,
And I called him Macaroni.

Aunt Beatrice gave me a pony party,
With lots of macaroni, ever so hardy.

Johnny introduced his new pony with a glow.
Macaroni was a hit and the star of the show.

Now, Johnny stopped asking for a real horse.
He now has a pony, of course, of course.

Note: *There is a wonderful book called "Hoofprints, Horse Poems" by Jessie Haas. The 104 poems go back in time, "through 65 million years of horse history." It tells the story of love between man and his horse. The real hoofprints are in our hearts (ages 10-12).*

Pony-Macaroni Buffet
Yield: Twelve

<u>Pony Menu</u>

Casseroles
Nugget's Corral Turkey Macaroni Casserole
Silverton's Chicken Delight Casserole
Velvet's Cheeses Macaroni
Bullet's Hardy Goulash
Haystack Casserole

Salads
Buckwheat's Chicken Macaroni Salad
Buttercup's Horseshoe Apple Salad
Bronco's Hee Haw Spinach Salad
Hee Haw Buttermilk Dressing

Desserts
Aunt Beatrice's Petal Bread
Prince's Ranch Torte
Muffin's Dream Carousel Birthday Torte
Dumpling's Apple Dumplings
Dreamcicle's Alaskan Apples
Sweet Oat's Cowboy Cookies

Note: *The casserole and salad recipes are designed for 10-12 people. Cut the recipe in half for 6 servings. Some children eat only boxed macaroni and cheese. Follow the box for quick and easy macaroni and cheese or buy Spaghetti O's for the kids. Select two or three of the macaroni dishes and serve in cowboy style.*

Note: *There is a book called "Macaroni & Cheese, 52 Recipes, from Simple to Sublime", by Joan Schwartz. The recipes are interesting and some are even different. Also look up "Picnics, Catering on the Move" by Pat Nekola. There are macaroni salad recipes, a how-to-cook macaroni chart, and a funny macaroni story on pages 25-27. Look this book up on www.patnekolabooks.com.*

Nugget's Corral Turkey Macaroni Casserole
Yield: Ten to twelve servings

Water
2 tablespoons olive oil
1 teaspoon salt
1 pound macaroni, (4 cups, uncooked)
1 pound fresh asparagus
1-8 ounce package sliced mushrooms
1 bunch scallions with tops, chopped
$\frac{1}{2}$ cup celery, diced fine
1 yellow pepper, cored and diced fine
1 cup shredded carrots
1 teaspoon black pepper
2 teaspoons minced garlic
$\frac{1}{2}$ teaspoon season salt
3 cups cheddar cheese, finely grated and divided
1-10$\frac{1}{4}$ ounce cans cream of chicken soup
2-10$\frac{1}{4}$ ounce cans (each) cheddar cheese soup
2-10$\frac{1}{4}$ ounce cans (each) cream of asparagus soup
1 cup milk
$\frac{1}{2}$ cup chicken broth
2 pounds turkey, cooked and cubed
No-stick baking spray

Bring a large pan of water to a boil. Add olive oil, 1 teaspoon salt, and the macaroni. Stir every few minutes to prevent the macaroni from sticking to the bottom of the pan. Cook macaroni until tender. Drain and rinse with cold water. Clean asparagus. Place in a large pot. Cover with water. Boil the asparagus only for a couple of minutes to barely tender. Remove from the heat. Drain the water and rinse with cold water. Cut the asparagus into $\frac{1}{4}$ inch pieces. In a large bowl mix the macaroni with the asparagus, mushrooms, scallions, celery, yellow pepper, carrots, black pepper, minced garlic, seasoned salt, and 1-$\frac{1}{2}$ cups cheddar cheese. In a second large bowl mix together the three soups with the milk and chicken broth. Pour over the turkey macaroni mixture. Stir until all ingredients are moistened. Spray the two casserole pans with no-stick spray. Divide casserole evenly into two pans. Top each casserole with $\frac{3}{4}$ cup cheddar cheese. Foil or cover with a lid. Bake at 350 F for 30-45 minutes or until bubbly. See Picture on page 7 in the color section.

Note: The Silverton's Chicken Delight Casserole is a take off on spaghetti.

Silverton's Chicken Delight Casserole
Yield: Ten to twelve servings

Water
2 tablespoons olive oil
1 teaspoon salt
1-pound macaroni (4 cups, uncooked)
2-13 ounce cans (each) chicken (packed in water), drained
1-8 ounce package sliced mushrooms
$\frac{1}{2}$ cup diced onion
1 leek cut into ringlets
1 tablespoon minced garlic
2–32 ounce jars (each) Tomato and Basil Pasta sauce
2 teaspoons Italian seasoning
1 teaspoon pepper
$\frac{1}{4}$ teaspoon salt
No-stick baking spray
2 cups mozzarella

Bring a large pan of water to a boil. Add olive oil, 1 teaspoon salt, and the macaroni. Stir every few minutes to prevent the macaroni from sticking to the bottom of the pan. Cook macaroni until tender. Drain and rinse macaroni with cold water. In a large bowl, mix together the macaroni, chicken, mushrooms, onions, leek, garlic, pasta sauce, Italian seasoning, pepper, and $\frac{1}{4}$ teaspoon salt. Spray a large lasagna pan with no-stick baking spray. Place the casserole into the lasagna pan. Sprinkle the mozzarella cheese over the top of the casserole. Cover with foil. Bake at 375 F for 45–55 minutes or until cheese melts and the casserole is bubbly.

Note: Colby and Monterey Jack shredded cheeses come in a package of 2 cups.

Velvet's Cheeses Macaroni

Yield: Eight to ten servings

Water
2 tablespoons olive oil
1 teaspoon salt
$^3/_4$ pound macaroni (3 cups, uncooked)
$^1/_2$ cup butter
4 cups milk
$^1/_2$ cup flour
2 cups Colby and Monterey Jack cheeses
No-stick baking spray
1 cup shredded cheddar cheese, divided

Bring a large pan of water to a boil. Add olive oil, 1 teaspoon salt, and macaroni. Stir every few minutes to prevent the macaroni from sticking to the bottom of the pan. Cook macaroni until tender. Drain and rinse with cold water. Pat macaroni dry with paper towel. Set aside. In a large pan, melt butter over medium heat. Microwave 4 cups of milk for two minutes. Whisk the flour into butter to form a smooth paste called a roux. Slowly add 3 cups of the warm milk to the roux, stirring constantly with the whisk. Add the Colby and Monterey Jack cheeses. Slowly add the remaining milk. Add one cup cheddar cheese and blend until cheese sauce is smooth and creamy. Gradually stir in the macaroni. Spray no-stick cooking spray into a large casserole dish. Place macaroni and cheese into the dish. Top with the remaining Colby and Monterey cheeses. Cover with a casserole lid or cover with foil. Bake at 375 F for 30-35 minutes or until cheese melts and macaroni dish is bubbly.

Bullet's Hardy Goulash

Yield: Ten to twelve servings

Water
2 tablespoons olive oil
1 teaspoon salt
1 pound macaroni (4 cups)
1-1/2 pounds ground chuck
$^1/_2$ cup onions, diced
$^1/_2$ teaspoon white pepper
$^1/_2$ teaspoon salt
1-14.5 ounce can chili tomatoes
2 cups cheddar cheese, divided
1-10$^3/_4$ can cream of rancho tomato soup
1 teaspoon chili powder

Bring a large pan of water to a boil. Add olive oil, 1 teaspoon salt, and the macaroni. Stir every few minutes to prevent the macaroni from sticking to the bottom of the pan. Cook macaroni until tender. Drain and rinse macaroni with cold water. Dry the macaroni with paper towel. Set aside. In a large frying pan, fry the ground chuck with the onion. Drain off excess grease and dab meat with paper towel. Add the macaroni, white pepper, $^1/_2$ teaspoon salt, chili tomatoes, 1 cup cheddar cheese, cream of rancho tomato soup, and chili powder. Heat through. Transfer goulash to large camping pot and serve from the pot, or place into a large casserole dish. Top with the remaining cheese. Bake at 375 F for 30-40 minutes or until cheese melts and the casserole is bubbly.

Note: The Haystack Casserole requires no milk or broth.

Haystack Casserole

Yield: Ten to twelve servings

Water
2 tablespoons olive oil
1 teaspoon salt
1 pound macaroni (4 cups uncooked)
2 pounds ham steak, diced
1 pound broccoli flowerettes, chopped
1 red pepper, diced fine
$^1/_2$ cup onion, diced fine
$^1/_2$ celery, diced fine
2 teaspoons minced garlic
$^1/_2$ teaspoon pepper
2-10$^3/_4$ ounce cans (each) cream of cheddar cheese soup
2-10$^3/_4$ ounce cans (each) cream of broccoli soup
No-stick spray
1 cup cheddar cheese, finely shredded

Bring a large pan of water to a boil. Add olive oil, 1 teaspoon salt, and macaroni. Stir every few minutes to prevent the macaroni from sticking to the bottom of the pan. Cook macaroni until tender. Drain and rinse with cold water. Dry the macaroni with a paper towel. In a large bowl, mix macaroni, ham, broccoli, red pepper, onion, celery, garlic, pepper, and soups. Spray a 13x9 lasagna pan with no-stick spray. Place the casserole into the pan. Sprinkle the cheddar cheese over the top of the casserole. Cover with foil. Bake at 375 F for 45-50 minutes or until cheese melts and the casserole bubbles.

Buckwheat's Chicken Macaroni Salad

Yield: Ten to twelve servings

Water
2 tablespoons olive oil
1 teaspoon salt
1 pound macaroni (4 cups, uncooked)
2-13 ounce cans (each) chicken, packed in water
1 pound frozen peas and carrots, thawed
3 teaspoons minced garlic
$1/4$ cup red onion, chopped
1 pound pasteurized processed cheese, cubed
1 teaspoon pepper
2 teaspoons Italian seasoning
2 teaspoons curry powder
3 cups light mayonnaise
2 tablespoons olive oil
1 teaspoon salt
Red leaf lettuce
Tomato slices or
Yellow pepper rings

Bring a large pan of water to a boil. Add olive oil, 1 teaspoon salt, and the macaroni. Stir every few minutes to prevent macaroni from sticking to the bottom of the pan. Cook macaroni until tender. Drain and rinse with cold water. Dry the macaroni with paper towel. In a large bowl, mix cooked macaroni with chicken, peas and carrots, garlic, red onion, cheese, pepper, Italian seasoning, and curry powder. Stir in mayonnaise to moisten all ingredients. Turn salad into a pasta dish. Chill before serving Garnish with red leafy lettuce and tomato slices or yellow pepper rings.

Buttercup's Horseshoe Apple Salad

Yield: Twelve servings

Water
1 tablespoon olive oil
1/2 teaspoon salt
1-8 ounce box macaroni, (2 cups,uncooked)
4 delicious apples
1 granny smith apple
1 pink lady apple
2 cups shredded carrots
1 pound seedless red grapes, halved
1 pound seedless green grapes, halved
1 pint blueberries
4-6 ounce (each) light fat free lemon cream pie yogurts
1/4 pound black cherries, with stems (optional)
1 bunch of fresh parsley

Bring a medium pan of water to a boil. Add olive oil, salt, and the macaroni. Stir every few minutes to prevent the macaroni from sticking to the bottom of the pan. Cook macaroni until tender. Drain and rinse with cold water. Chill the macaroni. Peel, core, and chop the apples into bite sized pieces. Add carrots, red and green grapes, blueberries, and macaroni. Moisten with the yogurt. Place the salad onto a platter in the shape of a horseshoe. Wash and dry the cherries. Garnish with parsley and fresh black stemmed cherries. See Picture on page 7 in the color section.

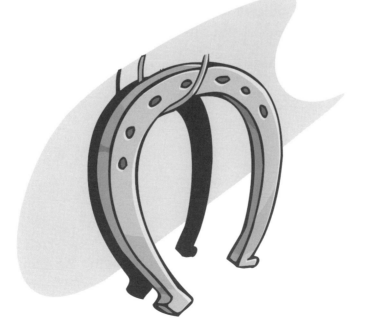

Note: If the eggs roll on the counter top, the eggs are cooked and the yolks should stay yellow.

Bronco's Hee Haw Spinach Salad

Yield: Twelve servings

3 hard cooked eggs
2 tablespoons lemon juice
1 teaspoon salt
1 pound romaine lettuce, chopped
2-5 ounce bags (each), baby spinach and red leaf lettuce mix
1 pound bacon
2 cucumbers
1 small red onion, sliced
2 pints grape tomatoes, divided
1-8 ounce package shredded Swiss cheese

Place 3 eggs into cold water. Add the lemon juice and salt. Bring eggs to a boil. Remove from heat. Cover eggs and let set for 30 minutes. Drain. Rinse in cold water. Peel the eggs and slice. Clean the vegetables, romaine and red leafy lettuce. Dice and fry the bacon. Drain off the grease with paper towel. Set aside. Peel and dice one cucumber. In a large bowl, mix spinach, red leafy lettuce mixture with romaine lettuce, onions, 1 pint grape tomatoes, diced cucumber, cheese, and half the bacon. Run fork down along the entire outside of the peel of the second cucumber. Slice into circles. Place the salad mixture into a large serving salad bowl. Garnish with remaining bacon, grape tomatoes, sliced cucumbers, egg slices, 1 egg flowerette in the center of the salad and one grape tomato flower in the center of the egg. Serve with Hee Haw dressing or bottled ranch dressing. See Picture on page 7 in the color section.

Hee Haw Buttermilk Dressing

Yield: Twelve servings

1 cup buttermilk
1 cup light mayonnaise
1-4 ounce package ranch salad dressing mix
1 tablespoon fresh parsley, finely chopped
$1/8$ teaspoon seasoned salt

In a medium size bowl, mix buttermilk, mayonnaise, salad dressing mix, parsley, and season salt. Refrigerate for 20 minutes or until serving time. Place into a salad dressing bowl. Serve cold.

Aunt Beatrice's Petal Bread

Yield: Twenty biscuits

2-12 ounce cans (each) buttermilk biscuits
1 egg, beaten
2 teaspoons cream
1 tablespoon honey
$1/8$ teaspoon cinnamon
2 tablespoons poppy seed
Honey
Butter

In a 12 inch pie pan, arrange biscuits into three circles, starting from the outside and working to the inside. With a fork, beat the egg, cream, honey and cinnamon together. With a pastry brush, spread the egg mixture over the top of the biscuits. Sprinkle poppy seed over the top of each biscuit. Bake at 375 F for 20-25 minutes or until golden brown and a toothpick inserted in the middle comes out clean. Serve warm with honey and butter. See Picture on page 7 in the color section.

Prince's Ranch Torte

Yield: Three 9 inch torte (1 whole cake)

No-stick baking spray
1-18.25 box yellow cake mix
1-2.6 ounce box (two packages) dry whipped topping mix
1-3 ounce package " Cook & Serve" vanilla pudding mix
3 eggs
$1^{1}/_{4}$ cup water
$1/4$ cup vegetable oil
$1/2$ cup mini chocolate chips (optional)
$1/2$ cup sliced almonds (optional)
3-10 inch cardboard cake circles

Preheat oven to 350 F. Spray 3-9 inch cake pans with no-stick baking spray. Mix cake mix, dry whipped topping mix, pudding mix, eggs, water, and oil in a mixing bowl. Beat at low speed to incorporate the ingredients. Increase speed to medium. Beat 4 minutes. Stir in mini chocolate chips and sliced almonds. Pour into prepared pans. Bake 20-25 minutes or until toothpick inserted in the center of the cake comes out clean. Cool on cake racks for 5 minutes. Turn each cake onto a cardboard circle. Continue to cool. Frost and decorate the cake corral style. See Picture on page 8 in the color section.

Note: The frosting recipe will frost two whole torte cakes, one 11x17 inch sheet cake or 3 quarter sized sheet cakes. Be sure the cream and milk are ice cold. Refrigerate the cake to prevent spoiling.

Note: The birthday boy candles will burn for 2 minutes and have lead-free wicks.

Prince's Ranch Torte Frosting

Yield: Frosting for two tortes

1-2.6 ounce box (2 packages) whipped topping mix
1-3 ounce package instant white chocolate pudding
1-3 ounce package instant chocolate pudding
1 cup 2% milk
1 cup coconut green food coloring
2 quart size bags
1-1.4 ounce milk chocolate English toffee bar
1 package of 11 pick candles (saying birthday boy)

In a large mixing bowl, place whipped topping mix, chocolate and white chocolate pudding, and the milk. Beat on low for about 3 minutes. Continue to beat on high speed about 10 minutes or until blended and fluffy. Frost the cake and refrigerate for one half hour to firm up the cake. Place coconut and green food coloring into a quart size bag. Seal and shake until coconut turns green. Place milk chocolate English toffee bar into the bag. Crush the candy bar with rolling pin. Sprinkle the coconut around the top and bottom to form the border. Sprinkle crushed candy bar over the top center of the cake. Do not sprinkle over the coconut. Place 5 corral pieces of the corral around the outside of the crushed candy. Place three horses inside the corral fence. Place "birthday boy"candles around the outside of the fence. Refrigerate until time for serving.

Muffin's Story

Muffin insisted that her entire cake had to be pink. Aunt Beatrice came up with her great grandmother's (Grammie) raspberry apple sauce cake. Grammie grew raspberries and had apple trees. Every year Grammie made homemade raspberry applesauce. Aunt Beatrice made the raspberry applesauce cake and Muffin was tickled pink.

Note: A couple drops of red food coloring brightens the raspberry color. There are 6-4 ounce apple sauce cups per 24 ounce package.

Muffin's Dream Carousel Birthday Torte

Yield: Three 9 inch cakes (one whole cake)

No-stick baking spray
1$\frac{1}{2}$ cups shortening
1$\frac{1}{2}$ cups sugar
3 eggs
1-24 ounce package raspberry applesauce
3 cups flour
1$\frac{1}{2}$ cups oatmeal
3 teaspoons baking soda
2$\frac{1}{2}$ teaspoons cinnamon
2$\frac{1}{2}$ teaspoons nutmeg
A couple drops of red food coloring
3-10 inch cake cardboards

Preheat oven to 350 F. Spray no-stick baking spray into three 9 inch round cake pans. Cream together the shortening and sugar. Add eggs. Beat until creamy. Add the applesauce and beat. Add the flour, a little at a time, and beat. Add the oatmeal, baking soda, cinnamon, nutmeg and beat. Fold in the red food coloring. Bake for 25-30 minutes or until toothpick inserted in the center comes out clean. Cool. Turn each cake onto a cake cardboard.

Aunt Beatrice made carousel hats with the same pattern for the carousel cake. She just sewed on 2-18 ribbons (one on each side of the carousel. The girls and the female guests wore the carousel hats. They tied the hat strings into a bow beneath their chins. They all looked so cute and very festive for the party.

Muffin's Carousel Top to Her Cake

Yield: One carousel top

1-10x10 inch piece white mat board (light weight)
1-10x10 inch piece of pink and white striped material
1¼ wide package double fold pink bias tape
1 spool pink thread
1 pink and white striped drinking straw
1-9x12 inch pink sheet of Foamtastic®
2 packages horse and daisy stickers (acid free)
1 glue gun (with glue stick)

Lay pink material across the construction paper. Outline a 10-inch circle onto the fabric. Cut out both thickness of the circle together. Make a line half way up the center of the circle. Cut on the line. Overlap the centerline about ½ to 1 inch to form the peak of the carousel. With a sewing machine, sew the material and cardboard together to form the centerline down and around the border of the circle. Sew on the pink bias tape around the bottom of the circle. Poke a small hole at the center peak of the carousel. Cut the straw down to 4 inches. Trace a flag out of the Foamtastic®. Cut out the flag and hot glue the straight edge of the flag onto the top of the straw. Push the bottom of the straw through the hole. Hot glue the bottom of the flag to the cardboard. Place a pony sticker onto the center of the flag and one onto the bottom of the straw just below the pony on the flag. Stick a daisy on the top of the carousel, on each side of the pony flag. Alternate a horse and a daisy sticker all the way around the bottom of the carousel to make the pony/daisy border. The carousel top is about the same size as the cake. You can also make extra Carousel Tops to use in the project below.

Muffin's Carousel Hat

Yield: One carousel hat

1 Completed Carousel Top to her cake
Two 1-18 inch pieces of gross grain ribbon

Use a completed Muffin's Carousel Top to Her Cake from the above project. Stich the 1-18 inch piece of gross grain ribbon on each side of the Carousel Top to use as ties to form the hat.

Muffin's Carousel Applesauce Fluff Frosting

Yield: One 9 inch frosted cake

1-12 ounce container non-dairy whipped topping
1 cup raspberry applesauce

Fold the applesauce into the whipped topping. Frost the cake. With a number 199 tip, pipe on the border around top and bottom.

Decorations for the Carousel Cake
Yield: One decorated cake

4 candles, carousel horses
4 pink and white striped cupcake candles
8-7 inch (each) pink and green striped candy sticks
1-13 ounce bag animal crackers
1 carousel top
Place one peppermint stick in the center of the cake and four more around the cake edge, equally spaced. Search through the animal crackers for eight horses. Place four animal horse crackers around the middle candy stick. Alternate 4 cupcake candles with 4 carousel horse candles. Place an animal cracker horse in front of each of the cupcake candles. Center and place the carousel top over the candy sticks just before the party. See picture of the completed cake on page 8 in the color section.

Note: See information about puff pastry on page 172 in the "Picnics, Catering on the Move Cookbook, by Pat Nekola. Puff pastry is a good substitute for piecrust.

Dumpling's Apple Dumplings
Yield: Twelve dumplings

12 small to medium cooking apples
1³/₄ cup plus 2 tablespoons brown sugar
²/₃ cup butter
¹/₂ cup honey
1 teaspoon cinnamon
3 tablespoons lemon juice
3 cups cold water
No-stick baking spray
2-17.3 ounce boxes (each) puff
    pastry sheets (2 per box)

Peel and core apples, leaving each apple whole. Mix brown sugar, butter, and honey together. Add cinnamon and beat until the mixture is smooth. In a large bowl mix together lemon juice and water. Dip apples into the lemon juice-water mixture. Dry apples. Lay out 3 puff pastry sheets on the counter top. Using scissors, cut each pastry piece into four equal pieces. Spray no-stick baking spray onto a baking sheet. Place one apple onto the center of each of the puff pastry squares. Fill the center of each apple with the brown sugar mixture. Bring the four corners of the puff pastry together at the top and pinch together to hold the apple in place. Serve with ice cream and caramel sauce. See Picture on page 8 in the color section.

Note: There is a wonderful butterscotch-caramel topping that comes in a 17 ounce jar. This product can be substituted for the caramel sauce recipe below. Vanilla can be substituted for caramel flavor.

Caramel Sauce

Yield: One cup

The extra apple dumpling filling
2 tablespoons butter
$^1/_2$ cup fat free half and half
$^1/_2$ teaspoon caramel flavoring
2-1.4 ounce (each) milk chocolate English toffee bars, crushed
1-quart size bag
1-12 ounce container non-dairy whipped topping
1 cup pecans, chopped fine, optional (per dumpling), optional
1-10 ounce jar maraschino cherries with stems
Vanilla ice cream

In a medium sized saucepan place the extra apple dumpling filling, butter, and half and half. Cook sauce on low heat stirring constantly until smooth. Remove from heat. Stir in the caramel flavoring last. Place one scoop of ice cream over each apple dumpling. Drizzle the caramel sauce over the ice cream. With a rolling pin, crush milk chocolate English toffee bars in a quart sized bag. Sprinkle two teaspoons of the chocolate English toffee bar over the caramel sauce. With a 199 cake tube, swirl on whipped topping. Sprinkle 2 teaspoons pecans over the whipped topping. Top with a stemmed maraschino cherry.

Alaskan Apple Story

When Nya was attending college, she was assigned to entertain the college president and his wife, as part of her class project. Six other students were living at the Home Management House sponsored by the University. The other students said they would help Nya. The students made a wonderful meal. Nya's assignment was dessert. She insisted on making apple dumplings for dessert. She thought they would go well with the pork dish and it was different. She made the pie crust and put too much shortening in the crust. After finally getting the crust around each apple, she baked the dumplings. When it was time to serve the dumplings, she discovered that the crust had slipped off of every apple. She pushed the panic button. She asked Miss Evans to come into the kitchen immediately. Miss Evans suggested placing every apple into a separate dessert dish. She also said to place a scoop of vanilla ice cream over every apple. Nya suggested the whipped cream and maraschino cherry with a stem. The dessert looked beautiful and every guest wanted Nya's recipe. The president asked Nya the name and the dish and she cleverly blurted out, "Alaskan Apple". He said, "very interesting, Nya. "My wife will have to make this dish for our family next Sunday". At this point Nya put her head down for her face was beet red.

Dreamcicle's Alaskan Apples

Yield: Twelve

2 cooking apples
3 tablespoons lemon juice
3 cups cold water
1 cup light corn syrup
$\frac{1}{4}$ cup sugar
$\frac{1}{4}$ cup dark brown sugar
3 tablespoons butter, melted
$\frac{1}{2}$ teaspoon cinnamon
No-stick baking spray
1-3 ounce container cinnamon décor (red hots)
$\frac{1}{2}$ gallon vanilla ice cream
1-17 ounce butterscotch caramel or extra corn syrup mixture
1 cup pecans, finely chopped
3-1.4 ounce (each) milk chocolate English toffee bars, crushed
1-10 ounce jar maraschino cherries with stems
Non-dairy whipped topping

Peel each apple only a fourth down around the apple, leaving the remaining peel in tack. Core the apple leaving the bottom core in tack. In a large bowl mix together the lemon juice and water. Dip the apples in the water. Drain and dry apples. In a medium size bowl, mix together corn syrup, sugar, brown sugar, butter, and cinnamon. Spray 13x9 inch pan with no-stick baking spray. Place the apples into the pan. Fill the cavity of each apple with the corn syrup mixture. Sprinkle 8 cinnamon décor (red hots) into the cavity each apple with the corn syrup mixture. Bake the apples at 350 F for 30-40 minutes or until tender. Cool slightly. Place each apple in a dessert bowl. Cut apple in half and cut off the bottom core. Place one scoop of vanilla ice cream onto each apple. Drizzle the butterscotch caramel or extra corn syrup mixture over the top of the ice cream. Top with non-dairy whipped topping. Sprinkle 1 tablespoon each of nuts and chocolate English toffee over the whipped topping. Top with a maraschino cherry with a stem. See picture on page 8 in the color section.

Note: These cookies are large and will spread. For best results place six cookies per 11x17 inch cookie sheet with two across and three down.

Sweet Oat's Cowboy Cookies

Yield: Fifteen cookies (5 inches each)

1 cup butter
$3/4$ cup granulated sugar
$3/4$ cup brown sugar
2 eggs
1 teaspoon maple flavor or vanilla
$1\frac{1}{2}$ cups flour
1 teaspoon cinnamon
1 teaspoon nutmeg
1 teaspoon baking soda
$1/4$ teaspoon salt
3 cups oats
1 cup coconut
1 cup white chocolate chips
1 cup craisins
1 cup pecans, chopped

Set oven to 350 F. Cream together butter, sugar and brown sugar. Add eggs and maple flavor and beat. Add flour, cinnamon, nutmeg, baking soda, salt, oats, coconut, white chocolate chips, craisins, and pecans. Beat until smooth. Using a number 12 scoop, place 6 cookies per ungreased cookie sheet. Bake the cookies for 20-22 minutes or until the cookies are firm. Cool on pan for a couple minutes. Remove from the cookie sheet and place on a cooling rack.

Sweet Oat's Cowboy Frosting

Yield: Fifteen frosted cookies

$1/4$ cup butter, melted
$1/2$ cup sour cream
2-1 ounce packages pre-melted unsweetened chocolate
$1/2$ teaspoon vanilla flavor
1 pound powdered sugar
2 packages (each) horses with corral fences.

Add the butter, sour cream, unsweetened chocolate, and vanilla to the powdered sugar. Beat until smooth and creamy. Frost the center of the cookie leaving about 1 inch of the edge of the cookie unfrosted. Place one horse in the center of the cookie and 1 corral fence in front of the horse. The horse and coral will adhere to the frosting. See picture on page 8 in the color section.

Setting up the Pony Macaroni Buffet

On serving surface lay down green tablecloth for grass. Place macaroni casserole dishes in a grouping. Lay out carrots, apples, and horse cookies at random across the entire buffet. Place a vase of flowers in the center of the table. Set the cowboy cake next to the casseroles as part of a centerpiece. Place the cold salad and petal bread in a grouping. Place the carousel cake at the end of the buffet line. Decorate the buffet with leaves and flowers. See picture on page 7 in the color section.

Suggested Activities

Using the pattern on page 150, help Muffin the horse count the shapes and objects. Follow the instructions and fill in the number of each item in the blank space to the right. Complete the work from 1-10. Use the chart below for more fun with Muffin.

Muffin's Learning Chart

1. Color half of the apples red and the other half yellow.
2. Color the carrots orange and the tops green.
3. Draw circles around four of the bells.
4. Color all the stars blue.
5. Draw a square around five horse saddles.
6. Color two hats of choice green.
7. Draw a diamond shape around two stars of choice.
8. Place a small star above the last four horse heads.
9. Place a circle around one carrot of choice.
10. Place a vertical line through the last two bells.

Other Activity Suggestions

Take the children to a farm to see the horses and learn how to care for the horses.

Feed the ponies at the horse farm.

Play the video "A Day with the Horses". See video under references on page 158.

Have a picnic at a horse farm.

Help Muffin Count and Color the
Following Shapes and Objects

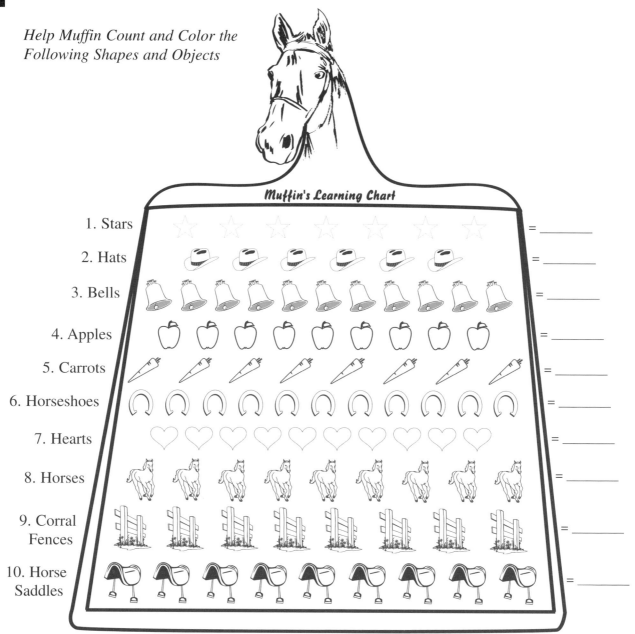

Muffin's Learning Chart

1. Stars = _____
2. Hats = _____
3. Bells = _____
4. Apples = _____
5. Carrots = _____
6. Horseshoes = _____
7. Hearts = _____
8. Horses = _____
9. Corral Fences = _____
10. Horse Saddles = _____

1. Name three objects on Muffin's learning chart.
2. Color 2 hats of your choice red.
3. Color all of the horses saddles orange.
4. Color all of the hearts red.
5. Color 4 stars blue.
6. Color 3 horseshoes pink and three horseshoes yellow.
7. How many horseshoes are not colored.
8. Place a horizontal line through the center of 4 of the hearts of your choice.
9. Draw a circle around the first 5 bells.
10. Color 2 of the corral fences black and 4 corral fences brown..

This exercise teaches children how to count, colors and how to identify shapes and objects.

```
K T I O P L M N U E W Q U C I M Q W E F T I U A R A B I A N
T T P O N Y T H Y U V B J I O W Q M N D O B B I N B I N W O
R B D F O A L Y Y K K I I E E C L I P P E R U P X S L O L I
U E I O L K M J U H Y G R R O P R O Y L K I R J H Y R F B F
R X J K J Y U J K M N B B A Y R T T B U C K S K I N B V F P
B E L G I U M N B O Y U I U Y R E W Q Z E B R A V G E R F U
Y K R F E D S W Q A S C O L T M K I U J M N Y H Y T N B V V
I R E U I U Y T R T Y T R E F H Y T R S T U D H U I R I U D
T T M A R E T G Y H U J I K R A C E R O I U E T G Y U J I D
Y I F R D F C V B H Y T G F R E S P A L O M I N O Q O I U Y
E K D K C A L I C O P O P L K N R G Y H Y G R F H O B B Y U
I D C L Y D E S D A L E O L I J U M N H Y T U E W S F T R J
L O G F R T R E W S D B R O N C O L P O I K F J M N U H Y K
V F S G S T A L L I O N O P O K J I U H Y T H R E D B H B W
D R A F T G R D E W S A C P O L M J U Y H Y U S T A B L E G
```

Types of Horses Word Search

Mare	Pony	Foal	Hobby
Stud	Racer	Zebra	Arabian
Bronco	Belgium	Palomino	Stallion
Colt	Calico	Clydesdale	Stable
Draft	Clipper	Dobbin	Buck Skin

```
K T I O P L M N U E W Q U C I M Q W E F T I U A R A B I A N
T T P O N Y T H Y U V B J I O W Q M N D O B B I N B I N W O
R B D F O A L Y Y K K I I E E C L I P P E R U P X S L O L I
U E I O L K M J U H Y G R R O P R O Y L K I R J H Y R F B F
R X J K J Y U J M N B B A Y R T T B U C K S K I N B V F P
B E L G I U M N B O Y U I U Y R E W Q Z E B R A V G E R F U
Y K R F E D S W Q A S C O L T M K I U J M N Y H Y T N B V Y
I R E U I U Y T R T Y T R E F H Y T R S T U D H U I R I U D
T T M A R E T G Y H U J I K R A C E R O I U E T G Y U J I D
Y I F R D F C V B H Y T G F R E S P A L O M I N O Q O I U Y
E K D K C A L I C O P O P L K N R G Y H Y G R F H O B B Y U
I D C L Y D E S D A L E O L I J U M N H Y T U E W S F T R J
L O G F R T R E W S D B R O N C O L P O I K F J M N U H Y K
V F S G S T A L L I O N O P O K J I U H Y T H R E D B H B W
D R A F T G R D E W S A C P O L M J U Y H Y U S T A B L E G
```

Types of Horses Word Search

Mare	Pony	Foal	Hobby
Stud	Racer	Zebra	Arabian
Bronco	Belgium	Palomino	Stallion
Colt	Calico	Clydesdale	Stable
Draft	Clipper	Dobbin	Buck Skin

Horse Crossword Puzzle

Across:
1. An orange vegetable eaten by a horse
3. Curved flat iron bars fitted to horses' hooves
7. A covering placed under a saddle (2 words)
8. Horse manure
9. A building to house horses
12. A young male horse
14. Footwear when riding a horse
16. A fruit grown on a tree and eaten by horses
19. A young horse under one year old
21. Grass that is cut and dried
23. A seat of padded leather for riding a horse
24. A leather strap used in guiding a horse
25. A small sturdy horse of various breeds

Down:
2. Two or more horses harnessed together to pull a wagon
4. Cereal grams eaten by both animals and humans
5. The skin of a horse
6. A sweet cube loved by horses
10. A long open receptacle for animal feed
11. Part of the bridle inserted in a horse's mouth
12. To move at a gentle gallop
13. Found at the back of the horse
15. A cattle herder on the range who works on horseback
17. A large piece of property owned by a rancher on which to raise horses
18. A female horse
20. A rope used for catching wild horses
22. A cowboy "yes"

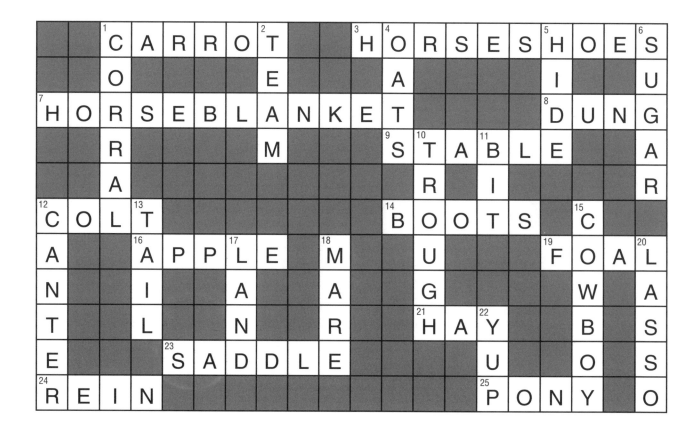

Horse Crossword Puzzle

Across:
1. An orange vegetable eaten by a horse
3. Curved flat iron bars fitted to horses' hooves
7. A covering placed under a saddle (2 words)
8. Horse manure
9. A building to house horses
12. A young male horse
14. Footwear when riding a horse
16. A fruit grown on a tree and eaten by horses
19. A young horse under one year old
21. Grass that is cut and dried
23. A seat of padded leather for riding a horse
24. A leather strap used in guiding a horse
25. A small sturdy horse of various breeds

Down:
2. Two or more horses harnessed together to pull a wagon
4. Cereal grams eaten by both animals and humans
5. The skin of a horse
6. A sweet cube loved by horses
10. A long open receptacle for animal feed
11. Part of the bridle inserted in a horse's mouth
12. To move at a gentle gallop
13. Found at the back of the horse
15. A cattle herder on the range who works on horseback
17. A large piece of property owned by a rancher on which to raise horses
18. A female horse
20. A rope used for catching wild horses
22. A cowboy "yes"

Pattern for Muffin's Carousel Top to Her Cake and Hat

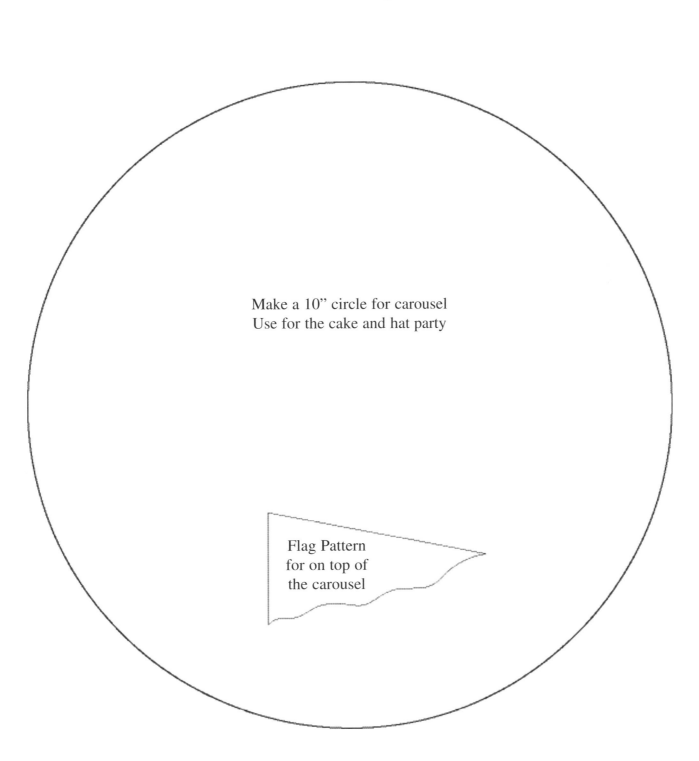

Make a 10" circle for carousel
Use for the cake and hat party

Flag Pattern
for on top of
the carousel

Pony Theme Related Book Resources

Alexander. Liza
"I Want to be a Cowboy"
Publisher: Western Publishing Company
Published Date: c1992
The book is a full color summary with straightforward and engaging text. There is a board spectrum of occupations. (ages 5-7)

Anderson, C.W.
"Blaze the Lost Quarry"
Publisher: Aladdin Paperbacks
Published Date: c1991
Blaze the horse and Billy have an adventure for the day by finding the lost quarry and exploring the area. (ages 4-6) Note: For more Blaze stories, look up the author's name at your local library.

Bang-Campbell, Monika
"Little Rat Rides"
Publisher: Harcourt
Published Date: c2004
This is a story about the rat who wants to ride on a horse. With encouragement from Pee Wee the horse, the rat's dream comes true. (ages 5-7)

Cooper, Jason
"Foal to Horse"
Publisher: Rourke Publishing
Published Date: c2004
The book talks about newborn foals, foals and horses growing up, and wild horses. (ages 4-5)

Goble, Paul
"Mystic Horse"
Publisher: HarperCollins Publishers
Published Date: c2003
This story is based on the unwritten traditions of Pawnee Indians. The story is about a legend of a special mystic horse and "Piraski Resaru", meaning "Boy Chief". The poor Pawnee boy is rewarded by the horse's mystic powers for his brave deed. (ages 7-8)

Haas, Jessie
"A Horse Lover's Alphabet. Appaloosa Zebra"
Publisher: Greenwillow Books
Published Book: c2002
The book goes through the 26 letters of the alphabet describing horses and horse terms. The back of the book has a section called, "More about Horses" and provides more information. (ages 4-5)

Hass, Jessie
"Birthday Pony":
Publisher: Greenwillow Books
Published Date: c2004
This is a story about a little girl named Jane. She is a horse Lover. Her Grandmother Aggie is also a horse lover. Jane gets to show off her pony and wins first prize. (ages 8-10)

Porte, Barbara Ann
"Harry's Pony"
Publisher: Greenwillow Books
Published Date: c1997
Harry wins a pony in a contest. Harry has to give the horse away to the pony farm because Harry lives in the city. Harry gets a trophy and also a newspaper write-up for his good deed. (ages 4-6)

Ransford, Sandy,
"Horse & Pony Care"
Publisher: Kingfisher
Published Date: c2002
The book has many pictures and explains how to care for your horse, such as stabling, feeding, and grooming. (ages 6-8) *Note: For More information on ponies by this author, check out resources at your local library.*

Sewell, Anna
"Black Beauty: The Graphic Novel"
Publisher: Puffin
Published Date: c2005
It is the classic heart-warming story about a horse that gets sold to several families. Black Beauty takes some abuse on the way, but in the end his friend Joe buys him and promises Black Beauty he will never be sold again. (ages 5-7)

Van Camp, Richard
"What's The Most Beautiful Thing You Know About Horses"
Publisher: Children's Press
Published Date: c1998
The author never saw a horse in person because he lives in Fort Smith in Northwest Territories in Canada. It is 40 below and too cold to have horses. (ages 3-5)

Western Music CD

"Songs of the West"
{Intersound}
Publisher: Rhino Records, Inc.
Published Date: c1993
The "Songs of West" includes the "Happy Trails" song by Roy Rogers and Dale Evans. Gene Autry also sings. The Children can sing along.

DVD

"American Black Beauty"
{Video recording}
Publisher: Sterling Entertainment
Published Date: c2005
"Black Beauty" is a timeless tale of love and courage and treating animals humanely. The movie is based on the novel of Anna Sewell (ages 10-12)

"Felicity" (An American girl Adventure)
{Video recording}
Publisher: Warner Home Video
Published Date: c2005
Nine-year-old Felicity is a spirited girl growing up in Virginia just before the revolutionary war. Felicity shows courage and even loses a friend for the support of her family. She also falls in love with a horse. (ages 8-10)

"The New Adventures of Black Beauty: Season One and Two"
{Video recording}
Publisher: Questar Entertainment
Published Date: c2004
The scene is set in New Zealand's rugged wilderness. Jenny and Vicki learn to get along with their new life and home. Vicki falls in love with Black Beauty and earns Black Beauty's trust. (ages 7-8)

The Saddle Club:
"Adventures at Pine Hollow"
{Video recording}
Publisher: Warner Home Video
Published Date: c2002
It is an adventure with horses and friendship with two girls form a saddle club. (ages 10-12)

The Saddle Club:
"Horse Crazy"
{Video recording}
Publisher: Good Times Entertainment
Published Date: c2005
The adventure takes place with horses and friendship. A male star, a female journalist, and a cowboy teaching a Western clinic, all arrive at Pine Hollow at the horse stables. (ages 10-12)

Note: For more DVD Saddle Club titles, look them up at your local library.

Video

"A Day with Horses"
Publisher: Vision Entertainment and Tidewater Productions Inc.
Published Date: c1994
Children learn about how to care for and feed horses. Sing along songs teach the kids on the topics of teamwork and being responsible while caring for the horses. I strongly recommend this video for kids at school or for an educational party. (ages 3-6)

Bowling Party

Bowling Party Story

Aunt Lavern's brother Tyler (Herman) told his grandnephew Tyler Herman he would fly to Milwaukee when he turned 10 for a grand birthday party at the local bowling alley. Uncle Herman didn't come to town very often, but he kept in touch by phone. He recently enrolled in a computer class and he took to the computer like a fish to water. He now sends e-mails like crazy to all the nieces and nephews. He said that it was the coolest machine ever invented on the planet earth. Aunt Lavern didn't agree. She didn't own a computer and she thought Herman was being very silly. She insisted they talk by phone. So, to please her, he calls Aunt Lavern once a month.

Uncle Herman was 6 feet tall with a lanky, lean, muscular body and a ruddy complexion. He had a white crowbar mustache with bushy eyebrows. If he were heavier, he could have played the part of Santa Claus. He seemed to always wear the same attire of bright plaid flannel shirts, and brown leather suspenders to hold up his baggy pants. His tall black boots were very worn and always muddy. Despite this, everyone looked forward to his yearly visit. His eyes sparkled as he told tales of his life as a lumberjack. No one minded him telling the same story every time he visited. The family found the stories fun and heart warming. He did a great rendition of "timber" that echoed in the ears for several hours after. He could yodel and do Indian dances from the old wild west. He told how he could tangle red-handed with the big black bears in the forest. We always knew Uncle Herman could stretch the truth a tad, but it did not matter. Our family was happy to see him.

Uncle Herman savored his desserts with a sweet passion. He said a person should always eat the dessert first so one could get the full benefit of every bite. If a person ate the large meal before dessert, he would be too full to eat the extra tasty dessert.

When Lavern and Herman were growing up, he always made a point to sit next to his sister especially, on holidays when Grandma made those wonderful pies. Pumpkin was Herman's favorite pie. He knew Lavern didn't care much for pumpkin pie. He buttered up Lavern to eat both desserts. He browned up his sister by telling her she was his favorite sister. Lavern did not catch onto his dessert tactic until they became teenagers. She still teases him about dessert to this day. She always makes him a pumpkin pie each year during his family visit. She enjoys watching his face as he enjoys every bite. Lavern just wishes he would shower more often and wear some different clothes. She always sent him back to California with fresh laundry and clean polished boots. She knows it won't last, but at least the people in the airplane won't mind sitting next to him on the trip back home.

Aunt Lavern is very petite with small bones and fine features. She is also very prim and proper. Uncle Herman said that she was small but mighty. When they were younger, he would pick up Lavern and almost squeeze the liver out of her. Basically, the two get along very well and show great concern for each other, particularly as they grow older. Both members loved family and it showed.

Uncle Herman was a star bowler, getting strike after strike. He won a large trophy and many awards in several bowling competitions. He likes to boast that he was the best bowler on the entire continent. He always helped many of the family members learn how to bowl.

Whenever he would take the younger family members bowling, he would hoot and holler if the ball created a split. He would spin his body around and yell, "Oh no!" if the ball rolled toward the gutter. Sometimes he would wave his hand in a back and forth motion as if he could stop the ball from rolling into the gutter. He gave you a high five if you made a strike.

Tyler was very excited about celebrating his birthday at the local bowling alley. Aunt Lavern insisted on making cupcakes because it was Ty's favorite dessert. She wanted to keep everything very simple so everyone could enjoy the party. She ordered cocktail sandwiches made with assorted meats from the local deli. She purchased baby carrots and baby dill pickle spears. She also purchased several bags of potato chips for the 12 people attending the family birthday party. She hand-made bowling pin tickets and gave each guest 2 tickets for two free sodas. She and Uncle Herman decided to split the bill and treat the entire family for this special birthday gathering. Everyone would meet at the bowling alley at 1:30 p.m. on a Sunday afternoon. Aunt Lavern came early to set up the buffet table. She loved parties whether it be as hostess or a guest. She always had fun. They celebrated Ty's birthday with enthusiasm and a few sets of bowling. Aunt Lavern was very pleased and said that keeping things simple at the family gathering is best. Uncle Herman gave Ty a new bowling ball for his birthday. He made Ty a very happy boy.

Bowling Menu

Assorted Cocktail Sandwiches

Mustard and Mayonnaise

Pickles and Carrots

Potato Chips

Bowling Cup Cakes

Assorted Sodas

Cupcake Bowling Alley

Yield: Twenty-four cupcakes

1-18.25 ounce devil's food cake mix
3 eggs
Water
Vegetable oil
24 cupcake liners
2 cupcake pans (12 each)
1 ounce bottle red sugar
1 ounce bottle blue sugar
1-1 ounce package yellow jimmies

Follow the directions on the cake mix. Place the cup cake liners into the cupcake pans. Fill each cupcake ⅔ full. Bake for 15 to 18 minutes or until tooth pick inserted in the cupcake comes out clean. Cool thoroughly on cooling racks.

Note: You can purchase the bowling pins and ball set at your local cake decorating store.

Supplies for the Bowling Alley Lane

1-18x18 inch white cardboard
1 black magic marker
1 yard stick
1 package of miniature bowling pins with bowling ball

Butter Cream Frosting

Follow the recipe on page 73. With a number 30 tip, pipe on frosting. Start at the outside and work cake tip to the inside going around in a circle. Sprinkle the various colors of the sugar and jimmies over the top of each frosted cupcake. Place one miniature bowling pin in the center of each of the ten cupcakes and one miniature bowling ball on one of the cupcakes.

Making the Bowling Alley

With the magic marker and yardstick for measuring, draw vertical lines from top to bottom of the cardboard about 2 inches apart. There will be a total of 11 vertical lines.

Make the bowling alley lane look life like by drawing in planks of flooring onto cardboard. Draw straight horizontal lines in an uneven pattern, 2 to 3 lines per 2 inch vertical space. Place bowling ball on top of one of the cupcakes and the remaining cupcakes with one pin each. Place the 11 cupcakes onto the bowling alley lane as described below. The children can color in each plank flooring with their favorite colors. I chose to leave the cardboard black and white. Place the other 13 cupcakes onto a tray.

Carry the cupcakes in a container to the bowling alley. Set up the table with the bowling print tablecloth. Place the cardboard bowling alley lane design onto the center of the table. Place one cupcake onto the center of the cardboard. Place two cupcakes behind the one pin. Place three cupcakes behind the two pins and four cupcakes behind the three pins. This makes 10 pins in the shape of a V to form the pin set up for the bowling lane. Place the cupcake with the bowling ball at the center end of the bowling alley cardboard.

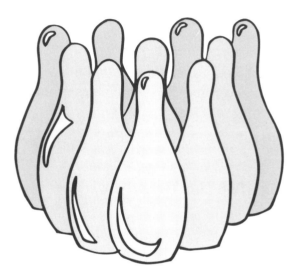

Items to Pack for Setting up the Buffet

2 spoons for condiments
2 tongs for pickles and carrots
1 platter for the extra 13 cupcakes
1 doily
1 large bowl for the potato chips
2 teaspoons for serving the condiments
2 small bowls for the mustard and mayonnaise
24-6 inch plates
2 packages of 16 (each) of cocktail napkins

Arrange the pickles and carrots on separate plates or bowls ready to be transported to the bowling alley. After arriving at the bowling alley, place mayonnaise and mustard into the two separate bowls. Place one spoon next to each condiment. Place the sandwich trays next to the condiments. Place the carrots and pickles near the sandwich tray. Fill the potato chips in the large bowl and place on the buffet. Place the napkins and plates at the beginning of the buffet line.

Ladybug Tea Party

Story of Miss Ladybug's High Tea

Miss Ladybug was born on Victoria Island, British Columbia in the 1900's. High teas were very common on this beautiful island. Her mother was very prim and proper and attended many high teas. She also gave several teas in their stylish Victorian home. The dining room had several tall narrow windows adorned with lacy curtains. The highly polished wood floor often creaked as the maids walked across the room. An ornate rug lay under the 12 foot long dining room table. The decorative wooden table with carvings of their family history had been handed down to her mother on her wedding day.

Mrs. Ladybug had an hourglass figure, with sparkling green eyes and naturally red curly hair. She was always dressed to perfection with every curl in place. Her clear complexion radiated with a warm smile as she greeted each guest at the tea party in her home.

Every person in the community adored Mrs. Ladybug because she was kind and gentle and knew how to talk to the town's people. She was very community-minded.

She taught her own children manners and wrote a book called "How to Socialize at a Tea". She never published the book, but she taught neighboring families about teas as well.

Some of the Rules Found in Mrs. Ladybug's Tea Book Are as Follows:

Sit up straight at the table while attending a tea.

Do not eat until everyone has been seated and served.

Take only a small portion of food. Remember it is a tea.

Do not chew with your mouth open.

Chew your food slowly and savor the taste.

Do not dominate the conversation.

Be interested in all guests' conversations at the tea.

Do not interrupt a person as she is speaking.

Remember to say, "Please", and pass the finger sandwiches.

Thank the hostess for the invitation.

Thank the hostess for the lovely tea party.

Do not gossip at the party.

Place your napkin on your lap.
When the tea has ended, don't stay beyond the
specified time in the invitation.
After the party send a thank you note to the hostess.
This is called a "bread-and-butter" note.

Mrs. Ladybug and Miss Ladybug

She wrote several stories and gave many examples of good manners and how to socialize.

Mrs. Ladybug gave birth to three sons. She longed to have a daughter. When her daughter was born, she was thrilled to have her wish come true. She named her Ladybug and called her Miss Ladybug. Her daughter was soft and cuddly and she enjoyed holding her.

Mrs. Ladybug couldn't wait until her daughter was old enough to attend her teas. She would teach her daughter everything about manners and high teas. When Miss Ladybug became five, her mother began her mission of training Miss Ladybug for the fancy high teas in the Ladybug family home.

Miss Ladybug had other plans. She disliked the ritual of high teas and made a fuss when she was required to attend a tea in one of those awful frilly dresses. Miss Ladybug loved animals and liked to play ball. Unlike her mother, she hated lacy dresses. She was rough and tumbling and had a passion for reading. Every year, against her will, Miss Ladybug attended several teas just to please her mother.

When Miss Ladybug grew up, she studied to be a librarian. She never married and saw no need to be tied down to a Mr. Right. Miss Ladybug had a very rounded face even as she aged. She had a big dimple in the middle of her chin and a ruddy complexion. She had silky white hair neatly combed into a bun. She wore Ben Franklin glasses that slid down to the edge of her nose. Her ears were large and very pointed.

She ran a tight ship in her school library and never missed a trick with her large ears. The students could not figure out how she knew everything going on in her library. She was always one step ahead of them to keep perfect order. There was a huge sign, handwritten by Miss Ladybug, that said "Be Quiet or Leave". It was in bold black letters with a border of ladybugs all around the edge of the sign. Every student knew her rules and one look from Miss Ladybug would devastate that student who tried to test or defy any of Miss Ladybug's rules.

She also had a heart as big as a bucket. She was very knowledgeable on most topics. The students knew they could rely on her help for their class assignments. She also had thought-provoking trivia questions to keep the students thinking. In fact, the students liked to go to the library for that very reason.

One of the students from the 6th grade class became very ill and was hospitalized. Miss Ladybug visited him every few days and encouraged him to get better. Without her realizing it, her mother had instilled good strong values. Miss Ladybug was also community-minded.

One day, the principal came into the library on Miss Ladybug's lunch hour. She was wondering what had happened because he never came into the library. Staff meetings were always held in the gym.

He said, "We need to teach the 8th grade football stars some manners. I think you are just the lady to make things happen at the Longfellow Strata School District. I'll give you a week to come up with a plan." Miss Ladybug asked the principal for time to think about it.

It was indeed thought provoking. She wondered if she could ever teach those football players anything, let alone manners. She was only a school librarian. After of week of thinking, she agreed to help. She shared her brilliant plan with the school principal.

She pulled her mother's book out of the box in her closet. She dusted it off and opened the book that had been neatly tucked away for 30 years. Her mother had willed it to her. Inside the front cover of the book, Miss Ladybug found this note in an envelope.

Dear Miss Ladybug,
I have loved you, my dearest child, since the day you were born and I held you in my arms.
You were always my beautiful and precious daughter. I knew that you did not like my teas and often
my ways of thinking. Sweetheart, you were always the apple of my eye and, in my own way,
I have admired you for your no-nonsense approach. I do hope that some day you will read and use
my book. Perhaps one day, as a school librarian, you may find this book useful for the students.

With love and great admiration,
Mother

Ladybug read this letter several times as tears streamed down her cheeks. She had never given a thought to look in this book before. Now, she had discovered a letter from her mother. It finally confirmed that her mother really loved her as the person she was. She felt very silly wanting her mother's approval after all these years. Isn't it funny, no matter his/her age, how every person looks for approval from a parent.

She placed the letter back into the envelope and put it into her large jewelry box with its ornate collection of ladybug jewelry. She thought of her plan to share with the principal and her work to do in carrying out her plan.

She decided to go to the football players and announce that a tea would be held for Mr. Wanamaker, the school principal. They were going to have to help her train the kindergarten children to be polite. She went to the kindergarten class and told the kindergarten students that they were going to learn manners in honor of the school principal and that the 8th grade football team was going to teach them.

She knew she had her work cut out for her. Every day for the entire semester, she spent her preparation period working with the 8th graders and the kindergarten class. After two months of hard work, she assigned a kindergarten student to each of the eighth grade football players. She was amazed how the young children and eighth graders bonded together. Both classes had learned their lessons on manners very well. Now she needed to prove it to herself by having the students participate in the actual tea party.

She set the tea date for May 22nd (one week before school ended for the year). An invitation was sent out with a ladybug symbol on the front of the invitation. Inside the invitation were the date, time, and place for the tea. The older students printed out the invitations. She arranged for three of the violin students from the school orchestra to play concert songs to simulate the music played at high teas just like on Victoria Island.

This was Miss Ladybug's last year at the school library. She decided that at age seventy she should move on and let someone else take over her position. She felt she had served the school, students, and community for fifty years with a job well done. Miss Ladybug did not realize how attached the students had became to her. They decided to also plan a surprise retirement party the same day as the tea. Everyone was sworn to keep the big secret. Miss Ladybug, with the help of the students, made hats and necklaces for the kindergarten class and pins for the football team involved in the tea.

The day before they set up the buffet table with a pink and white checked tablecloth with a ladybug pattern. She made cloth napkins for all the guests.

The students helped her select a simple menu. The students thought there was a lot of red. Miss Ladybug said, "Red is good and, besides red is my favorite color." So, the students agreed with her idea about red. The food department purchased and organized the food and the students prepared the food.

On the day of the party, the food buffet table is set up in the following manner. Cover the table with the ladybug print tablecloth. Starting from left to right, place the fruit bowl with the hat behind. Place the cupcakes on the cupcake dessert stand next to the fruit. The fruit punch is next to the cupcakes with the centerpiece in the center of the buffet. The ladybug stuffed animal, hats, flowers and chicken tartlets are in a grouping. The two ladybug cakes, mini cheesecakes, and hats are in the far right grouping. The hat nearest to the bottom ladybug cake also has ladybug candy around the brim of the hat. Feel free to place the food on the buffet table using your own judgment. See picture on page 8 in the color section.

As the guests arrived, the music flowed through the room and the guests were enjoying conversation. Everyone felt welcomed. They nicely greeted Mr. Wanamaker. Miss Ladybug thanked him for the great opportunity to help train the students. She felt her time spent was well worthwhile.

At the end of the party, the eighth grade football players stood up and chanted "We love you, Miss Ladybug!" Every person in the room stood and yelled, "Surprise! Miss Ladybug!" One by one, each student came up to her with a thank you card or a note. They had made a crown with ladybug pins. They placed the crown on her head and said she was queen for the hour. They also gave her a red vase of flowers with ladybugs on each flower and leaf. The teachers and principal also rallied around her and shook her hand and thanked her for 50 years of service. The principal said that she was always welcomed to return to school any time. Miss Ladybug was totally flabbergasted at the reception of the staff and students. She could barely speak. She said, "Well, I guess when in doubt, just say thank you." Zack, the team leader of the football team, read a poem in honor of Miss Ladybug.

At the end of the year, she packed up her things and took one more look at her library. The 50 years had passed quickly and had been filled with many blessings and she was happy to have been Miss Ladybug, the school librarian. She silently thanked her mother for her upbringing. She knew she was one lucky 70 year old woman. At night she kneeled at the side of her bed and thanked God for being Miss Ladybug. She had truly had a lifetime of beautiful experiences.

We Love you, Ladybug Poem
by the Class Football Team

Ladybug, you are no powder puff.
You sure know your library stuff,
And never let any student sluff.

You have big ears.
Always listening to hear,
And give us your experience of 50 years.

Once I told you a story with glee,
You laughed and helped me,
Prepare for my spelling bee.

With your white silky hair,
And your face always so fair,
You showered everyone with care.

With no time to pine,
You made sure all students would shine.
Your library was interesting and very fine.

Your library always decorated in red,
Your favorite color, so you said.
We bet you even have red on your bed.

You taught manners to the classes.
Watched us through your Ben Franklin glasses,
Checking the students' library passes.

With your career closing, today is your day,
For us to honor and respect you and say,
We love you, Miss Ladybug for your kind way.

Note: The neck of the vase is 10 inches long. Find the assorted buttons at a craft store. I found the bouquet of flowers taped together on one stem.

How to Make the Ladybug Centerpiece
Yield: One ladybug centerpiece

1 red vase, 18 inches tall
One bouquet of 9 red flowers, with brown centers and green leaves
1 package ladybug picks
1 package ladybug buttons
2 packages of assorted buttons with sunflowers, flower pots, ladybugs, and watering can

Arrange flowers. At random hot glue the sunflowers, flowerpots, water can and ladybug picks onto the leaves and edges of flowers. Hot glue one ladybug button to the brown center of the each of the nine flowers. Hot glue one ladybug pick onto one of two leaves located in front and the remaining seven glued at random onto the flowers. See picture on page 8 in the color section.

Note: Use your imagination to make a variety of ladybug hats.

How to Assemble Ladybug Straw Hats
Yield: One hat per child

Style One
Yield: One child's ladybug hat

How to make the band for the hat:
1-4$\frac{1}{2}$ inch wide by 46 inches long fabric strip using ladybug material
7 miniature garden flower clothespins
1 double string of red beads necklace
1 wooden ladybug

Cut the 46 inch long piece of material. Turn over the $\frac{1}{4}$ inch edge twice on the 4$\frac{1}{2}$ inch strip. Stick in place. Fold the 46-inch length strip in half with wrong sides together and press on the fold line. Stitch along the folded line. Turn the raw edges over $\frac{1}{4}$ inch and stitch the entire 46 inch length. Place the band around bottom of the crown of the hat and all around the hat. Tie the band into a knot at the back of the hat. Hot glue the necklace at the bottom of the hatband, all around the hat. Hot glue the wooden ladybug onto the top of the hat at random, clip on the miniature garden flower clothespins onto top of the hatband.

Style Two

Yield: One child's ladybug hat

⁷/₈ yard 1 inch wide white lace
¹/₂ yard ¹/₂ inch wide ladybug ribbon
1 ladybug appliqué
glue gun
glue

Run ribbon around the bottom of the crown of the hat and tie into a bow. Hot glue the ladybug appliqué onto the front center of the hat. Cut the lace into six 3-inch strips. Glue down each strip vertically across the brim of the hat with a 3-4 inch space between each strip.

Note: The children had fun making their own hat. They had their own ideas of how to design their hats.

Style Three

Yield: One child's ladybug hat

1⁷/₈ yard ⁵/₈ inch wide ladybug ribbon in red, blue and black
1 Raphael straw bow
1 wooden ladybug
3 ladybug buttons
2 sunflower buttons

Place ribbon around the bottom of the crown of the hat and crisscross the ribbon in the front. Hot glue ribbon in place. Center the wooden ladybug in the front of the hat and hot glue it into place. Hot glue the Raphael straw bow into place at the back of the hat. Hot glue the ladybug buttons across the top of the hat about 1 inch apart with one ladybug in the center of the top of the hat. Hot glue one sunflower in front and back of the ladybug in the center of the hat.

Note: There are many kinds of ladybug material. It does not have to be pink and white checked material. You can find the craft items at a Hobby Lobby or Michaels craft store. I special ordered extra ladybug fabric at Joann Fabrics. They shipped the material to my door. I cut out my own 12x12 inch napkins and folded each edge ⅛ inch twice. Stitch all four edges in place. The napkin holders are turned into door handles for each guest to take napkins are turned into door handles for each guest to take home and use as a door handle to remember the tea.

Door/Napkin Holders

Yield: Six door/napkin holders

6 wooden door handles
1-11 ounce can metallic finish spray paint
2-2.54 packages (each) 1 inch red pom poms
6- 13x13 inches (each) pink and white checked ladybug napkins
6-3½ wooden ladybugs
1½ yards ladybug ribbon
glue gun and glue

Spray paint the door handles, both front and back. Let each side dry for a couple hours. After 24 hours begin to assemble the napkin holders. Starting at the bottom the door hanger, glue on three pom poms in a row. Glue on a ladybug above the pom poms. Cut six 7-inch pieces from the ladybug ribbon. Glue on ribbon above the ladybug with the seams overlapping in the back of the door hanger. Cut out 6-13x13 inch napkins. Turn the raw edges over ¼ inch twice on all four sides and stitch each side. Press the napkins. Fold each napkin in half diagonally. Fold points of napkin toward the fold. Starting at the bottom of the napkin, fold the napkin in one-inch increments to form a band. Center the band around the top loop of the door hanger. Tie the napkin into a knot. The napkin looks like two rabbit ears.

Note: The straw hat pin is miniature size. The half eyes will be difficult for a child to make. It may be better for the adult to put the hats together in advance.

Straw Hat Pins

Yield: Six pins

6 miniature Straw hats
1 package of eight
1 inch pin backs
1 package of 24$\frac{1}{4}$ inch ladybug buttons
2 packages black half round eyes (1-16 inch)

Glue on twelve black half round eyes around the bottom rim of the crown of the hat leaving approximately a $\frac{1}{2}$ inch space between each set of three round eyes. Glue one ladybug button onto the $\frac{1}{2}$ inch space or a total of 4 ladybugs per hat. Glue on pin back to the back of the hat. Dry overnight.

Note: This is just a sample. Go creative and make up your own pattern. This is hard for a child to do alone. Get the child's opinion on how she would like to make her pin. Help her put it together.

Fence Ladybug Pins

Yield: Six pins

3-2 inch (50.8mm) packages (each) fence picket
1 package black half round eyes (1-16 inch)
1 box garden clothespins assorted-72 pieces (18 ladybugs in the above package)
1 package of eight 1-inch pin backs
glue gun
glue

Glue three fence pickets side by side to form the fence. Cut 6 fence pickets to one inch leaving the picket top. Angle and center the one-inch fence picket bar across the top of the fence. Glue this piece down. Glue a ladybug clothespin to the left side of the fence and a bumblebee to the right side of the fence above the angled fence picket bar. Glue three half round eyes across the fence picket bar and three below the bar. Glue on the pin back to the back onto the pin in the middle or top of pin.

Ladybug Necklace

Style One
Yield: One wooden necklace

1- 3^1/$_2$ inch wooden ladybug
^{7}/$_8$ yard ladybug ribbon
drill
^{1}/$_8$ inch drill bit

Drill two holes ^{5}/$_8$ inches apart across the top of the red part on the wooden ladybug. Cut a ^{7}/$_8$ yard strip of ladybug ribbon. String the ribbon through the two holes. Tie a knot to join the two ends together to form the necklace.

Note: Separate the 3 colors of beads for the children. They can share the dishes of beads. The beads can also be strung on the wooden ladybug using the black satin cord. Stringing the beads is an excellent project for the children, ages five to eight.

Style Two
Yield: One appliqué ladybug necklace

1 package each, red, yellow, and black pony beads
1 ladybug appliqué
1 package satin cord (2mm 5 yards)
3 custard cups or bowls

Place the cord through the back of the strings of the ladybug applique. Place each color of beads into a custard cup. String beads on each side of the satin cord. Tie a knot in the back to form the closure on the necklace.

Setting up the Guest Table
Yield: Six place settings

1 tablecloth with ladybug print

6 door hanger napkin holders

6 hatpins

6 luncheon napkins with ladybug print

6 fence ladybug pins

6 ladybug necklaces

6 ladybug hats

6 teacups with saucers

6–7 inch plates

2 bouquets of red flowers

1 candle

6 teacups

6 tea saucers

creamer and sugar set

Place the tablecloth onto the guest table. Pin on the ladybug pin into the middle of the knot of each napkin. Place the door hanger napkin holder to the left of each place setting. Place the cup and saucer to the right of the place setting. Place one hat in the middle of each place. Scatter the fence ladybug pins in the center of the table. Place flowers in the center of the table with the votive candles around the two bouquets. Place creamer and sugar set onto the table. See picture on page 8 in the color section.

Ladybug Menu

Mini Chicken Tartlets

Ladybug's Very Berry
Fruit Salad with Mint Garnish

Lazy Ladybug Cake

Ladybug Shaped Cake

Ladybug Cupcakes

Designer Ladybug Chocolates

Mini Cherry Cheesecakes

Miss Ladybug's Cherry Delight Cake

Raspberry Sherbert Punch

Note: Sandwich Spread is a product of Kraft ®. It comes in a 16 ounce glass jar. This product should be at your local grocery store. The mini filo shells come in a box and are found in the freezer section of the grocery store. There are 15 shells per box.

Mini Chicken Tartlets
Yield: Forty

1-13 ounce can chicken breast packed in water
2 teaspoons dehydrated onion
$^1/_4$ cup finely diced celery
$^2/_3$ cup sandwich spread
3-2.1 ounce packages (each) mini fillo shells

Garnish:
Dill weed
Paprika

Drain water off the chicken. Break chicken breast into small pieces. Add onion and celery. Stir in the sandwich spread, moistening and holding all ingredients together. Fill the shells level to the top of each shell. Garnish with dill weed and paprika. Arrange on a platter or tiered plate. Serve chilled.

Note: Reserve 6 strawberries for a garnish on top of the salad. "Picnics Catering on the Move Cookbook" explains and also has diagrams on how to cut a pineapple on page 64.

Ladybug's Very Berry Fruit Salad with Mint Garnish
Yield: Sixteen

1 fresh pineapple, cut into chunks
2-1 pound (each) containers strawberries, sliced
2 large bananas, sliced
1-3 ounce package sugar free strawberry Jell-O®
1 pint fresh blueberries

Stir together pineapple, strawberries, bananas, and the dry powder sugar free strawberry Jell-0®. Place fruit mixture into a large pasta bowl. Garnish with blueberries, mint leaves and the 6 whole strawberries. See picture on page 8 in the color section.

Note: If the chocolate chips stick to the bottom of the pan, scrape off the chips and frost the top of the cake with the warm melted chocolate chips.

Lazy Ladybug Cake

Yield: One 8 inch layer

1 cup flour
$^1/_4$ teaspoon salt
$1^1/_4$ teaspoons baking powder
1 cup sugar
1 tablespoon butter
$^1/_3$ cup cream
2 eggs
1 teaspoon almond flavor
1 teaspoon maraschino cherry juice
2 drops red flood coloring
No-stick spray
1-8 inch round cake layer pan
$^1/_2$ cup mini chocolate chips
12 inch cardboard circle
Foil
Tape

In a separate bowl mix together flour, salt, baking powder, and sugar. Add butter to the cream and scald. Cool. Beat eggs until lemon colored. Add the almond and cherry juice. Alternate the dry ingredients with the cream/butter mixture, ending with the dry ingredients. Mix in the red food coloring. Spray pan with no-stick baking spray. Place cake batter into the cake pan. Bake at 350 F for 30 minutes or until toothpick inserted in the center comes out clean. Cool cake for five minutes. Cover a 12 inch cake cardboard circle with foil. Tape the foil unto the back of the cake cardboard circle. Turn cake out onto the cake circle. Cool thoroughly before frosting the cake.

Lazy Ladybug Frosting
Yield: One 8 inch cake

$^1/_4$ cup butter
$^1/_3$ cup sour cream
$2^1/_2$ cups powdered sugar
$^1/_8$ teaspoon salt
2 teaspoons maraschino cherry juice
1 teaspoon almond flavor

Note: The "Half/Nuts Company" is willing to ship you the ladybug candies or any other candy or nut supplies anywhere in the country. Their website is <u>www.halfnuts.net</u> and phone number is (414) 476-NUTS. They are located at 9617 West Greenfield Avenue, West Allis, WI. 53214.

Supplies for Decorating the Cake

2 dozen ladybug candies wrapped in ladybug design foil
3 large red silk flowers with brown centers (sunflower style)
5 large green silk leaves
1 package $^5/_8$ inch ladybug buttons
1 box garden clothespin assorted-72 pieces (includes 18 ladybugs)
2-10 inch doilies
Glue gun
Glue

Cream together butter and sour cream. Add the powdered sugar and the salt. Beat. Add the maraschino cherry juice and almond. Beat until smooth and creamy. Frost the cake. Cut the center out of each doily. Place the lacy edge around the bottom of the cake. Place 17 foil wrapped lady bugs around the side of the entire cake. Place the remaining 7 ladybug candies to one side of the cake in a grouping. Hot glue one ladybug button into the center of each flower. Place the three flowers on the opposite side of the ladybug grouping on top of cake. Hot glue remaining ladybug buttons onto leaves at random. Place the leaves behind the flowers in a half moon shape. Place one garden ladybug on a clothespin on the pedal of each flower. Cover and refrigerate until serving time. See Picture on page 8 in the color section.

Ladybug Shaped Cake
Yield: One cake

1-18.25 ounce red velvet cake mix
1$\frac{1}{4}$ cups water
$\frac{1}{3}$ cup vegetable oil
3 large eggs
1 cake pan shaped into a ladybug
No-stick spray
1-12 inch cake cardboard circle
2-10 inch doilies

Follow the cake mix directions on the back of the box mix. Pour cake mix into prepared ladybug cake pan. Bake at 350 F for 30 minutes or until toothpick inserted in the center of the cake comes out clean. Cool cake for 10 minutes. Cover a 12-inch cake cardboard circle with foil. Tape the foil onto the back of the cardboard circle. Turn the cake onto the top of the foiled cardboard. Follow the butter cream frosting recipe on page 73. Divide the frosting coloring $\frac{1}{2}$ of the frosting red, $\frac{1}{4}$ black and leaving $\frac{1}{4}$ white. Cut the center out from each doily. Place the lacy edge of each doily around the bottom of the ladybug cake. With a number 15 star tip, pipe on the black to form the face, the oval spots, eyes, and dimples. With a number 15 star tip, pipe the red onto the body of the ladybug. With a number 5 writing tip, outline the eyes and mouth with the white. With a number 5 writing tip, outline the bottom of the smile with red in the ladybug mouth area. See colored picture in the ladybug cake pan insert and also in the book on page 8 in the color section.

Ladybug Cupcakes
Yield: Twenty-four

1-18.25 ounce super moist deviled foods cake mix
$\frac{1}{3}$ cup water
$\frac{1}{2}$ cup vegetable oil
3 eggs
24 cupcake liners

Follow the cake mix directions on the back of the box mix. Place cupcake liners into the cupcake pan. Evenly divide the batter to make 24 cupcakes. Bake at 350 F for 15-20 minutes or until center of each cupcake springs up with the touch of your forefinger. Cool cupcakes thoroughly. Make up a $\frac{1}{2}$ batch of butter cream frosting.

Butter Cream Frosting

Yield: One pound (one 8 inch cake)

$^{1}/_{2}$ cup butter
$^{1}/_{2}$ cup shortening
1 pound powdered sugar
$^{1}/_{2}$ teaspoon almond flavor
3 tablespoons water

Decorations for the Ladybug Cupcakes

2 packages (each) ladybug picks (12 count)
2 ounces red sugar or color of choice

Cream butter and shortening together. Add powdered sugar, almond flavor, and water. Beat until smooth and creamy. Using a number 30 cake tube, pipe frosting onto each cupcake. Sprinkle the red sugar over the top of the frosted cupcake. Place one ladybug pick into the center of each cupcake. Place onto a tray lined with a doily or into the cupcake dessert stand. See picture on page 8 in the color section.

Note: Extra crust will be leftover with this recipe. Freeze it and use it the next time you make the cheese cakes. Only half of the can of cherry pie filling will be used when making 40 mini cheese cakes. I made my husband a mini pie with the remaining cherry pie filling.

Mini Cherry Cheese Cakes

Yield: Seventy-two cheese cakes

Crust:
2$^1/_2$ cups graham cracker crumbs
$^1/_2$ cup butter, melted
$^1/_4$ cup sugar
1 package mini muffin baking cups (flower design, optional)
2 mini muffin pans (24 muffins per pan)

Filling: *Yield: Forty*
1-pound cream cheese, softened
$^1/_3$ cup sugar
1 teaspoon vanilla
2 eggs

Topping:
1-21 ounce can cherry pie filling

Combine cracker crumbs, butter and sugar. Stir thoroughly. Place the muffin liners into the muffin pan. Pack a teaspoon of crumbs into the bottom of each muffin liner. Cream together the cream cheese and sugar. Add the vanilla and eggs. Beat until smooth and creamy. Place the cream cheese mixture over each crust to fill the muffin cup almost full. Place one pie filling cherry into the center of each mini cheesecake. Bake at 375 F for 12-15 minutes or until toothpick comes out clean.

Miss Ladybug's Cherry Delight Cake

Yield: One 13x9 pan

1-9 ounce white cake mix, such as Jiffy®
1 egg
$\frac{1}{4}$ cup maraschino cherry juice
$\frac{1}{4}$ cup water
$\frac{1}{3}$ cup finely diced maraschino cherries
No-stick spray

Filling:
1-8 ounce package cream cheese, softened
1-1.5 ounce package vanilla instant pudding
2 cups cold milk
1-16 ounce container of non-dairy whipped topping

Decorations for on Top of the Cake:
12 whole maraschino cherries
48 whole pecans
1-ounce container red sugar

Add the egg, cherry juice and water to the cake mix. Beat until smooth. Fold in the 1/3 cup maraschino cherries. Spray the 13x9 inch pan with no stick spray. Place cake batter into the cake pan. Bake at 350 F for 15-20 minutes or until toothpick inserted in the middle of the cake comes out clean. Cool thoroughly.

Filling and Decorations

Yield: One 13x9 cake

Beat cream cheese. Add the pudding and cold milk. Beat until the pudding stands in peaks. Spread the pudding mixture over the top of the cake. Spread the non-dairy whipped topping over the pudding. Sprinkle red sugar over the non-dairy whipped topping. Place a cluster of four nuts into a circle to form the petals of the flower (three across and four down). Drain and dry the 12 maraschino cherries. Place one maraschino cherry in the center of each pecan flower. Refrigerate over night or until the pudding is firm.

Raspberry Sherbet Punch

Yield: Fifteen to twenty servings

1 gallon Hawaiian Punch
1 quart bottle 7up
1 quart raspberry sherbet
1 orange, sliced with rind

In a large punch bowl, mix together the punch and soda. Top with scoops of raspberry sherbet and orange slices.

Ladybug Theme Related Book Resources

Bono, Mary
"Ugh! A Bug",
Publisher: Walker
Published Date: c2002
The book talks about different bugs. It cites a saying, "If a Ladybug sat on your knee, would you offer some tea?"

Braker, Flo
"Sweet Miniatures, The Art of Making Bite-size Desserts"
Publisher: W. Morrow
Published Date: c1991
There are recipes with all kinds of miniature desserts. (ages-family baker)

Carle, Eric
"The Grouchy Ladybug"
Publisher: HarperCollins
Published Date: c1996
"The Grouchy Ladybug" takes flight and meets different animals asking if they want to fight. She does not want to share her lunch with the friendly ladybug. But after the journey, she flies back to the friendly ladybug and shares her lunch. (ages 2-5)

Coughlan, Cheryl
"Ladybugs"
Publisher: Pebble Books
Published Date: c1999
The author explains the parts of a ladybug and also explains that ladybugs are beetles. (ages 2-4)

Crewe, Sabrina
"The Ladybug"
Publisher: Raintree Steck-Vaughn
Published Date: c1997
The book explains the growth stages of a ladybug. There is a diagram of the body parts of a ladybug. The author has a map of where the ladybugs live and also a glossary with terms. (ages 6-8)

Finn, Isobel
"The Very Lazy Ladybug"
Publisher: Tiger Tales
Published Date: c2001
The story is about a ladybug that sleeps all day and all night. She is too lazy to learn how to fly. She tries to sleep on different animals but never feels comfortable. The lazy ladybug tries to sleep on an elephant. The elephant sneezes and brushes off the ladybug. Finally, the ladybug decides to fly. (ages 2-5)

Rowan, James P.
"Ladybugs"
Publisher: Rourke
Published Date: c1993
The book explains the life cycle of a ladybug. (ages 5-6)

Szekeres, Cyndy
"Ladybug, Ladybug, Where Are You?"
Publisher: Golden Books
Published Date: c1991
This is a very cute story. The ladybug is hiding on each page of the story. The children need to find the ladybug in the picture. (ages 3-5)

Ladybug Theme Related Cassette and Book

Zoehfeld, Kathleen Weider
"Ladybug at Orchard Avenue"
{Sound recording}
Publisher: Sound Prints
Published Date: c1996
The cassette goes along with the book. It explains that aphids are ladybug's favorite food. Aphids are found on leaves. They are green insects that are sweet and juicy. It tells the story of a ladybug preparing for the long winter months. (ages 3-4)

Dinosaur Party

Timmy's Dinosaur Story

Timmy loved dinosaurs from kindergarten up through 4th grade. He got interested in dinosaurs when he began watching the Dino Riders show. He had his mother read every dinosaur story to him very often. Everyone bought him dinosaurs of all sizes. His mother learned to pronounce every species of each dinosaur family. He took his dinosaurs to school for Show and Tell. The teacher was amazed at his knowledge of dinosaurs. Timmy is now in his early 20's and he still has his big collection of dinosaurs. Hopefully, he will be able to teach his children about dinosaurs and also share his dinosaur collection.

Read this poem at the party and help your guests learn how to pronounce the names of the dinosaurs.

Ask About the Dinosaurs Poem

I have to ask,
Did he wear a mask?

Were there species that were very small?
Were there actually dinosaurs 4 stories tall?

Were some dinosaurs really 90 feet long?
There large bones must have been very strong.

One night in my sleep, I had a dream,
A triceratops smiled at me, or so it did seem. (try-SAIR-uh-tops)

I saw the allosaurus's meat-eating jaws, (AL-a-saw-russ)
With jagged teeth shaped like saws.

I witnessed a 5 ton ankylosaurus eat, (an-KILE-a-saw-russ)
That made my heart pound and skip a beat.

I saw a shantungosaurus that looked like a duck (Shan-TOONG-o-saw-russ)
He came so close to me, and I was totally awestruck!

A diplodocus came to my school to play basketball. (dih-PLOD-a-kuss)
I saw him coming toward me in the upstairs hall.

After school I saw a omeisaurus near the local bowling alley. (o-may—SAW-russ)
He followed me for a distance but I escaped into the art gallery.

In the morning when I awoke I knew it had been only a dream in my sleep,
But my time with the dinosaurs was a memory I would keep.

Dinosaur Menu

Snacks

Cheese and Crackers

Partysaurus Dinosaur Cake

Dinosaur Cake

Party Dinosaur Cup Cakes

Apple Juice

Milk

Partysaurus Dinosaur Cake

Yield: One 14x14 cake

1-18.25 ounce cake mix
3 eggs
Oil
Water
1 dinosaur cake pan
No-stick baking spray
1-16x16 inch cake cardboard

Preheat oven to 350 F. Follow the package directions for mixing the cake. Beat the cake mix until smooth. Spray the partysaurus dinosaur cake pan with no-stick cooking spray. Place the batter into the pan. Bake for 35-45 minutes or until toothpick inserted in the cake center comes out clean. Let the cake stand 8-10 minutes to slightly cool. Cover a cake cardboard with foil. Tape the foil to the back of the cake cardboard. Turn the cake onto the cardboard. Follow the picture in the partysaurus cake pan and the suggested directions that come with the cake pan for best results. See the picture on finished product on page 9 in the color section.

Note: There are many books on dinosaurs. A person could spend hours researching the character-istics of dinosaurs. To save time, give each student an assignment on 2 types of dinosaurs and have each student give a report. There are also many pictures of dinosaurs in various books. The student can show the pictures of the two dinosaurs he reports on in the class-room. Take the students to the local library to select the books or the teacher can bring the books to the classroom or look up dinosaurs on the internet. There are many names of dinosaurs. Let each student select and report on his own favorite dinosaur. Work with the students on how to spell and pronounce the names of each dinosaur. Use the suggested reference books to learn about the various characteristics of each dinosaur.

Note: There is a dinosaur pronunciation website. Some of the dinosaur names in parenthesis show that the end of some of the dinosaur names end with end with (SAWR-us) or (saw-russ). I had several books on how to spell the names of the dinosaurs. They are listed in the dinosaur reference area in this chapter.

How to Spell and Pronounce the Names of the Dinosaurs

1. Tyrannosaurus (tuh-ran-uh-SAW-rus)
2. Allosaurus (al-lo-SAW-rus)
3. Barapasaurus (ba-ra-puh-SAW-rus)
4. Dipldocus (dih-plod-okus)
5. Iguanodon (I-GWAN-o-don)
6. Triceratops (try-SAIR-uh-tops)
7. Styracosaurus (sty-ra-co-SAW-rus)

8. Ankylosaurus (ang-KI-lo-saw-rus)
9. Spinosaurus (spin-o-SAW-rus)
10. Hardrosaurs (HAD-row-sawrus)
11. Mamenchisaurus (ma-men-ki-SAW-rus)
12. Apatosaurus (a-pat-o-SAW-rus)
13. Brachiosaurus (brack-ee-o-SAW-rus)
14. Shantugosaurus (shan-TOONG-o-saw-russ)
15. Supersaurus (SOO-per-saw-russ)
16. Utrasaurus (UHL-tra-saw-russ)
17. Ceratosaurus (sehr-uh-tuh-SAWR-us)
18. Brontosaurus (BRON-ta-saw-russ)

How to Spell and Pronounce the Names of the Smaller Sized Dinosaurs

1. Coloradisaurus (kol-or-ADD-ee-saw-russ)
2. Ohmdenosaurus (OHM-den-o-saw-russ)
3. Bactrosaurus (Back-tra-saw-russ)
4. Scelidosaurus (skel-EE-doe-saw-russ)
5. Coelophysis (SEE-low-FIE-sis)
6. Dravidosaurus (dra-VID-saw-russ)
7. Anchisaurs (AN-key-saw-russ)
8. Parksosaurus (PARKS-a-saw-russ)
9. Tylocephale (tie-lo-SEF-a-lee)
10. Oviraptor (oh-vee-RAP-tor)
11. Stenonychosaurus (sten-NON-ik-a-saw-russ)
12. Leptoceratops (lep-toe-CER-a-tops)
13. Struthiosaurus (STROO-thee-oh-saw-russ)
14. Hypsilophodon (hip-sil-LO-fa-don)
15. Lesothosaurus (le-soh-toh-SAWR-us)
16. Tatisaurus (Tat-ee-saw-russ)
17. Bagaceratops (bag-a-CER-a-tops)
18. Othnielia (oth-NEE-lee-ah)
19. Microceratops (mike-row-CER-a-tops)
20. Saltopus (SALT-o-pus)
21. Micropachycephalosaurus (mike-row-pak-ee-SEF-a-la-saw-russ)
22. Segisaurus (SEE-gih-saw-russ)
23. Mussaurus (moo-SAW-russ)
24. Psittacosaurus (SIT-ah-ka-saw-russ)

Find Out the Facts About Dinosaurs

Draw a line connecting the item in the left column to the correct description in the right column in each set of four. (ages 6-8)

Set One

1. Dinosaur

2. Scientists

3. Allosaurus

4. Barapasaurus

a. A large animal that has not been in existence for 65 million years

b. Walked on his two back legs and has two very short front legs

c. Found bones, eggs, skin, and footprints of dinosaurs which confirms dinosaurs existed

d. Had a very heavy body and walks on all four legs

Set Two

1. Apatosaurus

2. Tyrannosaurus

3. Mamenchisaurus

4. Hardrosaurs

a. The head looked like a duck's bill with webfeet

b. Had a very long neck

c. Had very sharp and pointed teeth like a saw and ate meat

d. Had rounded teeth and ate plants

Set Three

1. Spinosaurus

2. Ankylosaurus

3. Triceratops

4. Styracosaurus

a. Had a head six and a half feet long with three horns on its head

b. Had a large head with six horns on it and a big horn at its nose

c. Had a large fin on its back

d. Had a bony like ball the size of two basket balls on the end of his tail

Set Four

1. Iguanodon

2. Diplodocus

3. Brachiosaurus

4. Dinosaurs

a. Was the height of a four-story building

b. Revealed how they walked by its size and shape

c. Ate leaves and lived on land

d. Had one spike on his thumb

Set Five (Smaller Dinosaurs)

1. Psittacosarus

2. Struthiosaurus

3. Lesothosaurus

4. Microceratops

a. Was only $2^{1}/_{2}$ feet long

b. Was only 4 feet long

c. From the ankylosaur family and only 5 feet long

d. Only 10 inches tall, the size of a cereal box, with a beak resembling a parrot

Answer Key

Set One	Set Two	Set Three	Set Four	Set Five
1. a.	1. d.	1. c.	1. d.	1. d.
2. c.	2. c.	2. d.	2. c.	2. c.
3. b.	3. b.	3. a.	3. a.	3. b.
4. d.	4. a.	4. b.	4. b.	4. a.

Activity Suggestions

Take your party guests or family to the Chicago Science Museum. There is a wonderful display of dinosaurs. The Chicago Science Museum is very educational. It is difficult to see everything in one day. I live only 90 miles away from the museum. Every time I go to the museum, I learn something new.

Have a dinosaur hat day and hat fashion show.

Have a dino birthday party.

Suggestions for Dinosaur Visors and Hats

Note: This visor is a simple project for 3 and 4 year olds.

Simple Dinosaur Visor

Yield: One decorated visor

1 yellow foam visor with spring back
1 package dinosaur stickers (24 count)

Place 10-12 dinosaur stickers at random on the foam visor.

Note: Select the colors you desire. I am only giving you a suggestion. The green scales are a little longer than the yellow polka dot. This visor is an easy project for five and six year olds.

Decorated Dinosaur Visor

Yield: One decorated visor

1 yellow foam visor with spring back
1 package dinosaur stickers (24 count)
1 8x11 yellow sheet of paper with polka dots
1 8x11 sheet of paper with green background and wavy yellow V lines
All purpose glue

Trace and cut 6 pieces of the green paper and 5 pieces of the yellow polka dot paper to make a total of 11 scales. Place 10-12 dinosaur stickers at random on the brim of the visor. Starting at the side of the visor glue on the scales alternating the green with the yellow until all 11 scales are glued onto the

visor. See picture on page 9 in the color section.
Note: The Roaring Dinosaur hat is ideal for 5 year olds boys.

Roaring Dinosaur Visor

Yield: One visor

1 yellow foam visor with spring back
3 roaring dinosaurs
1 package dinosaur stickers (24 count)
Glue gun
Hot glue

Place stickers around the bottom sides and front edge of the visor. Evenly space the dinosaurs from left to right and hot glue the 3 roaring dinosaurs onto the visor. See picture on page 9 in the color section.

Note: The hat is ideal for a 3 or 4 year old birthday party. I showed the hat off to my little 4 year old friend at the YMCA. Her eyes lit up like a Christmas tree. You can use regular felt and glue the circles on with fabric glue. See picture on page 9 in the color section.

Dino Party Visor

Yield: One visor

1 blue visor
1 package dino party toppers (4 count)
1 bunch decorative plastic balloons
2-20 mm easy-glue eyes
1-9x12 sheet blue sticky felt
1-9x12 sheet yellow sticky felt
Hot glue
Hot glue gun

Using a penny, trace 6 circles on the yellow felt. Using a 50 cent piece, trace two circles on the blue felt. Cut out the circles. Take the paper off the back of each circle, one at a time. Stick the two blue circles on the bill of the visor to form the background for the eyes. Hot glue one eye, off center onto the blue. Place the yellow circles all around the brim edge of the visor. Hot glue the four dinosaur party toppers onto the bill just above the eyes. Hot glue the balloons onto the center of the back of the visor. See picture on page 9 in the color section.

The Spinosaurus Dinosaur Hat

Yield: One hat

1 pink baseball hat
1 orange spinosarus dinosaur
2 large puffy pom poms
2-20 mm easy-glue eyes
1-9x12 sheet (each) color lime, green, yellow, and orange
1-9x12 piece of white felt
Hot glue stick
Glue gun
Fabric glue

Trace the platelets onto single thickness of white felt. Cut out the platelets. Hot glue the platelets to the front edge of the bill of the baseball cap. Using a penny, trace 4 circles on the lime green felt and two circles on the yellow felt. Using a quarter, trace a circle on the orange felt. Cut out all 7 circles. Glue the orange circle onto the lower center of the cap, with one fourth of the circle glued onto the edge of the white platelet. Glue one yellow circle on each side at the bottom end of the bill of the hat with a ½ inch of the edge of the circle glued to the top of the white platelets. Glue two green circles in between the yellow and orange circle on the left and right side of the bill with a ½ inch of the edge of the circle glued to the top of the white platelets. Center the spinosarus and hot glue the dinosaur feet to the bill of the hat. Hot glue the tail to the center of the ball cap. Hot glue one eye to the center of each of the pom poms. Hot glue each pom pom onto the front of the ball cap near the back hind legs of the spinosarus to form his eyes. See picture on page 9 in the color section.

Note: This hat takes two hours of work. I made and wore this hat when reading stories to the children at the party. I received many good comments about the hat. With help, a 7-9 year old could make this hat. The tail wags back and worth as the person turns his head back and forth.

Note: Cut two pieces of material for the head and the tail and one piece for the platelets. Only use a dot of glue in the bottom center of each platelet. I folded the edge of the platelet up ¹/₂ inch and placed the glue on the bottom center of the edge of the platelet. This project is best suited for ages 8-10 years. An adult should help the kids put the hat together. The happy dinosaur head and tail hat is awesome. I got out the various dinosaur hats at our 35th wedding anniversary just for conversation's sake. Two of our guests volunteered to have their picture taken with me with the dinosaur hats. Everyone had a big laugh over how we looked. Even the adults can get into the dinosaur theme.

Note: See page 200-201 for The Happy Dinosur Head and Tail Hat pattern.

The Happy Dinosaur Head and Tail Hat

Yield: One Hat

1 green baseball cap
1-9x12 sticky felt (each color) yellow, orange, lime green, light blue, navy
1-9x12 piece fuchsia starched felt
1-9x12 piece purple starched felt
1-9x12 piece yellow starched felt
2-10 mm easy-glue eyes
Black permanent marker with a fine tip
Purple thread
Fuchsia thread
1 sewing needle with small to medium eye for hand sewing
Hot glue stick
Glue gun
1-6³/₄ inch piece electrical solid copper wire
1-7 inch piece electrical solid copper wire
25 cotton balls, regular size
1-8 inch x ¹/₂ inch/10.16 cm x 1.27cm package mounting strips (self-sticking)

Trace the pattern for the head on the purple felt, the tail on the fuchsia felt and the platelets on the yellow felt. Cut out the patterns. Hot glue the yellow platelets to the center of the baseball cap. Place the 6³/₄ wire through 12 cotton balls and the 7 inch wire through 13 cotton balls. Draw black horizontal lines on the tail. Place the 6³/₄ inch wire with cotton balls down the center of the tail. Place the second piece of tail over the top. With fuchsia thread, hand sew the edges of the tail with an overcast stitch. Leave the top of tail open. Place the bottom edge of the back platelet inside the top of the tail. Hand sew the top of the tail. Bend the tail in two places to give it a moving effect. Place the wire onto the dinosaur head, starting from the bottom up. Place the top of the dinosaur head over the bottom piece of the dinosaur. Hand sew the edges of the head with an overcast stitch. Leaving the back of the body open, place the front platelet edge into the back opening of the dinosaur's body. Stitch the back shut. Hot glue an eye onto each side of the head. Using a penny, trace and cut out 4 green, 4 orange, and 2 yellow circles of the sticky felt. Place the 5 circles onto each side of the body of the dinosaur. Use two green, 1 yellow, and two orange for each side. Using a quarter, trace and cut out three orange and two navy blue circles from the sticky felt. Using a fifty cent piece, trace and cut out 2 circles from the light blue sticky felt. Cut a 3 inch long mounting strip. Cut the mounting strip in half to make two 1½ inch mounting strips Fasten the mounting strip 1½ inches on the center of the cap and the remaining strip onto the brim of the cap. Attach two orange circles, side by side, on the cap at the top of the mounting strip. Attach the two navy blue circles to the mounting strip under the orange circles. Attach the two light blue circles to the mounting strip under the navy blue circles. Attach the third orange circle to the center of the blue circles. Position the body of the dinosaur in the center of the mounting strip with felt circles and hot glue the bottom to the circles with the mounting strip. Bend the dinosaur at the neck. See picture on page 9 in the color section.

Note: The Dinosaur picture is a great project for 5 and 6 year olds. It is a trace, cut and paste, and spell project. It also helps children learn how to follow directions. Remember to place the body of the dinosaur on the fold line to make a front and a back.

Dinosaur Picture

Yield: One picture

1-9x12 piece starched felt
2 sheets (each) wrapping paper with a print
1-10 mm easy-glued eye
1-4 fluid ounce bottle multi-purpose glue

Using the self-adhesive die, cut alphabet stickers and spell out the word dinosaur. At the top of the picture, stick the letters on the starched felt, so the letters look like they are dancing. Take a copy of the dinosaur picture pattern on page 202 and lay it on the paper. Cut out the pattern. Fold together the two pieces over $1/2$ inch across the top of the body of the dinosaur. Place the tail and head inside the two pieces of the body of the dinosaur with the tail on the right side and the head on the left side of the dinosaur. Glue the head and tail in place. Glue the three platelets across the top back of the dinosaur so that the dinosaur's body stands up. Glue an eye in the center of the dinosaur head. See picture on page 9 in the color section.

Note: The children can help paint the stars. The adult should hot glue the pin back and the dinosaur button. Children all ages enjoy these pins. It is a perfect party favor.

Dinosaur Pin

Yield: One pin

1-$1^7/_8$ x $1/2$ inch wooden star
1-2 U.S. fluid ounce 59 ml bottle acrylic red paint
1 green dinosaur button
1–$1^1/_2$ inch brass steel pin back
Glue
Glue gun

Paint the entire star red. Dry thoroughly. Break off the shank on the back of the dinosaur button. Hot glue the button onto the center of the star. Hot glue the pin back to the back of the star.

Note: Be sure to propose or use mild peppers. The hot peppers are harmful to the children. They can burn their hands or harm their eyes. This project is fun for 5 and 6 year olds. The pre-school kids like looking at and feeling the centerpiece. I ran each toothpick through the the back flesh of each vegetable. I also had the whole vegetables to show off to the children. We talked about eating our vegetables so we would be strong.

Vegetable Centerpiece
Dinosaur Mommy with Her Children Theme

Yield: One centerpiece

1 rutabaga
2 large baking potatoes
1 box round toothpicks
2 radishes
10 mild yellow chili peppers
1 red pepper
1 yellow pepper
1 baby carrot
1 yellow zucchini
1 green zucchini
10 green beans

Cut a slice off the bottom of the rutabaga and each of the potatoes. Place one baking potato on each side of the rutabaga. Toothpick a radish on the back end of each potato. Place one whole mild chili pepper at the front of each potato. Cut off the bottom of each of the 7 mild chili peppers. Cut the 7 mild chili pepper lengthwise to form the platelets. Cut 4 platelets from the red pepper and one platelet from the yellow pepper. Using toothpicks, alternate the mild green chili with the red pepper in the middle on both potatoes. Toothpick the two red and yellow pepper platelets down the center of the dinosaur and the mild chili peppers on each side of the center platelets. Cut a slit into the front of the carrot to form the head and mouth. Toothpick the carrot to the small front part of the yellow zucchini. Toothpick the opposite side of the yellow zucchini into the front of the rutabaga to make the head. Toothpick the green zucchini onto the back of the rutabaga to make the tail. Lay 5 green beans on the plate on each side of the bottom of the rutabaga to make the dinosaur's long toenails. See picture on page 9 in the color section.

Dinosaur Crackers and Cheese

Yield: Twelve servings

1-8 ounce box dinosaur shaped crackers
1-12.5 ounce can cheddar cheese spread
1 doily

Lay out dinosaur crackers on a tray with a doily. Top each cracker with a dab of cheddar cheese spread. Serve as a snack.

Dinosaur Party Cupcakes

Yield: Twenty-four

1-18.25 ounce yellow cake mix
3 eggs
Water
Oil
24 Cup cake liners

Preheat the oven to 350 F. Mix the ingredients per package directions and beat until smooth and creamy. Divide the batter into 24 cupcakes. Bake for 15-20 minutes or until a toothpick inserted in the middle of a cupcakes is clean. Cool thoroughly.

Chocolate Frosting for the Party Cupcakes

Yield: Twenty-four cupcakes

1 cup butter
1 cup shortening
4-1 ounce packages (each) pre-melted chocolate
1 teaspoon almond flavoring
$1/2$ teaspoon salt
2 pounds powdered sugar
$1/3$ cup water
1-8 ounce container of candy dino quins
6 package (each) dino
Party toppers
1 colorful tablecloth
1 box wooden ABC blocks

Beat the butter and shortening together. Add the chocolate and beat. Add the almond flavoring, and salt. Alternately, add the powdered sugar with the water. Beat the frosting until smooth and creamy. Using a number 30 cake tip, pipe on the frosting onto each cupcake. Top each cupcake with dino quins and one birthday party dinosaur. Place a colorful tablecloth to cover the dessert buffet table. Stack the blocks at different heights. Place one cupcake on each stack of blocks. Arrange other cakes on the same buffet table.

Note: Drain and squeeze the juice out of the pineapple tidbits so the layers of cake will not be soggy. The birthday cake is for a 5 year old. Ask the kids attending the birthday party this trivia question. How many pieces of pineapple are in the cake to represent the hidden platelets? (195-200 pieces) Quins are also called sprinkles.

Note: The cake mix calls for 3 egg whites.

Dino Hidden Platelets Birthday Cake

Yield: One 9 inch decorated torte

1-18.25 ounce white cake mix
3 egg whites
Water
Oil
2 drops of red food coloring
1-20 ounce can pineapple tidbits, drained
No-stick baking spray
1-16 ounce container non-dairy whipped topping
1-10 inch cardboard cake circle
1-8 ounce container of candy dino quins
2 packages (each) dinosaur birthday candles (4 count)
1 package plastic balloon clusters (3 count)

Preheat the oven to 350 F. Follow the package directions. Beat the ingredients together until smooth and creamy. Add the red food coloring. Fold in the pineapple tidbits into the cake. Spray three 9 inch pans with no-stick baking spray. Divide the batter among the three pans. Bake for 20-25 minutes or until a toothpick placed in the middle of the cakes comes out clean. Cool thoroughly. Place one layer of cake onto the cardboard. Frost with the cake with non-dairy whipped topping. Repeat 2 more times. Frost the top of layer with cool whip. Sprinkle the candy dino quins over the top and sides of the cake. Place the 5 dinosaur candles in a row across the center of the cake. Place the 3 sets of balloons behind the dinosaur candles at three different heights.

```
H T U Y D V U I O P L M N U E W Q P O W E R F U L B O D Y E
L A R G E F E E T U Y T H Y U V B J I M N D G B P I N B B I
R B I M T F M D F I A L Y Y K K I I E I G D U C K L I K E L
U E W S D P G I O L L I Z A R D L I K E Y L O N G T A I L R
R X S W O U P J K J Y I J K H O R N S O N T H E H E A D E B
B E X G I A N T C L A W S B O Y U I U W Q Z D N J A V G T E
Y K L A R G E B O D Y S W Q A S C A L I U J Z U D H Y T Y N
I R E B U I L T F O U R S T O R I E S T A L L O Y H U I W R
T T G F R Y B M A H U M O N G O U S T O E S M C E T G Y G U
Y I M J S A W L I K E T E E T H S G F P A S M A L L B O D Y
D F B O N Y T A I L I A R T H U M B W I T H A H O R N O H B
E K F S P I K E O N T H E N O S E O H W D U W S T T W S A F
B I G C O L L A R B O N E O S J E B E A K F A C E E W Y K J
L O P K I W K G G R T R E W R D B I O L P J J D F J M N A U
V F D T R G V L O N G N E C K H U G E F I N G E R N A I L S
D J A U T M T B V G T R D E W C R E S T H E A D U S Y A L F
```

Dinosaur Word Search

Large Feet	Long Tail	Huge Fingernails	Lizard Like
Big Collar Bone	Long Neck	Bony Tail	Humongous Toes
Large Body	Saw Like Teeth	Giant Claws	Horns on the Head
Small Body	Beak Face	Spike on the Nose	Thumb with a Horn
Duck-like	Powerful Body	Built Four Stories Tall	Crest Head

```
H T U Y D V U I O P L M N U E W Q  P O W E R F U L B O D Y  E
L A R G E F E E T  U Y T H Y U V B J I M N D G B P I N B B I
R B I M T F M D F I A L Y Y K K I I E I G  D U C K L I K E  L
U E W S D P G I O L  L I Z A R D L I K E  Y  L O N G T A I L  R
R X S W O U P J K J Y I J K  H O R N S O N T H E H E A D  E B
B E X  G I A N T C L A W S  B O Y U I U W Q Z D N J A V G T E
Y K  L A R G E B O D Y  S W Q A S C A L I U J Z U D H Y T Y N
I R E  B U I L T F O U R S T O R I E S T A L L  O Y H U I W R
T T G F R Y B M A  H U M O N G O U S T O E S  M C E T G Y G U
Y I M J  S A W L I K E T E E T H  S G F P A  S M A L L B O D Y
D F  B O N Y T A I L  I A R  T H U M B W I T H A H O R N  O H B
E K F  S P I K E O N T H E N O S E  O H W D U W S T T W S A F
B I G C O L L A R B O N E  O S J E  B E A K F A C E  E W Y K J
L O P K I W K G G R T R E W R D B I O L P J J D F J M N A U
V F D T R G V  L O N G N E C K H U G E F I N G E R N A I L S
D J A U T M T B V G T R D E W  C R E S T H E A D  U S Y A L F
```

Dinosaur Word Search

Large Feet	Long Tail	Huge Fingernails	Lizard Like
Big Collar Bone	Long Neck	Bony Tail	Humongous Toes
Large Body	Saw Like Teeth	Giant Claws	Horns on the Head
Small Body	Beak Face	Spike on the Nose	Thumb with a Horn
Duck-like	Powerful Body	Built Four Stories Tall	Crest Head

The Happy Dinosaur Head and Tail Hat Patterns

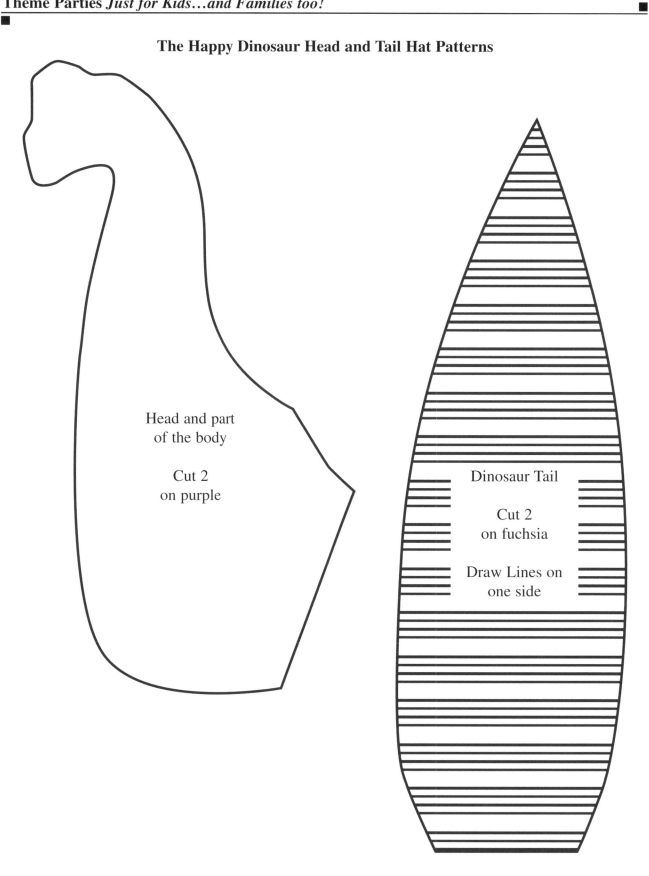

Head and part
of the body

Cut 2
on purple

Dinosaur Tail

Cut 2
on fuchsia

Draw Lines on
one side

The Happy Dinosaur Head and Tail Hat Patterns

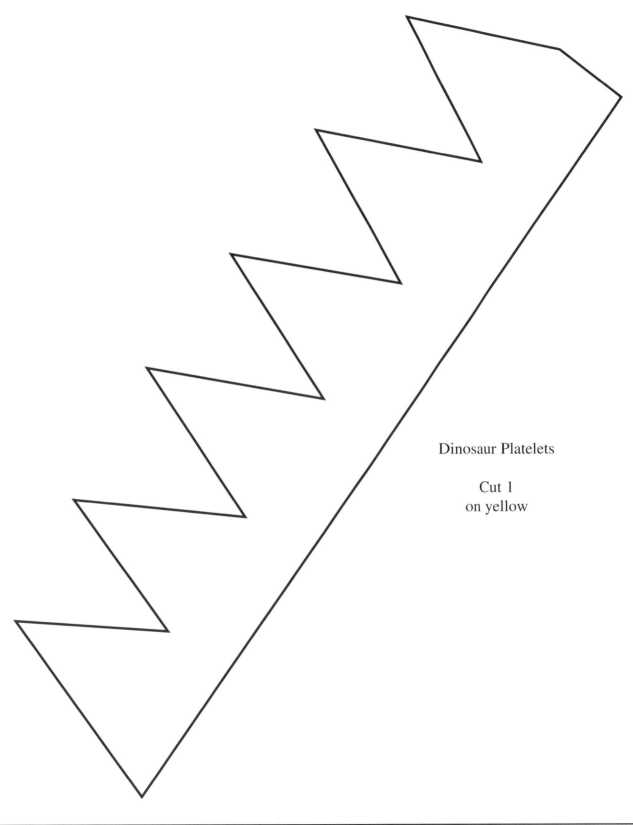

Dinosaur Platelets

Cut 1
on yellow

Dinosaur Picture Pattern

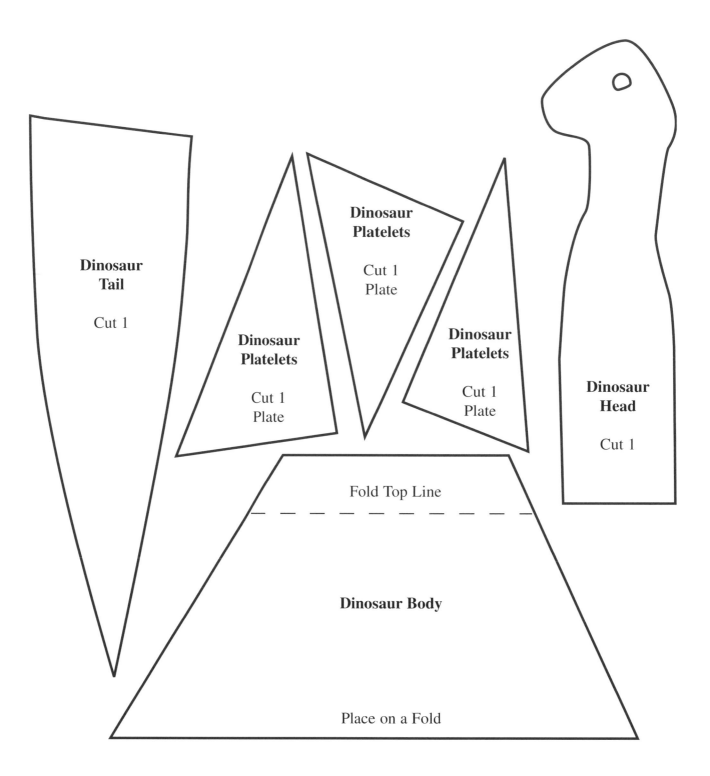

Dinosaur Theme Related Book Resources

Bennett, Christopher S.
"Pterosaurs, The Flying Reptiles"
Publisher: F. Watts
Published Date: c1995
There is an explanation about the pterosaurs and also pictures of each species (ages 7-9)

Berenstain, Michael
"The Biggest Dinosaurs"
Publisher: Western Publishing Company
Published Date: c1989
There are pictures and explanations about the biggest dinosaurs. (ages 4-6)

Berenstain, Stan
"Brother Bear Loves Dinosaurs"
Publisher: HarperCollins
Published Date: c2005
The board book tells the readers how much Brother Bear loves his favorite dinosaurs. Sister Bear learns that sharing means more fun for everyone. (ages 2-5)

Cohen, Daniel
"Tyrannosaurus Rex and other Cretaceous Meat-Eaters"
Publisher: Bridgestone Books
Published Date: c2001
The book goes into great detail about the meat-eating dinosaurs. (ages 8-9)
Note: Search the author for other books on the different species of dinosaurs at your local library.

Cole, Joanna
"The Magic School Bus: In The Time of the Dinosaurs"
Publisher: Scholastic
Published Date: c1994
The book explains the meaning of "prehistoric". It also describes the different dinosaurs and has a model of the dinosaur's skeleton. There is a school bus that takes the kids on an imaginary ride into the forest to see the different species of dinosaurs. (ages 4-6)

Dixon, Dougal
"Amazing Dinosaurs"
Publisher: Boyds Mills Press
Published Date: c2000
It describes the early dinosaurs. The book has many illustrations with bite-sized pieces of dinosaur information. Some topics are on the fiercest, tallest and smallest dinosaurs. (ages 3-5) Note: Search this author for more information on dinosaurs at your local library.

Foreman, Michael
"A Trip to Dinosaur Time"
Publisher: Candlewick Press
Published Date: c2003
This is a very imaginative book. Tom's mother gets a new timer. She instructs Tom not to play with the timer. He does not listen. The timer sends Tom to Dinosaur Land where he has an adventure. He brings home a dinosaur egg that hatches. He sends the baby dinosaur back to Dinosaur Land and can't think of how to tell his mom his story. (4-6)

Hoff, Syd
"Happy Birthday, Danny and the Dinosaur"
Publisher: HarperCollins
Published Date: c1995
Six-year old Danny invites his dinosaur friend to come to his birthday party. (ages 5-6)

Ingoglia, Gina
"Those Mysterious Dinosaurs"
Publisher: Golden Books
Published Date: c1989
The book explains about the common dinosaurs in very simply terms. (ages 4-6)

Lessem, Don
"Armored Dinosaurs"
Publisher: Lehner Publications
Published Date: c2005
The book explains the different species of armored dinosaurs. (ages 5-7)

Metzger, Steve
"Dinofours, It's Beach Day"
Publisher: Scholastic
Published Date: c1996
The mother dinosaur gathers the children dinosaurs to ride the bus for a day at the beach. Tara is afraid of the water but decides to join the other dinofours.(ages 3-5)

Metzer, Steve
"Dinofours, It's Time for School"
Publisher: Scholastic
Publisher Date: c1996
The book prepares a child for school as the mother tells her dinosaur baby he is growing up and ready for school. (ages 4-5)

Mitton, Tony
"Dinosaurumpus"
Publisher: Orchard Books
Published Date: c2003
There are pictures of the various dinosaurs, with the description words such as rump, bump, donk, clatter, swirl, twist, thwack, zoom, rattle, roar, and wallop. The story ends up with the dinosaurs in a heap and all of them fall fast asleep until the next day. It is a rhyming tale of triceratops, tryrannosaurus, and brontasaurus gathering at the swamp. (ages 3-5)

Most, Bernard
"How Big Were the Dinosaurs?"
Publisher: Harcourt Brace & Company
Published Date:
This book tells the name, and size of each dinosaur by comparing the species to the different size objects, such as a school bus It also teaches the child and the adult how to pronounce the name of each dinosaur. (ages 3-7)

Most, Bernard
"The Littlest Dinosaurs"
Publisher: Harcourt Brace & Company
Published Date: c1994
The book tells the name of the dinosaurs shows the size of the littlest dinosaur by comparing them to objects. (ages 3-7) Note: I used this book as a reference. Search this author for more information at your local library.

Ting, Morris
"Dinosaurs"
Publisher: F. Watts
Published Date c1993
The book has things to make, activities and facts. (ages 5-8)

Yolen, Jane
"How Do Dinosaurs Get Well Soon?"
Publisher: Blue Sky Press
Published Date: c2003
This book is very imaginative. It asks questions about how the different dinosaurs would react if they were sick. The inside front and back covers show all the different dinosaurs in bed. This book will warm your heart and make you laugh. Ask the children if they can identify the Styracosaurus in the last page of the book. (ages 3-5)

Zoehfeld, Weidner Kathleen
"Dinosaur Parents, Dinosaur Young"
{Electronic Resource}
Publisher: Clarion Books
Published Date: c2001
The author explains that we don't know much about dinosaurs as parents. She has an exercise called, "Make a Fossil Egg". The purpose of the project is to learn more about fossils. (ages 5-6).

CD References

"Dinosaur Rock"
{Sound recording}
Publisher: Rounder Kids
Published Date: c1998
There are two children are on vacation at the beach with their parents. The CD has songs that explain the different types of dinosaurs and also explains the job of the paleontologist. (ages 5-7)

"The Most Amazing Dinosaur Songs"
{Sound recording}
Publisher: Music for Little People
Published Date: c2004
The kids are singing the dinosaur alphabet and pronouncing the names of each dinosaur starting with each letter of the alphabet. They also go on an imaginary trip to explore dinosaurs. (ages 4-5)

Cassette

Hoff, Syd
{Sound recording}
"Danny and the Dinosaur go to Camp'
Publisher: HarperCollins
Published Date: c2001
Danny and good friend Dinosaur is accompanied by Danny to camp, and together the two enjoy racing, rowing, and hiking. (ages 3-5)

Website

www.google.com
Google Search Engine—Search Google to look up more information on dinosaurs for preschool. I was astonished by the amount of information on dinosaurs on this search engine.

Clown Party

The Story of Blinki the Clown

The name of Blinki's father was Bonzo the clown. He was the famous clown who performed on the flying trapeze. Blinki entered the circus tent with Bonzo for every performance. The audience knew Blinki as the cute little clown. Blinki would sit in the front row of the audience and watch his father perform day after day. Blinki wanted to go up on the trapeze with his father, but the answer was always "No". Bonzo would say, "Blinki, you are too young and too small." One day when Bonzo was performing, he missed the trapeze and Blinki threw his father a rope to break his fall. The crowd cheered for Blinki. He had saved his father's life. Suddenly, Blinki was the circus hero. Eventually, Blinki learned to perform with his father. They won the hearts of many circus crowds. When Bonzo retired from the circus, Blinki continued entertaining the audience with his son Blinko. The family tradition of circus- entertaining continued for almost 75 years. When the reporters interviewed Blinki upon his retirement, they asked him why he had performed for so many years. He said, "I loved pleasing the crowds of people, especially the children". It was a good life and a wonderful way of giving."

A Funny Clown Poem

He is a funny clown,
Even when he makes a frown.

Some clowns wear floppy shoes and polka dot pants,
They make people smile, laugh and want to dance.

The circus clowns are the talk of the town.
Children are pointing and saying, "There's the clown".

A clown wears a wig and paints his face,
Performing for young and old - The Whole Human Race!

Clowns make balloon hats,
All sizes, even into animals like cats.

A clown performs up in the air on a high trapeze.
The crowd watches and hopes he does not sneeze.

Clowns light up the children's eyes to a glow,
Clowns garner the attention at any circus show.

Note: I have given you many options on the food. Don't feel you need to make all of this menu.

Clown Menu

Sloppy Joes

Hamburger Buns

Clown-Faced Sandwiches

Quick and Easy Clown Cupcakes

Potato Chips

Dill Pickle Spears

Caramel Corn Clown Bags

Birthday Clown-Faced Cookie

Clown Donuts

Easy-does-It Clown Cake

Decorated Clown Raspberry Torte

Clown Birthday Honey Cake

Sloppy Joes

Yield: Five pounds or twenty-five sandwiches

3 pounds ground chuck, chopped
1 cup water
1 small onion, diced
$\frac{1}{2}$ large green pepper, diced
$\frac{1}{2}$ cup celery, diced
1 tablespoon minced garlic
1 teaspoons salt
1 teaspoon pepper
$2\frac{1}{2}$ teaspoons Worcestershire sauce
1 tablespoon yellow mustard
2 tablespoons lemon juice
2 tablespoons dark brown sugar
2 cups catsup

Brown the meat with water, onion, green pepper, and celery. Drain and rinse the meat. Pat dry. Add the minced garlic, salt, pepper, Worcestershire sauce, yellow mustard, lemon juice, dark brown sugar, and catsup. Stir all ingredients thoroughly every couple of minutes and cook the Sloppy Joes over low heat for about 5-8 minutes. Serve on your favorite style hamburger bun with chips and relishes.

Note: There are 5 whole bagels per 14 ounce package. I like to use the honey wheat bagels because of the extra fiber.

Clown-Faced Sandwiches

Yield: Ten bagel sandwiches

1¹/₂ teaspoons Worcestershire sauce
1 teaspoon onion powder
3-8 ounce packages (each) cream cheese, softened
1-14 ounce package plain or honey wheat bagels
10 slices deli turkey
10 cherry tomatoes
10 queen size Spanish olives stuffed with pimiento
10 cocktail-size Kosher dill pickles
1-10 ounce package shredded carrots
2 packages (each) of 8 balloon design paper plates 6³/₄ inch (each) in diameter

Add the Worcestershire sauce and onion powder to the cream cheese. Beat the mixture until smooth and creamy. Spread the cream cheese over each open faced bagel. Fold the deli turkey in half. Place the folded edge of the turkey to the bottom of the bagel. Place a dab of cream cheese in the center of the bagel. Top each bagel with one cherry tomato to form the nose. Cut the olives in half lengthwise. Place a dab of cream cheese above and slightly to the right and left of the cherry tomato. Place the olive half over each dab of cream cheese. The pimiento side should be facing up to form the two eyes. Place a dab of cream cheese below the nose. Top with one cocktail-size dill pickle to form the mouth. Using a number 234 hair tip, pipe cream cheese around the out edges of the meat to form the clown's hair. Sprinkle the shredded carrots over the piped on cream cheese. Get some of the carrots to stand up at the top of his head. Place each sandwich on the decorated balloon paper plate. Place sandwiches on the buffet table. See picture on page 9 in the color section.

Note: Use white cup cake liners to bake the cupcakes. Place each baked and cooled cupcake into a snappy stripe cup cake liner. The colors are bright and will not be dulled by baking the cupcakes in the snappy stripe color cupcake liners. Cupcake liners often come in packages of 50. Quins are sprinkles in various bright colors.

Quick and Easy Clown Cupcakes

Yield: Twenty-four cupcakes

3 eggs
$1/2$ cup oil
$1^1/_3$ cups water
1-18.25 ounce box cake mix
24 white standard-sized party cupcake liners
24 snappy stripe style standard-sized cupcake liners
4 packages (each) clown head picks (6 per package)
2-16 ounce (each) containers, French vanilla frosting
1-8 ounce container bright dot quins
1 cupcake dessert stand

Preheat the oven to 350 F. Add the eggs, oil, and the water to the cake mix. Beat the batter until smooth and creamy. Line the cupcake pans with the white cupcake liners. Fill each cupcake 2/3 full. Bake for 12-15 minutes or until a toothpick inserted in the center of the cupcake comes out clean. Cool thoroughly. Place each cupcake into a snappy stripe cupcake liner. Using a number 30 tip, pipe on the frosting, starting at the outer edge and going in a circular motion to cover each cupcake. Sprinkle the bright dot quins over each cupcake. Place one clown head into the center of each cupcake. Place the cupcakes into cupcake dessert stand. See picture on page 9 in the color section.

Note: Purchase non-acid stickers for the children's own safety. There are five cups of caramel corn in each 8 ounce container. You do not have to use the birthday party saying on each bag. You can use all balloons of various sizes at the bottom of each treat bag. The children really enjoyed making the treat bags. I hot glued all the clowns in each straw.

Clown Goodie Bags

Yield: Twenty bags

1 package snappy party bags (20 per package)
5 packages (each) happy birthday stickers (four per package)
2 packages (each) party theme stickers with birthday cakes, party hats, and confetti
2 packages (each) balloon stickers (24 per package)
4-8ounce containers (each) fat free caramel corn
4 packages (each) clown head picks (6 per package)
1 package 8-inch flex straws (100 count)
Glue gun
Glue stick
1 skein of yellow nylon yarn

Place a happy birthday sticker in the middle of each bag. Place balloons and other sticker decorations at random below the happy birthday sticker. Fill each bag with one cup of caramel corn. Cut the yarn into one $2^1/_3$ yards piece. Fold yarn in half and in half again. Cut off two inches of the bottom of each straw. Place a small dab of hot glue into the bottom end of the clown pick. Place the clown pick into the top of the straw, just above the flex area of the straw. Dry. Wipe off any excess glue. Place the straw into the bag through the middle of the caramel corn. The clown head will be facing up. Two and one half inches from the top of the bag, tie the yarn to form a bow and thus securing the straw with the clown head in place. Tying the bow will form the clown's collar and makes a clown's costume. See picture on page 9 in the color section.

Birthday Clown-Face Cookie

Yield: One 13x13 cookie

1 clown face cake pan non-stick cooking spray
1-16.5 ounce package sugar cookie dough
2-16 ounce containers (each) French vanilla frosting
Orange, blue and red food coloring
1-8 ounce package bright small dot quins
1 red jawbreaker

Preheat oven to 350 F. Spray the bottom of the clown face pan with no-stick spray. Spread the cookie dough over the entire bottom of the pan. Bake for 15-20 minutes or until a toothpick inserted in the center of the cookie comes out clean. Cool slightly. Turn onto a 14x14 inch round serving tray. Continue to cool the cookie thoroughly. Color 2 cups frosting with orange, $^1/_2$ cup frosting with red, and $1^1/_2$ cups frosting with royal blue. Leave the remaining frosting white. Prepare 4 decorating bags with each of the frostings. Using a number 501 tip, pipe on the orange frosting with squiggly lines to form the hair. Frost the nose, circles on the cheeks, hat, and collar with white frosting. Sprinkle the bright small dot quins over the white frosted areas. Using a number 15 tip, pipe in the smile-like mouth with red frosting. Using a number 30 tip, pipe on white frosting below the mouth and also to complete the clown's face. Using a number 15 tip, pipe in the blue frosting to form the eyes and also to outline the clown's hat, collar, chin, and face. Place the red jawbreaker to form the nose. Using the number 30 tip, outline the nose around the jawbreaker with red frosting. Sprinkle the bright small dot quins around the outline of the eyes and the nose. Enjoy! See picture on page 10 in the color section.

Note: I generally make up the clown donuts, 6 to a platter.

Clown Donuts
Yield: Twelve

1 dozen large glazed donuts with white frosting
2-16 ounce containers (each) French vanilla frosting
Orange food coloring
Yellow food coloring
1-16 ounce container fudge frosting
12 gummy peach-0-ring candies
12 malted milk balls
12 maraschino cherries, drained and patted dry
2-10 inch doilies

Place donuts onto the platters lined with the doilies. Mix 1 cup frosting with orange food coloring and 1 cup frosting with yellow food coloring. Place the orange and yellow food coloring into the same cake decorating bag with the number 234 hair tip. With the number 234 tip, pipe on the frosting half away around the sides and top of the donut to form the hair. Place gummy peach-0-ring off to the top left side of the donut over the frosting hair. Place a dab of frosting into the center of the gummy peach-0-ring. Place the maraschino cherry into the center of the peach-0-ring. Place a dab of white frosting into the center of the donut hole. Place the malted milk ball over the Frosting. With a number 13 tip, pipe on the eyes with frosting with color of choice and the mouth. With your forefinger rub a little chocolate and yellow frosting over the cheek area. See picture on page 9 in the color section.

Note: I found the red and yellow sugar decorations at my local grocery store in the baking aisle. The sugar decorations package has 5 balloons, 1 happy birthday saying, and 5 party cake swirls. The butter cream frosting recipe is found on page 73. Use a cake spatula with hot water to smooth out the top and sides of the cake.

Easy-Does-It Clown Cake

Yield: One decorated 9 inch cake

No-stick cooking spray
3-9 inch round baking pans
3 eggs
$1/_3$ cup oil
$1^1/_2$ cup water
1-18.25 ounce confetti cake mix
2 pounds butter cream frosting
1 package of sugar decorations
3 medium size clown head picks
Yellow food coloring

Preheat the oven to 350 F. Spray no-stick spray on three 9 inch round baking pans. Add the eggs, oil, and water to the cake mix. Beat the cake mix until smooth. Divide the batter among the three cake pans. Bake for 20 minutes or until a toothpick inserted in the middle of the cakes comes out clean. Cool for ten minutes. Turn out the cakes onto 3 separate plates or 3-10 inch cardboard cake circles. Make up the butter cream frosting. Frost each cake. Place the happy birthday letters in the center of the cake with "happy" above the "birthday" letters. Place the balloons and the cake swirls at random on the top and bottom of the cake. Color the white frosting yellow. With a number 30 tip, pipe on a border, both on cake top and around bottom of the cake. Place the three clown head picks toward the back of the cake, all three in a row to represent a third birthday. See picture on page 9 in the color section.

Amy's Story

Amy was born on July 19th on her mother and father's 10th wedding anniversary. The family adored Amy. She was a smart and well-mannered little girl. Amy loved clowns. The entire family read every clown story to Amy available from the local library. Amy had clown dolls and clown stuffed pillows. Her aunt even made her pajamas from clown print material. When Amy turned four, she asked to have a clown party for her half birthday. Her family said it would be a fun idea. So, the planning began. The party was the best ever. Just leave it to a child's imagination to come up with a Christmas clown theme party. I hope you will have as much fun at your next birthday party using the clown theme.

Note: I generally bake the torte a day before I frost it. I find that it holds together better. The butter cream frosting is found on page 73. Frosting on the cake plate holds the first layer of cake in place. I used purple and pink birthday candles because these are Amy's favorite colors. The clowns say 4 for her 4th birthday. The party icing decorations come in all shapes and are used for decorating cupcakes, cookies, cakes and ice cream. The individual pudding cups come in a four pack.

Decorated Clown Raspberry Torte

Yield: One 9 inch torte

1-18.25 ounce yellow or white cake mix
1-18-25 ounce red velvet cake mix
Eggs
Water
Oil
No-stick cooking spray
6-10 inch cardboard cake circles
2 pounds butter cream frosting
1-24 ounce jar red raspberry jam
2-4.35 (each) vanilla pudding cups
2 packages (each) clown heads (1 per package) (each had has a dial that turns for ages 1-6)
1 package small-size clown head picks
4-6 inch long birthday candles
1 package party hat icing decorations (12 per package)

Mix each cake mix separately. Follow the cake mix direction on each box. Preheat oven to 350 F. Prepare 6-9 inch round cake pans. Divide the yellow cake batter into three of the 9 inch pans and the red velvet cake batter into the remaining 3 cake pans. Bake for 20-22 minutes or until a toothpick inserted in the center of each cake comes out clean. Cool all 6 layers of cake for 10 minutes. Place the cardboard circle over each cake. Turn each cake onto a cardboard circle. Cool thoroughly. Make the butter cream frosting. Place frosting in the middle of the cake plate. Place the yellow cake with cardboard on the 10 inch cake plate. Frost the first layer of cake with the raspberry jam. Remove the red velvet cake from the cardboard and place this cake on top of the yellow cake. Frost the second layer with vanilla pudding. Remove the yellow cake from the cardboard. Place this cake on top with red velvet cake. Repeat these same steps with the last three cakes, ending up with the red velvet on top. Frost the top of the cake. This will make 6 layers to complete the torte. With a number 30 tip, frost sides and pipe on a the border around the top and bottom of the cake. Set the number for the age of the child on each of the clown heads. Place both clown heads into the center of the cake with the heads going back to back. Place the clown head picks evenly spaced around the top border of the cake. Place two candles on each side of the clown face alternating pink with purple. Place the party hats in groups of threes on each side and both the front and back. See picture on page 9 in the color section.

Note: The Clown birthday honey cake has two layers. The bottom layer is chocolate and the top layer is white. I put the unbaked chocolate layer over the unbaked white layer. The two colors slightly blend together, but also give the cake a look of having two separate layers after the cake is baked.

Clown Birthday Honey Cake

Yield: One 12x15 inch cake

1 teaspoon baking powder
1 teaspoon baking soda
$^1/_2$ teaspoon salt
$^3/_4$ cup sugar
$2^1/_2$ cups cake flour
$^1/_2$ cup butter
$^1/_2$ cup honey
1 egg
2-1 ounce (each) pre-melted chocolate (only include on layer one)
$^1/_2$ cup cream
$^1/_2$ cup sour cream
$^1/_4$ cup plus 2 tablespoons water
1 teaspoon vanilla
1 clown character cake pan

Preheat the oven to 350 F. Mix the baking powder, baking soda, salt, and sugar and the flour together. Beat in the butter, honey, egg, and chocolate. Blend in the cream, sour cream, water and vanilla. Grease and lightly flour the clown pan. Pour the chocolate cake batter into the clown cake pan. Repeat the Honey Cake again omitting the chocolate. Spread the white cake batter over the chocolate cake batter in pan. Bake for 40-45 minutes or until toothpick inserted into the center of the cake comes out clean. Cool for 10 minutes. Turn the cake onto a 16x16 cake cardboard, diagonally. See picture on page 10 in the color section.

Note: The 12x15 inch clown cake takes 3 pounds of frosting due to mixing several colors.

Note: Do not try to make this frosting with a little hand mixer. I use my Kitchen Aide® to mix the larger batch. See the three-pound butter cream recipe on page 216.

Note: Put the amount of birthday candles needed on the top left hand side of the clown above the clown's head.

Butter Cream Frosting

Yield: Three pounds

1¹/₂ cups butter
1¹/₂ cups white shortening
3 pounds powdered sugar
¹/₃ cup plus 2 tablespoons and 2 teaspoons water
1¹/₂ teaspoons almond flavor
1 teaspoon salt

Beat butter and shortening together until smooth and creamy. Add the powdered sugar alternating it with the water. Add the almond and salt. Beat frosting until smooth and creamy.

Chart for Cake Tip Sizes Used for Decorating the 12x15 Inch Clown Cake

Black—number 13 (small star tip)
White—number 30 (medium star tip)
Purple—number 15 (small star tip)
Orange—number 234 (hair tip)
Blue—number 15 (small star tip)
Yellow—number 13 (small star tip

Note: Do not feel you need to mix these exact colors if you wish to use other colors. This is just a suggestion. Every child has his/her own favorite colors.

Chart for Piping in the Colors of the Clown

Umbrella—yellow, purple, shocking pink
Umbrella handle—purple
Balloon—yellow with pink polka dots
Hat—purple and yellow
Hair—orange
Tie—purple and yellow
Coat—blue
Trousers—shocking pink
Shoes—black
Mouth and nose—pink
Eye—blue
Outline of the eye—black
Face—white

Sides of the cake and top—white

Where the candles are positioned—white

Hands—white

Small area below the umbrella-black

Note: When Missy attended the clown party she got all excited when she saw the crayon shaped candles. I was surprised at her reaction.

How to Frost the Clown Cake

Yield: One 12x15 inch clown cake

3 pounds butter cream frosting
5 crayon birthday candles
Pink, blue, violet, black, orange, and yellow food coloring

Reserve $1\frac{1}{2}$ pound of the white frosting. Mix the pink, blue, violet, back and yellow frosting in five separate small bowls. Fill each pastry bag with the different colors using the tips as directed on the chart above. Pipe on the various areas of the cake to make a clown cake.

Note: It is best to purchase the chocolate from a specialty company that sells chocolate for candy making for best results. Use the powdered food coloring. Do not use the liquid coloring sold in the grocery store. Purchase the small jars of powdered food coloring at the candy supply shop. Smaller lollipop molds with much detail makes for tedious work. I find that the big balloons are simple and excellent for younger children to make lollipops. Rinse out each paintbrush in warm water after each use. Run each paint brush between the thumb and fore finger to keep the paint brush point. Dry the paintbrush with a paper towel. It is best to use good quality camel hair or sable paintbrushes for best results. Store paintbrushes with a straw over the hair of the brush. Cover each baby jar of chocolate and store them in a box until next use or start fresh if you so desire.

Note: Sucker sticks come in 100 count and 1000 count.

Clown Themed Lollipops
Yield: Twelve lollipops

8 empty baby food jars
1 empty larger olive jar
1 electric burner
1-16 ounce package white chocolate wafers
1-16 ounce package chocolate wafers
1 package sucker sticks (100 count)
1-1ounce jar (each) red, green, lavender, yellow, and blue food coloring (powder form)
1 lollipop mold with clowns
1 lollipop mold with balloons party hat, happy birthday
1 lollipop mold with 4 large groupings of balloons.
Variety of small artist paintbrushes
1 small paring knife
1 stainless steel frying pan
Water
6 baby spoons
1 teaspoon
Plastic straws

Place water in the stainless steel pan. Place 6 baby food jars and 1 larger jar in the pan with the water. Add ¹/₃ to ¹/₂ cup of the chocolate wafers to the larger jar and ¹/₄ to ¹/₃ cup of the white chocolate wafers to the 6 smaller jars. When the white chocolate is melted, add the various food colorings (one color per jar). Stir each baby food jar to mix the food coloring. Select the color for each balloon. Paint the bottoms of the lollipop balloon to mold the colored white chocolate in the center, brushing out the colored chocolate to the sides. make sure the entire area is covered. Overlap the colors in the mold. Hold the mold to the light to be sure the colored chocolate is thick enough in the mold. This step will prevent the dark chocolate from seeping through the bottom layer. Freeze this layer of chocolate for about 10 minutes. Remove from the freezer. With the paring knife, scrap off any excess chocolate. Fill the lollipop mold with the melted chocolate by spooning the chocolate into the center of the mold. Brush the chocolate evenly across the lollipop mold. Tap the mold to be sure the chocolate is even. Place the sucker stick half way up and also down into the center of the lollipop. Twirl the sucker stick to cover the stick with chocolate. Tap the lollipop mold on the counter a second time to make sure the lollipop is even and the stick is centered and secured. Freeze the lollipop in the mold for 10 more minutes. Gently pop out the lollipops.

Note: The Styrofoam® ball should be between the size of a softball and soccer ball.
The circumference of the ball measures 20 inches.

A Circus Lollipop Theme Ball

Yield: Twelve lollipops and fifteen foiled clowns

1 Styrofoam® ball (6 inches in diameter)
4 clown lollipops
1 single lollipop balloon
4 large groupings of lollipop balloons
2 happy birthday lollipop balloons
1 party hat lollipop
1 package star balloons
1 package plastic balloons (3 count per package/5 balloons per grouping)
2 packages (each) medium size clown head picks
1 package small size clown head picks
15 chocolate foiled covered clowns
1-14x14 inch serving tray
1-12 inch doily

Place the star balloons in a circle near the top of the ball. Stick the single lollipop balloon into the top center of the ball. Stick the remaining lollipops at random all around into the Styrofoam® ball. Place the small and medium clown head picks around the bottom of the ball. Line the tray with the doily. Place the lollipop ball in the center of the tray. Place the 15 chocolate clowns on the tray around the ball. See picture on page 10 in the color section.

Note: I found the wooden stars at a local craft store. You can vary the Christmas ornament by gluing only one large clown head pick in the middle of the star instead of three small derby clowns. I sprayed both sides of each star in one sitting and then I hung the stars up in my husband's work shop. I used the clown ornaments for door prizes at the birthday party. I have a small artificial Christmas tree with a burlap bottom. I hung the clown ornaments on this tree and used the clown face print material for the tree skirt for Amy's birthday party as part of the decoration. You can also use miniature Christmas trees and hang just one clown ornament on each tree. This too can be a neat door prize for each child.

Note: These ornaments are for children 5 and older. Use non-toxic paint for best results. Amy will not stick the clown in her mouth. She knows it is not a toy and it is a cute decoration only to hang on her Christmas tree.

Craft Project Clown Christmas Ornaments

Yields: Six star ornaments

6-5 inch wooden 5 pointed stars with hanger
1-11 ounce can silver paint spray (fast drying) (non toxic)
2 packages (each) small derby clowns head on a pick (12 count)
2 packages (each) star balloons
1 package plastic balloons with (3 count per package)

Spray paint each star, front and back. Hang up to dry thoroughly. Hot glue one star balloon grouping to the left of the point of the star with the wire hanger. Glue three clowns onto the center of each star, either straight across or in a half circle. See picture on page 10 in the color section.

Games

Note: The clown game comes in a packaged kit.

Pin the Nose on the Clown Game

Yield: One clown face

1 17x18 inch clown face
1 blindfold mask
12 numbered noses

Cut out the clown and tape to a wall. Cut out all 12 numbered pink noses. Blindfold each player. The player that pins his nose on the clown's nose or comes the closest wins the prize.

*Note: I purchased the wooden stars already painted in yellow. If you need to paint the stars,
purchase the yellow acrylic paint or the color of your choice. Each clown pick tapers
at the end of the pick. Therefore it is wise to cut off the tapered end, leaving $^1/_4$ inch.*

Clown Tic-Tac-Toe
Yield: Twelve Tic-Tac-Toe game boards

6-6$^1/_2$ x 9$^1/_2$ x 1 inch pine blocks of wood
2-4 ounce cans (each) glitter gold spray
1-2 U.S. fluid ounce bottle Santa red acrylic paint acrylic paint
Drill
$^1/_4$ inch diameter drill bit head pick
5 packages (each) small size clown head picks (clown style 1/12 count)
5 packages (each) small size clown head picks (clown style 2/12 count)
6 clown heads with the movable numbers 1-6
1 yard of felt
Newspaper
Yard stick
Ruler
Fine tip permanent black marker
Glue
12 wooden stars
1 very fine artist paintbrush
1$^1/_2$ inch artist paintbrush
Pencil chalk marker
Pad and pencil to keep score
12-quart size bags

Spray all six front sides of each board with the glitter paint. Dry thoroughly. Paint the tops of the
board with the Santa red paint. Dry thoroughly. Drill one hole on a practice piece of wood to be sure
the clown head pick fits into the hole. Paint the holes red with a very fine brush and a dab of paint to
cover the holes. Let dry. Lay each board down onto one piece of felt. Trace a line along each piece
of felt to fit the size of the board. Cut out the six 6$^1/_2$ x 9$^1/_2$ inch pieces of felt. Place small dots of glue
at random and all four corners on each piece of felt. Place each board bottom onto the felt. Press to
glue the felt in place. Glue two stars at the top of each board, one on each side. Glue the clown onto
the center top of the board. Measure and mark off the board into 3 equal spaces across and 3 equal
spaces down, making a division to total of 9 spaces. Draw division lines with a black felt pen. Place
a ruler on each line and draw the black line with the permanent black marker. Mark a hole in the center of each space and drill. Place 10 matching clowns of one style into the bag and the second set of
10 matching clowns in the second bag. The object is to get three matching clowns to go across, down
or diagonally in one row to win the game. Keep score on a score pad or a piece of paper. See picture
on page 10 in the color section.

A Clown Doodle Pad

Yield: Six doodle pads

6-6$\frac{1}{2}$ x 9$\frac{1}{2}$ rectangular pieces of wooden boards
2-4 ounce cans glitter spray paint
1-2 U.S. fluid ounce bottle Santa Red acrylic paint
18-2$\frac{1}{2}$ inch (each) stars
1 package small derby clowns (12 count)
1 package small derby clowns (6 count) number 1-6
6-3$\frac{1}{2}$ x 8 inch doodle pad
1 drill
1-$\frac{1}{4}$ inch diameter drill bit
2 sets (each) colored pencils (20 count)
Hot glue stick
Glue gun
6-9x12 inch (each) black felt
4 U.S. fluid ounces tacky glue
1 pencil chalk marker

Spray the front and sides of each board with the glitter paint. Dry thoroughly. Paint the top of each wooden board red. Dry thoroughly. Glue on the three stars across the top end of each board, one on each side and one in the center with part of each star extended above the board. Drill one hole $\frac{1}{2}$ deep, slightly off centered in each star. Cut down each clown pick to $\frac{1}{4}$ inch. Hot glue each clown pick into the hole in each star. Glue on a doodle pad below the stars. Lay each board down onto a piece of felt and cut out the piece. Trace the felt to fit the board size. Place small dots of glue at random and all four corners of the felt. Set the backside of the board onto the side of the felt with the tacky glue. Glue the felt in place. Dry thoroughly. Each child can select pencils of choice. Ask each child to draw a simple clown head picture or to doodle something of his/her own choice. This activity is for ages 5-8. See picture on page 10 in the color section.

Note: I printed "Happy Birthday" on each bag with my happy birthday stamp. Once the children gathered the pennies, I tied the bag shut with ribbon and put the child's name of his bag.

Penny Scramble

Large pile of shredded paper
200 pennies
Small paper bags
Ribbon or yarn

Place shredded paper on a large mat or rug in your recreation room or your kitchen floor. Scramble the pennies into the shredded paper. Give each child a small paper bag. Let the children scamper to the pile, find pennies and put them in their bags. they will have a blast. The activity is good for children. (ages 4-6)

Note: I have a large picture of a clown. I told the children that this picture was only a sample. They could color the clown any color they so desired. The shoestring lacing clown project is good for ages 5 and 6.

Note: Be sure you punch the holes large enough so the child will have success at stringing the clown head and bow tie. Make as many clown faces as children at the party.

Color and Lacing Yarn Through the Clown Face Picture
Yield: Six clowns

6-14x14 medium heavy white poster board
2 packages (each) washable markers (20 count) assorted colors
Clown head picture
Medium size Philips screw driver
6-2mm x 60 inches (each) Satin Battail cord
Scotch tape

Draw a clown face on medium heavy weight white poster board. Using a Philips screwdriver, punch holes about $1^{1}/_{2}$-2 inches apart around the outline of the face, hair, and hat of the clown. Color in the clown's eyes, nose, cheeks, mouth, hair, hat, and collar with selected with washable markers. Measure the length of cord needed for lacing the clown's face, outer edge of hair, and hat. Tape each end of the cording to form the top of a shoelace. Thread the cord through the holes around the face, hair, and the hat. Tie the two ends of the yarn together on the back of the picture. See picture on page 10 in the color section and on page 225.

Circus Trivia
(for ages 6-10)

1. A person that teaches animals to do tricks is called a
      a. a lady trainer   b. an animal trainer   c. a male trainer

2. A tent or an enclosed area where circus folks perform is called
      a. an arena   b. a coral   c. a stall

3. A swing with a short bar that is held up with two ropes of equal length.
      a. seat   b. chair   c. trapeze

4. A show with many performers with various talents is called
      a. a variety show   b. a clowning show   c. an animal show

5. A person working behind the scenes to help set up a show is called
      a.volunteer   b. Roustabout   c. hard worker

6. In the early 1900's cotton candy was called
      a.fairy floss   b. fairy candy   c. a dentist's favorite candy

7. The first equestrian parade occurred in America and was performed by Philip Lailson and took place in the year of
   a. 1779   b. 1879   c. 1899

8. Baraboo, Wisconsin is famous for
   a. great stunt men   b. funny clowns   c. circus parades

9. The old-time parades mostly use what kind of theme
   a. Christmas   b. Fall   c. patriotic

10. The famous Hollywood star who comes to Milwaukee in July for the circus parade and dresses as a clown and walks in the parade
    a. Ernest Borgnine   b. Elise Borgnine   c. Billy Borgnine

11. People watching a parade are called
    a. spectators   b. participants   c. both answers

12. In 1903 a bandwagon was built for the season of Barnum and Bailey circus. How many horses can be hitched to this great American circus wagon?
    a. 20   b. 40   c. 60

13. The large animal dressed in circus costume that wins the hearts of the spectators is
    a. a lion   b. a giraffe   c. an elephant

14. The two countries known for circus performances are
    a. America & France   b. America & Africa   c. neither answer

15. The name of the famous horses in the parade in Milwaukee is
    a. ponies   b. Clydesdales   c. wild horses

16. The French usually have their national flag on their circus wagons. What are the three colors found in the French Flag?
    a. green, pink & blue   b. red, white & blue   c. yellow, red & blue

17. The circus person performing for the audience and who looks very tall is on
    a. stilts   b. tall wheels   c. neither answer

18. The clown that juggles is called a
    a. juggler   b. jiggler   c. jumper

19. The performers that often steal the show are
    a. opera singers   b. clowns   c. dog trainers

20. Clowns not only work in a circus under a circus tent, but also at a
    a. rodeo   b. carnival   c. a and b

Answer Key

1. b	7. a	14. a
2. a	8. c	15. b
3. c	9. c	16. b
4. a	10. a	17. a
5. b	11. c	18. a
6. a	12. b	19. b
	13. c	20. c

Color and Lacing Yarn Through the Clown Face Picture

Note: The Clown word search is for ages 6-10

```
G F U J I T I R I F L I M F R E C K L E S T Y I M M O O E D
J U M B O S E R T G B V C J I U O K M J U H Y T G F R E D W
R T Y H N J I K L M J N H Y G R F E D C G T R F E D B H J I
H U I J H B G T R F B I N G O P P L K I J U H Y T G R F D V
V Y I U J U Y T G R E O K I J J J N O O D L E S O L O I K U
O L M K J U B G T F R D E W S X C B O Z O I O K M J U H T G
I K M J Y C L A R A B E L L I K M J U H Y G T F R E D C V C
U J N H Y T G F R E D S W D F T G H Y U J K I Y O G I L O U
I U J N I U J Y H T R E D F T L U C K Y I K J U Y H T G F R
S S U U S T I T C H E S M K I U J Y H T G R F B Y U J H Y T
H Y H U J I K O L K I U J S M I L E Y P O I U Y H T R F E D
G H U J H Y T G F R D E D D F T Y J K I L P L W I G G L E S
T O T O K I N J U Y T G R F D E C A S E Y P L P L O I K M N
T Y U I U H A R P O I U J U H Y T G F R D E W S E D R F T G
I U J I K L O I M N Y R E W S D A I S Y L P O I U J Y G T F
T Y U I U D I M P L E S R D E F T G H J U J K O P O L I K J
Y U Y H O U K I L O I U Y L O L L Y P O P L O I U Y H N H G
U I M K J H Y T G F R E D G T Y H J P B L I N K Y R E D F G
T Y H U J K I M N H Y T R C H U C K L E S O P L M K I U Y T
F R E S N U G G L E S O P L O I K J U H N B I M B O S D C F
```

Clown Names Word Search

Blinky	Snuggles	Daisy	Bingo
Wiggles	Dimples	Noodles	Stitches
Clarabell	Jumbo	Yogi	Smiley
Lucky	Freckles	Casey	Lollypop
Bozo	Bimbo	Harpo	Chuckles

```
G F U J I T I R I F L I M  FRECKLES  T Y I M M O O E D
JUMBO  S E R T G B V C J I U O K M J U H Y T G F R E D W
R T Y H N J I K L M J N H Y G R F E D C G T R F E D B H J I
H U I J H B G T R F  BINGO  P P L K I J U H Y T G R F D V
V Y I U J U Y T G R E O K I J J J  NOODLES  O L O I K U
O L M K J U B G T F R D E W S X C  BOZO  I O K M J U H T G
I K M J Y  CLARABELL  I K M J U H Y G T F R E D C V C
U J N H Y T G F R E D S W D F T G H Y U J K I  YOGI  L O U
I U J N I U J Y H T R E D F T  LUCKY  I K J U Y H T G F R
S S U U  STITCHES  M K I U J Y H T G R F B Y U J H Y T
H Y H U J I K O L K I U J  SMILEY  P O I U Y H T R F E D
G H U J H Y T G F R D E D D F T Y J K I L P L  WIGGLES
T O T O K I N J U Y T G R F D E  CASEY  P L P L O I K M N
T Y U I U  HARPO  I U J U H Y T G F R D E W S E D R F T G
I U J I K L O I M N Y R E W S  DAISY  L P O I U J Y G T F
T Y U I U  DIMPLES  R D E F T G H J U J K O P O L I K J
Y U Y H O U K I L O I U Y  LOLLYPOP  L O I U Y H N H G
U I M K J H Y T G F R E D G T Y H J P  BLINKY  R E D F G
T Y H U J K I M N H Y T R  CHUCKLES  O P L M K I U Y T
F R E  SNUGGLES  O P L O I K J U H N  BIMBO  S D C F
```

Clown Names Word Search

Blinky	Snuggles	Daisy	Bingo
Wiggles	Dimples	Noodles	Stitches
Clarabell	Jumbo	Yogi	Smiley
Lucky	Freckles	Casey	Lollypop
Bozo	Bimbo	Harpo	Chuckles

Clown Theme Related Book Resources

Boase, Petra
"Painting and Dressing up for Kids: Step-by-Step"
Publisher: Anness
Published Date: c1995
{ages 54-55 show how to put on a clown's make up and how to make a simple clown costume.
(ages 5-9)

Bullock, Ivan
"I want to be A Clown"
Publisher: Thomas Learning
Published Date: c1995
The book teaches a child how to be a clown by getting dressed in clown attire. (ages 6-10)

Carter, Kyle
"Circus Stars"
Publisher: Rourke
Published Date: c1994
The book tells about different men and women circus performers. (ages 5-8)

Clement, Herbert
"The Great Circus Parade"
Publisher: Gareth Stevens Publisher
Publication Date: c1989
This book is about the great circus parade that comes to Milwaukee every year in July. People line
the streets of Milwaukee to watch the Museum's collection of over 100 Circuswagons in the
Parade. (6 and up)

Dodds, Dayle Ann
"Where's Pup?"
Publisher: Dial Books for Young Readers
Published Date: c2003
 The Pup is missing at the circus. The clown looks for pup. He asks everyone and finally gives up
only to see the sign that says, "Can't Find Pup? Just look up". (ages 2-3)

Herman, Gail
"Lowly Worm Joins the Circus"
Publisher: Simon Spotlight
Published Date: c1998
Lowly worm discovers that it isn't as wonderful to join the circus, especially since he is away from
his family. (ages 3-5)

Laden, Nina
"Clowns on Vacation"
Publisher: Walker
Published Date: c2002
Clowns make everyone laugh. When the circus is completed for the year , the clowns decide to go on vacation and never stop clowning around. (ages 3-5)

Littlesugar, Amy
"Clown Child"
Publisher: Philomel Books
Published Date: c2006
Olivia travels in the Crystal Caravan with her father in the year 1910. Olivia wants a real home to go to. Olivia has tea with the farm lady. Mrs. Thorstaad boiled water for a bath for Olivia. She is excited to soak in the tub. Olivia stays with Mrs. Thorstaad until her father came back for her. She is glad to be with her father again and back in the circus. (ages 4-6)

Radlauer, Ed
"Clown Mania"
Publisher: Children's Press
Published Date:c1981
The book talks about what clowns do as they perform for an audience such as singing, dancing, or working at a rodeo. It also shows how the clowns put on their makeup. (ages 7-9)

Rex, Adam'
"Tree Ring Circus"
Publisher: Harcourt
Published Date: c2006
There is a tree outside of town where a bear, chicken and a runaway clown get together. They have fun with the other animals on the tree. This full color text is part word game, part counting and party mystery. (ages 3-5)

Rey, Margret
"Curious George First Words at the Circus"
Publisher: Houghton Mifflin Company
Published Date: c2005
Curious George learns words like circus tent, popcorn, peanuts, cotton candy, circus ponies, trapeze, lion tamer, and clown band. (ages 1-3)

Cassette Circus Music

Merle Evans Circus Band
"The Circus is in Town: The Greatest Show on Earth"
Publisher: Shortland Publications
Published Date: c1988
It is a sing along book cassettes. The circus song is repeated twice. The cassette is perfect for playing musical chairs. (ages 3-6)

CD

"Circus Music from the Big Top"
{Sound recording}
Publisher: Legacy International
Published Date: Early 1900's
The CD has 12 songs with a March tempo. (ages 4-7)

"Screamers Circus Marches"
{Sound recording}
Publisher: Mercury
Published Date: c1991
The CD has a variety of circus marches. The music is played by the Eastman Wind Ensemble and conducted by Frederick Fennell. The CD has a total of 28 upbeat songs. (ages 4-7)

Great American Main Street Band (Musical Group)
"Under the Big Top"
{Sound recording}
Publisher: Angel Records
Published Date: c1993
The CD has 28 circus upbeat songs. (ages 4-7)

DVD

"Mister Rogers' Neighborhood: A Day at the Circus"
{Video recording}
Publisher: Anchor Bay Entertainment
Published Date: c2005
It is life lessons: self esteem, creativity and musical fun. (ages 3-5)

Pizza Party

The Story of Grandpa Frank and Grandma Maggie

Grandpa Frank and Grandma Maggie have been married 50 years and they are still going strong. He is a slender man with long legs and big feet. With his high cheekbones, hazel blue eyes, gray sideburns, the dimple in the middle of his chin, and fair complexion, he is still handsome and full of enthusiasm. Life is always good according to Grandpa Frank. Life wasn't always easy on the farm in Duluth, Minnesota. Grandpa makes the best of everything. He whistles like a canary. He says whistling chases the blues away. Grandpa Frank is a self made man and an avid reader. He believes in education. He continued to learn everything about farming to maintain a good farming sense. He believes in change and says, "change is good." One morning while working in his barn, he began reflecting on his life with Grandma Maggie. They have had a good life together.

Grandma Maggie is a little lady with dyed coal black naturally curly hair and big brown eyes. Grandma grew up on the farm next to Grandpa Frank. He was always so protective of Grandma Maggie from the 1st grade on up. Grandpa Frank is six years older than Grandma Maggie. It didn't seem to matter. Grandma Maggie married Grandpa Frank when she was only 18 years old. They seem to agree on just about everything except food.

She thought a hard working man should always eat comfort foods, such as turnip soup, beef and noodles, shepherd's pie, and good old-fashion beef stew with lots of homemade bread, hot from the oven. She has made many apple pies with apples from their apple trees. Grandpa Frank admits that Grandma Maggie is an excellent cook and a wonderful wife.

He spoke up to Grandma Maggie and said that a man should enjoy eating other foods like pizza. Who would ever want to come to a party to eat comfort food? At least that is how Grandpa Frank saw it.

After Grandpa Frank retired and let his sons take over the farming, he went swimming at the local YMCA daily. He and his swimming friends went for pizza at least twice a week. Having pizza was pure pleasure and Grandpa Frank enjoyed every bite. He just couldn't get enough of pizza.

One day his YMCA friends began talking to Grandpa Frank about pizza parlors. "Say, Frank, you ought to build a pizza parlor on your property for all the locals to enjoy". Grandpa Frank thought it was a splendid idea. He went to the library researched pizza parlors and the history of pizza.

Grandpa Frank was not only a good farmer, but is also an excellent finishing carpenter. He can build anything. When Grandpa Frank returned home, he sat Grandma Maggie down to talk about his plans. "Maggie, I have good news. I am going to build a pizza parlor right here. We can have parties for our families and friends and we will never get bored or lonely. We will be surrounded with the good smells of pizza every day". Grandma Maggie yelled, "Frank, have you lost your mind?" Grandma Maggie knew that he always had progressive ideas, but this idea took the cake. He said, "Maggie, I'll have lots of help building the pizza parlor. It would be neat and a great addition for the town's people and also the neighboring towns. It will be grand". Maggie stamped her feet, yelling, "No! No!"

Days went by and Grandpa Frank could only think of building his pizza parlor. Finally, after a lot of coaxing and lots of calls from friends and family, Grandma Maggie said "yes."

The pizza parlor would be in the old barn. Grandpa admitted that it was time for a big renovation project. He knew it would be a lot of work, but he could envision the finished project. Neighbors came out to put together the pizza parlor. Within three months the barn looked like a new place and the pizza parlor was fabulous. It was decorated with colorful ceiling lights. Grandpa Frank had a large framed picture of himself in his pepper-design chef hat and coat. He wore a smile that was almost as broad as his barn.

He had modern pizza equipment, a large restaurant style freezer and lots of counter space to make every kind of pizza. It was a pizza haven. He said, "If you can dream it, you can do it." Well folks, we did it.

He set a date for a big pizza party. Everyone in the area was invited, including the out-of- town family members. He was very excited about celebrating and showing off his new pizza parlor. A couple of hundred people showed up for the party. Grandpa took the time to thank everyone for helping to make his dream come true and sharing this most wonderful day with him, his wife and family. He made a toast, thanking everyonethere, and wishing everyone better tomorrows with more pizza parties. "Eat Lots of Pizza" became his slogan.

After the party Grandma Maggie talked to Grandpa Frank asking him if she could throw a January Thaw Party with her favorite comfort foods. Grandpa said yes as a compromise with Grandma Maggie. Grandma was very happy. Grandma saw Grandpa Frank put onion and garlic into everything. She said that he most likely would turn into an onion or a big bulb of garlic very soon. Grandpa Frank just smiled at her comment and said, "Oh Maggie, pizza and many other good foods must have these two ingredients."

Now Grandpa Frank is famous all over the county. He gives classes to anyone willing to listen on how to make his great pizzas with onions and garlic, of course. In his class, he continues to tell his students to eat lots of pizza and live life to the fullest.

Grandpa Frank's Pizza Parlor Poem
by Sue Schmitzer

What a great thing to be in town,
When a pizza party comes around.

Pizzas with every topping,
Just one slice and there is no stopping.

Sample each pizza. You are sure to enjoy,
Such a variety those taste buds will employ.

Try all the pizzas of every dish,
There is even one made with fish.

Come join our pizza party,
Bring your appetite and eat most hearty.

Have fun playing mind-boggling games,
While trying to remember all the guests' names.

Grandpa Frank's pizza can't be beat,
Made in his own pizza parlor, most complete.

The Ultimate Pizza Party at Grandpa Frank's Pizza Parlor

Grandpa Frank's Pizza Menu

Deluxe Crab Pizza

S.M.O.P. (Sausage, Mushroom, Onion, and Pepperoni) Pizza

Veggie Pizza

Shrimp Pizza #1

Shrimp Pizza #2

Open-faced Chicken Pizza

Open-faced Tuna Pizza

Ham and Double Swiss Cheese Pizza

Canadian Bacon Pizza

Taco Pizza

Taco Pizza Appetizers

Grandpa Frank's Chicken Appetizer Pizza

Liberty Bell Dessert Pizza

Note: Each 7 ounce pizza yields 4 servings.
Note: The pizza crust is found in the dairy department.

Deluxe Crab Pizza

Yield: Eight 7 ounce pizzas

1-16 ounce package hickory smoked bacon
³/₄ cup celery, finely diced
1-8 ounce package mushrooms, sliced
1 cup fresh broccoli flowerets, chopped
¹/₂ red pepper, diced
¹/₂ green pepper, diced
1 tablespoon minced garlic
³/₄ cup scallions, sliced into circles
1-12 ounce package imitation crab
1-6 ounce package shredded Parmesan cheese (1¹/₂ cups)
1-10³/₄ can cream of mushroom soup
3 packages (12 ounces each) 7 inch pizza crusts
2-8 ounce (each) Italian six-cheese blend or mozzarella cheese

Dice bacon and fry to medium crisp. Drain bacon on paper towel and crumble. Mix together celery, mushrooms, broccoli, red and green peppers, garlic, scallions, crab and Parmesan cheese. Stir in cream of mushroom soup to hold the mixture together. Divide the mixture among the 8 pizzas. Top with the crumbled bacon. Cover each pizza with a ¹/₂ cup Italian six-cheese blend. Bake at 375 F for 20-25 minutes or until cheese melts and ingredients are thoroughly heated.

S.M.O.P. Pizza
(Sausage, Mushroom, Onion, and Pepperoni)

Yields: Four 8x12 inch pizzas

The recipe is in the *Elder Activities, for People Who Care: Volume Two* on page 204-205 under November Activities. The children enjoy making this style of pizza. They like to roll out the dough and select their toppings of choice. It is very tasty. My five year old friend, Abby made pizza for the whole family. She rolled out all the crusts and did a great job. Even at age five, she likes to cook.

Veggie Pizza

Yield: One-half sheet pan

1-13 ounce can pizza crust
1-8 ounce package cream cheese, softened
2 teaspoons Worcestershire sauce
$1/4$ teaspoon seasoned salt
1 teaspoon garlic powder
$1/2$ cup broccoli, shredded
$1/2$ cup cauliflower, shredded
$1/3$ cup red onion, finely diced
$1/2$ cup julienne carrots
$1/3$ cup celery, finely diced
$1/2$ cup sliced radishes or one red pepper, diced

Place pizza crust onto a baking sheet. Stretch the pizza crust to line the pan. Bake the crust at 400 F for 8 minutes or until the crust is golden brown. Cool thoroughly. Beat the cream cheese. Add the Worcestershire sauce, seasoned salt, and garlic powder. Beat until smooth and creamy. Spread the cream cheese mixture over the crust. Sprinkle the broccoli, cauliflower, onion, carrots, and celery over the cream cheese. Decorate the pizza with the radish slices. Cut the pizza from the narrow end top to the narrow end bottom into 5 equal strips. Cut across the other way into 7 equal strips making a total of 35 pieces. Place appetizers on a doily lined platter and serve cold as an appetizer pizza.

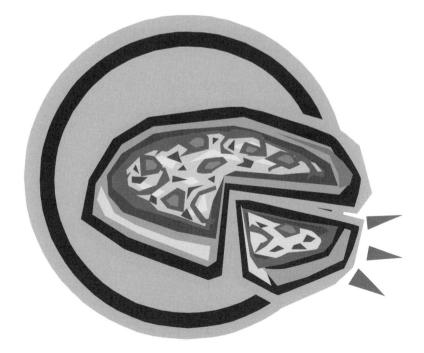

Shrimp Pizza Style One

Yield: One-half sheet baking pan

1-13 ounces can pizza crust
2 packages cream cheese, softened
1-12 ounce bottle chili sauce
1-16 ounce bag salad shrimp, washed and dried
$^1/_3$ cup red onion, finely diced
1 teaspoon minced garlic
$^1/_3$ cup green pepper, finely diced
$^1/_3$ cup celery, finely diced
1 cup cheddar cheese, shredded
1 cup carrots, julienne
1 cup broccoli flowerets, finely diced
2 Roma tomatoes, seeded and and finely diced

Place pizza crust onto a baking sheet. Stretch the pizza crust to line a 11x17 foil half-sheet pan. Bake at 400 F for 6-8 minutes or until the crust is golden brown. Cool thoroughly. Beat the cream cheese. Add the chili sauce and beat until smooth and creamy. Combine the shrimp, red onion, garlic, green pepper, and celery into the cream cheese mixture. Spread the cream cheese mixture over the crust. Sprinkle the cheddar cheese over the cream cheese mixture. Sprinkle the carrots, broccoli, and tomatoes over the cheese. Cut the pizzas into 5x7 inch pieces to make 35 pieces. Serve cold as an appetizer pizza.

Shrimp Pizza Style Two

Yield: Eight 7 ounce pizzas

Follow the Deluxe Crab Pizza recipe except substitute 1 pound of salad shrimp for crabmeat. Be sure to rinse the shrimp in cold water and squeeze out excess water or use half crab and half shrimp.
Note: Make and freeze these pizzas in advance. They make excellent party pleasers.

Open-Faced Chicken Pizza

Yield: Sixteen individual pizzas

2-5 ounce boneless, skinless chicken breasts
2 tablespoons olive oil
1 cup water
1 tablespoon minced garlic
2 tablespoons diced onion
1 yellow or red pepper, diced
$\frac{1}{2}$ pound asparagus, slightly steamed and cut into one inch pieces
2 teaspoons Italian seasoning
$\frac{1}{2}$ teaspoon black pepper
1-12 ounce can Dei Fratelli Presto Italian Dip®
1 teaspoon garlic powder
$\frac{1}{2}$ cup butter, melted
1 package English muffins
1-5 ounce package shredded Romano cheese

Dice chicken. Cook chicken in the olive oil and water until chicken is no longer pink. Add the minced garlic, onion, pepper, asparagus, Italian seasoning, and black pepper. Simmer for ten minutes and add a little more water if needed. When vegetables are softened and the water is absorbed, add the Presto Italian Dip®. Mix the Presto Italian Dip® thoroughly into the vegetables and chicken. Mix the garlic powder into the butter. Using two cookie sheets, place muffin halves, cut side up (eight per sheet). Brush each English muffin with the garlic butter and toast each English muffin for 1 to 2 minutes in the preheated oven at 400 F. Remove from the oven. Place the $\frac{1}{4}$ cup pizza topping over each English muffin. Top with pizza with 1 tablespoon Romano cheese. Return the open-faced pizzas to the oven. Bake at 400 F for 5 minutes or until cheese melts.

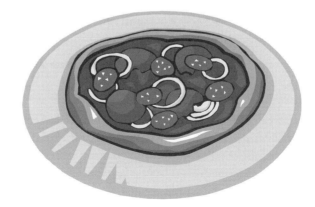

Note: 1- 8 ounce package of cheese has two cups and 1-16 ounce package of cheese has four cups.

Open-Faced Tuna Pizza
Yield: Sixteen pieces

2 loaves French Baguettes
4 tablespoons butter, melted
$^{1}/_{2}$ teaspoon onion powder
2-6 ounce cans solid white albacore tuna, drained
1-15 ounce can tomato sauce
1-6 ounce can tomato paste
1 cup fresh mushrooms, diced
$^{1}/_{3}$ cup celery, diced (optional)
2 teaspoons dehydrated onion
1 teaspoon minced garlic
2 teaspoons Italian seasoning
1-8 ounce package mozzarella cheese, shredded

Slice both loaves of bread in half lengthwise. Mix together the butter and onion powder. Brush the butter mixture on the cut side of each bread half. Cut the bread into 3-4 inch pieces. Mix together the tuna, tomato sauce, tomato paste, mushrooms, celery, onion, garlic, and Italian seasoning. Cook the mixture over medium heat for 6-8 minutes stirring every 2 minutes. Spread tuna mixture over the bread. Top with the cheese. Bake at 400 F for 4-5 minutes or until cheese melts or microwave for 1-3 minutes. Serve hot immediately.

Note: There are 3 gourmet pizza crusts in each 12 ounce package. I had only enough sauce to make 5 pizzas. I have extra cheese and vegetables for each pizza if you so desire to use the extras.

Ham and Double Swiss Cheese Pizza

Yield: Five 7 ounce pizzas

4 tablespoons butter
4 tablespoons flour
2 cups fat free half and half
1-16 ounce package Swiss cheese, shredded
1 teaspoon onion powder
1 teaspoon minced garlic
1 teaspoon black pepper
$^1/_4$ teaspoon seasoned salt
1 tablespoon Grey Poupon® mustard
1-16 ounce package ham, cubed
1-8 ounce package Swiss cheese, shredded
2-12 ounce packages (each) gourmet pizza crusts
$^1/_2$ cup plus 2 tablespoons broccoli flowerets, finely cut
1 cup mushroom, chopped
$1^1/_2$ cups French fried onions, optional

Melt butter and whisk in the flour. Gradually add the half&half, stirring constantly. Add 1 cup Swiss cheese to the white sauce/ham mixture. Reduce the heat and cook 2-3 minutes longer continuing to stir constantly. Add the onion powder, garlic, pepper, salt, and the Grey Poupon® mustard. Stir until smooth and creamy. Mix the ham into the cheese sauce. Sprinkle $^1/_4$ cup Swiss cheese over each pizza crust. Spread $^3/_4$ cup ham mixture over the cheese on each pizza. Top with 2 tablespoons of broccoli and 2 tablespoons mushrooms. Place $^1/_3$ cup Swiss cheese over the vegetables for each pizza. Bake at 375 F for 15-20 minutes or until cheese melts and the ingredients are thoroughly heated. Top each pizza with $^1/_4$ cup of French fried onions. Place pizzas back into the oven for 1-2 more minutes or until the onions are slightly crisp. Serve immediately. For best results do not microwave this pizza.

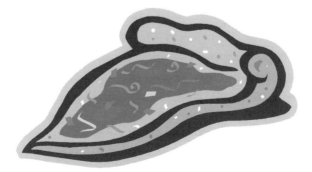

Canadian Bacon Pizza

Yield: Six 7 ounce pizzas

4 tablespoons butter
4 tablespoons flour
2 cups fat free half & half
1 teaspoon onion powder
1 teaspoon minced garlic
1 teaspoon pepper
$^1/_2$ teaspoon salt
1-11.5 ounce can cream of cheddar soup
1 pound Canadian bacon, chopped
2-12 ounce packages (each) gourmet pizza crusts
1-8 ounce package sharp cheddar cheese, shredded
$^1/_2$ cup red onions, diced
$^1/_2$ cup sliced black olives
$^1/_2$ cup green pepper, diced

Melt butter and whisk in the flour. Gradually add the half & half, stirring constantly. Reduce heat and cook 3-5 minutes longer. Add the onion powder, garlic, pepper, and salt. Stir until smooth and creamy. Stir in the cream of cheddar soup and whisk until the white sauce and soup are blended well. Add the Canadian bacon to the sauce and stir. Top each pizza crust with $^1/_2$ cup cheese sauce and then shredded cheddar cheese. Top sauce cheese. Sprinkle each pizza with onion, ripe olives, and green pepper. Place the pizzas on the oven rack. Bake at 375 F for 15 to 20 minutes or until cheese melts and the ingredients are thoroughly heated through. Serve immediately. For best results, do not microwave.

Note: Make taco pizzas with 10 inch or 6 inch tortilla shells. Purchase 1-1.25 ounce package mild taco seasoning. Use only 3 tablespoons from the package. I generally put chopped red and green pepper for color and garnishing on each pizza. The taco pizza meat mixture makes 15-6 inch pizzas. Each 6 inch taco pizza has 1/3 cup meat, 1/3 cup cheese, and 1 tablespoon each of red and green pepper. You may have to omit the green and red peppers because some children do not like peppers. They generally like lots of cheese. Place each taco on a 6 inch cardboard circle. Bake at 400 F for 6-8 minutes or until cheese melts and the crust is slightly crisp around the edges. If you freeze the 6 inch tacos before baking them, wrap individual taco pizzas with plastic wrap and place each one into a separate quart size bag; seal. Add at least 5-8 minutes extra baking time for frozen tacos. Two 6 inch tacos will fit on a 11x17 inch baking pan. You can microwave a 6 inch taco for 2-4 minutes on high, leaving the taco on the cardboard. However, I prefer to bake the taco for best results. Serve on the cardboard to save time for a great nutritious snack.

Note: There are 8-10 inch and 12-6 inch tacos per package.

Taco Pizza

Yield: Eight 10 inch pizzas

1 pound ground chuck
1 pound bulk pork sausage
1 small onion, diced
2 tablespoons minced garlic
1-15 ounce can tomatoes with chilies, and juice
1-15 ounce can black beans, drained and rinsed
1 cup water
1$\frac{1}{3}$ cups chunky salsa
2 teaspoons ground cumin
$\frac{1}{2}$ teaspoon black pepper
3 tablespoons taco seasoning
1-14 ounce package soft 10 inch tortilla shells
1-16 ounce package Mexican four cheese, finely shredded
1 cup diced red pepper, divided
1 cup diced green pepper, divided
8-10 inch cardboard pizza circles.

Taco Toppings

2 large tomatoes, diced
2-2.25 ounce cans (each) sliced black olives
2 bunches green onion, with tops, chopped
1-16 ounce container sour cream
1-16 ounce container avocado dip
1- 16 ounce jar mild or hot salsa
1-16 ounce package Mexican four cheese, finely shredded
1 head lettuce, cleaned, cored, patted dry, and shredded

Chop and fry the ground chuck and sausage with the onion and garlic. Drain the meat. Rinse the meats and squeeze off the excess grease. Add the tomatoes, black beans, water, salsa, cumin, pepper, and the taco seasoning. Stir ingredients thoroughly and cook until vegetables are softened and juice is absorbed. Place $3/4$ cup meat mixture over the each tortilla shell. Sprinkle $1/2$ cup cheese over the meat mixture on each taco. Top each pizza with diced red and green peppers. Plastic wrap each taco and place individual tacos into a one gallon storage bag. Freeze the tacos. On the day of the party, dice the tomatoes and drain the sliced olives. In separate bowls, place tomatoes, black olives, green onions, sour cream, avocado dip, salsa, extra cheese, and lettuce. Place the toppings on a buffet table. Remove the pizzas from the cardboard. Place one 10 inch taco on a lightly greased 11x17 inch baking sheet. Bake at 400 F for 10-15 minutes or until the cheese melts and the crust around the edges become slightly crisp. Remove pizzas from each pan. Place each pizza on a 10 inch dinner plate. Serve the pizza open-faced with taco toppings or fold the taco pizza in half with taco toppings. Enjoy!

Taco Pizza Appetizers - Style One
Yield: Thirty-two appetizers

Follow the recipe for taco pizza. Cut each 10 inch baked taco into 4 even pieces. Top with ripe olives Fold in half. Top with salsa of choice and a dab of sour cream. Garnish with one jalapeno pepper per appetizer. Serve on a platter lined with leafy lettuce. Serve the pizza warm. Pass appetizers to your guests.

Taco Pizza Appetizers - Style Two
Yield: Eight appetizers per 10 inch taco pizza

Follow the recipe for taco pizza. Cut each baked 10 inch taco pizza into 8 pie-shaped pieces. Starting at the wider side of the pie-shaped piece roll up each piece. Place the appetizers on a platter and garnish with ripe olives and jalapeno peppers. Serve the pizza warm.

Taco Pizza Appetizers - Style Three

Yield: Eight taco pizza appetizers per 10 inch pizza

Follow the recipe for the taco pizza. After the pizza is baked, roll the 10 inch pizza shaped into a cylinder. Cut the taco pizza into eight pieces to form a pinwheel appetizer. Place on a platter and garnish with onion flowerets and parsley. Serve the pizza warm.

Note: See page 63 in the Picnics, Catering on the Move Cookbook and Guide, to learn how to make the green onion garnish.

Taco Pizza Appetizers - Style Four

Yield: One pizza

Follow the taco pizza recipe using 6 inch tortillas. After the taco pizzas are baked roll up into a cone shape. Place cone shaped taco pizzas on a platter and garnish with ripe olives and Jalapeno pepper slices. Serve pizza warm.

Grandpa Frank's Chicken Appetizer Pizza

Yield: One 11x17 pan pizza

No-stick baking spray
1-13 ounce can pizza crust
2-13 ounce cans (each) chicken breast in water, drained
$^1/_3$ cup celery
2 teaspoons garlic
2 teaspoons dehydrated onion
$^1/_2$ cup cucumber, without seeds and diced fine
$^1/_3$ cup red pepper, diced fine
$^1/_2$ teaspoon black pepper
1 cup cheddar cheese
$1^1/_2$ cup Kraft® Sandwich Spread
$^1/_3$ cup soft margarine or butter
1 cup shredded carrots
1 cup broccoli flowerets, chopped fine
1-6 ounce can black olives, drained well, and sliced
1 cup queen size green olives with pimento, drained well, and sliced

Spray the cookie sheet with the non-stick cooking spray. Remove the pizza crust from the can. Spread out the crust to cover the entire cookie sheet. Bake at 350 F for 8-10 minutes or until the crust is golden brown. Cool thoroughly. In a large bowl, add the chicken, celery, garlic, onion, cucumber, red pepper, black pepper, and cheese. Add the sandwich spread and stir together to moisten all the ingredients. On the day of the party, butter the crust. Spread the chicken salad over the entire crust. Garnish the pizza with the carrots, broccoli, and the black and green olives. Cut into 30 square pieces. Place a doily on a 14-inch tray. Arrange the chicken appetizers on the tray. Wrap the chicken appetizers with plastic wrap and refrigerate until serving time.

Note: The pizza crust in a can is found in the dairy department. You can substitute all blueberry or all cherry pie filling. The two together make the bell look more festive. Use the blueberry filling at the top and bottom of the pizza and the cherry pie filling in the center of the Liberty Bell Dessert Pizza. You can serve the dessert pizza with non-dairy whipped topping or real whipped cream.

Liberty Bell Dessert Pizza

Yield: Ten to twelve servings

1-11x17 jellyroll pan
No-stick baking or cooking spray
1-13 ounce can pizza crust
1 piece of cardboard (12x20 inches)
2 pieces foil
Clear tape
1½ cups prepared vanilla pudding
1-21 ounce can blueberry pie filling
1-21 ounce can cherry pie filling
Patriotic tablecloth

Preheat oven to 375 F. Spray the jellyroll pan with non-stick baking spray. Unroll the pizza crust onto the prepared pan. Reserve two small pieces of crust for the bell handle and ball-shaped bell ringer. Shape the body of the bell. Connect the handle shape at the center of the top of the bell and the ball in the center of the bottom of the bell. Bake the crust for 8-10 minutes or until golden brown. Cool slightly. Cover the cardboard with the foil. Tape the foil to the back of the cardboard. Transfer the bell shaped pizza to the foiled covered cardboard. Continue to cool. Spread the vanilla pudding over the surface of the bell. Gently spread the blueberry pie filling over the pudding, both at the top and the bottom, and the cherry pie filling in the center. Cover the handle of the bell with a little pudding and a touch of cherry or blueberry pie filling. Place a patriotic tablecloth on your buffet table. Place the liberty bell pizza in the center of the table. See picture on page 10 in the color section. Enjoy!

Grandpa Frank's Pizza Party Trivia Questions

1. The Italian word for a person making pizza is
       a. pizzaollo   b. pizzaiolo   c. pizza man

2. Pizza began in the
       a. 1st century   b. 2nd century   c. 3rd century

3. Pizzo means
       a. place   b. person   c. point

4. The Italian restaurants call their pizza places
  a pizza parlors b. pizza joints c. pizzeria

5. The two countries that use the name "pizza parlor" are:
  a. U.S. & Canada b. France & Spain c. Spain & Japan

6. Leftover pizza is typically eaten cold at
  a. breakfast b. lunch c. supper

7. The first pizzeria established in the U.S. was in
  a. Chicago b. Los Angeles c. New York

8. A very thick pizza crust is known as
  a. Neapolitan style b. Chicago style c. Cincinnati style

9. "Hand-tossed" style pizza is the art of the
  a. French b. Germans c. Italians

10. Americans are noted for
  a. pan pizza b. rolled pizza c. neither answer

11. A pizza crust is known as
  a. French style b. Neapolitan style c. Greek style

12. The name of the first commercial pizza—pie mix produced in Worcester Massachusetts by Frank A Fiorello is
  a. Roma pizza Mix b. Roman Pizza Mix c. Romano Pizza Mix

13. American soldiers learned to eat and enjoy pizza in Italy during which war
  a. Civil War b. World War I c. World War II

14. The name of the singer who sang "when the moon hits your eyes like a big pizza pie, that's amore" is
  a. Frank Sinatra b. Joe DiMaggio c. Dean Martin

15. The three colors found in the flag of Italy is
  a. Green, white, red b. green, white, orange c. green, red, beige

16. Frozen pizza were introduced and found in the local grocery stores which began in the year
  a. 1950 b. 1955 c. 1957

17. Pizza actually came to Americans in the
  a. early 1900's b. late 1800's c. late1900's

18. For many Italian-Americans, pizzas were known as
      a. tomato pie   b. pepper pie   c. red sauce pie

19. Pizza became very popular with the teenagers when it was sold by the
      a. slice   b. ½ of a pizza   c. with choice of toppings

20. Most pre-school children like what toppings on their pizza
      a. lots of vegetables   b. cheese only   c. lots of sauce

Answer Key:

1. (b)
2. (a)
3. (c)
4. (c)
5. (a)
6. (a)
7. (c)
8. (b)
9. (c)
10. (a)
11. (b)
12. (b)
13. (b)
14. (c)
15. (a)
16. (c)
17. (b)
18. (a)
19. (a)
20. (b)

```
A S T U N A B C E R T O T O T Y U M O L K B G R E D I L O P
Y Y O O U J K L G H T R E W B K U T R F E D P L K V C R A B
A N C H O V I E S P P L L M J U Y T R E W S D J H G F C F C
M U S H I L O P P K I Y R B V F F N K M U S H R O O M S P K
U I R O T R E D G O P L L I D G O Y O R E D P E P P E R S G
P O L I J U H Y G B H J S A U S A G E S A Y G E M M N D R T
K K I P I Z Z A S A U C E I O P L M J U Y T U Y P I P I O O
T T Y U U J M N B G Y J I L O K M N H B L A C K O L I V E S
P E P P R R T Y U M O M N B O B G P E P P E R O N I K K L O
T O M T O O T O Y C A N A D I A N B A C O N T O P T A N E N
L P A R M E S A N C H E E S E O O N G H I T O T H E M O O N
S S R R T S H R I M P I O P R T H J I K L O P L K M N H T G
I O P R Y G V H J G R E E N P E P P E R S G L O O X Q G N B
O O P P P T R H N B V F R T G R E E N O N I O N S O I P L
K I M M N H Y U I O L K J H Y T G R F V R E D O N I O N S O
I L O K M N J Y H G M O Z Z A R E L L A C H E E S E O K M N
S A T U J I K K I J N H Y G F R C V Q B G T H J U M J H H A
I J U Y H T B A R B E C U E D C H I C K E N O P K I U J H Y
Y U J N H Y T G F R D E H A M A N D P I N E A P P L E O P L
```

Grandpa Frank's Pizza Toppings Word Search

Mozzarella cheese	Red peppers	Red onions	Crab
Parmesan cheese	Sausage	Black olives	Tuna
Mushrooms	Pepperoni	Pizza Sauce	Green onions
Green Peppers	Barbecued chicken	Ham and pineapple	
Anchovies	Canadian bacon	Shrimp	

```
A S T U N A B C E R T O T O T Y U M O L K B G R E D I L O P
Y Y O O U J K L G H T R E W B K U T R F E D P L K V C R A B
A N C H O V I E S P P L L M J U Y T R E W S D J H G F C F C
M U S H I L O P P K I Y R B V F N K M U S H R O O M S P K
U I R O T R E D G O P L L I D G O Y O R E D P E P P E R S G
P O L I J U H Y G B H J S A U S A G E S A Y G E M M N D R T
K K I P I Z Z A S A U C E I O P L M J U Y T U Y P I P I O O
T T Y U U J M N B G Y J I L O K M N H B L A C K O L I V E S
P E P P R R T Y U M O M N B O B G P E P P E R O N I K K L O
T O M T O O T O Y C A N A D I A N B A C O N T O P T A N E N
L P A R M E S A N C H E E S E O O N G H I T O T H E M O O N
S S R R T S H R I M P I O P R T H J I K L O P L K M N H T G
I O P R Y G V H J G R E E N P E P P E R S G L O O X Q G N B
O O P P P T T R H N B V F R T G R E E N O N I O N S O I P L
K I M M N H Y U I O L K J H Y T G R F V R E D O N I O N S O
I L O K M N J Y H G M O Z Z A R E L L A C H E E S E O K M N
S A T U J I K K I J N H Y G F R C V Q B G T H J U M J H H A
I J U Y H T B A R B E C U E D C H I C K E N O P K I U J H Y
Y U J N H Y T G F R D E H A M A N D P I N E A P P L E O P L
```

Grandpa Frank's Pizza Toppings Word Search

Mozzarella cheese	Red peppers	Red onions	Crab
Parmesan cheese	Sausage	Black olives	Tuna
Mushrooms	Pepperoni	Pizza Sauce	Green onions
Green Peppers	Barbecued chicken	Ham and pineapple	
Anchovies	Canadian bacon	Shrimp	

Pizza Theme Related Book Resources

Buehner, Caralyn
"A Job For Wittilda"
Publisher: Dial Books (For Young Readers)
Published: Date: c1993
It is an imaginative story. Whittilda has 48 stray cats. She needs a job to feed her cats. Her aunt hires her at the beauty shop. She doesn't do very well and is fired. She sees an ad in the paper to deliver pizza for Joe Dingaling. Many applicants come to apply for the job. He gives each applicant 5 pizzas to deliver. He states that the first one to come back from the delivery gets the job. Wittilda the witch gets the job and plenty of pizza to feed her cats. (ages 3-5)

Ellison, Emily
"Rocky Bobcky, The Pizza Man"
Publisher: Longstreet Press
Published Date: c1996
Rocky Bobocky is known to be the best pizza man in town. Passerby folks could see Rocky Bobocky spinning pizza dough. Rocky loves pizza and all Italian foods. He likes to sing and he loves his work. Rocky is not a businessman. He is good at his job, but he could not make enough money at what he loved doing so well. Betty, the neighbor, worked long hours for an accountant. She was too tired to cook, so she and her family went to Rocky's for pizza. Betty loses her job and becomes partners in Rocky's business. She keeps his books and her children make and deliver pizzas. They made the money to keep his pizza parlor open and Rocky continued to sing. (ages 3-6)

Flax, Larry
"The California Pizza Kitchen Cookbook"
Publisher: Hungry Minds
Published Date: c1996
The cookbook has instructions on how to make a good pizza crust for every kind of unusual and novelty pizza. (ages-adults cooking with children)

French, Vivian
"Mrs. Hippo's Pizza Parlor"
Publisher: Kingfisher
Published Date: c2004
This is a cute story about Mrs. Hippo's Pizza Parlor. She can't get clients to come to her pizza parlor until she advertises her business at the local beach. (ages 3-5)

Grunes, Barbara
"Skinny Pizzas"
Publisher: Surrey Books
Published Date: c1996
There are over 100 low-fat recipes in this book. Each recipe gives the nutritional data. There are a variety of pizza crusts and toppings. (ages-adults cooking with children)

Holub, Joan
"That Pizza That We Made"
Publisher: Viking/Puffin Books
Published Date: c2001
The cooks in this story are Suzanne, Max, and Jake. The book explains how to make a pizza and also has an excellent pizza recipe in the back of the book. (ages 5-6)

Hao, K.T.
"One Pizza, One Penny"
Publisher: Cricket Books
Published Date: c2003
Chris Croc is the baker of Heavenly Cakes and Ben Bear is the maker of wonderful pizzas. The two animal friends pass the gold coin back and forth as they share their pizza and cakes with each other, while competing on roadside stands. (ages 3-5)

Pienkowski, Jan
"Pizza! A Young pop-Up"
Publisher: Candlewick Press
Published Date: c2001
The animals make a pizza for the king. The king is a hungry lion. The flaps, tabs, and pop-ups are a movable feast. This book fascinates a small child. (ages 3-5)

Rey, Margret
"Curious George and The Pizza"
Publisher: Houghton Mifflin Company
Published Date: c1985
Curious George creates havoc in a pizza shop but redeems himself by making an unusual delivery. (ages 3-5)

Rockwell, Lizzy
"Angelina of Italy"
Publisher: Random House
Published Date: c2004
Angelina loves to eat pizza. She confuses the Leaning Tower of Pisa with pizza. Her father drives Angelina and her whole family to let Angelina to see the Leaning Tower of Pisa. Afterwards, the family went home and ate pizza (ages 4-6)

Trimble, Irene
"Ord Eats A Pizza"
Publisher: Random House
Published Date: c2000
A dragon is making a pizza. He isn't really sure what goes on a pizza, so he asks several people. Finally, with help, Ord makes his first pizza and shares it with his helpers. (ages 3-5)

50's Party

Mrs. Cola's 50's Story

I was born in the early 1940's and I remember many events of the 1950's. The fifties are reborn each year with parties, sock hops, and discussions about the 50's as a turning point to changing times. I remember my mother taking me to see Elvis Presley in Southern Michigan. We drove two hours to get to his show. He was not very well-known at the time. A half hour into the show my mother told me that the young man was a disgrace to society. She removed me from the crowd. As we walked back to the car, she lectured me and said, "A man wiggling his hips in such a suggestive manner is sinful." We drove home in silence. Little did my mother know that Elvis would soon be famous and rock and roll would be changing our lives forever. My husband and I watched the DVD "The Fabulous 50's." A woman interviewed in the 50's show spoke just like my mother. We found this clip to be funny as I could still hear my mother's words ringing in my ears from way back in 1958.

I have three 50's parties that I want to share with my readers in this chapter. I attended a 50's party for Grandma K. She turned 60 in January. The other two parties are a 50's party at home and a sock hop party at school.

I would like to start out with the fifties party with Grandma K. She sent out invitations to 90 of her favorite girlfriends and female family members. I might add that Grandma K is very popular because she is one of the most gracious and well-liked ladies I have ever met. I felt privileged to receive an invitation to participate in her party.

The invitation stated:
Grandma K was born on January 12, 1947.

On January 12, 2007,
Grandma K wants all her girlfriends
To help her turn sixty.

Please come at 11:30 a.m.
Grandma K's favorite Women's Club.
The address is:

r.s.v.p.
Grandma K's phone number or E-mail Address

Help Grandma K blow out the other fifty-nine candles.

Note: Tell the summary of the story or the poem because some of the facts are repeated.
I personally like the poem.

She has a picture of her first birthday with one candle. I never knew that Grandma K could be so cute in her high chair with those monstrous funny looking white tie shoes. At any rate, I arrived at 11:30 a.m. sharp for Grandma K's big 60th birthday bash as she celebrated with a 50's theme. Grandma likes things simple, but elegant. She is excellent at organizing any party. She had white tablecloths and a vase of red and white fresh flowers arranged in the center of each guest table. Grandma K greeted every guest and made everyone feel welcomed and very special. We had punch and conversation for about an hour. The lunch consisted of a very fancy salad with salmon, citrus fruit and a tropical salad dressing. Homemade rolls and mini pecan sweet rolls with butter accompanied the salad. A birthday cake and coffee were served for dessert. I purchased Grandma K a balloon saying 60 for her cake table. We also had plenty of ice water and conversation throughout the meal.

I thought that Grandma K had outdone herself but the party got better when she announced that a group called "Four Guyz in Dinner Jackets" were about to give everyone a thrill by singing all the old songs and imitating the ads and commercials in the 50's. They were excellent. The crowd got into the swing of the 50's and everyone had a great time. One of the young men from the group bent down in front of one of Grandma K's friends. He sang a favorite 50's song to her. She was in 7th heaven. The Four Guyz in Dinner Jackets called Grandma K up to the stage. She sat on a 50's stool as they sang her favorite 50's songs. She was wearing a red jacket suit and her 60's crown. Grandma K was full of smiles. Grandma K had to go bonkers to dream up such a fabulous 50's party.

I have often thought of Grandma K's birthday bash. It will stick in my mind for a long time. I have enjoyed all her fantastic parties, but this one was the best. Grandma K is really neat. I can't wait to see what she does for her 70th birthday party. Thank you Grandma K for such a wonderful time. I love you!

Grandma K Has Gone Bonkers at Her 60th Birthday Party Poem
Poem by Pat Nekola

Birthdays come and go-sometimes in a flash,
But Grandma K was determined her 60th would be a bash!

Grandma K turned sixty wearing her pretty purple crown,
She organized the 50's Theme party with her ideas down.

Round tables covered with linen cloths and pretty fresh flowers,
Takes your breath away as each guest enters the room at the hour.

She greets all her girlfriends in her pretty red outfit at the door.
Welcoming everyone and assures them there is more in store.

All guests were given name tags and became fast friends,
Visiting with each other until the party ends.

As we sit down at our assigned table,
One guest talks about her horse stable.

A German lady keeps the guests in stitches,
With all her funny stories and glitches.

Grandma K's mother-in-law is ever so sweet,
She is a beautiful lady that can't be beat.

After lunch the 50's entertainment begins with a 4-man quartet
Singing 50's music and reminding us of times we could never forget.

Professional pictures are taken for Grandma's K memory book,
Now all of her girlfriends and family can have a look.

Grandma K has gone bonkers and outdone herself,
As the memory book is placed on her shelf.

Grandma K your 50's party went by all too fast.
But I will always have memories with a trip to the past.

We thank you Grandma K for a great time,
We love you, because you are mighty fine.

```
G N M C D E S R P O P M U S I C S R O O T B E E R F L O A T
B J D V L I C J D O T S L V K W R M O D E R N I S M E E K W
H B K L R O E E K W H A M B U R G E R S H O T D O G S Q R J
Y B A N A N A S P L I T R S P G H U M P H E R Y B O G A R T
H C R S P G W Q R J H K A R O S O D A J E R K K J C P J K I
P K A R O S Q R T T N J J K J C P J K I Y G E G T F T T J H
S O D A P O P J K I Y G S O C K H O P H N A I J H V E J O F
Y G E G T F T T J H N A I J H V E J O F Y O T T J M T W Y J
N A I J H V P R E S I D E N T E I S E N H O W E R A H H I W
Y O T B I N G C R O S B Y H E L V I S P R E S L E Y N Y Q M
O I J H L M A R I L Y N M O N R O E Q M R O C K N R O L L R
I L O V E L U C Y M K L N E W L E I S U R E H F M H G G P L
K L C A R H O P E R C K H F M H G G P L I F G G H J W N W H
C K H F M H G G P L I E D S U L L I V A N S H O W G S F R I
C H O C O L A T E S H A K E S G S F R I L C B M G H F G O U
G M F S S G S F R I L C B M G H F G F R A N K S I N A T R A
L C B M G H F G O U U V H A F B U D D Y H O L L Y N K S W J
F R E N C H F R I E S Z M S Q N K S W J N M C D E S R Z L N
I Z M S Q N K S W J N D O C T O R S A L K D V L I C J D O T
```

50's Word Search

Humphery Bogart	Elvis Presley	Marilyn Monroe	RockNRoll
Popmusic	Frank Sinatra	Modernism	Doctor Salk
I Love Lucy	Ed Sullivan Show	New Leisure	Buddy Holly
Bing Crosby	President Eisenhower	Soda Pop	Sock Hop
Car Hop	Soda Jerk	French Fries	Hot Dogs
Hamburgers	Banana Split	Root Beer Float	Chocolate Shake

```
G N M C D E S R P O P M U S I C S R O O T B E E R F L O A T
B J D V L I C J D O T S L V K W R M O D E R N I S M E E K W
H B K L R O E E K W H A M B U R G E R S H O T D O G S Q R J
Y B A N A N A S P L I T R S P G H U M P H E R Y B O G A R T
H C R S P G W Q R J H K A R O S O D A J E R K K J C P J K I
P K A R O S Q R T T N J J K J C P J K I Y G E G T F T T J H
S O D A P O P J K I Y G S O C K H O P H N A I J H V E J O F
Y G E G T F T T J H N A I J H V E J O F Y O T T J M T W Y J
N A I J H V P R E S I D E N T E I S E N H O W E R A H H I W
Y O T B I N G C R O S B Y H E L V I S P R E S L E Y N Y Q M
O I J H L M A R I L Y N M O N R O E Q M R O C K N R O L L R
I L O V E L U C Y M K L N E W L E I S U R E H F M H G G P L
K L C A R H O P E R C K H F M H G G P L I F G G H J W N W H
C K H F M H G G P L I E D S U L L I V A N S H O W G S F R I
C H O C O L A T E S H A K E S G S F R I L C B M G H F G O U
G M F S S G S F R I L C B M G H F G F R A N K S I N A T R A
L C B M G H F G O U U V H A F B U D D Y H O L L Y N K S W J
F R E N C H F R I E S Z M S Q N K S W J N M C D E S R Z L N
I Z M S Q N K S W J N D O C T O R S A L K D V L I C J D O T
```

50's Word Search

Humphery Bogart	Elvis Presley	Marilyn Monroe	RockNRoll
Popmusic	Frank Sinatra	Modernism	Doctor Salk
I Love Lucy	Ed Sullivan Show	New Leisure	Buddy Holly
Bing Crosby	President Eisenhower	Soda Pop	Sock Hop
Car Hop	Soda Jerk	French Fries	Hot Dogs
Hamburgers	Banana Split	Root Beer Float	Chocolate Shake

The 50's Party in My Home

The second 50's party was in my home. We decorated our dining room walls with a 50's soda fountain theme plastic covering. The covering came in a package folded but is size 1-4x50 feet fifties scene. I used the same covering for the tablecloth. I used 3-9 inch plastic records, 6-13 inch and 1-22 inch dimensional 7 musical notes for on the wall and table, and 1 package containing 5-24 inch x 60.96cm hanging swirl record decorations for decorating the ceiling. We served hot dogs, French fries, ice cream drinks, tin roofs, and banana splits. We also had potato chips and popcorn served in bowls shaped from old 33 records by melting three of my husband's old records. The hot dogs, French fries and the dill pickle were served in an old fashioned boat dish with a piece of waxed paper to line the boat, just like in the 50's. I cleared out the dining room and placed the dining room table against the wall with the 50's theme. We had 50's music for the entertainment. We danced and sang the old 50's songs. We had a great time. See the picture on page 10 in the color section.

A 50's Party at School

The third party was at a school. We had a sock hop. We again decorated like the 50's. We used records for bowls. We served soda pop, potato chips, pretzels, and popcorn. The fifth graders had fun decorating the gym. We also talked to the students about the 50's decade and also how to be polite at a dance. The students also learned some of the old 50's dances and we had a hula hoop demonstration.

Sometime 5th and 6th grade age is a very awkward age for a dance. Some of the kids are shy, but, never the less, it is a good experience to learn socialization skills and have fun.

50's Party Menu Pop Up Signs
Yield: Six signs

6-2x2 inch (each) square wooden blocks
6- 3$\frac{1}{2}$ x 6$\frac{1}{2}$ inch (each) wooden signs
1 package size 4$\frac{1}{2}$ x $\frac{3}{8}$ x $\frac{1}{2}$ inch colored craft sticks (150 count)
1-12 ounce can gold metallic spray paint
3 packages (each) 1950's stickers
6-8$\frac{1}{2}$ inch lengths x $\frac{3}{4}$ inch wide (each) lime green or pink grosgrain ribbon
2 packages (each) 8 inch fabulous 50's plates (8 count)

Menu of the Day

Hot Dogs
French Fries
Root Beer Float
Tin Roof Sundae
Banana Split
Chocolate Shake

Spray paint the wooden signs and blocks on all sides with gold paint. Dry thoroughly. At random, place the fifties stickers on the wooden sign. Hot glue one craft sick 1½ inches onto the center back of the block. Hot glue the craft stick 2 inches down onto the center back of the sign. With hot glue, run a grosgrain ribbon horizontally around each block, midway up, joining ribbon on the back of the block. Place a 50's sticker in the front of each block, centered on the grosgrain. Hot glue the bottom of a fabulous 50's plate onto the front surface of the wooden sign. Run off 2 copies of the menu found on page 256 on pink paper. Cut out 2 of each food and 2 of Menu of the Day for each sign. There is a total of six menu items. Starting with the Menu of the Day, hot glue this label in the top center of the plate. Hot glue Banana Split, Chocolate Shake, and Tin Roof Sundae menu signs on the right side of the plate and French Fries, Hot Dogs, and Root Beer Float on the left side of the plate. Hot glue a second fabulous 50 plate onto the first plate, back to back. Place the 50's party menus on the decorated diner's soda bar. The guests can order off the menu as if they were at a restaurant. See the picture of the party guest table on page 10 in the color section.

Star and Poodle Napkin Holders

Yield: Three star napkin holders

3-5 x 5 x ½ napkin holders
3-4 x 6 inch pink and white stuffed animal poodles
3-24 inch long x 1 inch wide pink grosgrain
1-12 ounce can metallic gold spray paint
3 packages (each) sock hop beverage napkins (16 count)
1 package 50's stickers or pictures of movie stars from the 50's

Spray paint the outside, inside and bottom of each star napkin holder. Dry thoroughly. Place the right front foot of the poodle into the napkin holder. Tie a knot with the grosgrain ribbon going around the poodle's waist and entire sides of the napkin holder to hold the poodle in place. Decorate the star napkin holder with the 50's stickers or movie star's picture. Place the beverage napkins into the napkin holder next to the poodle. See the picture on page 10 in the color section.

Note: If you over bake the record, it will stick to the bowl and you will have to pry the record off the bowl. Stand by the oven and watch carefully. The record melts to the sides of the stainless steel bowl very quickly.

How to Make Bowls From 33 RPM Records

Yield: One bowl per 33 RPM speed record

1-33 RPM record
1-3 quart-size stainless steel bowl
1-50's beverage napkin per bowl

Preheat the oven to 350 F. Place the record over the stainless steel bowl and bake for 1 minute. The record will melt down the sides of the bowl. Shape the edges of records to form a ruffled effect. Remove from the bowl and cool thoroughly. See the picture on page 10 in the color section.

Note: A 3 pound box of hot dogs contains 30 hot dogs.

Food Served at a 50's Party

Hot Dogs

Yield: Eight hot dogs

1 package hot dogs (8 count)

Grill the hot dogs. Place a hot dog in a hot dog bun.

French Fries
Yield: Eight to ten servings

1-24 fluid ounce vegetable oil
1-28 ounce package shoestring French fried potatoes
Salt

Place 2 cups of oil into a deep frying pan. Heat the oil to 375 F. Place 3 cups of French fries into the hot oil at a time or fry French fries in a homestyle deep fat fryer. Fry the French fries until golden brown. Drain the French fries on a paper towel. Sprinkle with salt. Serve with a hot dog in a bun and a dill pickle spear stabbed with a long frilled toothpick in a paper boat-style 50's basket.

Root Beer Float
Yield: One root beer float

2 cups root beer
3 scoops vanilla ice cream
Two tall straws
1-50's beverage napkin

Place one cup root beer in the bottom of a tall glass. Add 3 scoops vanilla ice cream. Top with the remaining root beer. Serve with two straws and a 50's beverage napkin.

Note: I was not able to locate pineapple sauce at the grocery store. I made my own sauce. You may not need to use all of the cornstarch mixture to thicken the pineapple. Use your own judgment. I have two recipes for pineapple sauce. The first recipe is for a smaller crowd and the second pineapple recipe is for a larger crowd.

Pineapple Sauce Number One
Yield: One cup (4 servings)

1-8 ounce can crushed pineapple with juice
1 tablespoon sugar
1 tablespoon cornstarch
2 tablespoons cold water
$1/2$ teaspoon vanilla

In a small saucepan, mix together the crushed pineapple with juice and sugar. Bring to a boil. Mix the cornstarch into the water until the mixture is smooth. Slowly add the cornstarch mixture to the pineapple. Whisk the mixture while cooking until bubbly. Remove from the burner and stir in the vanilla. Cool thoroughly. Serve $1/4$ cup over each scoop of vanilla ice cream for each banana split.

Note: The larger can of pineapple has more juice than a smaller can.

Pineapple Sauce Number Two

Yield: Sauce for eight to nine banana splits (2$^1/_4$ cups)

$^1/_4$ cup sugar
1-20 ounce can crushed pineapple with juice
2 tablespoons cornstarch
$^1/_4$ cup water
1 teaspoon vanilla

In a medium saucepan, mix sugar with the crushed pineapple and juice. In a separate small bowl, whisk cornstarch into the water until smooth. Bring the pineapple to a soft boil and slowly whisk the cornstarch mixture into the pineapple mixture until slightly thickened. Remove the pineapple sauce from the burner. Stir in the vanilla. Cool thoroughly. Serve $^1/_4$ cup over each scoop of vanilla ice cream for each banana split.

Banana Split

Yield: One banana split

1 banana
1 scoop vanilla ice cream
1 scoop chocolate ice cream
1 scoop strawberry ice cream
$^1/_4$ cup pineapple sauce
$^1/_4$ cup hot fudge or chocolate sauce
$^1/_4$ cup strawberry sauce
Whipped cream
$^1/_4$ cup chopped nuts
3 maraschino cherries

Peel and split a banana lengthwise. Place a banana half on each side of the banana split dish. Place one scoop of each variety of ice cream (vanilla, chocolate, and strawberry) down the center of the dish. Top the vanilla ice cream with pineapple sauce; the chocolate ice cream with hot fudge; and the strawberry ice cream with the strawberry sauce. Put a small amount of whipped cream on top of each sauce. Sprinkle the nuts over the whipped cream. Top each scoop of ice cream with 1 maraschino cherry. See the picture on page 10 in the color section.

Note: Vanilla ice cream may be substituted for chocolate ice cream

Chocolate Shake

Yield: One tall glass (3 cup shake)

2 cups whole milk
3 scoops chocolate ice cream
$^1/_2$ cup chocolate syrup
$^1/_2$ cup chocolate malted milk powder
2 tall straws
1-50's beverage napkin

Place the milk, ice cream, syrup, and malted milk powder into the blender on medium high. Blend the ingredients together and pour into a tall glass. Serve with two straws and a 50's beverage napkin.

Note: You can substitute strawberry ice cream for the vanilla ice cream.

Strawberry Shake

Yield: One tall glass (3 cup shake)

2 cups whole milk
3 scoops vanilla ice cream
$^1/_2$ cup strawberry syrup
$^1/_2$ cup original malted milk powder
2 tall straws
1 50's beverage napkin

Place the milk, ice cream, syrup, and malted milk powder into the blender on medium high. Blend the ingredients together and pour into a tall glass. Serve with two straws and one 50's beverage napkin. See the picture on page 10 in the color section.

Vanilla Shake

Yield: One tall glass (3 cup shake)

2 cups whole milk
3 scoops vanilla ice cream
$^1/_2$ cup original malted milk powder
1 teaspoon vanilla
2 tall straws
1 50's beverage napkin

Place the milk, ice cream, malted milk powder and vanilla into the blender on medium high. Blend the ingredients together and pour into a tall glass. Serve with two straws and one 50's beverage napkin.

Tin Roof Sundae

Yield: One tin roof sundae

Two or three scoops vanilla ice cream
¹/₂ cup hot fudge
whipped cream
¹/₃ cup Spanish peanuts
1 maraschino cherry

Place the scoops of ice cream into a sundae dish. Top the ice cream with the hot fudge. Top the hot fudge with the whipped cream, Spanish nuts, and one cherry. Serve with a spoon. See the picture on page 10 in the color section.

50's Theme Related Book Resources

Hoobler, Dorothy
"The 1950's Music"
Publisher: Millbrook Press
Published Date: c2001
The book discusses music in the 1950's. (young adults)

Olivier, Suzannah
"Juicing Smoothies & Blended Drinks"
Publisher: Lorenz
Published Date: c2003
Check out the Banana and Berry Milkshake on page 17; Chocolate Brownie Milkshake on page 175; floats, a variety of milkshakes starting on page 161; drinks for kids pages 177-191 (ages-adults cooking with children)

Sharman, Margaret
"1950's"
The book takes the reader through the 1950's decade covering many topics such as movie stars and politicians.

Tchudi, Stephen
"Soda Popery: The History of Soft Drinks in America"
Publisher: Scribner
Published Date: c1993
"There are recipes for making and using soft drinks plus easy science experiments."

Warren, Dick
"The Complete Idiots Guide to Homemade Ice Cream"
Publisher: Alpha Books
Published Date: c2006
There are over 200 ice cream recipes including sundaes and drinks of the 50's. (ages-adult cooking with children)

Witzel, Michael
"Soda Pop! From Miracle Medicine to Pop Culture"
Publisher: Town Square books
Published Date: 1986
The book shows all the ads of the different sodas and tells how soda pop evolved from a medicine to a beverage. There are also old pictures of soda fountains at the pharmacy.
(ages-young adults)

A Theme Related DVD on the 50's Era

"The Fabulous 50's"
{Video recording}:
Publisher: Questar
Published Date: c2003
The two-hour show takes a walk through the era of 1950"s (ages-family)

Music CD's

"Billboards Top Rock 'n' Roll Hits, 1957"
{Sound recording}
Publisher: Rhino Records
Published Date: 1988

Presley, Elvis
"Loving You"
{Sound recording}
Publisher: RCA
Published Date: c1997

Presley, Elvis
"G.I. Blues"
{Sound recording}
Publisher: Paramont
Published Date: c1997

Note: The above sound recordings are ideal for a sock hop. (ages 10-14) For more information on Elvis Presley {Sound recordings} search his music at your local library.

Princess Party

The Story of Princess Oletta and Leonardo

Once upon a time there was a princess named Oletta who grew up in the castle with her parents and many helpers attending to her needs. Her Father, King William, and her Mother, Queen Victoria, adored and worshiped their little princess daughter. Her parents thought she could do no wrong. Life was good for their family. The peasants also loved the princess because she was so sweet and kind to everyone. Leonardo was one of the children who would play soccer in the courtyard. Princess Oletta watched Leonardo play soccer from her bedroom window. After the game she would meet Leonardo and they would sit and talk for hours. They became good friends. They seemed so young, but had many dreams. Leonardo thought it would be wonderful to be a famous knight while Oletta wanted to be close to her parents. She always wanted to please them and the people that loved her so much. Years went by and it was time for Oletta to marry. Her father called her to his chamber room and said, "We need to talk." I have a perfect prince picked out just for you. By next year my little princess will be married. Princess Oletta's heart ached. She never gave her parents a hard time. She wanted to honor her father's wishes but she loved Leonardo. She wondered how she could tell her father about her feelings. She remained silent and thought for now, that silence is golden. Princess Oletta returned to her room and wept. As far as she was concerned her happy life was over. Maybe she could pack up and run away, but where would she go? She wanted to marry Leonardo. She talked to the peasants about her predicament. They said, "we know, lets have a puppet show." The peasants suggested that she invite her father to watch her do her ballet act. Then in the show, they can tell the Queen and the King how much Oletta wanted to marry Leonardo. The princess agreed to the scheme. It would be worth a try. So, the schoolmaster stayed up several nights writing the script. The princess asked the master seamstress to make pink satin curtains for the stage and she checked with the scheduler to be sure the courtyard would be free. The date was set for November 4th. The cooks began to prepare a menu for the party. The princess never liked to eat meat, but she like any food with vegetables and fruit. Leonardo enjoyed eating chicken dishes of any style. The cooks agreed to come up with a great menu very soon. They promised the princess it would be a feast for her sparkling eyes and for the guests.

The seamstress began to make the curtains and the staff began to make the puppets and the stage setting. Some of the workers thought it would be a nice added touch to make silk bows to tie around the theater-style chairs for the performance. The finest silver goblets and serving pieces were polished to a shine for the special occasion. The cook's helper remembered that they had Princess Oletta's special tablecloth from her ballet party. It had been stored away for several years. He would check on the condition of the tablecloth and would try to use the cloth.

Everyone was so excited about the gathering in the courtyard. The entire castle crew was sworn to secrecy not to tell the king and queen the purpose of the party. The king and queen could not figure out why all the castle workers were in such good humor. Finally, the princess went to her father and mother to invite them to the ballet and puppet show. Her parents said that the party would be great fun.

The day came and everything was ready for the festive party and puppet show. The princess was hopeful that her father would understand her feelings and all would end in her favor.

Silent Thoughts from King William and Princess Oletta Poem
By Pat Nekola

With deep thoughts, I am convinced,
My Oletta will marry the selected Prince.

As I made my announcement to the princess,
My sweet and precious Princess Oletta only winced.

Oh what is a princess to do.
She absolutely had no clue.

The princess loved her father and wanted to obey,
Her heart ached as she wondered what to say.

The king's helper made a big guest list.
The princess wanted to run away and not be missed.

The queen arranged to make the bridal dress.
With satin material, pearls, lace and nothing less.

Princess Oletta said, "What about me"?
"I love another prince, can't you see?"

The baker volunteered to make a 7-foot wedding cake.
Princess Oletta said, "Please don't, my happiness is at stake."

The king planned to walk her down the aisle,
Wearing his finest jewels and dressed in style.

The castle workers worked hard to plan a puppet show.
They hoped the King would learn the wedding was not a go.

Courtyard Menu One

Prince Leonardo Chicken Snacks

Chicken Ala King in Potato Baskets

Princess Oletta's Garden Salad

Cook Roungie's Brown Bread and Decorated Butter Pad

Cook Gazel's Fig Pudding with Lemon Sauce

Queen Victoria's Favorite Éclair
Ring Adorned with Ballet Dancers

Baker Toozell's Princess Doll Cake and Quick Butter Frosting

Royal Petit Fours decorated with Rose Buds

Aunt Olestra's Pie Roll ups

Tea and Apple Juice

Prince Leonardo's Chicken Snacks

Yield: Fifty-six chicken snacks

1-13.8 ounce can pizza crust
$\frac{1}{2}$ cup margarine
2-13 ounce (each) chicken breast packed in water, chopped
2 tablespoons green onions,finely diced
1 cup julienne carrots
1 tablespoon minced garlic
$\frac{1}{2}$ cup celery, diced
$\frac{1}{2}$ cup cucumber, peeled, seeds removed, and diced
1 cup Monterey Jack Cheese
1-16 ounce jar Kraft® sandwich spread
1 cup broccoli flowerets, chopped
1 cup black olives, drained and sliced
1 cup large green olives with pimento, sliced
1 red pepper, diced
1-11x17 inch jelly roll pan

Preheat the oven to 375 F. Grease an 11x17 inch pan. Stretch the pizza crust out to fit the pan. Bake the crust for 6-8 minutes or until golden brown. Cool. Spread the butter over the crust. Drain the chicken breast. Add the onions, carrots, garlic, celery, cucumber, and cheese to the chicken. Moisten with the sandwich spread. Spread the chicken salad over the buttered crust. Garnish chicken snack with the broccoli, black olives, green olives and red pepper. Cut the chicken snacks into 7x8 squares to make 56 pieces. Serve snacks on a large tray lined with a doily.

Note: The Chicken Ala King can be served over rice or biscuits instead of inside the potato basket. Purchase the Potato baskets from your grocery store.

Chicken Ala King in Potato Baskets

Yield: Twelve servings

$^1/_2$ cup butter, melted
4 cups cooked chicken, cubed
1-8 ounce package mushrooms, sliced
1 bunch green onion, chopped
1 green pepper, diced
1 red pepper, diced
$^1/_2$ teaspoon salt
$^1/_4$ teaspoon pepper
2 teaspoons curry powder
2 cups fat free half and half
1 cup frozen peas, thawed
1 cup frozen carrots slices, thawed
1-14 ounce can chicken broth
6 tablespoons cornstarch
12 potato baskets

Melt butter in a large frying pan and sauté the chicken. Add the mushrooms, green onions, green and red peppers; cook until tender. Add the salt, pepper, curry powder, cream, peas, and carrots. Cook over low heat for about 5 minutes. Whisk the cornstarch into the chicken stock. Slowly add the cornstarch chicken stock mixture to the chicken dish, stirring constantly until thickened remove from the heat. Just before serving, fill the individual potato baskets with the Ala King dish. Serve hot.

Princess Oletta's Garden Salad

Yield: Twelve servings

1 pound broccoli flowerets
1 red pepper diced
1 red onion sliced
2 tomatoes, chopped
$^1/_2$ cup julienne carrots
2 cups mozzarella cheese, divided
1 cup Italian low fat dressing
10 black olives

Clean broccoli. Add the red pepper, onion, tomatoes, carrots and 1 cup of cheese. Pour dressing over the salad and toss. Place the salad into a bowl. Sprinkle 1 cup of cheese over the top of the salad. Garnish with the olives. Chill until serving time.

Cook Roungie's Brown Bread

Yield: Eight servings

2 cups flour
1 cup cold water
1 teaspoon honey
$^1/_2$ cup molasses
1 egg
$^1/_2$ cup dark brown sugar
1 teaspoon baking soda
1 teaspoon cinnamon
1 teaspoon cloves
$^1/_2$ teaspoon nutmeg
$^1/_4$ teaspoon salt
$1^1/_4$ cup raisins
2 tablespoons butter, melted
4 emptied and clean 16 ounce cans
1-12 inch doily

Preheat the oven to 350 F. Combine the flour, water, honey, molasses, egg, sugar, baking soda, cinnamon, cloves, nutmeg, salt, and raisins. Stir slightly cooled butter into the mixture. Grease and flour four 16 ounce cans. Divide the batter among the four cans and fill each can half full. Bake for 35-45 minutes or until toothpick inserted in the center of the bread comes out clean. Cool for 10 minutes. Cut the bottom of the can open and slide the bread through. Cool thoroughly. Slice bread and arrange on a 12 inch platter lined with a doily. Serve with decorated butter pads.

Decorated Butter Pads

Yield: Twenty-four butter pads

1 Pound butter

Cut 3 sticks of butter into 8 pieces. Place the butter pads on a glass plate. Beat the 1 stick of butter until creamy. Place a butter into the cake decorating bag. With a number 30 tip, pipe a star in the center of each butter pad. Chill the butter pads until just before serving.

Note: Each custard cup holds ¹/₂ cup water.

Cook Gazel's Fig Pudding

Yield: Twelve custard cups

¹/₂ cup shortening
¹/₄ cup butter
1 cup granulated sugar
2 eggs
2 cups flour
1 teaspoon baking soda
1 teaspoon cloves
1 teaspoon cinnamon
¹/₄ teaspoon salt
1 teaspoon white vinegar
¹/₂ cup sour milk
1 teaspoon vanilla
1-12 ounce package fresh figs, chopped (1-3/4 cups)
12 Pyrex® custard cups

Preheat the oven to 375 F. Cream the shortening, butter, and sugar together. Add the eggs and blend well. Add the flour, baking soda, cloves, cinnamon, and salt to the mixture and stir well. Add the vinegar to the milk. Slowly blend the sour milk into the batter. Add the vanilla and beat the mixture until creamy. Fold in the figs. Fill each greased custard cup half full with the batter. Place the custard cups into a 12x15 inch roasting pan in a water bath with ³/₄ hot water in the bottom of the pan. Bake for 1 hour and 30 minutes. The bottom of the pudding will be slightly soft. Cool in the custard cup for 5 minutes. Turn each fig pudding out of its custard cup onto a large plate. Serve with lemon sauce.

Lemon Sauce
Yield: Twelve servings

1 cup lemon juice
3 tablespoons cornstarch
$^1\!/_2$ cup honey
$^1\!/_2$ cup sugar
2 cups water
2 tablespoons butter
12 maraschino cherries, drained
1-2.25 ounce package sliced almonds
1-1 ounce package mint leaves

Place the lemon juice into a saucepan. Whisk the cornstarch into the lemon juice. Cook on medium heat. Add the honey, sugar, water and butter. Continue to whisk the sauce until the mixture is thickened. Drizzle warm lemon sauce over each fig pudding. Garnish with 1 maraschino cherry in the top center of the fig pudding with 7 sliced almonds around each cherry to form a flower and 2 mint leaves on each side of the flower. Place 3-3$^1\!/_2$ inch doilies in the center of each glass dessert plate to form a circle. Place one garnished fig pudding over the doilies in the center of the plate. Serve as a dessert.

Queen Victoria's Favorite Éclair
Ring Adorned with Ballet Dancers
Yield: One éclair ring

1 cup butter
$^1\!/_4$ teaspoon salt
1 cup boiling water
1 cup flour
4 eggs
Bundt pan
1 recipe of vanilla pudding
1 recipe of fudge glaze
6 ballet figures
1 wedding cake candle

Add the butter and salt to the boiling water. Stir over the medium heat and bring the mixture to a boil. Turn the temperature down to medium heat. Add the flour. Stir vigorously to form a ball. Remove the mixture from the heat and beat in the eggs, one at a time. Do not grease the bundt pan. Spread the éclair mixture around the bottom of the bundt pan. Bake at 400 F for 45-55 minutes or until firm to the touch and golden brown. Cool for ten minutes in an area where there is no draft. Gently remove the éclair ring from the bundt pan and cool the ring completely. When the ring is cold, cut crosswise the ring to form a top and bottom and remove any extra wet dough. Fill the bottom of the ring with the vanilla pudding. Place the top of the ring over the vanilla pudding. Frost the top of the éclair with the fudge glaze and garnish with ballet dancer figures on top of the éclair and wedding cake candle in the center.

Vanilla Pudding

Yield: One cream puff ring

4 cups milk
1 cup sugar
6 tablespoons cornstarch
$1/4$ teaspoon salt
4 egg yolks
1 teaspoon vanilla
1 tablespoon butter

In the top of a double boiler, add the milk. Bring the milk to a boil. Mix together the sugar, cornstarch, and salt. Slowly add the dry ingredients stirring constantly and cook until bubbly. Remove from the heat. Beat the egg yolks. Add at least $1/3$ cup pudding to the egg yolks and beat together. Return the egg yolk/ pudding mixture to the remaining pudding mixture in the top of the double boiler. Continue to cook the pudding, stirring constantly until thickened. Add the vanilla and butter. Cool thoroughly. Spread pudding over the bottom of the cream puff ring. Cover the pudding with the top of the ring. Frost the ring with the fudge glaze. Decorate with 6 ballet dancers in honor of the princess.

Note: Do not over beat the fudge frosting or the frosting will turn too hard to spread on the éclair ring. The frosting should be soft. It will firm up as the frosting sits on the éclair ring. You can also use Adele's Chocolate Frosting found on page 336 instead of the Chocolate Fudge Glaze.

Chocolate Fudge Glaze

Yield: Frosting for one cream puff ring

2 cups sugar
2 tablespoons corn syrup
3-1 ounce (ea.) pre-melted chocolate
$1/2$ cup evaporated milk
1 teaspoon vanilla
2 tablespoons butter
2 packages of decorative ballet dancers on a half ball (4 per package)
1 package wedding cake candles (2 count)
1-4 inch stout white candle
Glue gun
Hot glue stick

In a heavy saucepan, combine the sugar, corn syrup, chocolate and milk. Stir continuously until it forms a soft ball by dropping a little of the mixture into cold water. Remove the pan from the heat. Add the vanilla and the butter and stir. With the hand mixer, beat the frosting in the pan for only 1 minute or beat the frosting by hand. Frost the éclair ring. Decorate the ring with 6 miniature ballet dancers. Level off the top of the candle. Hot glue a wedding cake candle onto the top of the stout candle. Place a dab of frosting in the center hole of the cream puff ring. Place the candle in the center of the ring. See picture on page 11 in the color section.

Note: I use an old 6 cup size Jell-O® mold from my mother's collection. Doll cake molds can be purchased at a cake-decorating center. Follow instructions for best results. The copper tube placed in the middle of the cake lets out the steam so that the cake can bake evenly and will not be doughy in the middle of the cake.

Baker Toozell's Princess Doll Cake
Yield: One Doll Cake

2 cups flour
2 teaspoons baking powder
$^1/_2$ teaspoon salt
$^1/_2$ cup shortening
1$^1/_2$ cups sugar
1 teaspoon vanilla
$^3/_4$ cup water
4 egg whites
2 drops gel base pink food coloring
Doll cake pan
8 inch cardboard cake circle covered with light pink foil
6 inch copper tube

Preheat the oven to 350 F. Mix the flour, baking powder, and salt together. Cream the shortening with the sugar and add the vanilla. Beat until smooth and creamy. Alternate the dry ingredients with the water. Stir in the pink food coloring. Place a 6 inch copper tube into the middle of the cake pan. Pour the cake batter into a greased and floured doll cake mold around the copper tube. Bake for 55-65 minutes or until cake springs back up with touch. Cool the cake for 10 minutes. Turn out onto the 8 inch cake circle covered with light pink foil. See picture on page 11 in the color section.

Note: I pulled the hair away from the princess face. Be creative when decorating the doll cake.

Quick Crumb Coat Butter Frosting

Yield: One doll cake

$^1/_2$ cup butter
3 cups powdered sugar
4 tablespoons cream
1 teaspoon almond flavoring
$^1/_4$ teaspoon salt
1 doll pick cake decoration
1 miniature pink crown
Hot glue gun
Hot glue stick

Cream the butter with the powdered sugar. Add the cream, almond flavoring, and salt. Beat until smooth and creamy. Frost the cake with the crumb coat frosting. Refrigerate for 1 hour. Braid the sides of the hair and attach to the top of the doll's head. Hot glue the pink crown onto the head of the doll pick. Place the doll pick into the center of the cake. Make the Cake Decorating Frosting to complete the doll.

Cake Decorating Frosting

Yield: One pound

$^1/_2$ cup butter
$^1/_2$ cup shortening
1 pound powdered sugar
$^1/_2$ teaspoon almond flavor
$^1/_4$ teaspoon salt
2 tablespoons plus 2 teaspoons water

Cream the butter and shortening together. Add the powdered sugar, almond, salt, and water. Beat the frosting until smooth and creamy. With a number 30 tip, pipe frosting stars around the entire skirt of the dress and the doll's bodice. Color remaining frosting pink by adding 1 drop of pink food coloring and mixing well. Using a number 104 rose tip, make a bow around the doll's waist. Using a number 129 flower tip, at random, place flowers on the doll's skirt.

Note: Bake the petit fours at 300 F to prevent the cake from puffing up in the middle. It will take longer to bake at the lower temperature. To prevent waste, cut the entire 11x17 cake pan into 1x2 inch shapes. If you choose to cut cake into hearts and 1x2 inch pieces, you will have odd-shaped pieces of cake left over. You can use these extra pieces to make parfaits. Mix extra cake pieces into 1 pound of vanilla pudding. Divide the mixture among dessert goblets and top each with non-dairy whipped topping and a strawberry.

Royal Petit Fours Decorated with Rose Buds

Yield: Nine heart shaped and forty-six 1x2 inch petit fours

2-18.25 (each) French vanilla cake mixes
6 eggs
Water
Oil
1-11x7 sheet cake pan
No-stick baking spray
Heart shaped cookie cutter

Preheat oven to 300 F. Grease the pan with the no-stick baking spray. In a 5 quart mixer, mix together the cake mixes, eggs, water, and oil until smooth and creamy. Spread the cake batter evenly into the cake pan. Bake for 45-55 minutes or until the toothpick inserted in the center of the cake comes out clean. Cool cake thoroughly. With a heart shape cookie cutter, cut the petit fours into hearts and 1x2 inch pieces. Frost the petit fours with the glaze frosting below.

Note: As you work with the glaze you may have to reheat the glaze if it gets thick. Individual petit fours can be placed into small pink or white muffin liners. I personally prefer not to use the muffin liners.

Petit Four Glaze Frosting

Yield: Three pounds

3 pounds powdered sugar
$^3/_4$ cup water
$^3/_4$ cup light corn syrup
$2^1/_2$ teaspoons almond extract
2 tablespoons hot water
1-10 ounce jar strawberry jam

In a large pan, place powdered sugar, water, corn syrup, and almond extract. Stir the ingredients together until mixture is smooth. Add 1 tablespoon hot water at a time and stir until the mixture can be poured over individual petit fours. Lay two long pieces of waxed paper over the countertop. Place cooling racks over the waxed paper. Cut the hearts crosswise. Spoon the strawberry jam over the bottom layer of the heart. Place the top of the heart over the jam to make a sandwich. Drizzle the glaze over the top and sides of each heart and 1x2 inch petit fours. Excess glaze will run off of each petit four. Scrape off the excess glaze from the waxed paper and reheat to soften the glaze as needed. The glaze on each petit fours should slightly harden. Make the butter cream frosting on page 73 to decorate each petit four. Using a number 104 tip, pipe on each petit fours with a pink rose bud. Using a number 352 tip, pipe on two leaves per petit four (one leaf on each side of the rose bud). Just before serving, place the doll cake onto the middle of a large oval mirror and place the petit fours around the doll.

Aunt Olestra's Story

Aunt Olestra was a motherly type. She mothered every person in the castle. She particularly loved the children and would have little cooking classes for them. She thought the puppet show would be a great idea. To get the children involved she had them make pie treats. She also thought that she could please the queen and king with the treats. She learned that children do not like almond paste, but liked anything with apples and strawberry jelly or jam. The children made the apple and strawberry treats for the children and the almond treats for the adults. The children enjoyed rolling out the pie dough and filling the treats. They were very excited about participating in the party.

Aunt Olestra's Pie Roll-ups

Yield: Twenty-four pie roll-ups

Pie Crust Recipe
4 cups flour
1 teaspoon salt
2 teaspoon sugar
2 cups shortening
1 tablespoon white vinegar
1 egg, beaten
$\frac{1}{2}$ cup ice water
1-4 inch cookie cutter

In a large bowl, mix flour, salt and sugar. Blend shortening into flour mixture until pea-size pieces form. Add vinegar and the egg to the water and blend into flour mixture until dough holds together. In between two pieces of waxed paper or on a lightly floured counter top, roll the pie dough out to approximately $\frac{1}{8}$ inch thick. Cut out the dough with the cookie cutter into 24 circles. Put the extra dough back into the bowl. Fill the pie treats with one or two fillings of choice listed below.

Apple Jelly Filling

Yield: Filling for twenty-four pie roll-ups

1 cup apple jelly
2 tablespoons light brown sugar
2 tablespoons butter, melted
1 teaspoon apple pie spice

In a medium size bowl, combine the jelly, brown sugar, butter, and apple pie spice. Whisk the ingredients together. Spread apple jelly mixture over each pie circle within $\frac{1}{4}$ inch of the circle's edge. Starting at the edge of the pie circle, roll up the circle into a cigar shape and pinch the edges shut. Bake at 400 F for 15 minutes or until golden brown on the bottom of the pie roll-up.

Almond Paste Filling

Yield: Filling for twelve to sixteen pie roll-ups

$^1/_3$ cup sliced almonds
1 teaspoon butter, melted
1-1 ounce package pre-melted unsweetened chocolate
$^1/_2$ teaspoon almond flavor
l-8 ounce can pure almond paste

In a small bowl, add the almonds, butter, chocolate, and almond flavor to the almond paste. Beat by hand until all the ingredients are blended well. Roll the almond paste into a small cigar shape. Roll out the dough and cut the dough with the 4 inch cookie cutter. Place the almond paste in the center of the pie dough circle. Starting at the end of the pie circle, roll the circle into a cigar shape and pinch the edges shut. Bake at 400 F for 15 minutes or until golden brown on the bottom of the pie roll-up.

Note: The children liked using strawberry jam or red currant jelly. It is quick and easy. Follow the directions for cutting and rolling out the apple jelly roll-ups. Use a plain jam or jelly straight from the jar. The baking time is the same for all the pie roll-ups.

Note: It is best to mix the glaze in small batches for best results.

Pie Roll-up Glaze

Yield: Glaze for eight to ten pie roll-ups

$^1/_2$ teaspoon almond flavoring
1 tablespoon butter, melted
1 tablespoon water
$^1/_4$ teaspoon salt
1 cup powdered sugar
1-2 ounce jar red sprinkles

In a small bowl, add the almond flavoring, butter, water, and salt to the powdered sugar. Stir until smooth and creamy. Cover a cookie sheet with waxed paper. Place the cooling rack over the waxed paper. Drizzle glaze over each pie roll-up immediately after the pie roll-up is baked. Sprinkle red sprinkles over the top of the glaze before the glaze hardens. Place the pie roll-ups on a 14 inch serving tray lined with doily or use an oval glass mirror. Serve at room temperature.

Tea and Apple Juice

Yield: One gallon tea and apple juice

Purchase the apple juice and place the juice into a pitcher. Make up the tea according to the packaged directions. Serve the juice cold and the tea hot.

Simple Brunch

A simple brunch could be fun for the family. Basically buy everything pre-made. Cover the buffet. Arrange the food. Make a pot of coffee and brew some tea. I did a party with each menu. This simple party was lovely. We did the play at both parties. I like to cook and bake so I thoroughly enjoyed doing the more elaborate party. I must tell you that within one hour, the easy brunch buffet was ready for serving.

Courtyard Menu Two

Cheese and Meat Tray

Fruit tray with Cantaloupe and Green and Red Grapes

Wheat and White Bagels

Strawberry, Honey Nut and Salmon Cream Cheese Spread

English muffins, Butter and Jam

Cranberry Bread

Apple Kringle

Brown Bread with Butter and Margarine

Orange and Cranapple Juice

Coffee, Tea, and Milk

```
U J H Y T F R S H I R X U K M C I N D E R E L L A O M V A S
S L E E P I N G B E A U T Y A G P W O D Q S O W K I A Z W P
Y H G B V G D T D B K W S I E W O O P C H A R M I N G L E O
T F R D E V E I U C E L E B R A T I O N I T E T J O E X R I
A D M I R E J W L Y A L L P D O P P W P R I N C E I R O R C
J H Y G F F M O E S L C D C P X W O E O O C W O F U T R T W
T T G K I N G T W L Q K K J O J P W O O W O E I O R A T D E
K K I J Y T D B A E O A P A L A C E P R I N C E S S I M P T
Y T T R F Y U M I C V I A W C A P Z W I S O G W E W O G W O
I J J B G F P Q U E E N P E P O O A Y O U R H I G H N E S S
U Y H G F K I N G D O M L O O P W O O P M I O W S S W W O W
Y Y H N G R O Y A L F A M I L Y W P M W L I W E W O O P I O
U U H T G R F E O P C R O W N S P M P T A E E O O I E O X E
M J U Y H B G D S L E Y S S W R O Y A L B A L L E R A E C I
H Y T G R F S P I W U O L L D O M A I N X O G T I N A I E F
U U J H T G Z Y Q W R I F B Z C H A O P P W W G N H A J Q A
F A I R Y T A L E O F L K Q O J O W P W O L E N G A S A O O
I Y T O R Y W C W B J P N W P H J E W E L S O A S E C D I J
J U H F T F W E C A R R I A G E T S S H O S S W G M F E S
Q W E Y E T O E O M C A S T L E T G Y C G I C L E F N M W P
```

Princess and Prince Word Search

Prince	Princess	Palace	King
Kingdom	Celebration	Carriage	Your Highness
Fairy Tale	Royal Ball	Domain	Sleeping Beauty
Admire	Charming	Queen	Cinderella
Crown	Jewels	Castle	Royal Family

```
U J H Y T F R S H I R X U K M C I N D E R E L L A O M V A S
S L E E P I N G B E A U T Y A G P W O D Q S O W K I A Z W P
Y H G B V G D T D B K W S I E W O O P C H A R M I N G L E O
T F R D E V E I U C E L E B R A T I O N I T E T J O E X R I
A D M I R E J W L Y A L L P D O P P W P R I N C E I R O R C
J H Y G F F M O E S L C D C P X W O E O O C W O F U T R T W
T T G K I N G T W L Q K K J O J P W O O W O E I O R A T D E
K K I J Y T D B A E O A P A L A C E P R I N C E S S I M P T
Y T T R F Y U M I C V I A W C A P Z W I S O G W E W O G W O
I J J B G F P Q U E E N P E P O O A Y O U R H I G H N E S S
U Y H G F K I N G D O M L O O P W O O P M I O W S S W W O W
Y Y H N G R O Y A L F A M I L Y W P M W L I W E W O O P I O
U U H T G R F E O P C R O W N S P M P T A E E O O I E O X E
M J U Y H B G D S L E Y S S W R O Y A L B A L L E R A E C I
H Y T G R F S P I W U O L L D O M A I N X O G T I N A I E F
U U J H T G Z Y Q W R I F B Z C H A O P P W W G N H A J Q A
F A I R Y T A L E O F L K Q O J O W P W O L E N G A S A O O
I Y T O R Y W C W B J P N W P H J E W E L S O A S E C D I J
J U H F T F T W E C A R R I A G E T S S H O S S W G M F E S
Q W E Y E T O E O M C A S T L E T G Y C G I C L E F N M W P
```

Princess and Prince Word Search

Prince	Princess	Palace	King
Kingdom	Celebration	Carriage	Your Highness
Fairy Tale	Royal Ball	Domain	Sleeping Beauty
Admire	Charming	Queen	Cinderella
Crown	Jewels	Castle	Royal Family

Cast of Puppet Characters

Narrator: The class teacher or an older student

King William	Rose
Queen Victoria	Treasure Box
Trumpet Trio	Butterfly Halo
School Master	Leonardo
Princess Oletta	Tree I (Shade Tree)
Cousin Frog Princess	Tree II (Fir Tree)
Dragon	Clouds
Judge Diplomat	Mrs. Mouse
Dancing Tulips	Moon and Stars
Selected Prince	Bride and Groom
Rainbow	Happy Hearts/ sign saying The End

Note: The Castle workers are the actors from the audience.

Note: This play is ideal for the 3rd grade class. Have a teacher narrate the play and assign the children to an individual puppet. Give each child the script to follow along with the play so that each child will know when to hold up their puppet on the stage. Assign children to be the castle workers. Before doing the play, read the script out loud with the class. Rehearse the play. Invite families to come into school to see the play.

The Castle Script for the Puppet Show and Fairy Tale Play

<u>Scene I</u>

Castle Workers:	As they bow and wave flags, they yell, Hail to the king!
King:	The king waves and smiles at the crowd and takes his seat in the front row.
Queen:	The queen throws kisses to the castle workers as she walks down the aisle in the courtyard.
School Master:	Today Princess Oletta will perform a beautiful ballet dance. Let's hear it for the Princess.
Castle Workers:	Applaud

Princess Oletta:	Thank you schoolmaster for the fine introduction.
Ballet dance:	The nutcracker music begins as she does her dance.
Castle Workers:	After the dance is finished, the castle workers applaud again.
School Master:	Now here is a special puppet show in honor of the princess.
Princess:	I welcome everyone to the puppet show and thank all the workers for making it possible. Thank you, Mother and Father for being here today. I love you very much.
Tree Number I:	I am the tree that shades my beautiful princess.
Cousin Frog Princess: (Pink color)	I am the frog that saw the princess and Leonardo hold hands. You looked so happy together.
Tree Number II:	I am the big fir tree that helped you hide as you visited with Leonardo.
Tulips:	The tulips dance on stage to honor the princess and are hopeful Leonardo will be soon be Oletta's groom.
Mr. Dragon:	If you don't want to marry the selected prince, I can eat him alive.
Princess Oletta:	Oh please, Mr. Dragon, that isn't necessary or very nice.
The Rose:	I saw Leonardo give Princess Oletta a rose to confirm his love for her.
The King:	I have chosen a prince to be Princess Oletta's husband.
Castle Workers:	Let the judge handle this sticky situation!
Judge Diplomat:	Your Highness how did you come to pick this prince?
King:	The prince's father and I are good friends and businessmen. If my daughter marries my friend's son, I will inherit a kingdom and a huge treasure.
Treasure Box:	I am the large treasure. The treasure box laughs rudely and loudly.

Queen Victoria:	Oh! King William! You convinced me that the prince would be a wonderful and caring husband and that he would protect our little darling. You have deceived me. I am so sad. Tears roll down the queen's cheeks and with handkerchief in hand, the queen is sobbing and asking the King how could she ever forgive him for his greedy motives.
Judge Diplomat:	Where is this selected prince now, your Highness?
King William:	He was not invited to the party today. I have other plans for his introduction to my daughter.
Judge Diplomat:	Is Leonardo here today?
Princess Oletta:	The princess interrupts. He is hiding with the tulips and waiting patiently for the outcome of today. I love him and I want to be with him forever.
Judge Diplomat:	My dear princess, why have you not told your father of this until now?
Princess Oletta:	I have always obeyed my father. I never wanted to disappoint or hurt him. My happiness is at stake. All I want is to be with Leonardo and to be happy.
Castle Workers	Chanting and repeating the phrase: Bring in Leonardo now.
Judge Diplomat:	Very well, let's have Leonardo appear now. The judge turns to Leonardo and commands: State your name.
Leonardo:	My name is Leonardo.
Judge Diplomat:	How do you know the princess?
Leonardo:	I have known her since we were children.
Judge Diplomat:	Do you wish to marry the princess?
Leonardo:	Yes!
King William:	That can't be. Why didn't I know of this?
Castle Workers:	(Chanting) Princess, tell the king how you feel.
Princess Oletta:	I always loved Leonardo, but I never wanted to disappoint you, Father. I want to marry Leonardo.

Judge Diplomat:	King William, your selfish motives are not acceptable. Everyone must think of others and try to understand their feelings. Don't you agree, King William?
King William:	Well, I never thought of it like that before. I have always been in charge. I generally get what I want. Besides, it is unheard of to have a Princess select her own prince. As the King and as her father, I think I know best.
Judge Diplomat:	Really!! I don't think I quite understand your statement, your Highness.
Queen Victoria:	Please, darling William, if marrying Leonardo is what Oletta wants and needs to be happy, then we must let her marry the man of her choice. I will forgive you for your selfish act if our Princess is granted her wish.
Selected Prince:	Everyone is shocked when the selected prince arrives at the scene. He charges down the center aisle.
Castle workers:	Gasp loudly.
Clouds:	Shake and shiver
Judge Diplomat:	Present yourself, Selected Prince. What do you think about this situation?
Selected Prince:	A message was sent to me. I do not want to marry King William's daughter. I want to marry someone else. Oh please! Judge, please, listen to my plea.
Judge Diplomat:	Well, that settles things very quickly. Princess Oletta can marry Leonardo. Usher out the selected prince immediately. Thank you for coming and helping us solve this dilemma.
Trumpets Trio:	The trumpets play as the Selected Prince is ushered out the courtyard. Continue to play trumpets to support for the marriage of Princess Oletta and Leonardo.
Queen Victoria:	The food is ready for the big celebration in honor of the princess and her bright future with Leonardo. Raise your flags to the princess and hail to the king.
Castle Workers:	Hail to the king. We hope you will accept Leonardo as your son-in-law and we wish much happiness for Princess Oletta and Leonardo.
Trumpets Trio:	Trumpet players play a processional song as the audience leaves the area to go to the big celebration.

Castle Workers:	Whispering, the castle workers say, "Oh! Princess Oletta, we did it. Congratulations!"
The Trees & The Tulips:	The trees and tulips quietly talk amongst each other. Just think, we were instrumental in developing a beautiful romance.
Butterflies Halo:	Flutter their happy wings and make a halo as they fly over the princess's head and telling her you are going to have a very happy life.
The Rainbow:	Somewhere over the rainbow sweet Princess Oletta, you now have your wish granted.
Mrs. Mouse:	Runs back to her hole cheerfully singing Oletta will marry Leonardo

SCENE II

Day of Wedding;	The Princess and Leonardo beam with happiness. Her father finally consents to the marriage and takes her down the aisle to meet Leonardo. The couple lived happily ever after.
The Moon & Stars:	Oh princess Oletta and Leonardo, we do wish to give you many evenings with a summer breeze as you gaze at the stars and the moonlight.
Bride and Groom in the carriage:	Flash the bride and groom on the stage in the carriage.
Closing Song:	"Here Comes the Bride"
Happy Heart:	Flash the happy heart to end the show.

The End

Note: All larger puppets will be fastened to a wooden stake and the smaller puppets will be fastened to a wooden spoon.

How to Make the Pop-ups and Puppets

King William Puppet

Yield: One king puppet

1 Garfield stuffed animal dressed like a king with a crown
1-12x1 inch wooden stake
Glue gun
Hot glue stick
Thread

Hot glue the stake onto the back of the king. Wrap thread around the body of the king and the stake for extra support. See picture on page 11 in the color section.

Queen Victoria Puppet

Yield: One queen

1 leopard cat stuffed animal
2 sparkling gold pipe cleaners
30 inches long x 2 inches wide white fur
1-1 inch circle purple lace
1-12x1 inch wooden stake
Glue gun
Hot glue stick

With a pipe cleaner, make a 2½ inch circle. Intertwine the edges of the pipe cleaner together to hold the circle intact. Cut off the extra length of the pipe cleaner. At the side of the circle, bend the pipe cleaner to form 4 v peaks to complete the formation of the crown. Hot glue the crown onto the queen's head. Place a 10 inch plate onto the material. Trace and cut out the circle. Cut a 6½ inch slit down the center of the circle. Pinch 4-6 pleats to make the cape look gathered. Place the cape around the neck of the cat and hot glue in place. Wrap the fir around the neck of the cat and tie the fir into a knot. Hot glue the stake onto the cat on the front tummy area between the paws and underneath the fur tie. Wind thread around the stake and body of the cat for extra support. See picture on page 11 in the color section.

Note: Two trumpets go to the left and one trumpet goes to the right

Trumpet Trio Pop-up

Yield: One trumpet trio pop-up

1-12x1 inch wooden stake
1-12x12 inch sheet gold starched felt
1 pattern to trace trumpets
1 package ³/₄ inch resin butterflies (3 pieces per package but need only one)
1 package 10mm round pink rhinestones (20 pieces per package)
1 package 6x9mm heart pony pink beads (65 pieces per package)
Silver metallic spray paint
Glue gun
Hot glue stick

Spray paint the wooden stake, front and back. Dry Thoroughly. Trace one trumpet from the pattern on page 301 onto the gold starched felt, saying cut 1 Trace two trumpets from the pattern onto the gold starched felt, saying cut 2. Cut out the patterns. Following the picture, fill in the lines for the mouthpiece, the trumpet valves, the two lines around the valves, and the bottom of the horn. Measure and mark 1¹/₂ inches from the bottom of the trumpet that says cut 1. Hot glue the bottom of the trumpet to the top of the wooden stake. Slant the bottom of the trumpet to the right and the second trumpet to the left and hot glue the trumpets in place. Hot glue three rhinestones across the bottom of each trumpet. Hot glue two rhinestones and one butterfly on the wooden stake alternating one rhinestone with the butterfly in the middle of the rhinestones. These rhinestones and the one butterfly is on the stake below the trumpets. Hot glue two hearts to each trumpet above the rhinestones.

Note: One 11-ounce can of silver metallic spray paint will cover all the pop-up puppet stakes, wooden spoons, and wooden boards.

Schoolmaster Puppet

Yield: One schoolmaster

1 wise owl stuffed animal
1-4 inch black witch hat
1-18x18 inch black cloth napkin
1 package self-adhesive shapes fun foam shapes (stars,crowns, frogs)
1-4 inch witches hat
1-3¹/₂x6 inch strip white felt
1-6 inch long x ¹/₄ inch wide blue ribbon
Silver metallic spray paint
Glue gun
Hot glue stick

Spray the stake with the silver paint both front and back. Dry thoroughly. Adhere the small pink star onto the center of the yellow crown. Adhere the crown to the front point of the hat. Adhere the frog to the front point of the hat just below the crown. Adhere 9 pink stars around the brim of the hat. Hot glue the hat onto the owl's head. Starting at the neck, hot glue the stake to center back of the owl and the tail. Fold the napkin in half the long way. The folded edge goes to the top of the owl. Hot glue 3 pleats in the center back of the napkin (one pleat in the center and one pleat on each side of the center pleat). Hot glue the napkin with the pleats to the center back of the owl. Fold top edges of the napkin on each side to barely overlap and hot glue in place. Fold each side of the napkin at an angle ending up with three inches on the bottom part of the fold on each side for the front of the napkin to make a cape. The front cape fold is on the outside next to the owl's feet. With the glue gun, adhere a pink star to the yellow crown and attach it to the top of the cape to act as a closure to the cape. Adhere frogs, crowns, and stars down the front sides of the cape for the decoration. Roll up the white felt to make the diploma. Tie the diploma with the ribbon. Hot glue the diploma onto the top of the right foot of the owl. See picture on page 11 in the color section.

Princess Oletta Pop-up

Yield: One princess

1 5x6 inch wooden shape - $\frac{1}{16}$ inch thick board
1 pre-finished wooden princess in pink and white
1-12x1 inch wooden stake
Metallic silver spray paint
Glue gun
Hot Glue

Spray the board and stake on the front and the backsides. Dry thoroughly. Hot glue the board onto the stake. Hot glue the princess figure onto the wooden board. See picture on page 11 in the color section.

Cousin Frog Princess Puppet

Yield: One cousin frog princess

1 Pink Cousin Frog stuffed animal
1-12x1 inch wide wooden stake
1-14 inch length pink grosgrain ribbon
Silver metallic spray paint
Glue gun
Hot glue stick

Spray the stake on the front and backside. Dry thoroughly. Hot glue the cousin frog princess to the top of the stake. Tie the grosgrain ribbon around the waist of the cousin frog princess to give extra support. See picture on page 11 in the color section.

Judge Diplomat Puppet
Yield: One judge

1-10-12 inch white fluffy dog with one pink ear and a pink tail
1-12x1 inch wide wooden stake
1-3x4½ piece light pink starched felt cut into a pumpkin shape without stem
1 label saying Judge Diplomat
1-3½x3½ inch graduation cap
1 pink butterfly
Silver Metallic spray paint
Glue gun
Hot glue stick
1-18x1 inch strip pink grosgrain ribbon

Spray paint the stake. Hot glue the butterfly onto the center edge of the cap. Hot glue the graduation cap to the dog's head. Cut a sign out of the pink starched felt. Using the Algerian font on the computer, type up the words "Judge Diplomat," size 24 large print. Run off the copy of the sign and cut the sign out to be slightly smaller than the pink pumpkin. Hot glue the Judge Diplomat sign onto the pink shaped pumpkin. Hot glue the pumpkin shaped sign to the dog. Hot glue the dog onto the stake. Tie the grosgrain ribbon around the waist of the dog and knot the tie onto the back of the stake. See picture on page 11 in the color section.

Happy Heart Pop-up
Yield: One heart pop up puppet

1-12x1 inch wooden stake
1-8x8½ inch wooden heart, ¹/₁₆th inch thick
1-3½x6 inch pre-painted wooden red heart
Silver metallic spray paint
Glue gun
Hot Glue stick

Spray paint the 8x8½ wooden heart and the stake both on the front and back sides with the metallic spray paint. Dry thoroughly. Hot glue the center of the heart to the top of the stake. Glue the red heart to the center of the silver painted heart. See picture on page 11 in the color section.

Dancing Tulips Pop-up

Yield: Dancing tulips pop-up puppet

1-12x1 inch wooden stake
1-6^1/$_2$ inch by 1^1/$_{16}$ inch thick wooden circle
3-3 inch (each) tulips with 8 inch sticks attached to tulip
1-2 fluid ounce bottle pink acrylic paint
1-18 inch by 1 inch wide pink grosgrain ribbon
1-14mm round white pearl

Spray paint the stake and the wooden circle on the both sides. Dry thoroughly. Paint the tulips and the sticks attached to the tulips pink. Dry thoroughly. Center the stick and hot glue the circle to the stake 3 inches in from the edge of the circle. Hot glue one tulip down the center of the circle. Hot glue one tulip to each side of the tulip in the center. Tie the grosgrain ribbon around the three sticks of the tulips and make a bow. Hot glue the pearl to the center of the tied bow. See picture on page 11 in the color section.

Select Prince Puppet

Yield: One select prince pop-up puppet

1 prince frog in green and yellow
1-12x1 inch wooden stake
Silver metallic paint
14x1 inch wide lime green grosgrain ribbon
Glue gun
Hot glue stick

Spray paint the wooden stick both front and back. Dry thoroughly. Starting from the back of the neck, hot glue the stake onto the center back of the frog. Tie the grosgrain ribbon around the neck of the frog and stake to make a knot. The ribbon becomes his bowtie. See picture on page 11 in the color section.

Bride and Groom Pop-up

Yield: One bride and groom

1-12x1 inch stake
1 tissue paper bride with groom centerpiece
Silver metallic paint
Glue gun
Hot glue stick

Spray paint the wooden stake Dry thoroughly. Hot glue the stake between the front and back of the bridal tissue centerpiece. See picture on page 11 in the color section.

Bride and Groom in the Wedding Carriage Pop-up

Yield: One Bride and Groom, Horses,Wedding Carriage

1-12x1 inch stake
1-6x$^1/_{16}$ inch wooden circle
1 cake decoration "bride and groom"
1-2 inch pink-stuffed miniature heart pillow
2 horses
1 cake decoration "white carriage"
1 cake decoration "top to the carriage"
1-8x8 inch piece pink wrapping paper
Silver metallic paint
Glue gun
Hot glue stick

Spray paint the stake and the wooden circle on both sides. Dry thoroughly. Form the pink wrapping paper around the inside of the carriage leaving a dip in the center. Hot glue the bride and groom in the center of the carriage. Hot glue the carriage to the center of the wooden circle. Hot glue the heart to the outside of the back wheel of the carriage. Hot glue the carriage top to the front of the wooden circle next to the heart. Place the stake across the back of the carriage and hot glue the stake to the back of the carriage and the side of the horse. Hot glue the tail of the second horse next to the first horse. See picture on page 11 in the color section.

Treasure Box Pop-up

Yield: One treasure box pop-up puppet

1-2$^1/_2$x3 inches long x 3 inches wide wooden heart
1-1x1 inch wooden heart.
1 pre-finished King's crown
1-5x6x$^1/_{16}$ inch thick wooden board
1 strand of purple beads
1 strand gold beads
1-2$^1/_4$x4x2 inches high treasure box with latch
8 gold coins
Silver metallic spray paint
1-2 fluid ounce pink acrylic paint
Glue gun
Hot glue stick

Using silver spray paint the 2$^1/_2$x3 inch wooden heart, wooden board, stake, and the treasure chest, front and back, and also the bottom of the treasure chest. Dry thoroughly. Paint the handle of the treasure chest and the 1-1x1 heart pink. Dry thoroughly. Hot glue the king's crown in the center of the wooden board. Hot glue the pink heart onto the larger heart just slightly to the right edge and upper hand corner of the heart. Hot glue the point of the bottom of the heart onto the board above the point of the center of the crown. Hot glue the board from three inches to the top of the stake. Hot glue the coins to the top of the treasure chest along the. Hot glue 2 rows of purple and 2 rows of gold beads on the top of the treasure chest. Hot glue one row of purple beads across the top front of the treasure chest. Hot glue two rows of purple beads around the sides and front of the treasure chest. Hot glue the gold beads at the top sides of the treasure chest. Hot glue the treasure chest onto the stake. See picture on page 11 in the color section.

Butterfly Halo Pop-up

Yield: One butterfly halo pop-up puppet

1 gold pipe cleaner
2 packages (each) butterfly Papillion, self-adhesive (4 count)
1 princess tiara (silver color)
1 tulip on stick
1 half shelf with 1 butterfly design
1-18 mm round white pearl
2-14 mm (each) round white pearls
1-12x1 inch wooden stake
1 gold metallic pipe cleaner
Silver metallic spray paint
fluid ounce pink acrylic paint
Glue gun
Hot glue stick

Spray paint the shelf and stake front and back. Leaving $\frac{1}{4}$ inch, saw off the stick to the tulip. Paint the tulip pink front and back. Paint the front side of the butterfly pink. Dry each coat thoroughly. Touching the butterfly, hot glue the tulip down the center of the shelf with the top of the tulip sticking up off the shelf. Remove the ends of each side of the tiara. Hot glue the tiara onto each edge of the shelf over the top of the tulip. Hot glue one pink and purple butterfly on each side of the bottom of the tulip. Form a 3 inch circle at one end of the pipe cleaner. Secure. Bend down the remaining straight portion of the pipe cleaner, perpendicular to the circle. Hot glue three butterflies onto the front area of the pipe cleaner-shaped crown. Hot glue the vertical piece of the pipe cleaner to the back of the stake. Hot glue the stake to the back of the shelf. The butterfly halo will appear as if it is flying over the princess's tiara. See picture on page 11 in the color section.

Note: The fun foam crown has a stretch band attached to the back of the crown.

Leonardo Puppet

Yield: One Leonardo pop-up puppet

1-12x1 inch wooden stake
1 lion wearing a shirt with a "I love you" hearts and heart glasses
1 fun foam red crown with stretch band
1-2½x2½ pink heart made from starched felt
1-2x2 heart on copy paper with the name "Leonardo" centered in the heart
Silver metallic spray paint
Glue gun
Hot glue stick
Gold thread

Spray paint the wooden stake on both sides. Dry thoroughly. Fit the crown to the lion's head and hot glue in place. Stretch the crown's band over the crown and place the band around the front and each side of the neck. Hot glue the white copy paper onto heart in the middle front of the pink heart shaped felt. Hot glue the pink heart onto the center front of the crown. Hot glue the top of the stake to the back fur of the lion. Tie the thread around the bottom of the lion's upper thighs and stake to give extra holding strength. See picture on page 11 in the color section.

Note: The mouse is a little stuffed animal and the remaining figures are pre-finished wooden pieces shaped into the various shapes for each pop-up puppet.

Pop-ups for the Tree I (Shade Tree), Tree II (Fir Tree), Clouds, Dragon, Moon and Stars, Rainbow, Rose, and Mrs. Mouse Puppet

Yield: Seven pop-ups and one puppet

8-10 inch (each) wooden spoons
1-11 ounce can Metallic silver spray paint
1 shade tree (tree I)
1 fir tree
1 cloud
1-3½ with 2 inch tail pink mouse
1-14 inch strip 1 inch wide pink grosgrain ribbon
1 dragon sponge stamp
1 moon and stars
1 rainbow
1 rose
Glue gun
Hot glue stick

Spray paint the wooden spoons both front and back. Dry thoroughly. Hot glue the mouse onto the wooden spoon and tie the grosgrain ribbon around the waist of the mouse (with the knot in the back of the wooden spoon. Hot glue one shape to the remaining of the 7 wooden spoons. See picture on page 11 in the color section.

Princess Oletta's Ballet Dance Pop-up
Yield: One ballet dancer pop-up

1-6x14 inch strip pink tulle
1 gold pipe cleaner
1 ballet party favor
1 multi-colored wooden spoon
2-12 inch (each) metallic gold pipe cleaners
1-2x2 inch pink starched felt heart
1-2 inch strip pink colored beads
3-6x9 mm pink heart pony beads
1-2 inch pre-strung pink colored beads
Glue gun
Hot glue stick

At the right and left end of the tulle, make pleats to the middle. Tie the middle with one end of the pipe cleaner. Make a 2^1/$_2$ inch oval loop and tie the edge of the pipe cleaner to the top of the pipe cleaner underneath the center of the tulle. Hot glue the oval shaped pipe cleaner to the back of the wooden spoon. Hot glue the ballet dancer onto the middle of the pipe cleaner and tulle. Hot glue the heart onto the top of the spoon. Hot glue the oval shape pipe cleaner onto the back of the spoon. Hot glue three heart shaped pony beads onto the middle of the heart and the pre-strung pink colored beads across the top of the heart above the pony beads. Hot glue the heart onto the top of the back of the spoon. Shape the second pipe cleaner into 3 v's to form the princess's crown. Hot glue the bottom center of the crown onto the bottom of the ballet dancer. Hot glue each side of the top of the tulle to the lower v on each side of the pipe cleaner. See picture on page 11 in the color section.

Note: The Algerian font is optional. Judge Diplomat has the pumpkin-shaped sign. Instructions can be found under Judge Diplomat puppet heading. If you prefer, you can store the puppets on 3x12x18 inch Styrofoam® sheets and in 3 medium boxers. It may be easier and less bulky to store the puppets.

How to Label the Puppets and Pop-up Characters
Yield: Heart–shaped labels for the cast

1-3x3 inch heart shape cookie cutter
2-12 inch sheets (each) pink starched felt
2 typed sheets (each) with all the puppets names in
Algerian font # 22
Glue stick
Glue gun

Hot glue
1-12x36 inch (each) Styrofoam® sheet
1-12x18 inch Styrofoam® sheet
3-12x18 inch (each) starched felt
3-1 yard and 24 inch (each) 1 inch wide grosgrain ribbon

Using a cookie cutter, trace 20 heart shapes and cut out the hearts. Type up the names of the puppets on the computer. Cut out the names with an inexpensive pair of pinking shears and, using the glue stick or hot glue, glue the names onto the center of each heart. Hot glue the heart-shaped names onto each appropriate puppet. Hot glue the starched felt to the bottom of the Styrofoam® for extra durability. Hot glue the grosgrain ribbon around all four sides of the Styrofoam® to prevent damage to the Styrofoam®. Stand puppets stakes and wooden spoons into the Styrofoam® sheets. Cut out a second sheet of puppet names. Hot glue the names of each puppet onto the Styrofoam® in front of each puppet for identification of each puppet. Store the puppets in 1 large box and 1 medium box.

Labels for Puppets and Pop-up Characters

JUDGE DIPLOMAT	DANCING TULIPS	LEONARDO
		MOON & STARS
TRUMPET TRIO	BUTTERFLY CIRCLE	
		BRIDE & GROOM
TREASURE BOX	FIR TREE	
	SHADE TREE	MRS. MOUSE
COUSIN FROG PRINCESS	SELECTED PRINCE	DRAGON
ROSE		PRINCESS

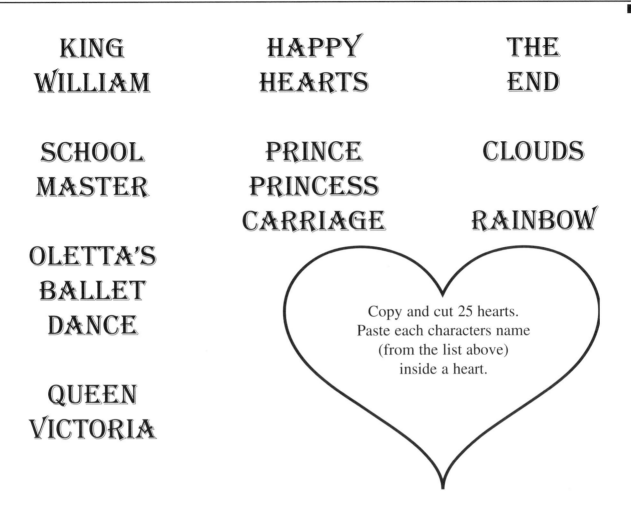

KING WILLIAM

HAPPY HEARTS

THE END

SCHOOL MASTER

PRINCE PRINCESS CARRIAGE

CLOUDS

RAINBOW

OLETTA'S BALLET DANCE

Copy and cut 25 hearts.
Paste each characters name
(from the list above)
inside a heart.

QUEEN VICTORIA

Note: There is already a front to the stage. The extra piece is only used for extra durability.

How to Make the Puppet Theater
Yield: One stage

1 large cardboard display box with two or three shelves
  (40 inches high, 36 inches across & 18 inches wide)
1 large piece of cardboard
3-2$^1/_2$x1$^2/_3$ yards rolls (each) purple with silver stars wrapping paper
2-5x30x12.5 square feet rolls (each) pink wrapping paper
10 yards 6 inch pink tulle
1 roll wide clear tape
2 packages (each) pink ballet dancers (4 count)

Measure and cut out the large piece of cardboard to fit the front of the stage. For extra strength, tape the second piece of cardboard to fit the front of the stage. Cover the sides and top of the box with the purple paper and the front of the stage with the pink wrapping paper. Tape the wrapping paper to the box to hold paper in place.

Note: If you do not want to make a stage, contact 1-800-SkyMall or their website www.skymall.com
    They have a stage called the instant doorway puppet theater. It weighs 5 1/2 pounds and it is
    30 inches wide and 60 inches high.

How to Make the Curtains and Decorate the Puppet Theater

Yield: One 44 inch x 3 yard curtain

3 yards of 44 inch wide pink fabric
2-44 inch strips (each) gold metallic wire ribbon 2½ inches wide (for the bottom of the curtain)
2-1⅞ yard (each) gold metallic wire ribbon 2 inches wide
1-8 inch strip pink grosgrain
2 packages (each) ballet dance party favors (pink color) (4 count)
2 packages (each) broken glass purple buttons (4 count)
1 package 14 mm round white pearls (12 count)
Hot glue stick
Glue Gun

Turn each 44-inch raw edge over twice ¼ inch each. Stitch the edge on both ends of the material.
Using a pinking shears, trim off ¼ inch of the ribbon to avoid fraying. Turn the edge of the ribbon
under. Lay the ribbon over the stitched edge of the fabric and sew on. Place small tucks on the wired
ribbon about 2 inches apart. Spray starch the curtain and press. Fold the material in half lengthwise
and shape the top of the curtains onto the top of box with curtains hanging down the sides. Make sure
each side is even. Tie the grosgrain ribbon around the center of the curtains at the top into a knot to
divide the curtain in half. Cut off the ends of the grosgrain ribbon. Fold the tulle in half, horizontally to form five yards and make 6 inch loops to look like many half bows on each side of the tulle with
each side of bows coming to the center. Hot glue the tulle bows in place down the center and center
front on top of the box. Hot glue one ballet dancer onto the knot of the grosgrain ribbon. Starting from
left to right and with a three-inch space between the ballet dancers, hot glue the dancers across the
top edge of the box. Using pink thread, on each side of the top of the curtain valence, hand sew tucks
to make a balloon valance. Hot glue 3 pearls in a vertical row to cover the thread. Hot glue the purple stone buttons onto the lower edge of the top of the box in a horizontal line evenly spaced. Tie the
gold wired ribbon into a bow on each side of the curtain. Bend the ribbon ties back and forth for a
wavy effect. Hot glue the sides of each curtain in place above the bow. See picture on page 11 in the
color section.

Princess Heart Shape Pin Style One

Yield: One princess heart shape pin

1 package 2x1¼ wooden hearts (2 count)
1 package diva memory mates (diamond hearts and pink dress)
1-11 ounce can silver metallic spray paint
fluid ounce bottle pink acrylic paint

1 purple bead
1-1½ inch gold pin back
Glue gun
Hot glue

Spray the heart silver on both sides of the heart. Dry thoroughly. Paint an outline of the heart in pink. Dry. Place the princess dress to the right hand side of the heart and hot glue the dress in place. On the left side of the heart, hot glue the three hearts in a circle to form a flower. Hot glue the purple bead in the center of the three hearts. Hot glue the pin back onto the center of the back of the pin.

Princess Heart Shape Pin Style Two

Yield: One pin

1 package butterfly papillon (4 per package) (self-adhesive)
1 gold bead
1-1½ inch gold pin back

Purchase the same supplies as for the pin style I. Using the memory mates (diva) package, hot glue on the princess high heel shoes onto the right side of the heart, one shoe above each other. Hot glue the gold bead between the shoes. Hot glue a butterfly onto the left side of the heart with half of the butterfly sticking off the heart pin. Hot glue the pin back onto the center of the back of the pin.

Note: I outlined the painted purse with pre-strung beads. I placed a butterfly on each side of the purse and, at random, placed the hearts around the butterfly. The picture will show different decorations on all of the six boxes. If you can not find ballet dancers, substitute a 1x1 inch heart and /or a crown made from pipe cleaners. The crown was explained under the Princess Oletta's Ballet Dance Pop-Up Puppet on page 295. Using the one inch heart pattern, trace the heart onto pink starched felt. Hot glue a pink heart pony bead onto the front center of the heart. Hot glue the heart in the middle of the tulle and pipe cleaner.

Note: The Princess wooden box treat is an excellent party favor. For 6 box treats you will 3-12 ounce bags of chocolate candy kisses.

Princess Wooden Treat Box

Yield: One purse

1-4x4x2 inch deep wooden box with handles
1-11 ounce can silver metallic spray paint
1-2 ounce bottle acrylic pink paint
1 artist paintbrush for kids
1 package butterfly Papillion (4 count) (self-adhesive)
1 package 6x9 mm pink heart pony beads
1 package designer metal sliders with pink crystals (9 count)
1 package jewels, acrylic oval multi-color 71x.51 inch rhinestones (32 count)
1 package 14 mm round white pearl (12 count)
2 strings of purple beads
1 pound of chocolate candy kisses
1-6 inch wide x 14 inch long piece of pink tulle
1-12 inch gold metallic pipe cleaner
wood glue or all purpose glue
1-12 inch pink pipe cleaner
1 pink ballet party favor
Glue gun
Hot glue stick
1-12 ounce package chocolate candy kisses

Spray silver paint over the entire wooden box except for the handles and bottom of the box. Dry thoroughly. Paint the handles and the bottom of the box pink. Have the children select decorations from several cups containing the rhinestones, pearls, butterflies, pony heart beads, and metal sliders with a pink crystal. Glue the selected decorations onto the front and back of the box. The child can outline the purse with the purple beads. Fill the box half full of candy kisses. Gather up the center of the tulle to form the center of the bow. Pinch 2 pleats from right and left, both going toward the center of the tulle. Wrap the top of the pipe cleaner around the center of the tulle tightly (twice) to hold the tulle together. With a separate pipe cleaner, make an oval loop and twist and tie the pipe cleaner at the top edge to to complete the oval shape. Turn the top wrapped center piece to lay as a platform. Hot glue the bottom ball of the ballet dancer to the center of the tulle and pipe cleaner. See the picture of the 6 decorated boxes with handles on page 11 in the color section.

Patterns for the Trumpet Trio Pop-ups

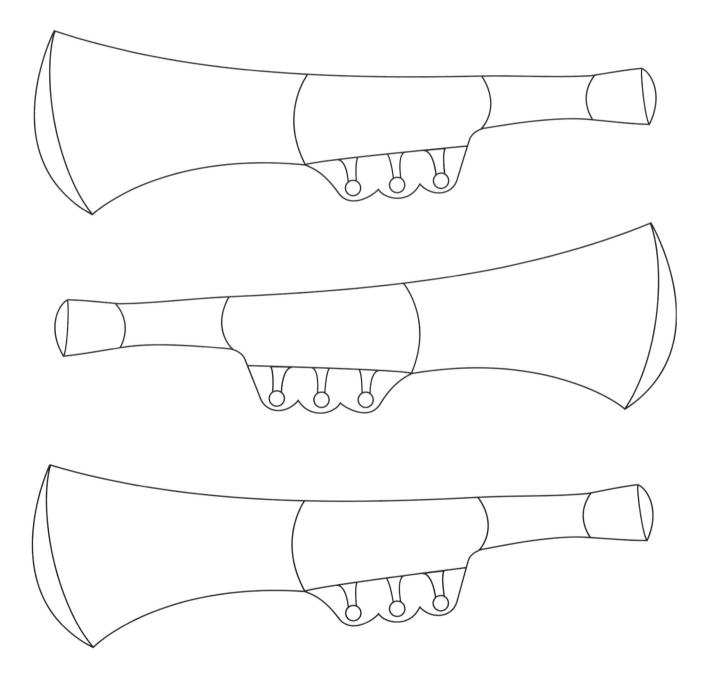

Princess Theme Related Book Resources

Cohen, Della
"Cinderella: A Read-Aloud Storybook, adapted by Della Cohen"
Publisher: Mouse Works
Published Date: c1999
This is a version of the Disney's animated classic, rags-to-riches story of Cinderella (ages 4-6)

Craig, Helen
"Angelina, and the Princess"
Publisher: Pleasant Company Publications
Published Date: 2000
Angelina went to ballet dance school and she practiced to perform before the princess. The day of the audition Angelina woke up sick. She went to the audition anyway and danced poorly. Her teacher told her she would have to take a smaller part. Although she was disappointed, she agreed to do so. She also studied the lead part. When the person assigned to the lead got sick, Angelina saved the day and all things ended well. (ages 4-6)

Disney, Walt
"Sleeping Beauty"
(1st American Addition)
Publisher: Groller Enterprises
Published Date: c1995
"Soft, dreamlike pastels are used to illustrate this reworking as the fairy tale", "Sleeping Beauty." (ages 3-7)

Lohnes, Marilyn
"Fractured Fairy Tales: Puppet Plays & Patterns"
Publisher: Upstart Books
Upstart Book: c2002
The book is filled with puppet plays and patterns. (ages 8-9)

McCullough, L.E.
"Plays from Fairy Tales"
Publisher: Smith and Kraus
Published Date: c1997
The book presents twelve original fairy tale plays from around the world. (ages 5-8)

McCourt, Lisa
"Good Night Princess Pruney-Toes"
Publisher:Troll/Bridgewater
Published Date: c2001
It is a cute story about the princess and her daddy. The little girl pretend to be a princess as she gets ready for bed. (ages 2-4)

Oram, Hiawyn
"Princess Chamonile's Garden"
Publisher: Dutton Children's Books
Published Date: c2002
The Princess was riding her bike in circles through the garden. She decided to help Melchoir the gardener. The nanny came to get the princess to scrub her up for her music lesson. The Princess dreams about her garden, while sitting in the tub. She could not think of music or anything else, just her future garden. The gardener helped her dream come true. She learned that gardening is hard work. The book cleverly uses a three-page picture to illustrate the end result. (ages 3-5)

Ordal, Stina Langlo
"Princess Aasta"
Publisher: Bloombury Children's Book
Published Date: c2000
This is a fairy tale story about a princess who wanted a white bear to love. She advertised in the newspaper. She selected Kvitebjorn because he was friendly. She picks apples and goes to the North with her Kvitebjorn. The bear was very kind to Princess Aasta. (ages 3-4)

Dale, Penny
"Princess, Princess"
Publisher: Candlewick Press
Published Date: c2003
It is a reworking of the fairy tale, "Sleeping Beauty".

Posner, Pat
"Princess Fidgety Feet"
Publisher: Gingham Dog Press
Published Date: c2003
Her parents arranged for Miss Posey to get the princess to stop her fidgety feet. Finally, the princess received permission to play soccer and became a star. Miss Posy became her soccer coach. When the princess is not playing soccer, her feet get fidgety.

Priceman, Marjorie
"Princess Picky"
Publisher: Roaring Brook Press
Published Date: c2002
There was a princess named Nicki. She lived in the castle with her family. The workers called her picky because she would not eat her vegetables. Her mother and father called a meeting and asked the workers to bribe her to eat her vegetables. She declined any offers and refused to eat her vegetables. The Wizard finally asked Princess Nicki what she really wanted. Due to her magic wish all the vegetables began to grow. She finally ate the vegetables and all her wishes came true. (ages 4-6)

■

Wilhem, Hans
"Anook: The Snow Princess"
Publisher: Barron's
Published Date: c2003
Anook is a princess bear. She lives with papa Polar Bear King and her other two siblings. The story teaches a child about honesty and sibling rivalry. Anook's loyalty to her father wins her the thorn in Northland and she becomes known as the Snow Princess. (ages 5-6)

CD Music

Giangiulio, Richard
"Music for Festive Occasions"
{Sound Recording}
Publisher: Crystal Records
Published Date: c1985
(ages 8-9) Use this CD for this music for the princess play.

Ronno
"Castles, Knights & Unicorns"
{Sound recording}: Action Songs for Fantasy & Fun
Publisher: Kimbo Educational
Published Date: c2001
The Sound recording takes the children through an imaginary ride with "Castles, Knights & Unicorns."(ages 3-6) The Ronno Website: www.ronnosong.com

Tchaikovsky, Peter Ilich
"Nutcracker Suite: op.71a"
"Serenade for Strings in C: op.48"
{Sound recording}
Publisher: Phillips
Published Date: c1982
The "Nutcracker Suite" music is ideal for the Princess ballet dance. (ages 8-12)

"Wedding Day"
{Sound recording}
Publisher: Intersound
Published Date: c1996
"The Mouret: Fanfare" ("Masterpiece Theatre" Theme) is excellent for the entrance of the King and Queen at the beginning of the play. (ages 8-9)

Video

"Angelina Ballerina: The Big Performance"
{Video recording}
Publisher: Hit Entertainment
Published Date: 2005
Angelina Ballerina is a little mouse that dreams of becoming a top notch ballerina. She is determined, headstrong, passionate, and feisty. The children will relate to her. Angelina is requested to dance for Queen Seraphina, but on the way she and Miss Lilly get lost. (ages 4-6)

"Sleeping Beauty, The Two Princesses"
{Video recording}
Publisher: Good Times Entertainment
Published Date: c 2005
"Alina appears first as a beautiful princess who cries pearls for tears, then again as an old and ugly goosemaid. First she hides in the deepest forest, next she appears in the castle's throne room. One moment her hair is blonde, then it's black...or is there more than one Alina?"

Kindergarten Graduation Party

Kindergarten Graduation Story

Students take pride in accomplishing their education even very early in their lives. Teachers, administrators, parents and entire family and friends celebrate the student's accomplishments.

Commencement acknowledges the student graduates, and they are presented with diplomas. The requirements for graduation are set by the state and school board. A typical commencement takes place at school in a gymnasium, football stadium, or an auditorium. The school band often plays the music for the graduation ceremony. The students march in to the song, "Pomp and Circumstances". An honor student is often recognized for his/her accomplishments.

There are many opinions about having or not having a kindergarten graduation. People argue that too much time is spent on rehearsing for the graduation and the demand too great that the graduation be picture perfect. Others complain about the cost. Others argue that we should not at any cost put a five year old on the spot with a graduation ceremony.

I personally was against a kindergarten graduation. My best friend, Ceil, attended her great granddaughter's kindergarten commencement. The children really got involved in learning about being recognized and how to socialize with their families. The kindergarten teacher asked the dads to loan a white dress shirt to their child. The children wore the shirt backwards. The children made their own graduation hats and tassels. They also wore a big bow for their tie. The children were very enthusiastic. They also helped make the plans for the punch and a marble cake. Families donated light refreshments.

At the beginning of the school year, each kindergartener was adopted by an eighth grade pal. Each eighth grader dressed the kindergartner for the ceremony and walked the kindergartener down the aisle. The children were told that there are no real mistakes and that they would do a good job.

The ceremony was a family affair. The children helped pour punch and pass the cake. Great Grandmother Ceil raved about ceremony. She bought in pictures at the YMCA to show off the ceremony. I also talked to her son and he felt it was a good experience. It was a way to congratulate kindergarteners for a job well done. No one kindergartener was singled out, but all were honored in a reasonable fashion. Afterwards the family went to dinner and visited for the evening. It was a great opportunity for a family gathering as the scattered around the country. They all came to show their support.

Food Supplies Needed for the Graduation Party

1 or 2 decorated graduation cakes
3 to 5 gallons of punch of your choice
Plates
Punch cups
Dessert forks
Dessert napkins
1 tablecloth
1 centerpiece

Supplies Needed for the Kindergartner's Graduation Outfit

1 of dad's white dress shirts
1 yard of ribbon in each of the school colors (supplied by the school)
Cardboard to make the hat
Yarn to make the tassel (supplied by the school)
$1^{3}/_{4}$x1 inch button per hat
Glue
1 piece white 8x11 copy paper
1-12 inch ribbon long, $^{1}/_{4}$ inch wide (school colors) or a rubber band
Congratulations saying for each child (supplied by the school)

Gather the kindergarteners with their eighth grade buddies. Measure each child's head. Cut a four-inch wide and a length, the size of the child's head. Overlap the edges of the cut out cardboard and staple the edges together. Cut out a square to cover the circle and glue in place. Hot glue a flat $^{3}/_{4}$–1 inch button in the center of the top of the square. Cut 6-20 inch pieces (per tassel). Place all six pieces together in one straight line. Fold all six pieces in half. Tie a loop of yarn around the top of the tassel, 1-1$^{1}/_{2}$ inches down to fit the button. Place the loop around the button and hot glue in place. Write the kindergartner's name on the inside of the cap. Glue the congratulations onto the copy paper. Have the eighth graders roll up each paper into cylinder shape. Print each kindergartner's name on the outside of the diploma. Tie the ribbon around the center of the diploma. Place them on the stage.

One kindergartner's father owned a digital camera. He volunteered to take pictures of each of the kindergartners with their cap and gown and also pictures of the ceremony. Pictures were displayed in school on the hallway bulletin. This same father donated the pictures and also helped order pictures for different families.

When I was only six years old, my father ran a grocery store. I stood on a sturdy wood box at the cash register and he taught me how to ring up the groceries, greet the customers, and sweep. I learned many social graces, and to this day, that experience has helped me to be successful in my own life. I learned to love people very early in life and be concerned for others. I also learned to share with others and be a part of a team. From that standpoint I feel honored to have learned early in my life the life skills needed to get through my daily life and to know how to love others on this earth. My father is now in heaven. I thank him for I feel honored to have learned those skills early on and use them in my daily life.

To conclude, in my opinion, if a kindergartner can learn life skills and how to be a part of a team, it would be worth the time and effort to prepare for a kindergarten graduation.

Chloe's Kindergarten Graduation Poem
By Pat Nekola

My name is Chloe and I am five.
I am trying to take graduation in stride.

Mom says, she is very proud of me.
She wants to invite family and host a tea.

Dad says, he will lend me his white shirt.
And then I will not have to wear a long skirt.

My brother, Josh will walk me down the aisle,
And he hopes I will give everyone a big smile.

I am suppose to make a homemade graduation cap,
I fear it will only fit the head of my dog, Hap.

Grandma says, she will attend and cry.
I get no answer, when I ask her why?

Grandpa is going to take pictures of me.
He says, "Chloe is five. That can't be".

My graduation Day is finally here
I walk in with Pomp and Circumstance playing in my ear.

As I look over my diploma, inside and out,
I want to say look everyone, and then give a shout.

Graduation truly is a kindergartener's milestone.
It is a memory I will keep with me even after I am grown.

I am saving my diploma to show to all mankind,
For my family and teacher told me I did just fine.

Mom says, "Never worry or fret.
Be happy when accomplishments are met."

I know I am off to a very good start,
And I thank my family with all my heart.

Graduation Attire

Bridal Shower Party

A Family's Daughter's Bridal Shower Party

Invitations were sent and the shower was hosted by the sister of the bride. A small crowd of family, neighbors, and close friends gathered to celebrate AnnMarie's engagement. You can see her picture on page 12 in the color section holding a beautiful serving dish and the picnic cookbook. AnnMarie received many beautiful kitchen and serving pieces. They were all so wonderful for entertaining. Her sister, Jenni, made several cakes for tasting. We sampled the different cakes and wrote down our favorite cake. Jenni is the cake decorator of the family. She promised AnnMarie that she would make her wedding cake. All the guests enjoyed selecting their favorite cake. Because we are all close friends and neighbors, it was easy to engage in conversation. Of course, whenever you get a bunch of women together, you will find there is no lack of conversation. The afternoon went all too quickly. It was a simple, but lovely gathering. We all walked away feelings good and excited about attending the wedding.

Bridal Shower Party Menu

Ham and Cheese Appetizers

Stuffed Mushrooms

Bruschetta

Small Dishes of Assorted Cut Fruits

Cream Cheese Fruit Dip

Assorted Chilled Relishes

Bridal Shower Cake

Assorted Beverages

Note: Purchase two 13.5 ounce cream cheese fruit dips at your local grocery store. Serve with assorted cut fruits.

Ham and Cheese Appetizers

Yield: Thirty-six

2 cups baking mix
$^3/_4$ cup finely chopped cooked ham
1 cup shredded Swiss or cheddar cheese (about 4 ounces)
$^1/_2$ cup Parmesan cheese
$^1/_4$ cup dairy sour cream
2 tablespoons fresh parsley, chopped
$^1/_2$ teaspoon salt
2 cloves garlic, crushed
1 egg

Heat oven to 350 F. Grease a 13x9x2 inch pan. Mix together the baking mix and all ingredients together. Spread in the pan. Bake until golden brown for 25 to 30 minutes. Cut into rectangles, about $2^1/_2$ inches long.

Note: One of the family members requested leaving out the ground cayenne. This recipe is from the kitchen of Jackie H.

Stuffed Mushrooms

Yield: Twenty

20 whole fresh mushrooms
$1^1/_2$ tablespoons olive oil
$1^1/_2$ tablespoons minced garlic
12 ounces cream cheese, softened
3 ounces grated Parmesan cheese
$^1/_2$ teaspoon ground black pepper
$^1/_2$ teaspoon onion powder
$^1/_2$ teaspoon ground cayenne, (optional)

Preheat oven to 350 F. Spray a baking sheet with cooking spray. Clean mushrooms with a damp paper towel. Carefully break off stems. Chop stems very fine, discarding tough end of stems.

Heat oil in a large skillet over medium heat. Add garlic and chopped mushroom stems to the skillet. Sauté until all moisture has disappeared, taking care not to burn the garlic. Set aside to cool.

When garlic and mushroom mixture is no longer hot, stir in cream cheese, Parmesan cheese, black pepper, onion powder and cayenne pepper. Mixture should be very thick. Using a little spoon, fill each mushroom cap with a generous amount of stuffing. Arrange mushroom caps on prepared cook-ie sheet. Bake for 20 minutes in the preheated oven, or until mushrooms are piping hot.

Note: Bruschetta are made with French Baguette bread, topped with pesto, mozzarella cheese, and fresh Roma tomatoes. They are very tasty and an excellent item for a shower. Have at least two servings per person.

Bruschetta

Yield: Eight per box

Purchase enough boxes of bruchetta for size of crowd. Follow the baking instructions found on the back of the box. The invitation explained that it would be a light supper. Janice got a couple of games off the Internet.

Note: The pre-made pesto with basil is made with extra virgin olive oil, walnuts, and Romano cheese. It can be purchased at your local grocery store.

Bruschetta

Yield: Twenty-four

1-12 ounce loaf of French Baguette
6 Roma tomatoes
$^1/_4$ teaspoon salt
1-7 ounce container Pesto
1-12 ounce package mozzarella cheese

Slice bread into 24 slices. Peel tomatoes and remove seeds. Finely dice the tomatoes. Place the tomatoes into a separate bowl. Sprinkle salt over tomatoes. Toss tomatoes gently. Spread a small amount of pesto onto the bread. Sprinkle a teaspoon of mozzarella cheese over the pesto. Top the cheese with $1^1/_2$ teaspoons tomato. Bake at 400 F for 8 to ten minutes or until cheese is melted and bread is toasted.

Note: You can substitute Italian seasoning for pasta seasoning. I personally like the pasta seasoning. This is a product of Penzey Spice.

Homemade Basil Pesto Bruschetta

Yield: Twenty-four

$1/2$ cup extra virgin olive oil
20 fresh basil leaves
$1/4$ cup finely diced onion
2 tablespoons minced garlic
1 teaspoon pasta seasoning
1 cup grated Parmesan cheese
6 Roma tomatoes
$1/4$ teaspoon salt
1-12 ounce loaf French baguette bread
1-12 ounce package mozzarella cheese, finely shredded

In a blender, add olive oil and basil leaves. Blend on high to pulverize. Turn the olive oil and basil mixture into a medium size bowl. Add the onion, garlic, pasta seasoning and Parmesan cheese to the basil mixture. Stir together. Peel the tomatoes. Remove seeds from the tomatoes. Finely dice each tomato. Place the tomatoes into a separate bowl. Add the salt and lightly toss. Spread pesto over each slice of bread. Sprinkle each bruschetta with 1 teaspoon mozzarella cheese. Top each bruschetta with 1-2 teaspoons tomato. Bake at 400 F for 8-10 minutes or until the cheese melts and the bottom of the bread is golden brown.

Note: I purchased a container of each of the bruschetta spreads.

Simple Bruschetta

Yield: Two and a half dozen

2-8 ounce loaves (each) Mini Twin French Bread
2-7 ounce containers (each pesto with basil with extra virgin olive oil)
2-10$1/2$ ounce classic or cuscan bruschetta spread
1-8 ounce package shredded 6 cheese Italian blend

Slice both loaves of bread into 28-30 slices $1/2$ inch thick. Spread the pesto over each slice of bread. Top with the bruschetta. Top each bruschetta with 1 teaspoon of cheese. Bake at 400 F for 8-10 minutes or until the cheese melts and the bottom of the bread is golden brown.
Note: I use olive oil spray to grease the baking cookie sheet.

Sun Dried Tomato Bruschettas

Yield: Twenty-four

1-16 ounce Loaf French Baguette Bread
$\frac{1}{2}$ cup extra virgin olive oil
1-3 ounce package sun dried tomatoes
12 fresh basil leaves
$\frac{1}{3}$ cup finely diced green pepper
$\frac{1}{3}$ cup pine nuts
1 cup freshly shredded Parmesan cheese
1 tablespoon minced garlic
$\frac{1}{4}$ cup finely chopped onion
$\frac{1}{4}$ teaspoon salt
$\frac{1}{4}$ teaspoon black pepper
1-5 ounce package finely shredded mozzarella cheese

Slice the bread into $\frac{1}{2}$ inch thick slices. Place on a greased baking cookie sheet. Blend together in a blender the olive oil, sun dried tomatoes and fresh basil leaves. Place the tomato and basil mixture into a medium size bowl. Add the green pepper, pine nuts, Parmesan cheese, garlic, onion, salt, and black pepper. Stir all ingredients together. Place the mixture onto each slice of French bread. Top each slice with 1 teaspoon of mozzarella cheese.

In order save time, the hostess purchased assorted precut fresh fruit and already prepared fruit dip at her local grocery store. Refer to Picnics, Catering on the Move cookbook for the Amaretto Fruit Dip on page 55.

When The Party Began

When we arrived, we were served a beverage of choice. Everyone received a clothespin. I placed mine on my shirtsleeve. The object of the game was that a person could not cross her legs at the knees. Anyone who caught a person crossing her legs could grab her clothespin. The one who collected the most clothespins won the prize. One guest in the crowd did an excellent job at collecting the most clothespins.

Games at the Shower

Another game was about a quiz about famous couples. One had to guess the TV Show that each couple appeared in. We also played a game called "Through the Years." The hostess gave AnnMarie's birth date. She then held up pictures of AnnMarie in a photo frame and we had to guess which year each picture was taken. The last game was Bingo. Fill in each square with an item you think AnnMarie will receive as a gift (i.e. Vase, Deep Fryer) as she opened her presents, we had to fill in the square. I am not a big game person but I enjoyed these games thoroughly. They generated a lot of conversation among the guests.

The light supper was perfect. We didn't need anymore to eat than the items mentioned above.

The Day Before the Wedding

The day before the wedding, the family gathered to help Jenni finish the cake. Her dad cut the dowels to be placed in the cake. I smiled and asked him how he was holding up. He answered, "fine. I just make myself very scarce." I just grinned.

The Day of the Wedding

Finally, AnnMarie's wedding day arrived. Her bridemaids wore simple black dresses with a red scarf around their arms. Jenni's daughter, Caitlin, carried a basket of red rose petals and she melted everyone's heart. (She is on the book cover of "Theme Parties Just for Kids and Family Too"). Candles adorned the end of the pews in the church. A runner of satin was rolled out minutes before the ceremony began. The other grandchildren were also in the wedding. Two of the grandsons handed out programs, and also bubbles in a bottle after the ceremony. One grandson was the ring bearer. The wedding ceremony was simple but elegant and very classy. My husband is a man of few words. He made a comment how beautiful the H Daughters looked for the wedding. He also thought the red scarves draped around their arms were a nice added touch. When he notices something like this, I know it is extra special.

The Wedding Cake

Jenni made the most beautiful and elegant three tiered square wedding cake. She also made the special frosting flowers. The cake was decorated with a simple border and a cluster of flowers on the top of the cake. Each corner of the cake had a simple flower with leaves and one flower in the center of each layer. A lacy tablecloth adorned the cake with a long string of pearls around the cake table. See picture on page 12 in the color section.

The Wedding Reception

Her reception was held at the local hotel. The arriving guests were greeted by the bride and groom and family as other guests grazed the appetizer buffet. The room was perfect for the reception. The kitchen staff from the hotel had set up individual stations with tables of Chinese, Mexican, Italian, seafood, along with a beef tenderloin carving station and a cake table. Two chefs cooked the pasta and tacos to perfection for each guest. At 9 p.m. miniature French pastries were also served. I assure you no one left hungry. The meal was the buzz of the room.

My husband and I personally tasted a little of everything. One gentleman wanted to taste the Italian food. I volunteered to select a combination that he and my husband might enjoy. The serving was enough to feed three people. It was fun watching the chef cooking the food.

Music was provided by a live band which all the guests enjoyed.

Thinking about the Past

AnnMarie was the last of the four daughters to get married. I thought back to their childhood and what these girls meant to me. I never could have children and they helped me fill a void. Aunt Jackie and I talked at AnnMarie's wedding. She remained single and felt lucky to have had her nieces be a part of her life. Now, she was a great aunt and she was even having more fun.

I remembered playing tag with Janice at age 3. She fell and skinned her knee on their driveway. I cried all the way home feeling horrible that she had fallen.

I went to their home on many Christmas days to see the girls' gifts. I rarely missed a 4th of July party watching the H daughters having fun at the party. I remember AnnMarie going to her Senior Prom. One by one, each daughter went off to college to study and prepare for her career. Each one received a degree and now holds a steady job. I ask myself, "Where has the time gone?"

When the first grandson was two, I played with him and his big red truck. I ran around and around the H's kitchen island and laughing with Alex.

A couple of the H teens worked with me in my catering service. They were hard workers because mom and dad insisted that should always give their best.

These four little girls grew up to be beautiful young women. No matter where I see them, they always acknowledge me and speak kindly to me.

I am ever so grateful to have the H family for my extended family. My husband and I are always welcome as part of their family for parties and very special celebrations.

Saying about Friendship

Friendship is a priceless gift and it should never be taken for granted.

Through the Years

Look at the picture of the bride-to-be in the photo frame and guess which year each picture was taken.

A. _____

B. _____

C. _____

D. _____

E. _____

F. _____

G. _____

H. _____

I. _____

Put a picture of the bride-to-be here

Famous Couples

Guess the TV Show that each couple is from.

1. Barney & Wilma _____

2. Lucy & Desi _____

3. Sam & Diane _____

4. Rachel & Ross _____

5. Niles & Daphne _____

6. Ward & June _____

7. Carrie & Mr. Big _____

8. Bo & Hope _____

9. David & Michelle _____

10. Homer & Marge _____

11. Stan & Wendy _____

12. Kevin & Winnie _____

13. Peter & Lois _____

14. Raymond & Debra _____

15. Samantha & Darin _____

16. Paul & Jamie _____

17. Joanie & Chachi _____

18. Cliff & Clair _____

19. Tim & Jill _____

20. Jonathan & Jennifer _____

Gift Bingo

Fill in each square with an item you think the bride-to-be will receive as a gift (i.e. vase, deep fryer). As she opens her presents, mark off the square with the item.

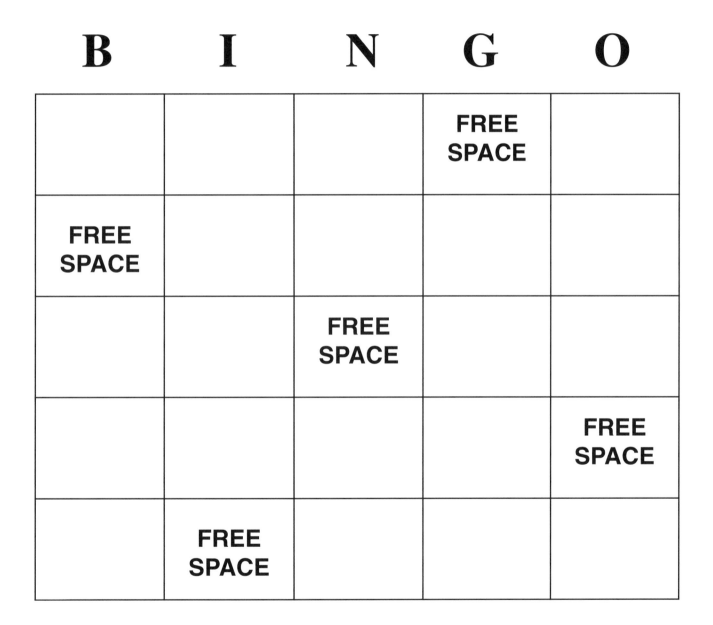

Reunion Party

About Reunions

Reunions take place all over the country. Some families see each more often than other families. A family reunion is a great way to get together for the day and share. Aunt Cassie brought pictures of family members when they were young and also, many pictures of ancestors. The family gathered around in the family room to see and enjoy the family pictures. Everyone brought a dish to pass. The family recipes are in this unit for your families to enjoy at your next family reunion. I set up the buffet with the various dishes. Everyone enjoyed the food and camaraderie.

When I went to visit Aunt Mary Margaret, she suggested that we have a reunion. She thought a reunion was long past due. Over breakfast, we began to plan the party. Since we have family living in the western part of Wisconsin, we felt it would be best to hold the reunion on one of the relative's apple farm. It is breath taking to see the hills, valleys and many beautiful trees. This family not only raises apples, but also has horses and other animals. The apple farm is filled with peace and tranquility. It is always a joy to visit the family at the apple farm. It is a great place to spend an afternoon meeting family members, and sharing conversation peppered with family stories, memories and the "what's new".

So, from our family to yours, please enjoy the recipes!!!

Family Reunion Menu

Steak Sandwiches
Hot Dogs
Condiments
Pickles, Olives, Carrots,
Grape Tomatoes on a Platter
Taco Chips and Salsa
Assorted Chips
Tortellini Picnic Salad
Vegetable Salad
Three Bean Salad (Baked Beans)
Baked Beans Supreme
Irish Coffee Cake
Deviled Eggs
Strawberry Applesauce Dessert

Note: If a family member is allergic to nuts, please delete the nuts.

Tortellini Picnic Salad

Yield: Twelve to fifteen servings
Recipe of Cousin Miki

Salad:
2-12 ounce packages (each) fresh three cheese tortellini
1-14 ounce can artichoke hearts packed in water, drained and cut into quarters
1 cup Roma tomatoes, chopped
1 cup (4 ounces) crumbled feta cheese
$^1/_2$ cup walnuts, chopped

Cook the pasta using the package directions; drain. Cool slightly. Combine the pasta, artichokes, tomato, cheese and walnuts in a bowl and mix gently.

Oil and Vinegar Dressing for the salad:
$^1/_2$ cup olive oil
$^1/_4$ cup white wine vinegar
$^1/_4$ cup chopped green onions
1 medium garlic clove, minced
1 tablespoon basil
1 teaspoon dill weed

Combine the olive oil, vinegar, green onions, garlic, basil and dill weed in a jar with a tight fitting lid and seal tightly. Shake to mix. Gently mix the salad dressing into the salad. Toss the salad to coat. Serve chilled. See picture on page 12 in the color section.

Vegetable Salad

Yield: Fifteen servings
Recipe of Aunt Mary Margaret

4 cups cauliflower
4 cups broccoli
1 cup sliced celery
1 cup frozen peas, thawed
1 small red onion, chopped
1 cup sliced water chestnuts, drained
$^1/_2$ pound bacon cut into small pieces, cooked until crisp

Dressing:
2 cups mayonnaise
$^1/_4$ cup sugar
2 teaspoons white vinegar
$^1/_4$ teaspoon salt
$^1/_4$ cup Parmesan cheese

Cut cauliflower and broccoli into small flower sizes. Combine the cauliflower, broccoli, celery, peas, red onion, water chestnuts and bacon. In a separate bowl, mix together the mayonnaise, sugar, vinegar, salt and Parmesan cheese. Pour over the vegetables and mix together to coat the vegetables. Marinate the salad in the refrigerator at least 4 hours or overnight or overnight. Served cold. See picture on page 12 in the color section.

Note: This is the genuine, gosh but it's so good, baked bean casserole Grandma always brought to the big family picnics.

Baked Beans Supreme

Yield: Fifteen to twenty servings
Recipe of Cousin Miki

1-28 ounce can pork and beans, do not drain
1-16 ounce can pork and beans, do not drain
1-15 ounce can butter beans, drained
1-15 ounces lima beans, drained
2 large onions, sliced into rings and halved
1 pound bacon, raw, cut into 2 inch pieces
1 teaspoon dry mustard
$1/2$ cup red wine vinegar
2 cups packed brown sugar

Preheat oven to 325 F. Combine beans, onion, and bacon in a 3 quart baking dish or small roaster. Combine the mustard, vinegar and brown sugar and add to beans. Bake uncovered for $3^1/2$ hours.

Note: Cynthia says that she likes the beans best cooked in her crock pot on low for 3 to 4 hours. Her family loves horses and this is a favorite dish she serves for her family and friends at the family's horse party gatherings.

Three Bean Salad (Baked Beans)

Yield:Twelve to fifteen servings
Recipe of Cousin-in-law Cynthia

1-28 ounce can baked beans with tomatoes
1-14.5 ounce can butter beans, drained
1-14.5 ounce can kidney beans, drained
$1/2$ cup ketchup
$2/3$ cup brown sugar
$1/4$ cup cubed mild cheddar cheese
6 slices bacon, fried, drained and crumbled
$1/4$ teaspoon garlic salt
$1/4$ teaspoon dry mustard

Mix together the baked beans, butter beans, and kidney beans. Add ketchup, brown sugar, cheese, bacon, garlic salt and dry mustard. Stir all ingredients together. Bake at 350 F, uncovered, for 45 minutes or until bean dish is piping hot and bubbly.

Note: To make a blueberry or apple coffee cake, add 1 cup of fresh blueberries or apples.
Fold in the fresh fruit at the end of the mixing process.

Irish Coffee Cake

Yield: Two 8x8 inch coffee cakes
Recipe of Aunt Alberta

$1/2$ cup butter
1 cup sugar
2 eggs
2 cups flour
$1/2$ teaspoon salt
1 teaspoon baking soda
1 teaspoon baking powder
1 cup sour cream
1 teaspoon vanilla
$1/2$ teaspoon cinnamon

Topping:

$1/4$ cup white sugar
$1/2$ cup brown sugar
$1 1/2$ teaspoons cinnamon
1 cup pecans

Cream butter and sugar together. Beat in one egg at a time. Beat well. Sift together the flour, salt, baking soda and baking powder. Alternate the sour cream with the dry ingredients. Add the vanilla and cinnamon. Stir the ingredients well.

Topping Directions:

Mix together the white and brown sugar. Add the cinnamon and pecans. Mix the ingredients together. Divide batter into two 8x8 inch pans. Divide topping and sprinkle over each coffee cake. Bake at 350 F for 30 to 40 minutes or until toothpick inserted in the middle of the coffeecake comes out clean.

Other Party Details

Family member Linda arranged the pickles, olives, carrots, and grape tomatoes on a tray. Another family member purchased a case of 30 individually packaged assorted chips. Taco chips were put out with a bowl of salsa. The salsa was purchased at the grocery store. Pat Nekola made three flan tortes. The flan torte recipe is found on page 156 in the *Picnics, Catering on the Move Cookbook*. Condiments of steak sauce, mustard and catsup was placed in a basket and placed on the table. Buns were placed in a basket and placed onto the serving table. My husband and cousin David grilled the steaks and hot dogs to order. The steaks were thinly sliced and especially designed for making a sandwich. Both meats took very little time to grill.

Deviled Eggs

Yield: Twelve deviled eggs
Recipe of Aunt Cassie

6 eggs
1¼ teaspoon salt
2 tablespoons lemon Juice
1 teaspoon prepared mustard
¼ cup mayonnaise
¼ teaspoon pepper
1 teaspoon horseradish (optional)
Garnish
Sprinkle with paprika
1 slice green olive per egg

Place eggs into a saucepan and cover with cold water, 1 teaspoon salt, and lemon juice. Bring to a boil and continue cooking approximately 7-10 minutes. Purge the eggs into cold water and when eggs are cool enough, remove the shells. Cut eggs lengthwise and remove the yolk. Place yolks into a small mixing bowl and mash them well. Add the mustard, mayonnaise, ¼ teaspoon salt, pepper, and horseradish. Mix together until smooth and creamy. Place yolk mixture into the hollowed portion of each cooked egg. Garnish as desired and chill. Serve and enjoy.

Note: The strawberry applesauce recipe can be made into a salad. Omit the graham cracker crust, whipped cream, and fresh strawberries. Place Jell-O® salad into a 9x13 inch pan. Refrigerate until firm. Cut the Jell-O® into squares and place on each lettuce leaf. Top each square with a dab of mayonnaise. Serve with the meal.

Note: Use Strawberry applesauce to give the Jell-O® a brighter red color or add a drop of red food coloring to the filling. Use the food coloring sparingly. To save on calories, omit the crust and use sugar free strawberry Jell-O® and sugar free non-dairy whipped topping. Also use sugar-free ice cream.

Strawberry Applesauce Dessert

Yield: One 9x13 pan
Recipe of Aunt Cassie's friend

Graham Cracker Crust:
$^1/_3$ cups sugar
$1^1/_3$ cups graham cracker crumbs
6 tablespoons butter, melted

Stir sugar into the graham cracker crumbs. Moisten the graham cracker crumbs with the butter. Stir all together and shape the graham cracker mixture into a crust in the bottom of the pan. Bake crust for 5 to 6 minutes at 350 F. Cool the crust.

Filling:
1 large package strawberry Jell-O®
1 pint vanilla ice cream
$^1/_8$ teaspoon salt, optional
$1^1/_2$ cups applesauce
1-8 ounce container non-dairy whipped topping, thawed
1 quart fresh strawberries, sliced

Make Jell-O® with 1 cup boiling water. Spoon in ice cream and stir until melted. Add salt and applesauce. Pour the Jell-O® mixture into graham cracker crust. Refrigerator for two hours or until firm. Top Jell-O® with non-dairy whipped topping and fresh strawberries slices. Cut the dessert into 4x4 size pieces to make 16 servings or 3x4 pieces makes 12 servings. Enjoy!

Music Camp Party

A Music Camp Luncheon

Every year in August the church music director plans a music camp. All ages of students participate in the event. I had the opportunity to work with Mr. MG, the Church Music director. Each year, I came up with a new idea for the luncheon. My job was to spend some time with the younger children teaching them manners and showing them how to go through a buffet line. The first year I worked music camp, I did a brunch. This food style of service was very foreign to many students. I had different egg dishes, various coffee cakes, juice and milk. Some students were reluctant to try some of the dishes, while others found the new food adventure tasty. The following year, I made an international buffet, made up of three individual tables with different foods from three different countries. I had Mexican, Chinese and Italian themes. The desserts were an American theme. The students were surprised that there was no waiting. They could pick up a plate in any line and help themselves to the food. They really enjoyed the lunch.

Two years passed without helping because Mr. MG moved to another church. I really missed his music and his diligent work at the music camp. He has a way of teaching the students to sing with their hearts and he helps them understand that singing is a wonderful way of praising our Lord. Every child is welcome to sing in Mr. MG's music camp. He is a great promoter and an accomplished artist. He knows his music well and it shows. God always asks every human being to share his/her talents. Mr. MG generously shares his talents, and all reap the benefits.

I made a surprise visit to the church where Mr. MG is presently working. I volunteered to help make the lunch at the summer music camp at his new location. The theme of the music camp for this year is "Journey." He agreed to have the luncheon.

When the day of the luncheon arrived, my neighbor set up his train for the younger children. This was a big hit with the kids. Our menu was very simple. Cheese and meat trays were ordered from our local deli, complete with buns and condiments. Potato chips, taco chips, and salsa along with assorted fresh fruit and relishes were also served with the meal. Homemade desserts were made up in shapes of a plane and a train. Other simple cakes were also served.

Another station was made up of lasagna, tossed salad, assorted dressings and garlic bread. My neighbor lady helped me prepare the lunch and the custodians set up the tables. Family members helped serve the lunch. My husband helped me clean up. The children were very polite and thankful for the lunch.

It was fun to see the children's faces when I announced that there were three tables of food. They had my permission to go to the dessert table first as long as they ate something nutritious. The smallest little girl got into the dessert line first and enjoyed every bite. To all of our surprise, she even ate a sandwich and some fruit.

For this year's luncheon, it was wonderful to see all the children, young adults, and staff socializing and enjoying the meal, train exhibit, the American ladybug picnic, and Italian theme tables.

See other setups of buffets on pages 188-191 in the *Picnics, Catering on the Move* book by Pat Nekola.

Some of the leftovers were served at break time. The teenagers especially enjoyed the snacks.

In the afternoon a church member kept the younger children occupied with arts and crafts while different groups practiced their parts for the upcoming performance. At one of the breaks, three young boys talked to me about the height of a giraffe. One boy thought a giraffe was 12 feet tall. When they asked me the height of the giraffe, my answer was, "I do not know". I went to the library and came back the next day with the answer. Matt was surprise that the average giraffe was 17 feet tall. Some grow as tall as 18 feet. I ran off a copy of the information about the giraffe for Matt and his friends. Do you know that a giraffe sleeps standing up?

Matt informed me that he was very good in math. So I posed a math question. If a giraffe is 17 feet tall, how many inches tall is a giraffe? I gave him a formula that 12 inches equals a foot. He came back with the answer of 204 inches. We both decided that the giraffe is very tall.

It was fun for me to sit on the floor and listen to the children talk and express themselves while waiting for their turn to sing.

At the end of the week, families gathered at church to listen to the children and young adults sing with zest. The church was packed and the children did not let Mr. MG down. Everyone felt the benefit of a successful week. It warmed my heart to see and listen to the children from surrounding churches singing their hearts out. It was another successful year for music camp. The music goes on forever and continues to ring in my ears with the sweet melodies and memories. I continue to give praise to God with a huge thank you to Mr. MG, the staff, and volunteers for sharing their talents.

Music Camp
A Journey Sent With Spirit Poem
by Pat Nekola

It is Monday; we're off to a good start.
With voices in unison, each of us singing our part.

Singing with songs and signing with our hands,
Playing our instruments while reading the music on our stands.

Remembering to always be a part of the team,
Our bright and shining faces with spirit beam.

Working hard to be good shepherds to meet our goal,
At the end of music camp, we each have learned our role.

The journey sent praising our God might be very long.
It is beautiful when music is sent to God in a song.

Spending the week practicing with songs for the Journey,
Fills our hearts with spirit and love throughout the Journey.

High school teens and young students ringing the bells,
Expressing a meaningful message which we have learned well.

Acting as servants for God, our work ahead symbolized with our lit candle,
We feel confident there is nothing in life we can't handle.

On Thursday, our group practices to record,
With happiness we sing, praising the Lord.

The shining and lingering memories of music camp,
It is a blessing to everyone like an indelible stamp.

God sees the message in each person and child's mind,
For the journey of music continues throughout a lifetime.

Bell Party

The Bell Family Birthday Parties

Julie worked for us in our catering business in her teenager years. She learned how to decorate wedding cakes, do food preparation and she also worked many catered parties. She went to college and studied to be a teacher. She came back to visit my husband and me during her semester breaks. When she was engaged she called our catering business to ask if she could make her own wedding cake. I agreed to give her the space to fulfill one of her wedding wishes. I volunteered to set up her wedding cake because I didn't think she should try to tackle such a project on her wedding day! The cake was beautiful and Julie made a lovely bride. I am especially proud of Julie because she had taken her catering job very seriously and she learned some life skill, which she applied in her own person life.

She and her husband Bronco have been married for several years with two great kids. Megan is an accomplished pianist and Robert is our little builder. As parents, they both have strived to make a loving home for their family, and they also have taught their children to be responsible and to respect others. They have good solid values in their home.

Julie said, she would have birthday parties for each child until they turned ten. I attended all 20 birthday parties. There was always a phone call or a computer invitation inviting my husband and I to attend each child's birthday party. Other friends and mostly family came religiously, year after year to show their support. We looked forward to attending and watching all the cousins playing together and enjoying their day at the Bell family gatherings. Both grandmothers also attended and we enjoyed conversing with them. The uncles often watched the football game while the ladies just visited. Sometimes the young adults gathered around the dining room table and chatted, played games, and/or enjoyed the piano playing.

Megan and Robert would thank each person for their gift at the party. In addition, each year Megan and Robert sent us their own version of a thank you note, when they became old enough to print or write. I have saved several of the notes because it has touched my heart and created a lasting memory.

Whenever I stop to visit, I am always welcomed and I feel like part of their family. It has been a pleasure to watch Megan and Robert grow and become young adults.

The food at the Bell parties is very traditional. The following recipes have always been a part of the Bell gatherings. The family has been most generous in sharing their recipes. We always start with appetizers and end up with the sandwiches and every family's favorite potato dish. Of course, it wouldn't be a family gathering party without dessert. I hope you can enjoy making and eating their family favorites at your next party.

The Traditional Recipes for the Bell Parties

Hot Artichoke and Spinach Dip
Yield: Sixteen to twenty

1-(6½ ounce) jar marinated artichokes hearts, drained, coarsely chopped
1-10 ounce package frozen creamed spinach, thawed
¼ cup mayonnaise
¼ cup sour cream
1 small clove of garlic, pressed
½ cup grated fresh Parmesan cheese
1 large red bell pepper, diced, optional
1 large tomato, diced, optional
2-8 ounce packages (each) rye chips
1-28 ounce loaf of rye bread, cut into squares

Preheat oven to 375 F. Combine chopped artichoke hearts, spinach, mayonnaise, sour cream, garlic, and Parmesan cheese. Mix well. Place the artichoke mixture into an oven safe baking dish. Bake for 20-25 minutes or until heated through. Garnish with red bell pepper or chopped tomatoes or both vegetables. Serve with rye chips or rye bread squares.

Artichoke Dip (no Spinach)
Yield: Sixteen to twenty servings

2 cans artichoke hearts, chopped
1 cup mayonnaise
1 cup shredded Parmesan cheese
1-8 ounce package mozzarella cheese, finely shredded
¼ teaspoon garlic salt
1 teaspoon dehydrated parsley flakes
1-8 ounce package rye chips
1-6 ounce package bagel chips

Mix together, artichoke hearts, mayonnaise, Parmesan cheese, and mozzarella cheese, garlic salt, and parsley flakes. Bake in a 3-quart slow cooker on low heat until heated through and cheese is melted, or bake at 375 F for 15-20 minutes. Keep hot while serving. Serve with rye chips or bagel chips or both.

Some of the family members also like cold shrimp. The hostess generally purchases a couple of shrimp rings (20 count) with the shrimp sauce. The shrimp rings are located in the frozen meat department at your local grocery store. Generally, the hostess purchases salami and cheese, fruit and vegetable platters to serve twenty people.

Note: Every family always has a simple and favorite dish. The Bell family enjoys Ruffles® potato chips and onion dip. In fact the family often makes a double batch of dip. They go to Sam's and buy the 3 pound box of Ruffles® potato chips. You can also purchase Ruffles® potato chips in 11.5 ounce bags at your local grocery store.

Easy-Ruffles® Potato Chips and Onion Dip
Yield: Sixteen to twenty servings

1-16 ounce container sour cream
Ounce Lipton® onion soup packet

Mix the sour cream and onion soup well. Serve with Ruffles® style potato chips.

Note: Julie suggests 1-2 packages of taco seasoning depending on how spicy a person likes their taco salad.

Taco Salad
Yield: Twenty servings

1-8 ounce cream cheese
1-16 ounce container of sour cream
1 or 2-1.25 ounce packages (each) taco seasoning
$^1/_2$ head of iceberg lettuce, finely shredded, and patted dry with a paper towel
2 cups finely shredded taco or cheddar cheese
1 small onion, chopped
1-2.25 ounce can, sliced black ripe olives
2 large ripe tomatoes, chopped
1-24 ounce bag taco chips

Soften the cream cheese. Beat the cream cheese. Add the sour cream and taco seasoning. Mix together until smooth. Spread the mixture on the bottom of a dish or round platter. Layer in order: shredded lettuce, shredded cheese, chopped onion, chopped black olives, and chopped tomatoes. Serve with taco chips.

Italian Beef
Yield: Fourteen to sixteen servings

4 pounds sirloin tip roast
1-1 ounce package Good Seasons® Italian dressing
1-16 ounce jar pepperoncini, (whole)

Place the sirloin tip roast in a 6-quart slow cooker. Add the Italian dressing. Pour the pepperoncini peppers and juice over the roast. Cook on low for 8-10 hours. Shred the meat when done. Enjoy on a fresh hoagie roll!

Beef Tenderloin

Yield: Fourteen to sixteen

1-4 pound tenderloin
4 tablespoons butter, melted

Preheat oven to 325 F. Place the tenderloin in a roaster pan. Pour the butter over the meat. Bake for 20 minutes.

Ingredients for the Marinade:

$^1/_2$ cup onion, diced
4 tablespoons butter
4 tablespoons soy sauce
2 teaspoon Grey Poupon® mustard
$^3/_4$ cup cooking sherry
$^1/_8$ teaspoon pepper
1-16 ounce package sliced mushrooms, optional

Sauté the onion in the butter. Add the soy sauce, mustard, cooking sherry, and pepper. Bring all the ingredients to a boil, and cook for one minute. Pour over the meat and bake at 300 F for 30 minutes. Baste often. Slice the meat (approximately $1^1/_2$ inch slices). Add the sliced mushrooms to the meat and continue to bake for another 30 minutes or until desired tenderness and doneness of the meat. Serve the tenderloin on a Kaiser® roll.

Note: O'Brien® potatoes have green peppers and onions. The Bells usually make two batches of this style of potato because it is the family's favorite. The recipe was passed down from their good friends (Diane and Bill).

Cheesy Potatoes

Yield: Ten servings

1 cup sour cream
1 10³/₄ ounce can of cream of chicken soup
1 small onion, chopped
1 tablespoon freeze dried chives
1-16 ounce package shredded cheddar cheese
¹/₂ teaspoon salt
1 teaspoon pepper
1 package O'Brien® potatoes (frozen)

Topping:
2 tablespoons butter, melted
2 cups cornflakes, crushed
Coat the cornflakes with the melted butter.

Preheat oven to 350 F. Combine sour cream, soup, onion, chives, cheese, salt, and pepper. Mix well. Add the frozen potatoes and mix. Place in a lightly greased oven safe dish. Cover with a layer of corn flake mixture. Bake covered for 40 minutes, or until heated through. Uncover the potatoes and bake for 10-15 minutes more or until the topping is slightly browned.

I often bring cole slaw and plain Jell-O® to each party. The recipes are found on the following pages in the Picnics, Catering on the Move book by Pat Nekola.

Cole slaw-pages 31-32
Jell-O®-pages 52-53

The children especially like the plain strawberry Jell-O® and the grandmothers like the cole slaw.

Due to time constraints, Julie normally orders a birthday cake from her local grocery store. Last year Megan made the sheet cake for Robert. They like white cake. She decided to color one layer of the cake pink and the second layer blue. She frosted and decorated it for Robert as a gift. It was a special birthday cake and it also was very tasty.

Aunt Cindy brought a most delicious chocolate cake. She calls it Adele's Chocolate Cake. It is an unusual cake because it does not have eggs. Adele was Cindy's neighbor when she was growing up. Her father really liked Adele's chocolate cake. The family begged Adele to please give their family the recipe. Adele made it clear it was her family's secret recipe from years ago. When Cindy's father got sick he craved for Adele's chocolate cake. Adele was very kind and made him the cake. Before Cindy's father passed away, Adele finally gave the family's secret recipe to Cindy so her father could have this wonderful cake often. Adele has since passed away and I have received permission to share this great chocolate cake with my readers.

Note: Adele's Chocolate Cake has no eggs. Due to the amount of water, you may have to turn down the temperature to 300 F after 30 minutes of baking if the center of the cake is still not baked to prevent the sides from drying out or burning. It is helpful to bake the cake in the center of the oven rack.

Adele's Chocolate Cake

Yield: One 9x13 cake

3 cups flour
2 cups sugar
$\frac{1}{2}$ cup cocoa
1 teaspoon salt
2 teaspoons baking soda
2 tablespoons white vinegar
$\frac{2}{3}$ cup canola oil
2 teaspoons vanilla
2 cups lukewarm water

Preheat oven to 350 F. Place flour, sugar, cocoa, salt, and baking soda into a mixing bowl. Add the vinegar to the water. Add the oil and the vanilla. Stir in the vinegar and water mixture into the dry ingredients. Grease and flour the 9x13 pan. Pour batter into prepared pan. Bake for 35-45 minutes or until toothpick inserted in the center of the cake comes out clean.

Note: The frosting makes for a very tasty cake. I use hazelnut flavored coffee. No one can figure out why the frosting is a little different. However you can use regular or decaf coffee instead of the hazelnut flavored coffee.

Adele's Chocolate Frosting

Yield: Frosting for one 9x13 cake

$^1/_2$ cup butter
$^2/_3$ cup cocoa
3 cups powdered sugar
$^1/_4$ teaspoon salt
1 teaspoon vanilla
1 teaspoon coffee
$^1/_3$ cup milk minus 1 teaspoon

Cream the butter. Add the cocoa, powdered sugar, salt, and vanilla. Slowly add coffee/ milk mixture to the frosting. Beat until smooth and creamy. Frost the top of the cake. Serve with vanilla ice cream.

To conclude, family and extended family are the most priceless gifts. All the material goods will never replace friends, family or extended family. So, I am happy to say I am blessed to be a part of the Bell family.

Baptism Party

Life in our Neighborhood

My husband and I were married in the early 1970's. Like most young couples, we wanted to have our own home and raise a family. We decided to build our home out in the country. We still reside at this same home over 30 years later. We were one of the first couples to settle in our subdivision. We met the new families, one by one, as they built their homes and started their families.

We would take our neighborhood walks and watch each home being built and welcome the families. My husband got the nickname "Digger" because he moved this overwhelming pile of dirt around our one acre lot. No one could believe he would accomplish the job. However, one year later the dirt was in place in our yard.

We couldn't have children so we became friends to the neighbors and their children. Little Jeff loved to bake and make pie dough sticks. He would come to our home and say Mrs. Cola, "wherries, please! please!" He couldn't say cherries. He loved maraschino cherries. I gave Jeff a gallon jar of maraschino cherries as one of his wedding gifts.

I made a castle cake for his brother Tommy's 5th birthday. Good ole Jeff piped up and asked, "Mrs. Cola, where is the moat?" We still laugh today about his question. Now he is the father to his own beautiful daughter.

Many of the moms in the neighborhood elected to be stay-home-moms. As we became acquainted, the women became friends and a strong support group developed. We celebrated each others birthdays in our homes. As the children grew up, most of the women went back to work. Our neighborhood group continued to meet at a restaurant of choice for each birthday. We just enjoy each other's company and we have an unusual relationship. We all lead our own lives, but we are there for each other and have maintained that great support system. As each family was raising their children, we all cheered each other on and assured each other all our problems would be resolved and our children would grow up just fine.

When I had breast cancer, they were there for me. When anyone from the group gets sick or a mother or a father dies we always band together. Three of us from our group struggled with moms with Alzheimer's. We again showed a strong support for each other.

When our 8 year old neighbor was struck down and killed by a drunk driver we helped. Several neighbors washed and ironed clothes. Some neighbors cooked for the family. We helped each other in whatever ways we could. This was one of my toughest assignments. Losing someone so young was hard to take. No matter the circumstance we are always there for each other. We laugh and cry together and we continue to support each other through good times and bad.

I personally enjoyed watching the neighbor children grow up. We had many neighborhood gatherings. Just this past summer, Debbie and Bob had a great party. We wanted to welcome our new neighbors. For several months many old neighbors cheered on our new neighbors as they built their large garage. It was delightful to meet them. The gathering was informal. We swam, had a cook-out, and great conversation. One of our neighbors is very quiet. He likes to travel. I took the time to listen to his adventures with his wife. I learned a lot about Mexico and other countries. It was a joy to take the time to gather and spend a relaxing day.

I remember my neighbors for being generous and helpful whenever needed. Our neighbor man will help move furniture or pick up the mail when we are out of town. One of the ladies in our birthday group is an exceptional seamstress. She sews bridal gowns and also does alterations. She always has been very generous in giving her time as a seamstress to the ladies in our birthday group. Another lady is very knowledgeable about medicine and she will give advice with medical tips or suggest which doctor is best to treat you. She and her husband gave a lovely party for their daughter's high school and college graduation. When we stop over to their home they take time to visit with us.

We often organized holiday parties or informal open houses. We would set out a buffet line and just visit. One of the ladies is an artist and does exceptional artwork. She has won many awards. Her buffet tables looked like a holiday picture found in a food magazine. Her husband is also very talented and finished their entire home using their living room as his work area. One of the ladies from our birthday group wanted a plaid wool skirt to wear at the party. She was very clever. She bought a man's Pendleton wool bathrobe for pennies. She took the robe apart and she made herself a skirt. I remember how lovely she looked at the party.

I have enjoyed parties from a very young age. It meant we could interact and have fun. I also have given a few open house parties for the neighborhood. I would like to share some of my open house appetizer recipes. They are some of my favorites and they are very easy to prepare and serve.

Note: There are several Triscuit® recipes. I usually did two varieties of Triscuits®.

Sausage Triscuit®

Yield: Thirty Triscuits®

$^1/_2$ pound butter, softened
1-13 ounce box Triscuits®
1 medium onion, finely diced (optional)
8 slices American cheese
1 pound precooked smoked sausage

Butter each Triscuit®. Sprinkle a scant amount of onion onto each buttered cracker. Cut each American cheese slice into 4 even squares. The cheese must fit each Triscuit®. Slice the smoked sausage into 30 slices. Top each Triscuit® with one smoked sausage slice. Bake on a cookie sheet at 400 F for 1 to 2 minutes or until the cheese melts or microwave for 30 seconds. Serve hot on a platter lined with a doily.

Ham and Cheese Triscuit®

Yield: Thirty Triscuits®

$^1/_2$ pound butter, softened
1 tablespoon poppy seed
1 tablespoon yellow mustard
$^1/_2$ teaspoon horseradish (optional)
1-13 ounce box Triscuits®
8 slices deli ham
8 slices Swiss cheese

Blend together the butter, poppy seed, yellow mustard and horseradish. Butter each Triscuit® with this mixture. Cut each piece of deli ham and Swiss cheese into four sections. Place one piece of ham over the buttered Triscuit® and one piece of cheese over the ham to fit the Triscuit®. Bake on a cookie sheet at 400 F for 1-2 minutes or microwave for 30 second. Serve hot on a platter lined with a doily.

Note: There are approximately 60-65 whole Triscuits® per 12 ounce box.

Pizza Snacks

Yield: Sixty snacks

1 cup butter, softened
1-12 ounce box Triscuits®
2 teaspoons oregano
$^1/_2$ teaspoon garlic powder
$^1/_4$ teaspoon onion salt
2-6 ounce cans (each) tomato paste
1-16 ounce package mozzarella cheese, finely shredded

Butter Triscuits® the day of the party. Add the oregano, garlic powder, and onion salt to the tomato paste. Mix well. Spread an approximate teaspoon of the seasoned tomato paste on each Triscuit®. Place a teaspoon of cheese on each Triscuit®. Bake on a cookie sheet at 400 F. or until the cheese melts, (about 1 minute) or microwave for 15-30 seconds. Serve hot on a platter lined with a doily.

Crab Triscuits®

Yield: Forty appetizers

1-13 ounce box Triscuits®
$^1/_2$ cup butter, softened
2 cups grated Swiss cheese
1-12 ounce package imitation crabmeat, flaked style
$^1/_4$ to $^1/_2$ cup mayonnaise

Butter Triscuits® the day of the party. Add the cheese to the finely flaked crabmeat. Moisten with the mayonnaise to hold the ingredients together. Spread 2 teaspoons of crab mixture onto each Triscuit®. Bake on a cookie sheet at 400 F for 1 to 2 minutes or microwave for 15 to 30 seconds. Serve hot on a platter lined with a doily.

Ham Roll-ups

Yield: Sixty

2-8 ounce packages (each) cream cheese, softened
1 teaspoon Worcestershire sauce
$^1/_2$ teaspoon onion powder
9 slices deli ham
1-16 ounce jar green olives with pimentos

Beat cream cheese with Worcestershire sauce and onion powder. Lay out the ham slices onto of a cutting board. Pat the ham dry with a paper towel. Spread the cream cheese over the ham slice. Drain the olives and gently dry each olive. At the narrow end of each piece of ham, line up 5 to 6 olives in a row. Starting from this end of the ham, roll the ham and olives tightly to form a cylinder. Chill for two hours. With a sharp wet knife cut each ham roll crosswise into 7 pieces resembling a pinwheel. Each pinwheel should have the olive pimento in its center. Serve cold on a platter with a doily.

*Note: The filo dough pieces are very thin and will dry out if the dough is not kept in a 1 quart bag.
    Work each appetizer very quickly to keep from cracking.*

Greek Appetizers

Yield: Forty appetizers

2-16 ounce cartons ricotta cheese
1-16 ounce package feta cheese
3 eggs
1 pound butter, melted
1-16 ounce box frozen filo dough, thawed

Beat cheeses and eggs together. Melt butter. Put the filo dough into a 1 quart storage bag. The filo sheets remain flat. Butter a breadboard. Lay one piece of filo dough down onto the board. Cut the filo dough into 6 strips; brush each strip with melted butter. Place 1 teaspoon filling onto the bottom end of each strip. Roll up as if folding up a flag. The Greek appetizer looks like a triangle when completed. Repeat with remaining filo dough sheets. Bake the Greek at 400 F for 8-10 minutes or until golden brown. Serve hot.

Note: Make 1 to 2 days ahead of the party.

Cucumber Mousse

Yield: Fifty servings

5 packets plus 1 teaspoon unflavored gelatin
2 cups chicken stock, heated
2 cups mayonnaise
2 cups evaporated milk
3 tablespoons sugar
3 tablespoons Worcestershire sauce
8 cucumbers, peeled, seeded, and chopped fine
2 tablespoons onion, chopped fine
1 bunch fresh parsley, chopped fine
1 bunch fresh parsley for garnishing
1 red bell pepper, cut into strips

Dissolve gelatin in the chicken broth and cool. Mix together the mayonnaise, evaporated milk, sugar, and Worcestershire sauce. Add the mixture to the cucumbers, onion and 1 bunch of fresh parsley. Pour mixture into two 2-quart molds and refrigerate. Remove the cucumber mousse and place onto two platters. Garnish with parsley and red Bell pepper strips. Serve with crackers.

Vegetable Tree

Yield: Twenty

1 Styrofoam® cone
Foil
1 head romaine lettuce, cleaned
1-8 ounce package baby carrots
1 head cauliflower, cleaned
3 pounds broccoli, cleaned
1 bunch of celery, cleaned,
2 packages radishes, cleaned
2 bunches fresh parsley, cleaned
2 packages frilled toothpicks

Wrap a Styrofoam® cone with foil. Cover with romaine leaves, fastening the lettuce with frilled tooth picks. Cut up the cauliflower and broccoli into flower-like pieces. Cut celery into three inch strips. Make radish roses. Toothpick the vegetables onto the tree and toothpick the parsley in between the assorted vegetables. Place the vegetable tree in the middle of a 16 inch round tray. Arrange the remaining vegetables around the tree to fill the tray. With a toothpick, place a radish onto the top of the tree. Serve with Dill Dip. The recipe is found on page 51 in *Picnics, Catering on the Move*.

Smoked Salmon

Yield: Thirty

1-8 pound smoked salmon
1 head romaine lettuce
3 fresh lemons
1 red bell pepper, cleaned and cut into strips
1 bunch parsley

Cut off the skin from the smoked salmon on both sides. Clean the romaine and separate the leaves. Pat the lettuce dry. Place the romaine lettuce on a tray especially designed for salmon. Lay the salmon onto the romaine lettuce. Score the salmon on both sides. Slice the lemons and place around the salmon. Garnish with the red bell pepper strips and parsley. Serve with crackers of choice.

Note: I generally purchase two cocktail buns per guest.

Beef Teriyaki

Yield: Twenty servings

5 pounds tenderloin
Kitchen Bouquet®
Onion salt
1 cup oil
2 cups water
$^1/_2$ cup soy sauce
1 cup brown sugar
1 teaspoon ginger
$^1/_2$ cup dehydrated onions
1 cup green peppers, diced
Cocktail buns

Remove the silver skin from the top of the tenderloin. Brush Kitchen Bouquet® over the top of the tenderloin. Sprinkle onion salt over the tenderloin. Bake at 275 F until baked to desired doneness. Mix together the oil, water, soy sauce, brown sugar, ginger, onions, and green peppers. Slice the meat about one inch thick. Pour the sauce over the meat. Refrigerate and marinate for 2 hours. Bake at 300 F for 30 to 40 minutes or desired doneness. Serve on cocktail buns.

Note: The seasoned flour recipe is from my mother when she ran her own restaurant. She made many chicken strips for snacks and become very famous in her town for her great chicken strips.

Chicken Strips

Yield: Twenty servings

5 pounds boneless, skinless chicken breast cut into strips
3 eggs
1 quart buttermilk
15 ounces Lawry® seasoned salt
1 ounce garlic salt
Seasoned flour
5 pounds flour
2 ounces pepper
Oil for deep frying

Cut each chicken breast into strips. Beat the eggs into the buttermilk. Set aside. Mix together the seasoned salt, garlic salt, and dip the chicken strips into the buttermilk egg mixture. Mix together the flour, season salt, garlic salt, and pepper. Working with a small amount at a time, place seasoned flour onto a dinner plate. Dip the chicken strips into the buttermilk/egg mixture. Roll the chicken strips into the seasoned flour. Deep fry the chicken strips until strips are cooked through and golden brown. Place on a cookie sheet with lined paper towel. Keep warm. Serve a few at a time on a platter lined with a doily.

Note: I also made the broccoli salad. The recipe is found on page 37 in the Picnics, Catering On the Move.

Note: I always make finger dessert for Christmas. I also make the Christmas wreath a small size.
I place my finger desserts on a tiered pinecone tray which makes a great impression.

Christmas Wreaths
Yield: Twenty

½ cup butter
1-15 ounce jar Marshmallow creme
1-28 ounce box of cornflakes
A couple drops of green food coloring
1 teaspoon vanilla
1-3 ounce container red cinnamon decors

Melt butter. Add marshmallow creme, cornflakes, food coloring, and flavoring. Mix well until cornflakes stick to the marshmallow cream. Shape cornflake mixture into a hollow circle to form each Christmas wreath. Decorate each wreath with 3 cinnamon decors.

Chinese Christmas Cookies
Yield: Twenty cookies

1-12 ounce package butterscotch chips
1-12 ounce package chocolate chips
1-12 ounce can Chinese noodles
1-11½ ounce can cashews
Butter

Melt chips in the top of double boiler and add remaining ingredients. Form the mixture into cookies. Place 1 teaspoon mixture to form the cookie on buttered waxed paper.

Spritz Cookies
Yield: Twelve to eighteen cookies

1 cup butter
½ cup plus 1 tablespoon sugar
1 egg
¾ teaspoon salt
1 teaspoon vanilla
2 teaspoon almond extract
2½ cups all-purpose flour
1 ounce jar red and green (each) colored sugar

Cream butter. Add the sugar. Blend in the egg, salt, extract, and flour. With hands, knead the dough in hands until soft and pliable. Do not grease the cookie sheets. Press the dough through a cookie press onto the cookie sheets. Decorate as desired with colored sugar. Bake at 375 F for about 8 to 10 minutes.

Mexican Wedding Cakes

Yield: Five dozen cookies

1 cup butter
$1/2$ cup powdered sugar
$1/2$ teaspoon salt
1 teaspoon vanilla
2 cups all purpose flour
Powdered sugar

Cream butter. Add $1/2$ cup powdered sugar gradually. Blend in the salt, vanilla, and flour. Mixture is stiff. Pinch off a small piece of dough and roll a ball into your hand. Place each ball onto un-greased cookie sheet. Bake at 400 F for about 8 to 10 minutes. Roll in powdered sugar while hot. Place each cookie on a cooling rack to cool. Place onto a platter with a doily.

Pecan Fingers

Yield: Four dozen cookies

1 cup butter
$1/2$ cup powdered sugar
$1/2$ teaspoon salt
1 teaspoon vanilla
2 cups all purpose flour
1 cup finely chopped pecans

Cream butter. Add sugar gradually. Blend in salt, vanilla, and flour. Mixture is stiff. Pinch off a small piece of dough and roll into a ball in your hand. Roll each ball into a thin short cigar shape. Bend each cookie slightly to form a finger. Place each pecan finger onto an un-greased cookie sheet. Bake at 400 F for 8 to 10 minutes. Roll in powdered sugar while hot. Place each cookie on a cooling rack to cool. Place onto a platter lined with a doily.

Note: I generally make two batches of caramel snappers. I also buy my chocolate frosting to frost the top of each caramel snapper.

Caramel Snappers

Yield: Twelve

1 cup pecan halves
36 light caramels
1-8 ounce container chocolate frosting

Arrange pecans with the flat side down in a group of 3 on a greased cookie sheet. Place 1 caramel on each cluster of pecans. Bake at 325 F until caramels soften, about 4 to 8 minutes. (Watch the caramel snappers very carefully; various brands of caramels melt differently). Remove from the oven. Flatten caramels over the pecans with a buttered spatula. Cool slightly. Remove from the pan and place onto buttered waxed paper. Frost each caramel snapper with chocolate frosting. Chill slightly. Place onto a dessert platter.

Note: Neighbors often bring their favorite dessert. We never lack for food and fellowship.

The Baptism

My neighbor had been very excited and animated when she announced the news that she was going to be a grandmother. After the baby's birth, the family had a large gathering to celebrate the baby's baptism. My neighbor's daughter-in-law and new mother is the oldest of eight children. Her daughter-in-law is an excellent cook and is used to cooking in quantity. She made most of the food for the baptism celebration. The proud grandmother took lots of pictures at the baptism. My neighbors are just delighted to be grandparents and enjoy their time with the new baby.

Blessing From the Neighbors

It is truly a unique blessing and an everlasting treasure to continue to be a part of our neighborhood. As we age, we continue to support each other and show our love and concern for each other. Most of us have been married for over 35 years to the same mate and we enjoy getting together. It is a great feeling to say that I live in a neighborhood with such caring people. We are a family!

35th Anniversary Party

A 35th Wedding Anniversary Party

Many people in the world celebrate 25, 50, or 75 years of marriage. There are very few couples that make their 75th anniversary. My husband and I decided to celebrate our 35th anniversary in December by having a party at our home. For many years we had a very tiny kitchen and dining room. It was difficult to do much entertaining for a large crowd due to the lack of space. A couple years ago we decided to take down the wall leading from the kitchen to the family room. We did not really need a living room and a family room for just two people. We put a plan together and expanded our kitchen into the family room. The expense was minimal because we did not have to expand any outside walls. We also had a carpenter build a 13 foot buffet top with cupboards below. We already had a rock fireplace in our existing family room. We added more windows to give the dining room an open feel and also new lighting. We are very pleased with the results.

Finally, I could have 35 people in the house and not feel over-crowded. I laid out my buffet on the 13-foot buffet counter top. We pushed my dining room table against the wall on the opposite side of the buffet top. We set up the beverages in our garage just off of the dining room. We set up a coffee bar on one of the kitchen counter tops. Snack tables and plenty of chairs were positioned in our living room and kitchen dinette. The arrangement worked out very well. My husband and I could visit all the guests and make them feel very welcomed because we did not have to work the party. All foods were laid out ahead of time just before the guests arrived. We always set a time for our guests arrival and departure. Our invitation says the date, day, the purpose of the party and the time. We like to entertain on a Sunday afternoon from 2-6 p.m. Most guests are off on Sundays and they enjoy socializing and grazing. People tend to eat and drink less on Sundays, especially if they are going to go to work the next day.

We set up the main courses on the dining room table and the snacks and wedding cake on the buffet top. We kept the soup hot in our large crock-pot and the two main dishes hot in a large chaffing dish with Sterno® burners that burn for a four-hour block. We placed all the desserts in one area and snacks in another area to form two or three groups of food. The snacks make great fillers. We place napkins on all serving areas with the snack plates. We put the main courses and salads on the dinning room table. We put soup bowls and spoons near the soup and the larger 9 inch plates by the food in the chaffing dish. See pictures of the buffet on page 12 in the color section.

An Anniversary Menu

Food on the Dining Room Table

Turnip Sausage Soup

Bean Soup

Swedish Meatballs

Italian Pasta Casserole

Oriental Salad

Sweet and Sour Salad Dressing

Cheese Balls

Crackers

Rolls and Butter

Snacks on the Buffet Counter Top

Snacks and Veggies

Pretzels

Sweet and Tangy Mustard

Taco Chips and Salsa

Caramel Corn

Cashew Nuts

Vegetable Tree and Vegetable Platter

Dill Dip

Seafood

Crab Dip and Crackers

Herring

Shrimp with Cocktail Sauce

Desserts

Wedding Anniversary Cake

Lemon Bundt Cake

Mini Cherry Cheese Cakes

Hello Dolly Bars

Holiday Fudge

Beverages

Raspberry and Pineapple Punch

Assorted Sodas

Note: My husband has a large garden for six mouths of the year. He grew better than 100 turnips. We had so many turnips that I took several to the YMCA and gave them to anyone willing to try our turnips. I got several negative reactions to the thought of eating turnips even though these people had never eaten turnips. I decided to make turnip soup for our party. I cooked the turnips in vegetable juice to get rid of the strong taste. One of the gentlemen working the front desk at the YMCA decided to make the turnip soup and reported that it was so delicious. My guests thought the turnips were potatoes and had no idea there were turnips in the soup. I made 3 batches of turnip soup for the party. This soup freezers very well. Remove the soup from the freezer 24 hours before serving.

Turnip Sausage Soup

Yield: Twelve servings

1 package mild Italian sausages (5 to a package)
1 quart chicken stock
4-12 ounce cans (each) vegetable juice
2 bay leaves
2 tablespoons minced garlic
½ cup onion, diced
2 cups turnips julienne
1 cup of carrots julienne
½ cup celery, diced
1-8 ounce package frozen mixed vegetables
ounce package fresh basil, chopped very fine
2 teaspoons Italian seasonings

Boil the sausages until cooked through. Drain and remove the skin from the sausages. Dice the sausage and set aside. Place the chicken stock and vegetable juice in a large stockpot. Add the bay leaves, sausage, garlic, onions, turnips, carrots, celery, mixed vegetables, basil and the Italian seasonings. Simmer for two hours. Remove the bay leaves at the end of the cooking time.

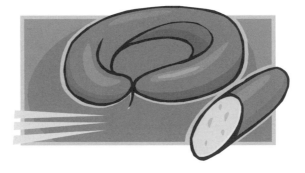

Note: You can serve bean soup instead of turnip soup.

Bean Soup

Yield: Eighteen cups

1 quart vegetable juice
1-14 ounce can beef broth with onions
1 cup water
$^1\!/_2$ cup burgundy cooking wine
1 ham bone with ham
1-14.5 ounce can diced tomatoes with juice
1 small onion, diced
1 leek, cut into ringlets without the green top
1 tablespoon minced garlic
1 cup celery, chopped
1 teaspoon black pepper
1 teaspoon cumin
1 teaspoon oregano
2 bay leaves
1 teaspoon onion powder
1-48 ounce jar of pre-cooked mixed or northern beans

Using a large crock pot, pour in the vegetable juice, beef broth, water, cooking wine, and ham bone with ham on the bone. Cook for one hour. Add the tomatoes with juice, onion, leek, garlic, celery, pepper, cumin, oregano, bay leaves, and onion powder. Cook on low for about 6 hours, stirring occasionally. When the ham begins to fall off the bone, remove the ham with the ham and cool slightly. Remove the ham from the bone and dice the ham. Return the ham to the soup. Discard the bone. Rinse off the beans. Add the beans to the soup. Continue to cook for another half hour. Serve with cheese slices or your favorite crackers.

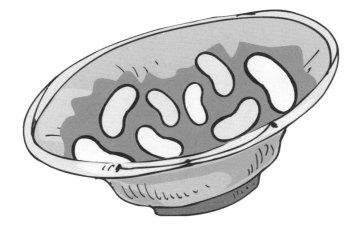

Note: I like to use 1¹/₂ teaspoons shallot pepper instead of the pepper, onion and garlic powder. The shallot pepper gives the meatballs a great flavor. I normally purchase the shallot pepper from the Penzey Spice Company in Milwaukee, Wisconsin. They ship spices all over the country and have a catalog.

Swedish Meatballs

Yield: One hundred, twenty-eight Swedish meatballs

1-32 ounce box 99% fat free beef broth
1-14 ounce can 100% lower sodium beef broth
¹/₃ cup cornstarch
1 cup water
1 cup sour cream
2 tablespoons dill weed
¹/₂ teaspoon pepper
¹/₂ teaspoon onion powder
¹/₂ teaspoon garlic powder
2 teaspoons browning & seasoning sauce
2-2 pound packages (each) ¹/₂ ounce size Swedish meatballs
1 package frilled toothpicks

In a large stockpot add beef broth. Add the cornstarch to the water and wire whip until the cornstarch is dissolved in the water. Bring the beef broth to a boil. Slowly add the cornstarch mixture and wire whip until the broth is thickened. Remove from the burner and add the sour cream, dill weed, pepper, onion and garlic powders, and the browning and seasoning sauce. Wire whip the mixture until all ingredients are blended and becomes gravy. Stir in the meatballs. Serve hot with frilled toothpicks.

Italian Pasta Casserole

Yield: Twenty servings

4 tablespoon olive oil, divided
1 teaspoon salt
1-16 ounce box rotelle
5-8 ounce boneless, skinless chicken breasts
Water
1 cup chicken stock
4-12 ounce cans (each) Presto Italian dip
1-26 ounce jar premium spaghetti sauce
2 small zucchini, sliced
1 small red onion, diced
1-8 ounce package sliced mushrooms
$1/2$ teaspoon pepper
2 teaspoons Italian seasoning
1 cup grated Romano cheese
No-stick cooking spray
2 cups mozzarella cheese

In a large pot, bring 10 cups water to a boil with 2 tablespoons olive oil and salt. Add the rotelle and cook the pasta until tender. Drain and rinse the rotelle in cold water. Dry off the pasta. Clean and cube the chicken. Add one cup water, chicken stock, and 2 tablespoons olive oil to a large frying pan. Cook the chicken until the chicken is no longer pink. Rinse the chicken. In a large pot, add the Presto Italian dip, spaghetti sauce, chicken, zucchini, onion, mushrooms, pepper, Italian seasoning, and Romano cheese. Spray no-stick cooking spray into a half pan or two casserole dishes. Sprinkle mozzarella cheese over the casserole. Cover with foil. Just before the party, bake the casserole at 350 F for 45-60 minutes.

Note: To save time I purchased two cheese balls from our local grocery store deli and also a 1½ pound tray filled with assorted cheese slices. I also purchased a 1-14.5 ounce Wheat Thins® and 1-13 ounce box of Triscuits® I put the crackers into 2 separate Santa sleighs with green and red cloth napkins.

Oriental Salad

Yield: Twenty servings

1 head romaine lettuce
1 head Boston head lettuce
1 head leafy red lettuce
4 cups baby spinach
1 small red onion, sliced
2 cups pea pods, cleaned, cut into small pieces
1-4 ounce can sliced water chestnuts
2-12 ounce cans (each) mandarin oranges, drained
1-12 ounce package chow mein noodles
1-3.75 ounce package honey
Almond accents

Clean and tear the romaine, Boston and leafy lettuce into bite size pieces. Clean and trim off the tails on the spinach. Dry the lettuce and spinach with paper towel. Place the lettuce and spinach in a large wooden salad bowl. Add the red onion, pea pods, water chestnuts, and mandarin oranges. Stir the ingredients into the lettuce. Refrigerate the salad. Just before serving time, sprinkle on the chow mien noodles and the honey almond accents.

Sweet and Sour Salad Dressing

Yield: Twenty servings

1 cup sugar
1 cup honey
1 teaspoon sesame seeds
¾ cup cider vinegar
1 teaspoon dehydrated onion
¼ teaspoon pepper
¼ teaspoon salt
2 drops green food color

Mix together the sugar, honey, sesame seeds, vinegar, onion, pepper, salt, and green food color. Serve in a small pitcher or a gravy boat.

Snacks on the Buffet Counter Top

Yield: Twenty servings

2-14 ounce packages (each) pretzels

2-8 ounce jars (each) sweet and tangy mustard

2-14 ounce packages taco chips

2-12 ounce jars (each) medium chunky salsa

1 pound caramel corn

1 pound 6 ounce container fancy cashews

Vegetable Tree and Vegetable Platter

Yield: Twenty servings

1-12 or 15 inch Styrofoam® cone
Foil
1 head romaine lettuce
2 pounds broccoli
1-2 pound head cauliflower
Pound package baby carrots
1 bunch radishes
1 bunch celery
2 bunches fresh parsley
Frilled toothpicks

Wrap the cone with foil. Clean and dry the lettuce. Toothpick the lettuce leaves to cover the foil on the cone. Clean the broccoli, cauliflower, radishes, and celery. Make broccoli and cauliflower flowerets. Rinse off the carrots. Make radish roses and celery sticks. At random, toothpick the various vegetables onto the cone. Toothpick a radish rose on the top of the cone. Clean the parsley. Toothpick the parsley onto the cone, in between the vegetables. Wrap wet paper towel around the tree and place the tree into a plastic bag until serving time. Remove the bag and paper towel. Place the tree into the center of the 14 inch serving tray. Alternate the variety of vegetables around the tree. Serve with dill dip. The dill dip recipe is found in the *Picnics, Catering on the Move* cookbook on page 51.

Note: I received a long narrow serving piece for olives. I did not know what to do with this dish until I began to use it for my cheese dips. It makes a nice impression and it is just a little different from the normal way of serving dips.

Crab Dip and Crackers
Yield: Twenty servings

2-8 ounce packages (each) cream cheese, softened
1-8 ounce package imitation crab
1 teaspoon dehydrated onion
¼ cup celery, diced
1 teaspoon Worcestershire sauce
1 teaspoon minced garlic
1 bunch fresh parsley

Beat the cream cheese until smooth and creamy. Add the crab, onion, celery, Worcestershire sauce and garlic. Beat the ingredients together. Place into a serving dish and garnish with fresh parsley.

Herring
Yield: Twenty servings

1-32 ounce jar Herring

Place herring into a dish and refrigerate until serving time.

Note: I buy the already prepared shrimp at Sam's Club in the frozen food department.

Shrimp
Yield: Thirty servings

2-2 pound bags (each) cooked medium shrimp

Thaw the shrimp and rinse with cold water. Dry the shrimp with a paper towel. Arrange on a tray with the cocktail sauce in a bowl in the middle of the 14 inch tray. Refrigerate until serving time.

Cocktail Sauce
Yield: Thirty servings

2-12 ounce bottles (each) chili sauce
2 teaspoons horseradish
1 teaspoon lemon juice
1 teaspoon Worcestershire sauce

Mix together the chili sauce, horseradish, lemon juice, and Worcestershire sauce. Place cocktail sauce in a small glass bowl. Serve with the shrimp.

Note: Each wedding torte has three layers. I can mix up both 18.25 cake mixes all at the same time in my Kitchen Aid® mixer. If you own a hand mixer do one cake mix at a time.

Note: I purchased a tiered cake stand and made two small 9 inch tortes. I ordered two fresh flower cake toppers to decorate the cake. I kept the frosting decorations very simple to make an elegant cake presentation. I received many compliments from our guests. The butter cream frosting is found on page 216.

Wedding Anniversary Cake

Yield: Two 9 tortes

2-18.25 ounce deep chocolate cake mix
6 eggs
Oil
Water
No-stick baking spray
6-10 inch (each) cake cardboard circles
1-16 ounce container prepared chocolate frosting
1-20 ounce can raspberry pie filling
2 pounds butter cream frosting
6-9 inch round layer cake pans
1 tiered cake holder.

Preheat the oven to 350 F. Add the eggs, oil, and water to the two cake mixes per package directions. Beat until the cake batter is smooth. Spray 6-9 inch cake pans with no-stick baking spray. Bake for 20-25 minutes or until toothpick inserted into each cake come out clean. Cool for 8 minutes. Turn each onto 6 separate 10 inch cake cardboard circle. Leave on cake on two of the cake circles. Remove the other four layers from the cake circles when frosting each layer. Frost chocolate frosting in between the layer on each torte. Spread a thin layer of the raspberry pie filling on top of the chocolate frosting for each layer. Place all three layers together for each torte. Frost the top and sides of both tortes with the butter cream frosting. With a number 30 cake tip, pipe borders around the edge and bottom of each cake. Put together the tiered cake holder. Just before serving time, place one cake on each tier. Decorate each tier with arranged cake flowers. See picture on page 12 in the color section.

Note: My guests enjoyed this very light lemon cake.

Lemon Bundt Cake

Yield: One bundt cake

1-18.25 ounce box lemon cake mix
2 eggs
Water
Oil
1-10 inch cake cardboard circle
2-15.75 ounce cans (each) lemon pie filling
1-16 ounce container non-dairy whipped topping
1-12 ounce jar red maraschino cherries with stems
1-10 ounce jar green maraschino cherries with stems

Preheat the oven to 350 F. Mix cake mix per package instructions. Place cake batter into a greased and floured bundt pan. Bake for 45-60 minutes or until toothpick inserted in the middle of the cake comes out clean. Cool. Turn out onto a cake cardboard circle. Place into the refrigerator over night to firm up the cake. Slice the cake horizontally through the cake three times to form 3 thin layers and fill between each layer with lemon pie filling. Frost the cake body with a thin coating of the pie filling. Frost over the entire cake with the non-dairy whipped topping. Decorate the top of the cake with the maraschino cherries.

Mini Cherry Cheese Cakes

Yield: Seventy-two mini

Refer to the Ladybug chapter on page 179 for the mini cherry cheesecakes in the *Theme Parties Just for Kids, and Family Too*.

Hello Dolly Bars

Yield: Three different Pan sizes

See the Hello Dolly Bars recipe on page 146 in the Picnics, Catering on the Move Cookbook. The pan sizes are 9x9x2 inch, 13x9x2 inch, and 1 half-sheet cake pan. The recipe calls for margarine, but I often use butter.

Note: My mother made this rich tasting fudge each year at Christmas.

Holiday Fudge
Yield: One Christmas wreath

1-12 ounce package chocolate chips
1$\frac{1}{2}$ cups butterscotch chips
1-14 ounce can sweetened condensed milk(reserve empty can)
1 teaspoon hazel nut flavoring
1 cup dried craisins
1 cup pecans, chopped
12-14 whole pecans
1-16 ounce jar red maraschino cherries
1-10 ounce jar green maraschino cherries

Melt chocolate chips and butterscotch chips in the top of a double boiler. Stir in sweetened condensed milk, hazel nut flavoring, craisins, and pecans. Wash out and dry the sweetened condensed milk can. Place the can into the center of a 12 inch platter. Form a wreath around the can. Decorate the wreath with maraschino cherries and whole pecans. Place the fudge into the freezer for 10 minutes. Remove from the freezer and remove the can. Wrap with plastic wrap and refrigerate until one hour before serving time. Pre-cut the fudge into wedges for easy self-serving.

Note: The recipe below fits into my punch bowl. I buy 1 gallon of fruit punch, 2 quarts of 7up, and 2 quarts of raspberry sherbet. I refill the punch bowl as needed.

Raspberry and Pineapple Punch
Yield: Two and a half quarts punch

2 quarts fruit punch
$\frac{1}{2}$ quart 7up
1-16 ounce can pineapple slices with juice
2-1 quart (each) raspberry sherbet
Punch cups

Mix together the fruit punch, 7up, and pineapple juice. Scoop 1 quart of raspberry sherbet balls into the punch bowl. Float the pineapple rings in the punch. Set out punch cups and let the guests serve themselves.

Cover a table with a tablecloth. Place the remaining beverages on the table with 2 buckets of ice and two ice tongs. Also, have various sizes of glasses for serving the sodas.

Extra Recipes

Blue Cheese Ball
Yield: Two cheese balls

2-8 ounce packages (each) cream cheese
1 cup blue cheese, crumbled
2 teaspoons minced garlic
1 teaspoon Worcestershire Sauce
$^1/_2$ cup celery, diced
2 teaspoons dehydrated onion
1 cup pecans, chopped finely

Beat cream cheese and blue cheese together. Add minced garlic, Worcestershire Sauce, celery, onion and $^1/_2$ cup pecans. Beat together ingredients until smooth and creamy. Divide the mixture into two cheese balls. Press $^1/_2$ cup chopped pecans onto each cheese ball. Place each cheese ball on a separate plate. Serve crackers.

Note: For best results, cook the chili over low heat.

Chicken Chili
Yield: Twenty one-cup servings

1 quart tomato juice
1 quart chicken stock
1-15 ounce can tomato sauce
1-13 ounce cans (each) chicken breast, packed in water, drained
2-14$^1/_2$ ounce cans (each) diced tomatoes
2-15 ounce cans (each) crispy corn
1 bunch scallions with tops, diced
1 leek, cut into ringlets
2 tablespoons fresh garlic, minced
1 small onion, diced
$^1/_2$ cup celery, diced
1-8 ounce package sliced mushrooms (optional)
1 green pepper (diced) (optional)
2 teaspoons chili powder
2 teaspoons cumin
$^1/_2$ teaspoon pepper
1-48 ounce jar Great Northern beans (fully cooked, drained and rinsed)

In a large stockpot, add the tomato juice, chicken stock, tomato sauce, chicken breast, tomatoes, corn, scallion, leek, fresh garlic, onion, celery, mushrooms, green pepper, chili powder, cumin, and pepper. Stir all ingredients together. Cook over low heat for 2 hours, stirring every half hour. Add the Northern beans last and cook for one more hour. Serve with cheese and crackers.

El Rancho Chicken Sandwich Casserole
Yield: Ten servings

1 tablespoon olive oil
³/₄ cup wild and white rice mixture or brown rice, cooked
Water to boil rice
4-6 ounce chicken breast, boneless, skinless, grilled or baked
1-15 ounce can 99% fat free chicken stock
1 pound extra lean turkey bacon, diced
1 red pepper, diced
1 cup fresh mushrooms, chopped
¹/₂ cup celery, diced
¹/₃ cup red onion, diced
¹/₄ cup fresh chives, chopped
2 teaspoons minced garlic
1-15 ounce can black beans, drained
1-14.5 ounce can diced chili tomatoes, with chili spices.
1-15 ounce can southwestern corn'n peppers, extra crispy, drained
1 teaspoon black pepper
1 teaspoon chili powder
2 teaspoons cumin
¹/₂ teaspoon Ancho chili powder
¹/₂ teaspoon fajita seasoning
1 can Campbells® creamy Ranchero tomato soup
2 cups taco cheese
No-stick baking spray

Add the olive oil and rice to water. Cook until tender. Drain excess water. Rinse. Set aside. Bake or grill chicken breasts until cooked through. Cool and slice chicken into strips. Set aside. In a wok add 1 can chicken stock. Add the turkey bacon and cook for about 5 minutes. Add all the fresh and canned vegetables, seasonings, and the Rancho tomato soup. Stir together and cook until soup is bubbly. Spray no-stick baking spray in the 13x9 pan. Add half of the mixture in the pan. Layer ¹/₂ the chicken strips across the casserole. Top with 1 cup of taco cheese. Repeat, by layering casserole over the cheese, top with chicken strips and then the cheese. Bake at 375 F for 15-20 minutes or until cheese melts. It optional if you would like to garnish the casserole with black olives, and fresh diced tomatoes.

Oriental Chicken Wok

Yield: Eight servings

1 head Chinese cabbage leaves, chopped
$^1/_2$ cup sliced almonds, toasted
3 tablespoons sesame seeds toasted
2 pounds boneless, skinless chicken breast tenderloins
2-14 ounce (each) 100% fat free chicken stock
1 cup Sake (Chinese cooking wine)
1 cup celery, cut into diagonal pieces
1 medium onion, cut into strips
2 cups fresh pea pods, cleaned, ends snipped
1 red pepper, diced
2 cups fresh bean sprouts, washed
1-8 ounce packaged sliced mushrooms
3 cloves fresh garlic, peeled and minced
$^1/_4$ cup fresh ginger, peeled and minced
1-8 $^3/_4$ ounce can whole baby sweet corn, drained
1-8 ounce can sliced water chestnuts, drained
1-8 ounce can bamboo shoots, drained
2 teaspoon Chinese five spice
$^1/_2$ cup Veri Veri Teriaki Sauce®
2 teaspoons soy sauce
3 tablespoons cornstarch
1 cup cold water
Extra soy sauce
2-3 ounce cans, (each) rice noodles

Prepare vegetables. Clean the Chinese cabbage. Cut the end of the cabbage off. Using a kitchen scissors cut the leaf off on each side of the cabbage core center for each piece. Discard the core. Chop the cabbage. Drain the cabbage well in a colander. Set aside. Place almonds and sesame seeds on a cookie sheet. Do not grease the sheet. Bake at 375 F for 3-5 minutes or until almonds and sesame seeds are golden brown. Set aside. In a large stock pan or wok, add chicken to chicken stock and Sake. Cook until chicken is no longer pink. Add almonds, sesame seeds, celery, onion strips, pea pods, red pepper, bean sprouts, mushrooms, garlic, ginger, baby sweet corn, water chestnuts, and bamboo shoots. Cook slowly, stirring occasionally until the vegetables are tender. Add cabbage leaves, Chinese Five spice, Veri Veri Teriaki Sauce® and soy sauce. Simmer only a few more minutes. Add the cornstarch to water. Whisk the two ingredients until smooth. Bring the chicken dish to a boil and slowly add the cornstarch mixture. Whisk the chicken dish until thickened. Remove from the heat. Serve the chicken dish with rice. Top with soy sauce and rice noodles.

INDEX

Completed
Rocket Cake
from page 7

Rocket Party from page 1

Rocket Party from page 1

Rocket Project from page 9 & 10

Rocket Sandwiches from page 13

Windmill S'mores from page 24

Kite Pizza Snacks from page 23

Windmill Cookies from page 18

Pin the Tail on the Kite Game from page 22

Kite Cake from page 24

A Kite Cake with a Number 5 Birthday Candle and Red Fish from page 24

Heart Shaped Sugar Cookies, Radish Rose Centerpiece, White Chocolate Truffles, Heart Shaped Open-Faced Sandwiches and Mini Muffins from the Valentine Party on page 32

Fruit Kabobs from page 35 and Mini Pecan Tarts from page 38

Valentine Party Guest Table from page 40

Mini Heart Cheese Cakes from page 37

Mini Apple Muffins from page 36

Two Guests Seated at the Valentine Table from page 32

Mrs. Cola Reading a St. Valentine Story to Her Guests from page 41

Lasagna from page 45

Red and Green Grapes with Strawberry Garnish from page 47

Half Birthday Party Buffet Table with Balloons from page 44

Half Birthday Card from page 49 with Green Bear

Romaine Lettuce Salad from page 47

One Half Chocolate Cake from page 48

Indy 500 & NASCAR® Party Buffet Set-up from page 65

How to Make the Checkerboard Cake from page 61

Indy 500 & NASCAR® Party Buffet Set-up from page 65

Checkerboard Cake from page 61

Indy 500 Centerpiece from page 62

Southwestern Style Cheese Dip from page 60

Indy 500 & NASCAR® Party Taco Chips, Salsa & Dips from page 57

Racecar Party Favors from page 64

Train Party Food Table Set-up from page 79

Train Visors from page 87

The Half Train Sheet Cake from page 72

Individual Crisped Rice Cereal Trains page 85

The Thomas the Train Table page 87
Pretend Horns from page 86

Decorated Cream Cheese Box page 86

The Train Quarter Sheet Cake from page 73

The Smile Candy Train page 74

Airplane Cake from page 99

The Airplane Luncheon Napkin, Lunch Box and Food
in each Lunch Box from Airplane Party page 95-102

Aircraft
Landing
Sandwiches
from page
101 with
Carrot
Airplane
Relish from
page 95

Airplane
Cupcake
Tree from
page 100

Apple Basket
from page 100

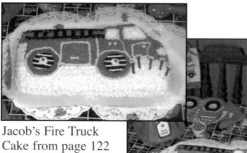

Jacob's Fire Truck
Cake from page 122

James' Fire Truck Cake from page 120

Guests Attending the
Fire Truck Party from
page 113

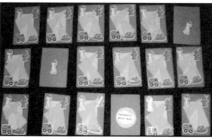

Jon's Fire Truck Cake
from page 118

Firemen Theme Guest Table page 123

Fireman's Memory Drill Card Game
from page 124

Raspberry Party Hobo Buffet Set-up from page 129

Mrs. Cola's Picnic Raspberry Pie from page 129

Guest at the Raspberry Party from page 128

Guests Picking Raspberries at the Raspberry Party from page 128

A Bowl of Black Cherries at the Pony Party from page 149

Pony Party Buffet Set-up from page 149

Prince's Ranch Torte, Sweet Oat's Cowboy Cookies and Buffet Set-up of the Pony Party from page 149

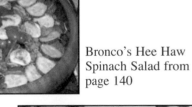

Bronco's Hee Haw Spinach Salad from page 140

Pony Party Buffet Set-up from page 149

Nugget's Corral Turkey Macaroni Casserole from page 133

Buttercup's Horseshoe Apple Salad from page 139

Aunt Beatrice's Petal Bread from page 141

■

Prince's Ranch Torte from page 141

Muffin's Dream Carousel Birthday Torte from page 143

Dumpling's Apple Dumplings from page 145

Dreamcicle's Alaskan Apples from page 147

Sweet Oat's Cowboy Cookies from page 148

Ladybug Party Guest Table from page 172

Ladybug Party Buffet Set-up from page 172

Ladybug Centerpiece from page 168

Ladybug's Very Berry Fruit Salad with Mint Garnish from page 174

Lazy Ladybug Cake from page 175

Ladybug Shaped Cake from page 177

Ladybug Cupcakes from page 177

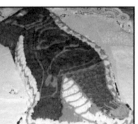

Partysaurus
Dinosaur
Cake
page 186

Decorated Dinosaur Visor from page 189

Dinosaur Party from page 184

Dinosaur
Picture from
page 194

Dino Party Visor
from page 190

Roaring Dinosaur Visor from page 190

Vegetable
Centerpiece-
Dinosaur Mommy
with Her Children
Theme from page
195

The
Spinosaurus
Dinosaur
Hat from
page 191

The Happy Dinosaur Head and Tail
Hat page 192

Clown Donuts from page 212

Clown Party Dessert and Sandwich Buffet
from page 207

Quick and Easy Clown
Cupcakes from page 210

Decorated Clown
Raspberry Torte
from page 214

Easy-Does-It Clown Cake
from page 213

Clown Goodie Bags
from page 210

Clown-Faced Sandwiches
from page 209

Birthday Clown-Faced
Cookie from page 211

Craft Project Clown
Christmas Ornaments
from page 220

Clown Tic-Tac-Toe
from page 221

A Clown
Doodle Pad
from page 222

Clown Birthday Honey
Cake from page 215

A
Circus
Lollipop
Theme
Ball
from
page
219

Color and Lacing Yarn
Through the Clown Face
Picture from page 223

A Clown Joins the Clown
Party from page 207

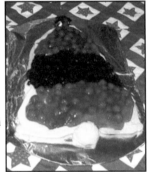

Liberty Bell Dessert
Pizza from page 244

Buffet Set-up for
the 50's Party
from page 256
with 50's Party
Menu Pop Up
Signs

Strawberry Shake from
page 261, Hot Dog and
French Fries pages 258
& 259

33 RPM Record Bowls
from page 258

Star and Poodle Napkin
Holder from page 257
and Record Bowl

Tin Roof Sundae from page 262

Banana Split from page 260

The Puppet Theatre/Stage from
page 297-298

The Puppet Show and Fairy Tale Play from the Princess Party
page 282-298

King William
Puppet page 287
and Judge
Diplomat Puppet
from page 290

King William and Queen Victoria
Puppets from page 287

Fir Tree, Cloud Pop-ups from page 294
and Cousin Frog Princess Puppet from
page 289

Baker Toozell's Princess Doll
Cake from page 273

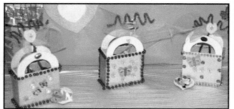

Bride and Groom in the Wedding
Carriage Pop-up from page 292

Princess Wooden Treat Boxes from
page 300

Queen Victoria's Favorite Éclair
Ring Adorned with Ballet Dancers
from page 271-272

■

H Daughters at the Bridal
Shower Party from page 310

Bridal Shower Party from
page 310

AnnMarie at her Bridal
Shower Party

The Wedding Cake from
page 315

Vegetable Salad from
page 322

Reunion
Party Buffet
Set-up from
page 320

Reunion Party Buffet Set-up from page 320

Tortellini
Picnic
Salad
from page
321

Family Enjoying the Reunion

Family
Enjoying
the Bell
Party

Bell Party Buffet Set-up from page 330

Megan Entertains the
Family at the Bell
Party from page 330

Baptism Party from page 337

Wedding Anniversary
Cake on page 357

35th Anniversary Party
Buffet Set-up from page 348